BASED ON THE HIGHLY POPULAR AOL FORUM

Business

Know-How

An Operational
Guide for
Home-Based
and Micro-Sized
Businesses with
Limited Budgets

by
Janet Attard

Adams Media Corporation
Holbrook, Massachusetts

Published by
Adams Media Corporation
260 Center Street, Holbrook, MA 02343
www.adamsmedia.com

ISBN: 1-58062-206-2

Printed in the United States of America.

J I H G F E D C

Library of Congress Cataloging-in-Publication Data

Business know-how / by Janet Attard.
p.   cm.
ISBN 1-58062-206-2
Includes index.
1. Small businesses—Management. I. Title.
HD62.7.A875   1999
658.02'2—dc21   99-28883
CIP

This publication is designed to provide accurate and authoritative information
with regard to the subject matter covered. It is sold with the understanding that
the publisher is not engaged in rendering legal, accounting, or other professional
advice. If legal advice or other expert assistance is required, the services of a
competent professional person should be sought.
— From a *Declaration of Principles* jointly adopted by a Committee of the
American Bar Association and a Committee of Publishers and Associations

Cover illustration by Laura Tedeschi.

This book is available at quantity discounts for bulk purchases.
For information, call 1-800-872-5627.

Visit our exciting Web site at www.businesstown.com

Contents

Acknowledgments →→→ v

Introduction →→→ vii

Part 1: Getting Your Act Together

Chapter 1/Finding the Real Opportunities→→→→→→→→→→→→→→→→→→ 3

Chapter 2/Business Research, Simplified→→→→→→→→→→→→→→→→→→→ 19

Chapter 3/Finding suppliers →→→→→→→→→→→→→→→→→→→→→→→→→→→ 37

Part 2: Marketing Magic—Big Results from Micro-Sized Budgets

Chapter 4/Make a Big Impression on a Small Budget →→→→→→→→→→ 51

Chapter 5/Shoestring Marketing Secrets →→→→→→→→→→→→→→→→→→ 73

Chapter 6/Getting Publicity →→→→→→→→→→→→→→→→→→→→→→→→→→→ 89

Chapter 7/Advertising Tips and Tricks →→→→→→→→→→→→→→→→→→→ 101

Chapter 8/Using the Mail to Build Business →→→→→→→→→→→→→→→ 131

Chapter 9/Mailing and Shipping Strategies →→→→→→→→→→→→→→→→ 145

Chapter 10/Trade Show Savvy →→→→→→→→→→→→→→→→→→→→→→→→→→ 155

Chapter 11/Selling to the Government →→→→→→→→→→→→→→→→→→→→ 179

Chapter 12/Bringing in Sales→→→→→→→→→→→→→→→→→→→→→→→→→→→ 197

Part 3: Operating in the Internet Age

Chapter 13/Increase Productivity and Profits on the Web →→→→→→ 219

Chapter 14/Build and Promote Your Web Site
  Without Going Broke →→→→→→→→→→→→→→→→→→→→→→→→→ 239

Chapter 15/Creating and Working in Your Home Office →→→→→→→→ 261

Chapter 16/Choosing and Using Office Equipment →→→→→→→→→→ 269

Chapter 17/Making More Profitable Connections →→→→→→→→→→→ 281

Part 4: You, the CFO

Chapter 18/Travel →→→→→→→→→→→→→→→→→→→→→→→→→→→→→→→→→→ 303

Chapter 19/Playing Hardball →→→→→→→→→→→→→→→→→→→→→→→→→→ 325

Chapter 20/Keeping the Tax Collector at Bay→→→→→→→→→→→→→→→ 333

Chapter 21/Making Cash Flow →→→→→→→→→→→→→→→→→→→→→→→→→→ 361

Chapter 22/Growing Your Business →→→→→→→→→→→→→→→→→→→→→→ 369

Glossary→→ 377

Index →→ 386

ACKNOWLEDGMENTS

If I were to list all of the people who made this book possible, I'd need to include a disk with a database listing of all the people who have ever shared their business experiences with me and all of the people who help and who have ever helped out on the staff of my online forums.

Although that's not possible to do, there are several people who deserve special recognition. At the top of my list are Angelia Hayes and Lisa Freeman who filled in for me on many occasions so I could make the time to write this book. I'd also like to thank Sonsie Conroy, John McAlister, and Sharon Porpiglia for their research and editorial assistance, and Adams Media senior editor, Jere Calmes, who has been so enthusiastic about the book from the day he first saw the proposal.

Finally, I'd be remiss if I didn't mention America Online and two people who worked so hard to champion small and home business through the service's WorkPlace Channel: Alex Whalen and Tim Driver. While there are many ways for homebased and small business owners to gather information on the Internet, America Online's WorkPlace Channel was the first service to make it easy and convenient for small and homebased businesses to find information—and to find one another.

INTRODUCTION

"**B**usiness as usual" is a phrase you don't hear much these days. That's because business is anything but usual in the electronic age. Corporate downsizings, reorganizations, and budget crunching have made job security an oxymoron. Superstores and the Internet have changed retailing forever. Jobs in every industry and at all levels from rank-and-file employees to top executives require computing skills. Shrinking workforces, increasing employer and client demands, and the need to keep up one's general knowledge and job skills have all combined to make time management a joke in many industries. One manager in a large accounting firm has her staffers send out their laundry and bill the expense to the firm so they can spend more hours at work instead of at the laundromat.

But as in every era, change brings new opportunities. Corporations that reduced their workforce now hire big and small independent contractors to do work that used to be done by their employees. That creates new opportunities for small businesses like yours. And it means new job opportunities for workers who have been tossed out of jobs in big companies.

The omnipresent computer has made it possible for more people than ever before to start businesses. More than half of the families in the United States own home computers—computers that are powerful enough to start and run many types of businesses. For under $2,000, you can buy a computer, monitor, and printer powerful enough to turn your spare bedroom—or even a spare corner of a room—into a business that brings in hundreds of thousands of dollars in sales each year. Using the Internet, that spare-room business can easily interact with customers, employees, independent contractors, and other suppliers who are located thousands of miles away.

That kind of success doesn't happen overnight, of course. Nor does it have anything to do with the type of wild income claims made by some companies whose business is selling income opportunities. But it does happen. People do make good incomes in their own businesses. You can, too, if you learn and apply the secrets to success presented in this book.

You don't have to be in a high-tech business, hire a slew of employees or contractors or work full-time to make money from self-employment, either. Neither do you have to be young to succeed in a business of your own. Men and women in their forties, fifties, and older start and run successful businesses. In fact, more than twenty million people are already making some or all of their income from full-time or part-time self-employment in the United States. According to the U.S. Department of Labor, half of all small businesses in the U.S. are homebased. Millions more people located in other countries are self-employed, as well.

So, what *are* the secrets to success? Hard work and good products are part of the formula. But as anyone who has ever started a business will tell you, they are not enough.

To be successful, you need to know how to *do* business. You need to know the best ways to find customers, to sell to them, to use technology, to cut costs, and to deal with problems that inevitably arise. And you need to know how to do it all on a shoestring.

That's what *Business Know-How* is all about.

Business Know-How picks up where start-up books leave off. Instead of telling you the steps you need to take to start a business, it tells you what you need to do to make your business work.

I've included a chapter on business ideas and one on researching business ideas, not because this is a book about starting a business, but because no business can remain stagnant. If you don't examine your products, services, and operating methods at least once a year to make sure they still meet your customers' needs, you won't be in business very long.

If you rely on other businesses to provide products and services you resell, you should be continually on the lookout for new suppliers, too. You won't be able to stay competitive if you don't. If your main supplier goes out of business, you won't be able to operate at all if you don't know where to find products or services to take their place. Chapter 3 will help you find suppliers.

To run your business successfully you have to know how to find customers and get them to pay attention to you—and how to find those customers without going broke. One of the biggest surprises to many new small business owners is just how much time and money can be spent on marketing. Knowing how to market your products and services efficiently and economically can spell the difference between success and failure. That's why I've included hundreds of suggestions that will make your small business look big and help you find customers who will build your bottom line.

You'll also find extensive Internet information in *Business Know-How*. That's because it's hard for any small business today to operate witho using the Internet. It is often the fastest and least expensive way to fin resources, suppliers, and customers.

Depending on the line of business you are in, you may find that some of your customers and suppliers won't work with you at all if you can't interact over the Web. If you aren't using the Internet regularly now, it's definitely time to get started.

Finally, since the bottom line for small businesses *is* the bottom line, being successful in your own business means knowing how to keep money coming in faster than it goes out. And how to keep it from going out at all. That's why you'll find hundred of tips and hints related to taxes, insurance, legal issues, collections, and other money matters in *Business Know-How*.

Because time is money, the book has been written so you don't have to wade through chapter after chapter to find those gems of wisdom that will make your business more profitable, either. The index, table of contents, and subheads in each chapter will guide you quickly to the information that you are looking for.

Whether you are just starting your business or have been running a home-based or small business for many years, the ideas, tips, and hints in *Business Know-How* could help you bring in tens of thousands of dollars of extra income each year. The book will also save you thousands of dollars every year by showing you how to avoid costly mistakes. I've personally used many of the strategies in this book to grow and profit from my own small business as an online content provider and Web developer. So I know that they work. I hope you'll put the tips and hints you find here to good use in your business, too.

Part 1

Getting Your Act Together

Chapters

▶ 1 **Finding the Real Opportunities**

▶ 2 **Business Research, Simplified**

▶ 3 **Finding Suppliers**

Chapter 1

FINDING THE REAL OPPORTUNITIES

Business ideas are all around you.

They are lurking in your garage, in your basement, in your kitchen, and in your children's room. You'll find them in magazine ads, at your neighbor's house, and at work. They are right there in the vegetables you brought in from the yard . . . in the stack of papers next to your laser printer . . . in the back of your truck . . . and at the back of your mind.

You don't need to be a genius or an MBA to spot those ideas and turn them into profits, either. Identifying business opportunities is often as easy as identifying problems many people share and finding a way to solve them. When Matthew Osborne, an entrepreneur from Columbus, Ohio, wanted a way to make money, he found one right at his feet: dog dirt. Unlike most people who just gripe about stepping in it or having to clean it up, he started a business removing dog waste from homeowners' yards. The business was an immediate success, and after several years, he sold the business for a quarter of a million dollars. Even then, however, he continued to make money from his idea by writing a booklet about how to start a pet waste removal business and selling the booklet on the Internet.

Other business owners have turned their hobbies, interests, and skills into satisfying and often lucrative businesses, simply by seeing a need in the world around them and finding a way to fill it. You can, too.

Do What You Love to Do

Businesses don't just happen. They are made.

Whether you plan to profit by twisting balloons into smile-generating shapes or orchestrating the growth of multimillion-dollar, multinational companies, your success relies on what you bring to the business. If you love what you do, your passion for the business will drive you to be knowledgeable, creative, and persistent. On the other hand, if your feeling for what you do is lukewarm, your success will be, too.

Turn Old Standbys into New Products

Truly new concepts are few and far between. Most new products or new business ideas are simply spin-offs of old ones. Inline skates is one good example. Essentially, they are ice skates on wheels or, depending on your point of view, streamlined roller-skates. Other new business ideas are nothing more than new ways of marketing mundane products. Take Dial-A-Mattress, for example. Furniture and bedding stores have always sold mattresses—but not by phone. Not until a furniture salesman by the name of Napoleon Barragan started a business selling mattresses over an 800-number phone line. The idea took hold, and today, Dial-A-Mattress sells some $70 million worth of mattresses each year.

You may not have the money, management ability, contacts, or desire to launch a major new product like inline skates or the energy or desire to build a multimillion-dollar sales organization. But you don't have to launch anything that large to start a business or introduce a new product.

Years ago when my kids were little, I made money selling beanbags. The twist? I designed them in the shape of frogs and I filled them with birdseed instead of beans to make them pliable and less lumpy to the touch. To attract attention at craft shows, I displayed them in various human poses (sitting up, laying on their side resting their head on their hand, or hugging each other, for instance). I could produce them quickly and kept my costs low by making the frogs from inexpensive fabric remnants. That allowed me to price the frogs low enough to make them great impulse buys.

You can spin almost any skill or industry knowledge into marketable new products or services.

A neighbor turned his skill at fixing cars into a repair and tune-up service. His angle? He was mobile. Customers didn't have to drop their car off at the shop. Instead, the "shop" (a van outfitted with tools and auto parts) came to them. Another acquaintance built a business by purchasing large quantities of chemicals and repackaging them in smaller quantities.

And several paper suppliers have created businesses by preprinting colorful brochure or flier designs on paper stock. The preprinted papers are then sold to businesses and individuals who use their laser printers to print out their own sales literature and fliers on an as-needed basis.

Look for Avalanches

Marketing avalanches, that is.

"Drag your products into the path of an avalanche and you'll be swept along with it," says Alan Kaufman. Kaufman was the executive vice president of sales for Cheyenne Software when it was a small, vertical market software company that had big ambitions.

Cheyenne's owners had been keeping a close eye on trends in the computer industry in the late 1980s. They felt that Novell local area networks (LANs) were about to snowball and started developing enhancement products for Novell LANs. Within six years, the avalanche (combined with good products and heads-up management) turned their little company into a $127 million operation before it was sold to Computer Associates. Cheyenne was the 13th largest software company in the United States and employed nearly 700 people at the time of the sale.

Look for Mundane Moneymakers

You don't need to create exciting new products or services to go into business, either. Millions of business owners profit by selling routine and sometimes unglamorous services such as window washing, car repair, sandwich making, building maintenance, house cleaning, and plumbing. The key to making money with the mundane is to sell something your customers can't do, don't want to do, don't have the time to do, or can't get done well elsewhere.

> ▶ Tip
> One way to make really big money with mundane services is to develop a unique and reproducible method for marketing and delivering the service and then open up multiple offices, or franchise the concept. If you plan to franchise your idea or sell it as a business opportunity, retain an attorney early on who is familiar with franchise law and can help you steer clear of the pitfalls.

Spin off a More Lucrative Business

The business you start today may not be the business you run tomorrow. Entrepreneurs and self-employed individuals sometimes find that their initial attempts to start a business don't bring in the profits they had hoped for. Nevertheless, they often benefit by discovering new profit-making opportunities because of contacts or knowledge they pick up running their first business.

Las Vegas resident Beth Waite used to make $7 an hour as a self-employed dressmaker. Her customers often asked her for advice on choosing clothes, and she discovered that information available in books often was confusing and not really helpful. Because of her research, though, she heard of Beauty Control, an image consulting firm. After taking the company's training course, she started an image consulting business, charging clients $50 an hour for her advice. She supplements the consulting income with profits from the sale of Beauty Control products.

Sell Training Seminars to Corporate America

Don't limit yourself to training individuals or private groups of people. Look for ways to polish up your act and cash in on the $50 billion corporate training market.

What kind of training do corporations buy? Everything from sales, management and computer training courses to self-defense courses.

To locate training opportunities, contact the human resources department and ask to speak to the person in charge of training programs. Introduce yourself to that person and make an appointment to discuss the company's needs and your ability to fill them. If you get the assignment, be sure to have handouts for the class so they know how to reach you for more intensive training on their own.

Turn That Hobby into Cash

Do people ooh and ah at your handiwork? Whether you are a whiz at creating floral arrangements or at writing software, look for ways to turn your hobby into a business. You might want to manufacture your items in quantity; license them to other manufacturers; sell them by mail order, at flea markets, or on consignment; or open your own retail outlet selling supplies to others with similar interests.

Ask the reference librarian at your public library to help you find trade magazines pertaining to your hobby; then read them to generate new business ideas.

Learn a Trade

If you are just entering the job market or have found that skills you had are no longer needed in the workplace, learn a trade or skill that you can develop into a business. Look for programs that teach skills you can use to perform frequently needed services such as appliance repair, plumbing, printing, or word processing and typesetting. And don't forget computers need repairing. More than 50 percent of homes and virtually every business in the United States owns one or more computers.

Plan on bolstering your book learning with practical, on-the-job experience.

"You probably won't be able to go directly from a training course into your own business if you don't have any actual experience in the business," says Steven McPheters, a locksmith in southern Maine. "Working for other businesses first will help you gain the experience, confidence, and contacts you'll need to succeed on your own."

McPheters started his business after completing a National Radio Institute (NRI) correspondence course in 1990. He took the course, which cost about $1,600, to supplement his knowledge of locksmithing that he'd picked up doing door installations for a general contractor. When he completed the course, he contacted contractors he had worked for, gave them a business card, and told them he'd like the opportunity to give them quotes on jobs they had.

McPheters's business isn't likely to be huge; like many self-employed individuals, he would rather keep the business small.

Others who enjoy managing employees do turn services like locksmithing into larger businesses. The beauty of owning a business is that you have the opportunity to create exactly the kind of business and the lifestyle *you* prefer.

Correspondence courses aren't the only way to learn a trade. Other options include on-the-job training alone and taking courses at general vocational schools, community colleges, and trade schools. On-the-job experience is considered so important for long-term success that some trade schools won't take students who haven't worked in the field they hope to enter.

Reach Out and Teach Someone

Do you have a skill others want to acquire? Do you have a knack for explaining things so that others can understand them? If so, don't give your expertise away. Start charging for it!

For instance, if you are a karate expert, you might teach at a karate school or open your own karate school. If you're a talented artist, you could teach art at home or in a school.

> ▶ **Tip**
> Get a sales tax permit and make money selling books, supplies, or other items your students will need to buy to complete the course.

Mass-Produce Your Advice

Selling your product or service one on one limits the amount of money you can earn to the number of people you can personally see. To increase your profits without significantly increasing your work, consider turning your expertise into booklets, books, computer programs, audiotapes, or videotapes that you can market in quantity.

You can use your computer to produce camera-ready copy or complete copies of printed materials. You also can generate computer diskettes and have professionals produce your materials if the volume warrants.

Don't try the "loving hands at home" approach for audiotapes or videotapes, though. The result is likely to be an amateurish product.

Lloyd de Vries, a producer at CBS News, suggests that if you're on a tight budget, you may be able to produce master tapes economically by having them done by students in broadcasting courses at local colleges.

De Vries also suggests taking a broadcasting course yourself. "That way, you can polish your skills and at the same time gain access to whatever studio facilities are on campus as part of your course fee."

Another option is to contact your local radio or cable TV stations to see if they'll rent you studio time and provide a crew to make a tape.

If you have a proven concept and will be pumping a lot of cash into marketing your tapes, have them prepared professionally. Look in the Yellow Pages under video production services for names of companies to contact for both audio and video production. Be sure your concept is tested and saleable before going this route, though. Depending on where you live and what quality you seek, the cost of producing videotapes professionally runs between $500 and $1,000 per minute of finished videotape time.

Be an Industry Consultant

This is another great way to increase your bank account. If you can solve business problems (such as how to bring waste water into compliance with EPA regulations) or answer important business questions (what steps should be taken to increase market share in a target market or how to manage inventory more efficiently), you can earn substantial hourly fees selling your advice to corporations.

Downsized corporations can be a good source of consulting business since they may no longer have experts they need on staff.

A big key to success is to be an expert with years of experience or highly specialized knowledge. If you are newly self-employed, market yourself as an expert rather than as a worker.

Turn a Former Employer into a Valuable Source of New Business

Just because you leave a company doesn't mean it doesn't need your services. Companies often retain the services of former workers on a freelance or consulting basis. That way they get the benefit of trained personnel without having to pay payroll taxes and benefits. If you leave a company on good terms, ask about contract or freelance opportunities. Don't stop with contacts who work with the former employer, either. Call your former employer's suppliers and customers and tell them about your capabilities. Call their competitors, too. Stress your industry knowledge, contacts, and skills. You may soon find that the income you earn exceeds what you made as an employee.

Find a Need and Fill It

That old advice still works like a charm.

When Beth Cherkowsky, of Penndel, Pennsylvania, had trouble finding an affordable source for the toy action figures her son wanted for his collection, she discovered kids weren't the only people who bought action toys. Adults collected them, too. So, instead of just buying figures for her son, she found sources for the toys and set up a small mail-order business selling them from her home.

Modify One of Your Existing Products

Sometimes all it takes to create a "new" product is a slight change in an existing product.

Harrison-Hoge Industries is a mail-order company in Port Jefferson, New York, that sells fishing lures, inflatable boats, and other outdoor gear. In 1993, the company added a wide-brimmed, canvas hat called the Campesino to its catalog. The hat was a big success, but the owners of the company thought there might be more they could do with it. And there was.

They discovered they could adapt the hat to sell in specialized markets just by changing the hat band. Now, in addition to selling the original Campesino hat themselves, they supply the Museum of Natural History and the Guggenheim Museum (both in New York City) with hats. Each museum's hat has its own distinctive hat band.

Start a "Green" Business

Green businesses use and sell environmentally aware products and services. As the need for environmental responsibility and the laws enforcing it have become more widespread, so has the potential for profit grown.

Testing laboratories, environmental cleanup companies, printers, lawyers, recycling companies, engineers, writers, and others are cashing in on environmental profits.

Look at federal, state, and city government environmental contracting and subcontracting opportunities as well as targeting big and small businesses that want or must buy environmentally safe products or environmental cleanup services.

Think Digital

You can use your computer to give a new twist —and a new name—to traditional service concepts. For instance, instead of starting a business as a typist or answering service or office support company, start a business as a Virtual Assistant. You could perform just about all the services an administrative assistant might perform in a traditional office, but you would work from your own office (or home office) instead of at the customer's place of business. You could even answer their phone calls, faxes, and e-mail using call forwarding and e-mail forwarding services.

Develop a Recycling Business Aimed at Cost-Conscious Customers

Recycling can do more than just help the environment.

When recycling means reusing costly materials that would otherwise have been thrown away, it also becomes an effective cost-cutting strategy. Entrepreneurs who develop processes for recycling discarded items can make tidy profits if there is a market for the process and they know how to reach that market.

Michael Lewy, an engineer and inventor from Gloversville, New York, is a good example. In 1979, he sold an outdoor power equipment company he had owned and was looking for a new, more interesting business to buy. A local orthodontist who'd been a customer at the power tool business wanted a way to recycle the brackets and bands he used in treating patients. He knew Lewy was good at tinkering with things and asked him if he could develop the machinery and processes to recycle the brackets and bands. Lewy agreed to tackle the task and formed a partnership with the orthodontist. (Lewy later bought out his partner.)

Today, Lewy's company, Orthotronics, Inc., recycles hundreds of thousands of brackets and bands per year. His service has been so successful because it saves orthodontists $1,000 a month if they start 150 new cases a year.

Export Your Products to Build Sales

If your product or service sells well in this country, there's a good chance there's a significant market for it elsewhere. Close to 40 percent of Orthotronics' recycling business now comes from overseas sales.

For information on international sales opportunities, contact the International Trade Administration at 800-872-8723. For local contacts on exporting, call a regional economic development agency or local Small Business Development center. They should be able to point you to local programs to help businesses get started in exporting.

Steer Clear of Invention Promotion Frauds

If you are an inventor, don't get taken in by companies that promise to patent and market your invention. Many of these companies use deceptive advertising and sales practices and do little or nothing for the money paid to them. Before you submit any idea to such companies, send for the Federal Trade Commission's free booklet, *Invention Production Firms*. The booklet is available by writing to:

Federal Trade Commission
Office of Consumer and Business Education
600 Pennsylvania Avenue, NW
Washington, DC 20580
http://www.ftc.gov

If you have an idea for an invention you think is marketable, get a bound notebook (the kind with sewn-in pages) and write your idea down. Have two nonfamily members sign and date your entries in the notebook as you make them. Keep a record of what you do and whom you talk to about the invention. Have each entry witnessed.

Do preliminary market research (determine who would buy the product, if anything similar is being sold now, and what people would pay for it). If the idea appears marketable in sufficient quantity to be profitable, then do a preliminary patent search.

If you are a belt-and-suspenders type of person, you could also file an Invention Disclosure form with the U.S. Patent Office. This form is *not* a patent application and does not give your idea patent-pending status. It merely establishes a date for the creation of your invention. (Documenting the date can prove useful in cases where two or more independent researchers are working on similar ideas and need to prove who actually invented a device first.) If you do not begin the registration process within two years, the disclosure information you sent will be discarded.

Invention Disclosure forms are available from the Patent Office and may be downloaded from their Web site (http://www.uspto.gov). The filing fee is $10.

The next steps are to build a model or working prototype, get a patent, interest buyers and investors, and manufacture and market the item. "Marketing the invention is the most important part of the process," says

---

▶ **Warning**

Warning! Of all the possible ways to start a business, inventing a new product and bringing it to market is the most difficult and most expensive. In addition to design, and for the manufacturing and quality control issues, you will have to overcome many other obstacles you may never have thought about. Among them, the need to hire and manage a staff, the difficulty in building brand awareness and the sky-high fees to get popular mail-order catalogs to include your product. If all of that isn't enough to give you ulcers, if your product proves highly desirable you can count on having it copied and sold by competitors, or you might even have your notes, equipment, and plans stolen. Many of the problems can be solved by the one thing most inventors quickly find is in least supply: money.

Thomas O'Rourke, an intellectual properties attorney of Wyatt, Gerber, Meller and O'Rourke located in New York City. "Many inventors believe that hordes of people will come knocking on their door just because they secure a patent, and that's not the case at all. You have to do a lot of legwork." That legwork may include going to trade shows, showing it to manufacturers, and trying to market the product yourself.

If you need help at any stage, contact inventors clubs, legitimate invention assessment services or a Small Business Development Center (SBDC). SBDCs are jointly run by the Small Business Administration and state governments.

Capitalize on Demographic Trends

Keeping an eye on demographic trends can help you spot opportunities, too. It's no secret that the population of the United States is aging, for instance.

Businesses can profit by marketing products and services that appeal to people who are fifty and over. Minorities are growing in numbers and in buying power also. In 1994, African Americans represented a $300 billion market and the purchasing power of Latinos in the United States exceeded $206 billion.

The ever-growing numbers of people who work at home, the numbers of people with home computers, the growing use of the Internet and online services for sales and publicity, the changing national and local job markets are just a few trends that could potentially affect your business.

To stay on top of these and other trends, read news magazines, trade journals, and local newspapers. If you subscribe to an online service, see if it offers an electronic news-clipping service. These services will hunt incoming news stories by keywords you specify, and send any matches directly to your electronic mail box. You save time and benefit by knowing the latest developments in your field.

Look for online newsletters that can be delivered to your mailbox. Subscriptions are often free or low cost because the publishers don't have to pay any postage costs.

▶ **Tip**
The secret to successfully targeting these and other cultural markets is to pay attention to your audience's heritage and lifestyle. Don't just replace pictures of white people with pictures of African Americans or Latinos, and don't translate English word for word into any other language. Your marketing efforts will fail if you do. Instead, tailor the sales literature or ads to accurately reflect the lifestyle of the targeted market.

And, listen to your customers if you are already in business. They may alert you to profitable new products or services you could add to your offerings.

Get off to a Good Start in a Business Incubator

It takes a lot more than a good idea to hatch a viable business. If you've been wobbling along trying to develop a business on your own but have been hindered by lack of support services or lack of financial or management know-how, consider applying for a spot in a business incubator.

Business incubators, as their name suggests, nurture businesses, helping them develop so they can stand on their own. Some work with entrepreneurs who are just starting to develop products. Others prefer businesses that are ready to come out of the basement or the garage, but not quite ready to stand on their own.

Incubators typically offer budding businesses a package of services at prices that are lower than buying them separately. Depending on the specific incubator, these may include office space, shared receptionist or switchboard services, shared equipment and business development training, marketing assistance, or legal and accounting resources.

But the real value of an incubator is the mentoring and access to business contacts that takes place. The National Business Incubation Association (NBIA) says regional studies put the five-year success rate for incubator graduates at between 80 and 90 percent. A study conducted in October 1997 by the University of Michigan, NBIA, Ohio University, and the Southern Technology Council under a grant from the U.S. Department of Commerce Economic Development Administration shows that, on the average, incubator firms' sales increased by more than 400 percent from the time they entered until the time they left the incubator. In addition, the average annual growth in sales per firm in all types of incubators was $239,535.

In 1998, there were approximately 550 incubators in the United States. For help locating one near you, contact the National Business Incubation Association at 740-593-4331 or visit their Web site at http://www.nbia.org/.

Skip the Startup Headaches: Purchase an Existing Business

When you start a business from scratch, you have to jump through hoops to find and train employees, build up a customer base, and find suppliers. But when you buy an existing business, much of this infrastructure will already be in place.

Don Pelham is the owner of MasterCare Cleaning Services in Seattle, Washington, a service he bought from another businessperson. He explains the advantage of purchasing a business this way:

In a start-up you have to pound the pavement while you wait for your ads to appear in the phone books (and hope they get the phone number right). But when you purchase a business, the phone rings from day one. Ads are in place and working. Schedules are already made. When I took over the cleaning service, there were about twelve jobs already scheduled, three or four a week, and the phone was ringing a new job every two or three days.

Be sure to find out why the buyer is selling; don't rely on what he or she tells you. Investigate the business yourself. Find out how much traffic it actually gets. Check newspapers and town records for information about any proposed highways, superstores, or zoning changes. Check for liens against the business or other problems that could have an adverse effect on the business. Consult an accountant and an attorney before you sign on the dotted line and follow his or her advice.

> ▶ **Important**
> If you want your noncompete agreement to stand up in court, you must have the agreement written by an attorney familiar with your state's laws regarding the issue. The rules vary in every state, and if the agreement doesn't conform to state laws, it won't be enforceable. One other note: talk to your attorney about ways you can protect your business from employees who might copy it. In at least one state (California), noncompete agreements can't be enforced against employees.

Get a Noncompete Agreement Signed

When you buy an existing business, the seller is likely to tell you he or she wants to retire, to move on to other pursuits, or to leave the area.

But what the owner says and what he or she actually does can be two quite different things. To prevent the former owner of your business from becoming your newest and most dangerous competitor, ensure your sales agreement includes a valid noncompete agreement. The agreement should specify that the former owner cannot open up a competing business within a set period of time and within a certain area. Without this agreement, the former owner could open up shop across the street from you.

The agreement should give you breathing space and time to get established, but the terms have to be reasonable. An agreement that says the former owner couldn't open a competing business in the states of Michigan or Illinois for a period of twenty years would probably not stand up in court. Generally, the agreement should not extend more than 5 years or a 100-mile radius. Have an attorney whose practice focuses on small businesses write the noncompete agreement and review the entire purchase agreement. This is not the time to try to avoid legal fees.

Turn Your Competitor into Your Business Partner

Competitors don't have to be adversaries. In fact, as Greg Amy will tell you, teaming up with a competitor can turn a wannabe business into a million-dollar baby.

In 1993, Amy was laid off from his $40,000-a-year job as a computer-aided design (CAD) draftsperson in the aerospace industry. He worked as a job shopper (someone who gets contract work through temporary agencies known as job shops) for a year, and then decided to build his own computer services business focusing on companies that used AutoCAD. He spotted an ad for a night AutoCAD instructor that had been placed by Richard Allen, the owner of a business that competed with the business Amy was trying to start.

"I decided to try it for extra cash and to scope out what [the competitor] was doing," Amy says.

When Allen later needed a full-time instructor, Amy worked out an agreement to work on contract for Allen. Later, they pooled their resources to operate under the name Allen had established, OrthoCADD Services, Inc. The resulting jointly owned company had six employees and did about $2 million in sales in 1995.

Seize an Opportunity

Sometimes business opportunities seem to drop in your lap. When one does, picking it up and running with it can be a moneymaking move.

Brian Nelson is a supervisor at a factory in Michigan. He likes his work and the company, but he wanted a second source of income to allow his family to live more comfortably and to put some money away for the future. He also wanted to learn what running a retail store was all about, so he took a part-time job in a party store. The store offered customers the usual assortment of party goods and video rental services. But the store didn't own the tapes or display racks; they were owned by a third party who gave the owner a percentage of the rental fees in exchange for providing the space and handling rentals.

The arrangement should have been a win–win situation. The party store could offer its clientele a desirable service without having to buy inventory or hire extra employees. The owner of the videotapes and racks had a sales outlet without having to sign a lease, pay rent, or staff a store.

The arrangement worked for a while, but then the owner of the video rental service tired of the business. He didn't keep the racks stocked with new releases and lost many tapes because he didn't show up often enough to review the rental records and check on returns.

When he went on vacation, he asked Nelson to manage the party store rentals and rentals at several other locations. That gave Nelson a chance to learn more about what was involved in running the service. That experience, combined with research into the video rental industry, led Nelson to believe he could do a better job managing the rental service than the owner was doing, and before long he made an offer to buy out the video rental business at the party store location. The owner accepted, and Nelson was in business. His company, Midnight Video, has since expanded, adding profitable video rental concessions in several towns.

Buy a Franchise

If you want to start a business but don't want to develop your own products or methods of doing business, franchising could be your ticket to business ownership. That's because when you buy a franchise, what you get is essentially a build-your-own-business kit.

Depending on the amount of money you invest and the franchise opportunity you choose, you get rights to use the franchise name, distribute a branded product or service, and perhaps use the franchise's methods of operations. Customer leads, help locating your business, and other services may be part of your package, too.

The benefit of this approach is that it simplifies startup and may also help reduce the chance of failure.

A 1991 study of 366 franchises in 60 industries conducted by Arthur Anderson & Company found that 86 percent of the franchise units were still in operation five years after they had been started. By comparison, a 1992 SBA study of all businesses in the United States showed the five-year survival rate was only 37.6 percent.

Buying a franchise won't actually put you in business. You have to do that yourself. But if you choose your franchise carefully, the franchise's products and methods can give you the leg up you need to succeed.

Scott Wallace started his commercial cleaning business in Eden Prairie, Minnesota, this way.

"I had been fired from my job and decided I never wanted to go through that experience again," he says, "so I chose to go into business for myself. I decided to go with a franchise because of my previous business experience—none!"

After researching several types of franchises, Wallace concluded that the best one for him to buy would be a cleaning franchise because the investment was small (prices started under $5,000), no special knowledge was required, and the profit margins were good. He bought a Coverall franchise in 1994 because their Minnesota regional office seemed more interested in having him as a franchisee than other franchisors he contacted.

For his money, Wallace got a package of supplies, equipment, and customers. Then it was up to him to keep the customers and grow the business. A year after he had started, not only was he making a profit, he was considering buying a second cleaning business.

Wallace is one of hundreds of thousands of individuals who have turned to franchising as a way to get into business. According to the International Franchise Association (IFA), approximately 600,000 franchise units in the United States generate more than $800 billion in sales each year, accounting for more than 40 percent of all retail sales.

Despite the large number of franchise outlets and the huge dollar volume of sales, franchising isn't without its pitfalls. One New Jersey couple lost nearly $20,000 when the owners of a startup bread and roll franchise they had invested in went bankrupt. A West Coast man sunk his retirement funds into a mailbox/office center franchise and discovered to his dismay that the income didn't come near the claims the company's sales staff had made.

Other problems can arise, too. Franchise territories may not be large enough, or competing franchises or private businesses may open, making inroads into your selling area. Licensing fees may be excessive compared to

▶ **Tip**
There are many different types of franchises available. One quick way to search through them all is to use the Franchise Finder featured on Inc. Magazine's Web site at http://www.inc.com/virtualconsult/databases/franchise.html.

the services rendered, supplies may be too expensive, or you may find you personally don't want to conform to the franchisor's way of doing business.

To minimize the risk, learn as much about franchising as possible. Evaluate your own motives, needs, interests, and willingness to follow someone else's methods of doing business. Research several types of franchises and compare their profitability and appeal. Consider their track record and your ability to afford the franchise. Remember, you'll need money to live on as well as to get the business rolling.

Once you narrow your choices, call and visit as many current and past owners as you can. Get copies of the franchise's Uniform Franchise Offering Circular (UFOC) and read it cover to cover.

You can get copies of franchise UFOCs and get a mailing list with names of more than 100,000 franchises by contacting FranData at 800-793-8640.

For help with startup questions or problem solving after you are in businesses, contact:

The American Franchisee Association
53 West Jackson Blvd., Suite 205
Chicago, IL 60604
312-431-0545

Women in Franchising
53 W. Jackson Blvd., Suite 205
Chicago, IL 60604
800-222-4943
http://www.vaxxine.com/franchise/wif

You can get information about the franchise industry from:

The International Franchise Association
1350 New York Avenue, NW., Suite 900
Washington, DC 20005-4709
Phone: 202-628-8000
http://www.franchise.org/

The Franchise Annual Online
http://infonews.com/franchise

Chapter 2

BUSINESS RESEARCH, SIMPLIFIED

Research is the key to success in every aspect of your business. Whether you want to start a business, find investors to expand an existing business, or just write more effective sales letters, the result of your efforts will hinge on how much you really know about your industry, customers, and the specific issue at hand.

Research is so important that big business typically spends millions of dollars a year gathering the financial and market data necessary to make decisions. By comparison, small businesses often find it difficult to come up with just a few thousand dollars to purchase off-the-shelf industry studies sold by market researcher firms.

Fortunately, you don't have to spend huge amounts of cash to gather the information you need. Neither do you have to be a mathematical genius or experienced market researcher to collect useful data and analyze it; you can gather a lot of research information just by learning to talk and listen to the right people. Here are strategies that work for small businesses like yours.

Define Your Objective

Major research projects that aren't focused don't get done. Either they never get started because the task seems too vast or they are never completed because the researcher doesn't know what to research or when to stop.

To avoid either pitfall, carefully define your research objectives at the start of the project. Write a simple, one- or two-sentence statement describing why you are doing the research and what you want to accomplish. Then list the questions you want to address. For instance, if you were considering opening a pizza restaurant, your objective might read: Find out if it would be profitable for me to open and run a pizza restaurant in Springfield.

The questions you would want to answer might include:

What are the average sales of pizza restaurants in the United States?
How many other pizza restaurants are there in the Springfield area?
How well are they doing?
What is the population of Springfield?
How often does the average person order pizza from a restaurant?
What will rent and equipment cost?
How many employees will I need?
What salaries will I have to pay?
What would I have to do to advertise the restaurant?
What will ads cost?
How often will I have to run them?
Where will I buy ingredients and paper goods? What will they cost?
How many pizzas will I need to sell a week to make a profit?
Can I find enough steady customers here to make a profit?

Once you sketch out an outline like this, completing the research is then a matter of gathering the information needed to answer each question and seeing how the answers relate to your objective.

Set Time and Dollar Limits for Your Research

One of the hazards of the Information Age is how easy it is to get distracted from your goal. One source for facts may lead you to five more, and each of those five may point you to still more sources of information. If you attempt to track down each tidbit of information, you'll quickly lose control of both your time and your out-of-pocket costs. To avoid this problem, assign a specific amount of time and specific dollar limits to each part of the research project. Then, keep a running tab of the time and dollars you are putting into the work. Compare those figures frequently to your budget.

Make Sure Research Is Part of Your Regular Routine

Business research shouldn't be a one-time thing. Although you won't want to conduct major research studies every week, you do need to allocate time on a regular basis to keep up with your industry, your community, and the people in both. Without such regular research, you won't be able to spot trends or to make wise and profitable decisions. Free weekly trade magazines and online news services forums and list servers can help you get the information you need to stay current. They can also provide research information that is invaluable for creating business plans, developing strategy, and spotting trends. If you clip and file the pertinent facts or store them in a database, you'll have them on hand when you need them.

Get to Know the Reference Librarian

If you're not an experienced researcher, the most valuable "tool" you have for completing your research in an efficient manner is the reference librarian at public libraries. The reference librarian is trained to know where to look for various kinds of information and is paid to use that training to help you find the books or publications that are likely to contain the information you need. Be polite and patient, and most will happily help you locate the information you seek. All you have to do is ask.

> ▶ **Tip**
> If you file your research away in a traditional filing cabinet or if you store it in word processing documents on your computer, you may have trouble finding specific facts when you need them. Solve the problem by storing the information in the memo field of a simple database. That way, when you need facts at some later time, you can search the memo field for key words and quickly find what you tucked away.

Cut Research Costs by Using Student Researchers

If you don't have time or the skills to do your own market research, check with nearby colleges to see if they have any programs in which marketing or business students are assigned to conduct research for local businesses. At some colleges, the research is done by students at no cost to you other than out-of-pocket expenses. At institutions where marketing professors supplement their academic income by doing consulting, you may pay a fee, so be sure to ask. If the work is done by students, however, the fees should be considerably less than what you'd pay a market research firm. If they aren't, call other universities in your area.

Be sure to allow plenty of time for your research to be completed if you are working through the school. The work may progress over the course of a semester.

Don't stop with college students, either. Look for help at the high school level as well.

Advertise for a Freelancer in Student Newspapers

If you don't require a marketing professor to supervise your research, advertise in the college newspaper for one or more marketing students to help with a one-time project. Students are often willing to work for low pay to gain experience that can help them land jobs in their chosen profession when they graduate.

Get the Government to Pay for Your Research

If your business requires original technical or scientific research, you may be able to get the U.S. government to share the cost—or pay all of it. If you do such research, two federal programs to investigate are the Small Business Innovative Research (SBIR) program and the Small Business Technology Transfer (STTR) program. The SBIR program is the bigger of the two. In 1996, SBIR awards totaled $916 million. The STTR program awarded some $64 million for research that same year.

The SBIR program, which was enacted into law in 1982, awards funds to help develop products that will improve the nation's defense, protect our environment, make improvements in health care, and improve the ability to manage information and manipulate data.

Each year, ten federal agencies are required to set aside part of their research and development (R&D) budget for small business. Awards are made based on a number of factors, including the technical merit of the project and the future commercialization of the concept. Once projects are selected for funding, they go through up to three phases: a feasibility phase, actual research and development, and finally, commercialization. Awards of up to $100,000 are made during the feasibility phase (phase I). In phase II, up to $750,000 may be awarded to fund the actual research and development. During phase III, businesses have to get any needed funding from the private sector.

The ten agencies are:

Department of Agriculture
Department of Commerce
Department of Defense
Department of Education
Department of Energy
Department of Health and Human Services
Department of Transportation
Environmental Protection Agency
National Aeronautics and Space Administration
National Science Foundation

The STTR program focuses on public–private sector partnerships, providing funding for small businesses to collaborate with nonprofit research institutions. The program is similar to the SBIR program, except for the requirement for collaboration with the research institution. The upper level of funding in phase II is $500,000 rather than $750,000. Ownership of the intellectual property rights has to be negotiated with the partnering research institutions.

Five federal agencies participate in the STTR program. They are:

Department of Defense
Department of Energy
Department of Health and Human Services
National Aeronautics and Space Administration
National Science Foundation

You can get additional information about both the SBIR program and the STTR program from:

U.S. Small Business Administration
Office of Technology
409 Third Street, SW
Washington, DC 20416
202-205-6450
http://www.sbaonline.sba.gov/SBIR/

Gather Data from Free or Low-Cost U.S. Government Publications

The federal government is the world's largest publisher. It conducts research into everything from the size of industries to the number of unwed mothers, and it's all published. These reports are available free or at relatively low cost; the trick is discovering what reports are available.

The U.S. Government Printing Office (GPO) lists some 16,000 books, maps, posters, reports, microfiche, and subscription services among its for-sale publications. These documents are relatively low cost and contain facts and data that can be indispensable for your market research. Since most data produced by the U.S. government is in the public domain, you may even find information that you can repackage and resell to your customers. If you have access to the World Wide Web, you can conduct a free search for government publications through the GPO access site at http://www.access.gpo.gov.

You can also locate government information posted on the Web by searching from The FedWorld Information Network (http://www.fedworld.gov).

If you don't have access to a computer, you can get free catalogs listing publications by calling the GPO superintendent of documents at 202-512-

> ▶ Tip
> Many government publications can be downloaded directly from the Internet. Longer reports are often available only in Adobe Acrobat PDF format. You can download the Adobe Acrobat Reader (a program that lets you open, read and print files, but not change them) free from the Adobe Systems Web site at http://www.adobe.com/

Newspapers and Magazines

Don't forget about mass circulation newspapers and magazines as a source of research data. Articles in publications like *BusinessWeek*, *The Wall Street Journal*, the *New York Times*, *Fortune*, and *Forbes* can help you get statistics, keep up with trends, and gather names of useful contacts and leaders in a wide range of fields.

1800. Describe the kind of information you need and ask what catalogs they could send you. Some that might be of interest to you are a catalog of U.S. government subscriptions, a catalog of U.S. government information for businesses, and a catalog of information available in electronic format.

In addition to making government publications available via mail, the GPO also operates bookstores in major cities throughout the United States.

Get Population and Employment Data Free

Dig into the data at either the U.S. Department of Commerce's Census Bureau or the U.S. Department of Labor, and you'll find a mother lode of facts and figures to help you plan and run your business.

The Census Bureau is the agency that publishes population counts and economic indicators. Here you'll find county, state, and federal economic profiles and summary reports on everything from aging in America and the number of women over fifty giving birth, to the amount of municipal waste recovered or recycled per person in 1993. In fact, it's the first place you should look for the demographic, social, and economic data you'll need in order to predict the market for new products and services.

The Department of Labor publishes employment statistics, reports of workplace trends, occupational descriptions, and information about complying with workplace regulations. There you'll find everything from OSHA regulations, a study of 401k plan expenses, and wage, hour, and workplace standards, to a plain-English handbook explaining the federal labor laws that affect your business.

Census and Department of Labor information is available in many public libraries. But a faster and cheaper way to get the same information (considering the cost of all those photocopies you'd have to make) is to access the data through the Internet. The Census Bureau is accessible from the World Wide Web at http://www.census.gov. The Web site for the Department of Labor is located at http://www.dol.gov.

Get Research Data, Trade Leads, and Procurement Notices for Less Than 50 Cents a Day

If you need economic data or industry data, or are looking for opportunities to do business globally or with the U.S. government, STAT-USA/Internet, an agency in the Economics and Statistics Administration,

U.S. Department of Commerce, can help. The agency maintains an Internet database service at http://www.stat-usa.gov that pulls together data from hundreds of federal offices. The data falls into two broad, searchable categories: economic research and business opportunities.

Unlike other government Web sites, you have to pay to use STAT-USA. The fee is $50 a quarter or $150 a year. Some of the economic research is free from other sources, but if you use the service to get import or export leads or as a single source to keep a watch for government business opportunities, it can be well worth the fee. Sample documents and reports can be viewed for free on the STAT-USA/Internet Web site.

Buy U.S. Government Statistics in Print or on CD-ROM

You don't need a modem to get U.S. government statistics, of course. You can get publications such as *The Statistical Abstract of the United States* in print.

You can order *The Statistical Abstract* or other government publications by calling the superintendent of documents, U.S. Government Printing Office, at 202-512-1800.

In addition to print, some government offices are starting to make their data available on CD-ROM, too. If you will be referring repeatedly to certain government research sources and don't need today's facts today, purchasing government-produced CDs can be useful. However, if you will be using the information only once (say, for a business plan) or if you need very current information (such as trade leads, procurement opportunities, or real-time economic news), the Internet would be a better choice.

Get *The Statistical Abstract* for Less Than the Government Charges

Some third parties repackage government information and charge you more than the government does. But *The Statistical Abstract* is an exception. You can save 35 percent of the cover price by purchasing *The Statistical Abstract of the United States* from Hoovers, Inc. The company publishes a number of other products that can be helpful to you in planning (or marketing) your business. For a catalog of their products, call 800-486-8666.

Get For-Sale Government Publications for Free

Whether or not you have to pay a fee for a U.S. government publication sometimes depends on where you get it.

You can get various publications put out by the Department of Defense (DoD) for a fee from the GPO, but if you visit or call a nearby DoD office, you can get the same publication for free if they have it in stock. The same is true for many publications from other agencies.

If you can't get a government agency to give you a free copy of a report, you may be able to read the publication for free by looking it up in a public library or at a federal depository library.

Federal depository libraries are reference libraries that are often part of a college or university. They house large collections of pamphlets, books, and documents published by the federal government. If your own public library doesn't have the government publications you need, ask if there is a federal depository library in your vicinity.

Do Research on Commercial Online Services Free of Connect-Time Charges

If you have a computer and modem, but don't already subscribe to an online service, consider signing up. Look for offers that give you extra hours or a month of free time to try the service. Many of the services offer extra free time or usage credits that can be used during the first month you belong. Compare the deals, choose the best, and then use your free hours to do your research. Be sure you clarify in advance whether there are any restrictions on how you can use any free time you get when you sign on. There could be restrictions that prevent you from applying such credit to special research areas on the service.

Don't limit your search for information to research databases alone, however. Explore the forums or special interest areas online. Many can be a source of not only industry data, but also facts such as which groups of businesses or consumers make the best target customers and what advertising and marketing methods work best for a particular type of business. That type of insider information can put you on the fast track to success.

If you have friends or family members who have online accounts but don't normally use up all of their free time each month, ask them if they'd look up some of the information you need. Again, make sure that what you ask them to get is in an area that they won't be billed an extra fee to use. Have them give the information to you on disk. (Virus-check any disks your friends give you no matter how much you trust them.)

Get In-Depth Reports Quickly, but for a Price

If the data you uncover through free government and library sources isn't sufficient for your needs, or if you need to keep up with late-breaking news in your industry on a daily basis, you may want to use fee-based electronic research services targeted at corporate users.

If you can gather the information you need from newspaper articles, magazines, and trade journals, one of the best-priced online research services around is the Electric Library. Available on the Internet and through America Online, Compuserve, and Prodigy, the Electric Library lets you search and view an unlimited number of articles for a flat fee. Monthly and yearly subscriptions plans are available.

If you need to do trademark searches or want specialized, industry-specific research, expect to pay more—sometimes a lot more. You may have to pay $5 to $10 and up to view individual articles or listings, for instance. And you can expect to pay thousands of dollars for the latest industry analysis and projections prepared by market research firms.

▶ **Tip**
The Penn State Population Research Institute maintains a list of organizations that produce demographic data. You'll find a motherlode of Web links to demographic resources at this page on their Web site:
http://www.pop.psu.edu/Demography/demography.html.

Get Key Findings Without Paying Thousands of Dollars for Market Research Reports

Market research companies often issue press releases outlining some of the key findings of major research studies. This gets them free publicity, which helps them sell the detailed, high-priced reports to major corporations that can afford them. If you're doing preliminary research or don't need in-depth analyses, these press releases (published in newspapers and trade magazine articles) may provide you with all the statistical information you need. You can find these releases-turned-into-articles by searching magazine and newspaper indices in the public library for topics of interest. Or if you are using an online database, search for your subject matter and the words *study*, *research*, or *report*. If you know that one or two market research companies regularly issue reports about the topic you are researching, add the name of the market research company to your search terms.

Publications such as *American Demographics* are often a good source of cheap or free data, too. You can search back issues of *American Demographics* at the magazine's Web site at http://www.demographics.com. Articles include the name of the company, individual, or organization that provided the data along with contact information in case you need additional information. If you don't have a computer, see if your public library has Internet access or ask the reference librarian to show you how to find the research data you want using the facilities they do have available.

Encourage Your Customers to Give You Feedback

If you want to know how to improve your products to stay competitive or what new products to introduce, your customers can be your best source of information. Encourage them to report their experiences to you and be sure you keep a record of difficulties they report. Look for ways to solve these problems and keep your ears open for commonly requested features your product doesn't have.

If your sales are contract sales and you've lost out to a competitor, ask the customer for a debriefing. The information will give you the facts you need to determine how your offerings compare in price and quality to the competition and perhaps guide you to easy fixes you can make so you do get the contract the next time.

Look Up Comparative Financial Data in Library Reference Books

Whether you are writing a business plan or just want to keep your business on target, it's important to know how your income, assets, debt, and operating costs relate to each other and how they compare to similar businesses in your industry. Such comparisons can help you spot financial strengths and weaknesses. How your figures stack up to industry averages can also determine whether you get the bank loan or convince investors to put money into the business. Your accountant may be able to provide you with relevant industry financial information. Or you can look it up on your own for free at nearby public libraries. Three good reference books to look for are *Annual Statement Studies* (Robert Morris Associates), *Industry Norms & Key Business Ratios* (Dun & Bradstreet Information Services), and *Almanac of Business and Industrial Financial Ratios* (Prentice Hall). Not all libraries carry these, so call before making a trip. If the first library you call doesn't have these books, ask if they know if any nearby library does.

Read Business and Trade Magazines Regularly

Business and trade magazines that cover your field are essential reading. They'll alert you to industry trends and issues, regulatory changes, sources of supplies or new products, news about your competitors, demographic data, news of upcoming trade shows, statistics on salaries, and a wealth of other information that is vital for planning.

Many of these trade magazines are considered "controlled circulation" publications. That means they will be delivered to your office free if you appear to be a qualified buyer of the products and services advertised in the publications. To prove you are qualified, you'll have to fill out a lengthy application form that will have multiple-choice options for indicating your job function in your company, the type of equipment and products you are responsible for buying or specifying, the dollar amount or number of various types of products you purchase during the year, and other similar information. One tip: If your office is in your home, and the subscription card asks if this is a home or business address, check off business. Otherwise you might not qualify.

Contact Trade Associations

If you need industry information that you can't find in printed articles, call industry trade associations. Ask them where to find the information. They may have published studies on the subject or be able to refer you to experts in the field or other sources of information.

Quickly Locate Trade Associations and Trade Publications in All Fields

Quickly locate trade associations, trade publications, and experts in all fields. No matter what your industry or field, there is likely to be one or more industry associations and trade publications that cater to the field. There are also likely to be experts at colleges and universities around the country who study the industry. But how do you find these resources quickly? The easiest way is to go to the public library and look them up in one of the many directories you'll find there. Some likely sources:

The Standard Periodical Directory
Oxbridge Communications, Inc.
150 Fifth Ave., Suite 302
New York, NY 10011

Encyclopedia of Associations
Gale Research Inc.
The Gale Group
27500 Drake Road
Farmington Hills, MI 48331

Gale Directory of Publications and
Broadcast Media (formerly called
Ayer Directory of Publications)
Gale Research Inc.
The Gale Group
27500 Drake Road
Farmington Hills, MI 48331

If these don't provide the information you need, ask the reference librarian for help. He or she will know what other directories the library has that will help you find the contact information you need.

Read General Business Publications for Information on Industry Trends

Fortune magazine, *Business Week*, the *Wall Street Journal*, and other general business publications can provide valuable clues about industry trends and specific problems. The easiest and least expensive way to find articles is to use the *Magazine Index* or *Periodical Index* published by Information Access Company. Most public libraries have these available.

Search out Newspaper and Magazine Articles About Your Competitors

Reporters are usually good at digging up facts and figures. Thus, if you can find articles about your competitors, you may uncover a lot of competitive information all neatly summarized.

For instance, a couple of years ago, a North Carolina newspaper ran an article discussing the importance of destroying sensitive documents by shredding them rather than just throwing them in a trash can where industrial spies or disgruntled employees might get at them.

The article featured information about a local company that manufactured paper shredders. Ironically, it included a considerable amount of competitive information about the company that manufactured the shredders. Any competitor that read the article would immediately know the number of employees the company had, number of units it manufactured each year, price ranges, total market size, company's market share, names of customers, best-selling products, and locations of suppliers.

Use a News-Clipping Service to Keep Up with Trends

If your desk is piled high with industry publications you never have time to read, or if trying to keep up with all of them makes you feel snowed under, try one of these alternatives:

▶ Assign a staff member to browse through the publications and clip out important articles. Be sure to have him or her use a highlighter to mark the parts of articles that are pertinent so you don't have to read the entire article to find one or two important sentences.

▶ Subscribe to industry newsletters that summarize key information and report it in a timely fashion.

▶ Subscribe to an online clipping service. These are available on several of the major online services and let you set up a profile describing the kind of information you want to read. What you put in your profile might be a general industry term, such as pharmaceuticals if you wanted to get copies of all articles about that industry coming across the newswires, or it could be more specific, such as the name of a competitor you'd like to track.

Check Local Resources for Demographic Information

If you sell products or services to the local community, your best source of up-to-date demographic information about the area may be close at hand. Regional or city economic development centers, the gas and electric company serving your area, SCORE, the local Chamber of Commerce, and even daily and weekly newspapers may have population, income, or other demographics figures that will give you vital planning information. Look in the government listings in your telephone book for contact information.

Hire a Professional

If you will be putting significant sums of money into a project or if you require information that neither you nor any of your employees are trained to find quickly, hire a professional to do your research.

Depending on what kind of information you need, you may want to hire a market research consultant or firm, an information broker, or even a private detective. Although the hourly fees may be high ($60–$100 an hour or more), the professional will know where to get the information you need and how to do it in the fastest, most efficient manner. If you don't know where to find a market research professional, check in the public library for *The Green Book*, the industry directory published by the American Marketing Association.

One caveat: Be sure to check the professional's references thoroughly. Corporate downsizing has set loose not only a lot of good talent, but also a lot of deadwood. You need to make sure the expert's knowledge of your field is equal in quality to the brochure he or she hands out. Find out who he or she has worked for before and call them to find out if they were happy with the results. If this is your expert's first foray on his or her own, ask for names of former employers or coworkers you can call.

Tap Your Network of Friends and Acquaintances for Information

Your personal address book could be just as valuable in your quest for information as a corporate executive's Rolodex of business contacts.

Each person in it possesses a wealth of knowledge and experiences and might be able to provide leads to the information you seek. In addition, each of those contacts knows other people who may be able to help you.

Flora M. Brown, owner of Gift Baskets by Flora in Fullerton, California, has learned to use this technique to her advantage. Whenever she starts a new project, the first thing she does is get out her personal address book.

"I call everyone I know who might have any kind of connection with what I need to know," she says. "Once I get a little bit of information, it has a ripple effect. Everyone always seems to know someone else. . . . "

Brown used the ripple effect to gather information when she was starting her gift basket business. She didn't

Learn to Be Nosy

As a child, you were probably taught that it's rude to ask a lot of questions about other people's activities. As an adult, you will have to unlearn that lesson. To succeed in your own business, you'll have to make continuing efforts to keep informed about how your competitors are operating and what your customers really want to buy. You may feel uncomfortable trying to retrieve information you know your competitors don't want you to have. But you'll be left in the dust if you don't constantly keep tabs on how profitable they are, what new products they plan to introduce, what new manufacturing techniques they are using, what they do to make employees like working for them (or dislike their jobs), or what their customers think about their operation.

know anyone in the industry but did remember a friend who knew someone who sold gift baskets. By following up that lead, Brown learned about the Los Angeles Gift Mart, which is a building where manufacturers' sales representatives maintain showrooms. Someone at the Gift Mart told her about the gift trade show, a major industry show that is held at the Los Angeles Convention Center twice a year. She attended the show and came away with a wealth of information about suppliers, trade magazines, and training seminars.

Build Ongoing Relationships with Friendly Competitors

Whereas some competitors may be cold, hostile, and unwilling to share information, others in your field may be more than willing to share tips and tricks of the trade. This is particularly true for very small retailers and services providers. In fact, if there's a work overload, some competitors will refer customers to one another.

There are several ways to connect with your competitors. One way is to attend local chapter meetings of trade associations for your industry. (This also can be a good way to meet business prospects; corporate workers in a position to hire independent contractors often attend such meetings.)

Another way is to become active in local or regional business groups that are not industry specific. Chambers of Commerce, Toastmasters, Lions Clubs, and regional business associations are examples. If your product or service is sold to local businesses, you are very likely to meet competitors (as well as sales prospects) at such meetings. Seminars at trade shows held in your area are still another way to meet local competitors.

Know How to Play the Game

Just attending business meetings isn't going to get you very far. Although you may gain useful tips listening to speakers at a meeting, you'll learn a lot more by becoming a familiar face and striking up conversations with your competitors about common interests or problems you have.

How successful you are at gathering information (or making friends) this way will depend on how your competitors and other business owners perceive you.

If you seem genuinely in need of help, or genuinely interested in sharing ideas and concerns, you are likely to establish a good rapport with one or more of your colleagues. As you get to know them over time, you may exchange phone calls or meet for informal luncheons or breakfasts to talk shop. Such meetings with your direct competitors can help you learn about new suppliers, new production or manufacturing methods, new regulations, and other information that's vital to your success.

On the other hand, if you come on too strong, you'll have little success gaining information. If you aggressively pump small competitors for information, brag about your expertise (implying you are somehow better than the people with whom you want to network), or give them the impression that you can't be trusted, your attempts to get information will fail. Worse, you may develop a reputation for being unlikable or unethical that could hinder your attempts to get business.

Follow Discussions in Online Forums or Internet Newsgroups

> ### More Dirty Tricks
>
> Unscrupulous businesses and disgruntled employees will sometimes create fictitious online identities and use them to bad mouth their competitors or employers or spread lies such as the company is going bankrupt, or the owner is an alcoholic or drug addict. If allegations pop up out of the blue, if there seem to be just one or two people who make such claims, or if there are several e-mail addresses commenting, but they all write messages the same way and all misspell the same words, suspect sabotage.

An inexpensive way to research what customers like or dislike about products or what they wish they could find is to monitor the messages in online forums or Internet newsgroups discussing your industry. Comments from outspoken users can help you know what features to add, what to discard, and which you should be promoting more in your advertising. You may even get ideas for products you should consider developing.

Monitoring such discussions may also give you some indication of the reputation and reliability of vendors you are considering. However, before jumping to conclusions based on what you read, try to determine just who is making the comments. It's a dog-eat-dog world out there, and some vendors will do anything they can to win sales, including signing on under false identities or hiring shills to either praise their own products or discredit their competitors.

Conduct Your Own Market Research Survey

You can gather the numerical information you need to answer questions about your market by conducting your own market research study.

The survey could be a printed form you ask customers or prospects to complete and return, a telephone survey, or a poll conducted at a location where you might expect to find typical customers. Ideally, it should be conducted by a professional researcher, but if you can't afford to have a professional firm do all the work, consider hiring a professional to do part of the work for you, says James Smith, owner of Smith and Company, a consulting firm based in Chicago. "You could do the actual interviewing yourself, he says, but "let the professional write the survey for you, show you how to get a random, unbiased sample for interviews, and explain how to calculate the results."

You'll need to complete at least 100 interviews to have a reasonable sample, Smith says. If you plan to subdivide responses into age, sex, or other categories, you'll need a minimum of thirty responses in each sub-sample group.

Network with Bankers, Real Estate Agents and Local Politicians

If you derive most of your business from the local community, get to know the people in the community who are usually first to know about business deals. These are the people who rent property, insure property, review zoning compliance, and loan money. Schmoozing with these individuals can alert you to new business possibilities and get you introductions to key contacts before your competitors have a chance to throw their hat in the ring.

Come Right Out and Ask

You can gather a lot of research data and competitive intelligence just by asking the right people the right questions. Here are a few examples:

▶ Ask your competitors what they are up to. If they like to brag about their accomplishments or show off, they may volunteer a lot of information you can use to build your own business

▶ Ask your competitors' clients about your competitor. Ask what made them choose your competitor over you and whether they are completely satisfied with the competitor. If you have a good, personal relationship with the customer, ask him or her to show you any sales literature or samples the competitor is giving out. If any of your customers are good friends, they may go so far as to feed you everything the competition sends them.

▶ Ask your competitors' suppliers for information. The answers to simple questions like "What's hot?" or "How's business this month?" might give you important clues about what your competitors are up to.

▶ Ask your competitors' employees for information. If asked, they may be willing to talk about working conditions, overtime, salary, or new projects in the works.

Buy Your Competitor a Drink or Two

Some people schmooze it up in bars as a way of building camaraderie with potential customers. Others do it in hopes that the liquor will make a competitor or one of their employees drop his or her guard and leak important information about company procedures or projects. On the flip side of the coin, have your gin and tonic without the gin.

Hang Out Alone at Hotel Cafes and Bars

Find out when and where your competitors are holding sales meetings and what trade shows they will be attending, suggests Joanna Strohn, president of Electronic Motorcyclists, Inc. "Drop by the hotel or even get a room. Listen to the conversations in restaurants and on elevators." Strohn, who spent many years working in marketing for a Fortune 100 company, adds that breakfast and the bar are great for eavesdropping.

Pose as a Customer

You can find out what your competitors are selling, what they are charging, what special offers they make, what their delivery times are like, and more— all by posing as a customer. All you have to do is call or send for their literature or attend conferences and seminars they host. Don't forget to ask for a list of satisfied customers. Every name on it is a sales prospect for you.

To avoid detection when spying on the competition, some companies have employees assume fake identities and have mail sent to post office box numbers or to friends' and relatives' homes. They sidestep legal problems and even gain the ability to open a checking account with the fake ID by filing a fictitious name statement with appropriate state or local offices. Still another option: Hire a private investigator to do your undercover work.

▶ **Note**
If you plan to go to these extremes to gain competitive information, check with your attorney (and your conscience!) before carrying out your spy mission.

Test-Market New Products to Find Out What Customers *Really* Think

You've developed a new product you are sure will gain widespread acceptance. Your spouse thinks it's terrific. You neighbor wants to order several for gifts. So, now, it's time to beef up production and roll it out to the marketplace, right?

Not quite.

"There is no substitute for the opinions of real, live, air-breathing consumers—and your mother-in-law won't cut it," says Roy Bernstein, owner of Demand Research Corp. in Columbus, Ohio.

Just like major corporations, you should test-market your product on a wider scale before investing a large amount of time or money to produce it.

"If you do nothing else, take your product to at least 100 people who would be targets—not folks whose judgment you like," Bernstein advises.

Distribution Patterns

Don't conclude your research until you have a clear picture of both distribution patterns and buying preferences. You may have a great idea for a new product or service, but if you can't get it distributed through the channels customers normally use to buy, you'll have a long, hard path to travel to success. If you need to be in mail order catalogs, for instance, find out what you need to do—and to spend—to get there and plan accordingly.

Another way to gather useful information is to test-market your product by giving away free samples of it at trade shows, fairs, Chamber of Commerce mixers, stores, or shopping malls. If you offer a service such as artwork or Web design, do some work for free to develop a portfolio of samples.

Count Customers

If you're thinking about starting a business or buying one, try to determine how many customers the business (or similar ones) now gets. One way to do that is to park yourself on a bench or car within viewing distance of the business and actually count the number of people who go in, and how many come out carrying a purchase. Vary the times you watch so that you have records from midweek, midday, morning, evening, weekends.

Subscribe to the Newspapers in the Communities Where Your Competitors Are Located

Strohn also suggests keeping up with your competitors by subscribing to the local papers in the communities where they have major divisions or plants. In addition to stories about the company that appear in the papers, check the help wanted ads regularly. "It's amazing how companies that are normally secretive will give away a lot of information about future plans when they describe the skills and projects planned for new hires," Strohn says.

Warning: Competitive Intelligence Is a Two-Way Street

Be careful how much information about your future plans you give trading partners, employees, or curious customers. Your trading partner may unintentionally leak your plans to a competitor (or adapt your ideas themselves!); the employee you chastise may go to work for a competitor; and the inquisitive customer may be someone who works for your competitor and is using a phony name to gather information about your plans, products, or methods of doing business.

Chapter 3

FINDING

SUPPLIERS

Better, faster, cheaper.

Those three magic words can turn your hot prospects into happy customers. But in order for you to give your customers better products, faster service, and lower rates, you have to develop a core group of reliable suppliers who cut you good deals on the products and services you buy.

Finding reliable suppliers who will sell to you at low cost is no easy task. In fact, it's not unusual for small businesses to find they can buy certain products cheaper from WalMart than they can from a wholesaler. Nor is it unusual for a wholesaler or distributor to refuse to sell to a very small business. That's because it will take their sales staff the same time to process your $150 order as it would to process a $5,000 order.

Nevertheless, you can develop a core group of suppliers you can trust. Here are tips that help.

Be Persistent

Good suppliers and good deals don't just show up on your doorstep. "You have to really do some digging to find good suppliers," says Cheryl McMahon. Cheryl owns American Disabled Workshop, a for-profit workshop located in Tamarac, Florida. The company, which employs disabled workers, retirees, and people in 12-step programs, sells imprinted paper floor mats, auto litter bags, key tags, and plastic steering wheel covers. Cheryl has found she's had to pour considerable energy into finding suppliers and building good relationships with them.

"Nobody out there is going to tell you where to find the best products or how to find the cheapest printer. Shop around for the best deals. I use phone, read magazines and newspapers . . . sometimes I feel like a detective!"

Shop the Ads in Trade Magazines

Whether you want to buy a pump to use in your laboratory, shredded paper to use as filler in decorative baskets, or silver earrings to sell at flea markets, you're likely to find the products you need advertised in a trade magazine for your industry.

If you are just starting out in business and aren't sure what trade publications exist, ask your librarian to help you find the association and periodical directories mentioned in Chapter 1.

Once you find trade publications for your field, be sure to browse through all the ads. Small display ads at the backs of the magazines and new product listings can help you find new suppliers. If you are scouting out merchandise to sell, look over ads to see if there are any minimum purchase requirements.

Don't forget about regional publications of large national associations, either. The smaller regional publications often contain ads from local vendors who do not find it profitable to take out ads in their association's national publication.

Let Your Fingers Do the Walking

Before you place an order from any of the advertisers in a trade magazine, check your local yellow pages to see if you can find a local supplier. If those widgets that cost a fortune to ship and take up to ten days to arrive are available from a local supplier, the shipping cost may be less. Or you may be able to get them now and eliminate the shipping costs by picking them up from the manufacturer or distributor.

▶ **One Caution**
Using local suppliers can be particularly helpful when you need items you don't regularly stock to fill special orders. But if you have to make a special trip to buy supplies for a single customer, remember to factor in the cost of your time into your price for the job.

If you can't find suppliers in the regular yellow pages, call the telephone company and ask them if there is a separate business-to-business directory for your region. If there is, have them send it to you. It should be free, and it may contain ads from local suppliers who don't advertise in the yellow pages distributed to homeowners.

Search for Manufacturers in Directories on the Internet

If you have a computer, modem, and access to the World Wide Web, you can search a number of electronic databases for manufacturers and suppliers.

The first place to look is the Thomas Register on the Internet (http://www.thomasregister.com). This resource contains the entire database of the well-known Thomas Register of American Manufacturers, with the names of 155,000 companies organized into 55,000 product and service headings. The site also has online supplier catalogs with detailed buying and specifying information.

Other major business directories are available on the Internet as well. Among them are NYNEX's national yellow page listings and AT&T's 800 directory. To search the yellow pages, you'll need an area code or city name to narrow down your searches. AT&T's directory lets you search by category of goods.

You can reach the NYNEX yellow pages at the following URL: http://www.niyp.com/. The URL for the AT&T 800 directory is http://www.tollfree.att.net/tf.html. To find more directories on the Internet, use any of the major search engines (Yahoo, Lycos, AOL NetFind, and so on) and search for the words *manufacturer and directory.*

Search CD-ROM Yellow Pages for Suppliers

Get extra mileage out of the CD-ROM business directory you bought to help market your business. If the product allows you to search by Standard Industrial Code (SIC) or type of business, use it to locate the addresses and phone numbers of potential new suppliers for your company. Several products that let you search by business category or SIC are:

InfoUSA, Inc. CD-ROM Products
800-321-0869
http://www.infousa.com

American Yellow Pages
American Business Information
800-555-5666

Look for others in computer software mail-order catalogs, computer superstores, and online computer software stores.

Ask for Details Before Ordering a CD-ROM Directory

CD-ROM directory listings may include anything from simple name and address listings to details, including industry, SIC, annual sales, and number of employees. Some of them allow you unlimited use of the information on the CD; others restrict the number of names you can display or export for use in mailings.

Make sure you get what you expect and know what rights you are purchasing before spending your money on a product. If packaging or ads don't make it clear what rights you get and what listings will look like, call the CD-ROM publisher and ask them to mail or fax you a sample listing from the directory along with any pricing or usage information you need.

Look for Wholesalers, Distributors, and Manufacturers in Printed Directories

The reference section of your public library holds a lot more than the financial data and statistics mentioned in Chapter 2. In most libraries, you'll also find a variety of directories containing contact information and descriptions of wholesalers, distributors, manufacturers, and suppliers for your business.

Among the reference books and directories that can help you find products to sell, parts, or supplies that you can't find locally are:

Thomas Register of American Manufacturers
Thomas Publishing Company
5 Penn Plaza, 15th Floor
New York, NY 10001

The American Wholesalers and Distributors Directory
Gale Research Inc.
27500 Drake Rd.
Farmington Hills, MI 48331
800-877-GALE

If your public library doesn't have these directories, it will have others. Ask the reference librarian to help you find directories that will be of use to you.

▶ **Tip**
If your business is big enough that you need frequent access to information in these directories, contact the publishers and ask for the price of printed copies and CD-ROM versions of their material.

A smaller directory that features variety merchandise wholesalers is:

Directory of Wholesalers, Importers and Liquidators
Sumner Communications
24 Grassy Plain Street
Bethel, CT 06801-1725
http://www.sumcomm.com

It can be purchased for $32.90 from the publisher, who also publishes several magazines for variety retailers and flea market merchants.

▶ **Tip**
If the library where you live is small or doesn't have a large collection of business reference books, ask the reference librarian to help you locate another library in the area that better meets your needs. You may find that one library in your county is known for its collection of craft books, whereas another has a better collection of business directories.

Search for Manufacturers, Distributors, and Wholesalers in Online Directories

Search for suppliers in the Thomas Register on the Internet (http://www.thomasregister.com). If you don't have access to a computer and the Internet, visit your public library. Many have the Thomas Register on CD-ROM in the reference rooms.

Look for Directories of Catalog Vendors

Directories of catalog vendors can also help you locate the products you need to run your business. If you can't find suppliers or are looking for new sources, look through directories such as:

The Catalog of Catalogs
Woodbine House
6510 Bells Mills Road
Bethesda, MD 20817
800-843-7323

Wholesale by Mail Catalog
Lowell Miller and Prudence McCullogh
Harper Collins
10 East 53rd St.
New York, NY 10022

National Directory of Catalogs
Oxbridge Communications, Inc.
150 Fifth Avenue
New York, NY
800-955-0231

The National Directory of Catalogs is available on disk and CD-ROM as well as in print.

In addition to these or other publications with national listings, look for regional industrial or manufacturing directories and for directories that list wholesalers and suppliers by industry.

Attend Industry Trade Shows

Whether your business sells maps or Mother Mary's Mouthwatering Marmalade, there are trade shows that can help you find suppliers for ingredients, packaging, or new products. These trade shows are generally advertised in industry trade publications. In fact, if the industry you are in has a lot of trade shows, the trade magazines may even have a monthly column listing upcoming events. You can also find trade shows by searching the trade show directory at http://www.tsnn.com.

Ask Your Suppliers for Help Finding Alternate Sources for Products and Services

If you can't get what you want in the quantity you want from a distributor or wholesaler, ask them if they know any other company that can help you. They may know of sources you haven't thought of. When Flora M. Brown, owner of Gift Baskets by Flora in Fullerton, California, couldn't find the palm leaves she wanted to decorate a basket order, she asked one of her regular suppliers if they knew any place to get the leaves. They referred her to a local company that supplied dried flowers, vases, and decorative accessories to the floral industry. Brown not only got the palm leaves she was looking for, but also discovered a new source of other types of supplies she might not otherwise have found since she hadn't realized floral suppliers would have items she could use in baskets.

▶ **Tip**
Although the low prices at which buying clubs and superstores are able to offer merchandise have hurt some small businesses, others have found that they can profit by purchasing in bulk from these outlets and then reselling the merchandise in smaller quantities to their own customers.

Shop the Office Superstores and Buying Clubs and Warehouses

Superstores are changing the way both consumer and business products are sold. By cutting out the middlemen and buying large quantities of items directly from the manufacturer, superstores and warehouse clubs reduce their costs for merchandise enough so that they are able to offer it for resale at close to what small retailers have to pay to buy the same merchandise wholesale. As a result, if they carry the supplies you need for your office, store, or shop, they may offer the best available prices.

As with every other buying situation, however, it pays to shop around. Although the big warehouse chains and superstores can usually buy at the lowest possible prices, not all of them resell at the lowest possible prices. You may find some items at superstores are priced higher than you can get them from other sources.

Shop at Auctions

If you aren't in a hurry to purchase items, watch for notices of auctions. If you're looking for inventory items to purchase or industry-specific equipment, look for notices of auctions being held to sell off assets of businesses in your industry that have closed.

Don't Wait for an Auction

If you hear a business or a department of a larger corporation is being shut down, don't wait for the auction notice to appear in papers. Call the business and ask how they are going to dispose of furniture, equipment, and supplies you may be able to use. One laboratory owner I know got most of the equipment he needed to expand his testing facility for pennies on the dollar by purchasing it from a large corporation that was closing down a laboratory they had maintained in one of their offices.

Don't Rely on One Supplier

Having only one supplier for items you sell customers is risky. If that supplier has a problem and can't fill your order, you won't be able to service your customers.

"I learned the importance of this the hard way," says Cheryl McMahon. She had been using just one printer to imprint floor mats her company sells, and that printer developed equipment problems that lasted several weeks. "Now I have a different printer and use the first as backup," she says.

Network with Other Business Owners

Look for other businesses in your industry and in other industries with whom you can trade supplier information. If you can't find other businesses locally with whom you can share supplier information, search for discussions about your industry on commercial online services or on the Internet. Chances are there are groups of people in your field who regularly discuss such issues in online forums or in electronic mailing lists. (For more information, see Chapter 14.)

Buy Surplus or Used Goods from the U.S. Government

The U.S. government buys billions of dollars worth of goods and services each year, but sometimes they don't use everything they buy. Or it replaces old, but still serviceable, items with newer goods. When it does this, it sells off the old or surplus items at auction. These items may be perfect for use in your office or, in some cases, for resale. You can get on a mailing list to receive notices of auctions being held in your vicinity by calling the Defense Reutilization and Marketing Office (DRMO) at 800-468-8289. Or visit their Web site: http://www.drms.dla.mil.

Keep Your Eye on the Hidden Cost of Purchases

The actual cost for supplies you buy for your business isn't the only expense you incur in purchasing them. In addition to any direct expense, your cost includes the cost of time spent making the purchase. Even if you run a one-person business, that cost can be considerable. For instance, if you bill your services at $75 an hour and spend two hours to drive to two office supply stores in your area looking for the best price on toner cartridges, the cost of your time for doing so is $150! Therefore, if your time is limited, and the total purchase price of any item relatively little, you may find that shopping around for the best price is not cost efficient.

Cut Costs by Teaming Up with Your Competitors to Buy Supplies

Wholesalers often have minimum purchase requirements. For instance, they may require you to buy by the case or bundle, or refuse to process orders unless they exceed a certain dollar amount. Though such specifications make sense from the wholesaler's perspective (they are in business, after all, to sell in quantity), it isn't always practical for very small businesses to tie up cash by purchasing more stock or supplies than they can use up in a short time. To get around this dilemma, consider linking up with your competitors to purchase frequently needed supplies. If you can locate a large number of people in your industry locally, a formal cooperative could be the right approach. If there are just a few others with whom you network, call them and ask if they want to split an order when you have to order in quantity.

Find New Suppliers by Reading Packaging

One of the provisions of the U.S. Fair Packaging and Labeling Act requires all consumer products to bear a label that indicates the name and address of the manufacturer, packer, or distributor of the merchandise. This requirement allows consumers to identify the manufacturer or distributor should a problem arise with the product. It can also help enterprising small retailers identify new suppliers. Whenever you shop and see items that would fit in with the products you sell, copy down the manufacturer's name and address, and if available, phone number from the packaging. (If the phone number isn't on the packaging, look the company up in Thomas Register of American Manufacturers.) Then call the company and ask how to purchase the products.

Store Suppliers' Names in a Database

When you find good suppliers or service technicians, be sure to write down their contact information in a permanent database or address book. Business cards or scraps of paper that you jot notes down on tend to get lost. Even if they don't get lost, they may not contain enough information to help you remember why you saved a business card or other contact information. If your contact has given you directions to his or her establishment, be sure to include the directions in your database or address book. That way you won't have to ask for them again if you want to return to the same place.

▶ **One Caution**
When your suppliers drop-ship, you don't have the same control over the shipment of an order as you would if you keep inventory and ship the goods yourself.

Look for Reliable Suppliers Who Will Drop-Ship Merchandise

A drop shipper is a supplier that will mail merchandise you order directly to your customers instead of shipping it to you. When you can find drop shippers, the arrangement is beneficial because it lets you expand the line of products you offer your customers without forcing you to tie up cash in inventory or to find the physical space to store inventory on your premises.

Some companies let you know that they will drop-ship orders, but many don't advertise that fact in their catalogs or sales literature. Before assuming suppliers don't or won't drop-ship orders for you, call and ask what their policies are.

Ask for Other Types of Discounts

Quantity purchases aren't the only ones that can qualify for discounts. Depending on the source and the nature of the product or service, you may be able to get discounts for prepayment of orders or for payment of invoices in just a few days; for buying unused merchandise or unused advertising space (called "remnant space"); or for buying items that are slightly damaged (they may have a scratch, say) or that are in packaging that is damaged.

Eliminate COD Charges on Shipments

COD charges add to your costs of doing business and should be avoided whenever possible by establishing a line of credit with the vendor or, if necessary, ordering the merchandise using a personal credit card.

Ask About Stock Balancing

Stock balancing is a practice that lets you return an inventory item to your supplier, usually in exchange for a new, improved version of the product. James Ogawa, who once worked as a buyer with a large computer retailer, says stock balancing helps you avoid getting stuck with a lot of old inventory sitting on your shelf. If items don't move well, or if a company (such as a software company) upgrades its products, says Ogawa, stock balancing would let you return unopened inventory and get new merchandise back in its place.

Stock Your Shelves Without Risking a Cent of Your Own Money on Inventory

Buying inventory outright isn't the only way to get products to sell. Many small stores around the country get some or all of the products they sell from vendors who provide them on consignment. Under a consignment arrangement, you don't pay the vendor anything until a sale is made. Then you keep a percentage of the selling price and remit the remainder to the vendor. The percentage of the sale retailers or gallery owners keep ranges from a low of about 25 percent to a high of 50 percent, but usually falls in the middle of those figures.

If you decide to take merchandise on consignment, be prepared to work out a foolproof method for tracking the sales and paying vendors, advises

Marlo Miyashiro. Miyashiro, of Gardena, California, has had extensive experience with consignment sales from both sides of the counter. The owner and sole employee of Marlo M. Jewelry Design, Miyashiro sells many of her jewelry creations on consignment. She's also worked in the past as the manager of a craft and folk art gallery in southern California.

Miyashiro comments, "You have to keep track of each item sold for the month, take it out of your inventory as well as out of the artist's account inventory, list the items sold, cut a check, and remember to mail it on the first of the month. Then you have to hope that when the inventory is low, the artist will be willing to put more items in the store so as to not let the display look too sparse."

Using a computer to record sales and vendor data as sales are made can help ease the accounting headaches. If you use a DOS or Windows computer system, a program called The Consignment Store may prove useful. It's available from SCR Corporation in Alpine, Texas. The company can be reached by phone at 915-837-7180, or by e-mail at 76166.2320@compuserve.com. Be sure to back up records daily and store a backup copy in a safe place.

Buy Close-out or Used Merchandise

If you have a good sense about what items people will use and what will turn them off, you may be able to profit buying close-out merchandise. Typically, you'll have to buy in large quantities and won't be able to return the goods. But if you know your market and are fully aware of the time, space, and money it will take to dig the cash out of the trash, you can make money this way.

Recycled or used merchandise is another potential source of merchandise and profits. Greendisk, Inc. (http://www.greendisk.com), which is based in Preston, Washington, is a good example. They buy up obsolete and returned software from software

Don't Be Afraid to Ask for a Lower Price

Most people who have grown up in the United States have been taught that the price listed in a catalog or printed on a merchandise price tag is the price they will pay for an item. In fact, most of us have probably been taught to look over the receipts we get when we make a purchase to make sure we haven't accidentally been overcharged.

What most people are never taught, however, is that it's OK for suppliers to charge *less than* the printed or quoted price. In fact, for some reason, people who are new to business often seem embarrassed to ask any questions about the purchases they want to make. As a result, they wind up paying more than they need to for the inventory or office supplies they buy.

To avoid this pitfall and uncover hidden discounts, remember to use these eight magic words before making any major purchase for your business:

Can you do any better on the price?
If they say no, then ask one of these questions:
Do you offer quantity discounts?
What quantity would I have to buy to get a discount?

manufacturers, recycle the disks, and then sell the recycled, blank media to consumers.

Be sure to research the companies you buy from before sending checks. Some scam artists advertise close-outs, accept orders (and the payment) for them, and disappear, never delivering the advertised goods. And don't forget that you'll need warehouse facilities if you plan to buy truckload quantities of merchandise.

Magazines that include information about close-outs and recycled merchandise are as follows:

Bargains & Deals
5545 Broadmoor Bluffs Drive
Colorado Springs, CO 80906
800-530-7281
http://www.bargains-deals.com

Cover Magazine
Sumner Communications
24 Grassy Plain Street
Bethel, CT 06801-1725
http://www.sumcomm.com

Sumner Communications' Web site, WholesaleCentral.com, includes current ads for close-outs as well as wholesale ads. Close-out dealers are also listed in the company's Directory of Wholesalers, Importers, and Liquidators.

Be an Importer

If you've been running your business for a while and are looking for alternative sources of supplies, you may find it profitable to import goods to sell. The best way to learn the ropes (and learn to steer clear of pitfalls) is to contact the nearest office of the U.S. Department of Commerce and ask them about services available to help you locate and work with overseas contacts. Look in the U.S. government listing of your telephone book to locate an office near you. Once you know the ground rules, you may also want to search out your own leads using the resources available through Stat-USA/Internet (described in Chapter 2).

Part 2

Marketing Magic—Big Results from Micro-Sized Budgets

Chapters

▶ 4 **Make a Big Impression on a Small Budget**

▶ 5 **Shoestring Marketing Secrets**

▶ 6 **Getting Publicity**

▶ 7 **Advertising Tips and Tricks**

▶ 8 **Using the Mail to Build Business**

▶ 9 **Mailing and Shipping Strategies**

▶ 10 **Trade Show Savvy**

▶ 11 **Selling to the Government**

▶ 12 **Bringing in Sales**

Chapter 4

MAKE A BIG IMPRESSION
ON A SMALL BUDGET

When you run a small office, the last thing you want to do is to look small. Although you may be the company president, sales department, programmer, secretary, and shipping room clerk as well as the family taxi service, fast-order cook, and cleaning service, if that's the image you convey, you'll lose sales.

But how can you look big when you're not? How can you make the customer confident that your company is big enough to provide quality goods and services on time and within budget? And how can you do that without lying about the size of your business or its capabilities?

Here are a variety of strategies to consider.

Choose and Use a Business Name

If you are running your business activities using your own real name, consider switching to a business name. Although there will be some red tape* and costs involved, using a business name can help you gain important selling advantages. To understand why, picture this scenario.

You are a manager at a company with fifty employees. You have to find someone to network all the computers in your company's order department. Because of the importance of the department, the work must be done right the first time. If your company can't take orders or loses billing information, it's out of business. Furthermore you want the work done by a company that will be able to work with you down the road as the business expands.

---

* Some states require you to register as a business even if you operate under your own real name. Furthermore, in most states, you cannot open a bank account in a business name or cash checks made out to the business unless you register the business with appropriate state or local authorities.

Two salesmen give you similar estimates on the cost of the job, and each seem equally knowledgeable and interested in gaining you as a customer. Which of these two would *you* give the job to? John Smith, who sets up computer networks, or Bob Anderson, president of Corporate Edge Computer Solutions?

All other things being equal, chances are you'd pick Bob Anderson from Corporate Edge since his use of a business name makes it sound as though he plans to stay in business for many years.

Include Words That Imply Size and Stature in Your Business Name

Potential customers are likely to make certain assumptions about the size and scope of your business based solely on the business name. Take advantage of those assumptions by picking a business name that conjures up the image you want to establish for your company. For instance, if you live in a town called East Podunk, and being a "local" is important for bringing in business, you might want to call your electrical supply company East Podunk Electrical Supply. But if you wanted to sell to a wider region and sound like a big operation, you'd probably be better off with a name like Eastern Regional Electrical Supply.

Similarly, if you sell career guides to schools, you might do far better with a business name of Career Planning Institute than you would with the business name of Smithville Publishing.

Use Multiple Surnames as Your Business Name

It's traditional for many businesses to use the last names of the principles of the company as the name of the business. The resulting long name makes the firm seem established and big. If you run a family business, you may want to use the same strategy. Simply make up a business name that includes your last name plus the last name of one or more relatives involved in the business.

Michael Holzschu, a Michigan-based personnel consultant, is one of many home-based business owners for whom this strategy works. His business name, Holzschu, Jordan, Schiff & Associates, is made up of his own last name, his wife's maiden name, and the last names of his wife's children, all of whom work in the business when needed. He tacked on "& Associates" because he has a small group of other independent contractors he can call on to handle work he can't do.

Holzschu says the long name has helped disguise the fact that the business is home based, and has also helped distinguish his services (writing employee handbooks and procedures manuals) from those of headhunters. He also found the name has a hidden sales benefit: Because the name sounds as though it might be the name of a law firm, secretaries often put him straight through to the boss without asking why he is calling.

> ### ▶ Caution
> Use this technique only if you really do have multiple people working in your company to avoid any possibility of being accused of deceptive trade practices. In addition, never purposely mislead a client into thinking you are an attorney or accountant.

Give Yourself an Impressive Title

If you want to look big, give yourself an impressive title. If you use an occupational designation such as bookkeeper or chemist or engineer for a title, prospects will immediately think of you as a one-person business. Although that may be the appropriate image to convey at times, a title that indicates an occupation rather than a management position could also make prospects view you as someone to give orders to rather than as someone to call on to solve problems or manage jobs. If that's the way they see you, they won't be willing to pay you top fees or award you major contracts.

To solve the problem, give yourself a title such as president or director that sounds as though you are in control of an organization and are used to managing major projects. If you don't feel comfortable using those designations, or if customers seek you out because of your name and well-established reputation, use the word *consultant* as your title.

Have Two Sets of Business Cards Made Up

Business cards are among the most inexpensive and effective marketing tools available to you. Therefore, there's no reason not to have more than one set of business cards made up if you run multiple businesses. If you try to cram information about each business on one card, you look like the proverbial jack of all trades and master of none.

You might want to have two sets of business cards made up for other reasons as well. Larry R. Kraus, owner of LaRK Communications in Durham, North Carolina, has one set of business cards designating his title as president and another calling himself consultant. He hands out the president card to executives and the consultant card to technical employees because he's found that technical people tend to dislike executives, and executives generally like to deal with other executives. "I use whichever is appropriate for the level of communications going on," Kraus says. "I want to give the impression that I'm in whatever club the person on the other side of the table is in."

Use the Editorial "We" in Conversations and Sales Letters

If you are running a one-person business and want to look bigger than you are, don't use the word *I* in talking about what your business can do for your clients. Always use *we* or *us*. If you say, "Call me for a free estimate," or "I can set up your customer database," you've immediately positioned yourself as a small, one-person business. If you change the wording to "Call us for a free estimate," or "We can set up your database," your business will appear larger and more stable to prospects.

Put an Answering Service on Your Team

Customers who can't reach you to leave an order or make an appointment won't stay customers very long. If your business phone is frequently busy or you are frequently out of the office, consider using an answering service to pick up your incoming calls. A good answering service will keep you from missing orders and give you the advantage of appearing to have a staff of employees ready to serve your customers. Depending on your needs, you can arrange to call forward your calls to the service when you will be out of the office or have the line tied up, or you can have the service take all of your incoming calls.

In addition to just answering your phone calls, some answering services will fax out your product literature on request, let you use their mailing address as your own, and provide a variety of additional office and mailing services.

Prices of answering services vary by geographic area. In some parts of the country, you can get an answering service to take up to forty calls for $50 a month. In other parts of the country, the fee is triple that amount for the same service. Prices and quality can vary locally, too, so shop around, and if possible get recommendations from other businesspeople in your community.

Use an Out-Of-State Answering Service to Give Yourself an "Office" in a Distant State

Modern technology makes it possible for many businesses to work with customers thousands of miles away from their own home office. If you do a lot of business in a distant location—say, Washington, D.C., New York City, or Los Angeles—you may be able to give yourself a marketing advantage and command a higher fee by giving clients both your regular address and phone number and the address and phone number of your "office" in their city. If clients won't expect to visit your office, an answering service in the distant city may be the only office you need. If clients would want to come to your office for meetings, look in the yellow pages and newspaper ads in that city for the names of companies that rent desk space.

Use an Answering Machine or Voice Mail Service When You Want to Keep Costs Down

If you don't take orders on the telephone and don't need to have a live person answering the phone to keep your clients happy, an answering machine or voice mail will be more economical to use than an answering service. An answering machine, which can usually be purchased for under $70, is the cheaper of the two options since it's a one-time expense. The voice mail service, which costs approximately $6 to $7 per month from the telephone company, offers the advantage of being able to answer your phone calls if your telephone line is busy.

How Do You Sound?

Call the phone number that your answering machine picks up periodically to check how you sound and to be sure the outgoing message hasn't gotten garbled or erased. Leave yourself a message, too, to be sure the system is working properly.

Keep It Businesslike

Whether you use an answering machine or the telephone company's voice mail, keep your message simple and talk slowly enough so people can understand you. If you aren't sure what to say on the outgoing greeting, a good message to use is one like this:

> Hello, this is Joan Martin. I'm either on the phone or away from my desk. Please leave your name, phone number, and a brief message, and I'll call you back as soon as possible.

Don't say you are not home, and don't try to use fancy background effects unless you are in the entertainment business. Whistles, horns, jazz, and bongo drums—all of which I've heard as background noises on "business" answering machines—may seem appealing to you, but they are not businesslike, and they can annoy repeat callers.

Disguise Your Real Address by Having Your Business Mail Delivered to a Different Location

If your mailing address is a dead giveaway that your business is home based, and if customers would shy away from dealing with you if they knew that, have your business mail sent to a post office box number or to a mail receiving service. The U.S. Postal Services charges for a standard size box was $44 in 1999. Renting a mail box at a mail receiving service ran approximately $95 a year.

The receiving service offers several advantages the post office box does not. Among them: It will let you use a street address rather than a post office box number; it will accept packages for you from private mail shippers such as Federal Express or Airborne; and you may be able to call the mail receiving service to find out if there is mail for you, saving a trip out if there isn't.

Private mail receiving services often offer additional office services such as fax transmission and reception and photocopying, making them a handy one-stop source for many office needs.

Move up a Notch in the Business World

If clients will expect you to have a receptionist, conference room, and all the trappings of a "real" office, consider renting office space on a monthly basis in an executive suite or sharing an office with other noncompeting businesses. Check the commercial real estate listings in a large daily newspaper or look in the yellow pages under headings such as "office" or "mail" placed by businesses offering space-sharing arrangements.

Look Big with an 800-Number for Incoming Sales Calls

Your small mail-order business can look bigger by having a toll-free 800-number customers can use to place orders. The major long-distance phone companies offer 800-service for residential phones for as little as 9 to 10 cents per incoming call. Some plans tack on an additional monthly fee. Other don't. Compare all the details before selecting a service. One successful home-based software company finds that incoming sales calls cost an average of 30 to 60 cents apiece and that their total 800-bill each month is usually under $100. If you use your 800-line only for taking orders and you keep the calls short, the extra sales you make should more than offset the cost of the toll-free service.

Get a Separate Fax Number

In the general public's mind, "real" businesses have separate voice and fax telephone lines. If you give one phone number for both voice and fax, you immediately appear to be a very small business in prospects' eyes. If you can't get a separate fax line, consider purchasing distinctive ring service from your telephone company. This is one telephone line coming into the house, but with two phone numbers. Each number makes a distinctive sound when called (hence the name of the service) even though they come into the same telephones. By referring to one number as your fax number and the other as your voice number, you immediately make your business seem bigger for a minimal cost each month.

Use Attractively Designed Business Stationery

Your customers' impressions about the professionalism of your company can be influenced positively—or negatively—by the look and feel of your business stationery. If your stationery does not need to have a unique look, the easiest, fastest, and often least expensive way to get your business stationery printed is to choose a design, type style, and logo from a sample book or catalog. You can view samples at print shops or see samples in catalogs of mail-order companies, such as Nebbs, RapidForms, and Quill, that supply businesses with business stationery and preprinted forms. To keep costs down, look for specials where you get lower prices if you order envelopes, business cards, and letterhead at once.

Create a Logo on the Cheap

Choosing a logo and letterhead design from a catalog isn't everyone's cup of tea. Among the potential problems are that a local competitor might choose a similar logo to use for his or her business. If you have a little bit of design ability and access to a computer, you may want to try your hand at creating your own distinctive look. A relatively easy logo to create is a square or circle with your company initials enclosed.

If you own any desktop publishing or word processing programs, look to see if they have style templates or clip art that you can use to create your special look. If you have a laser or ink jet printer, print your stationery out in small quantities and "live" with it a while before having a large quantity printed professionally.

> ► **Tip**
> If you don't have time to get to a print shop during normal working hours you can order custom printing on the Web at http://www.iprint.com.

Make Sure Your Business Card Leaves the Right Impression

The look and feel of your business card says as much about your business as the words you have printed on it. In effect, your business card is the first example of the kind of work your company does that many people will see. If your card is well designed, makes judicious use of color, and is printed on a linen or other good, heavy card stock, the subconscious message it will send out is one of permanence and substance and careful attention to detail.

On the other hand, if the card looks cluttered, is hard to read, has an address crossed out, or looks dog-eared, it will give your contacts the impression that your business is unorganized and conducted rather haphazardly. If the card feels flimsy or looks as if you printed it yourself on a cheap printer, it will leave people with the impression that they are dealing with a small company that will disappear as soon as the owner finds a real job.

Although some of the preprinted paper that you can buy to create your own business card is heavy enough to pass for a "real" business card, most people will get better results by having their cards professionally typeset and printed. There may not be much difference in price, either. The price of business cards from the printer starts at about $25 for 500 cards; the heavier weight preprinted business card stock that you use to print your own business cards is about $20 for 500 cards, plus the cost of your laser toner or ink to print them.

Give Your Image a Boost with Color Printing

One inexpensive way to enhance your image is by having your business stationery, brochures, or fliers printed in color rather than in black. If you choose a single standard color—say, dark brown, dark blue, or maroon—printers typically will charge only about $15 extra to run off your job in color. This added fee is a "wash up fee" charged to cover the time it takes them to change the color ink on the press.

Get High-Quality, Low-Cost Artwork to Use in Fliers, Newsletters, and Brochures

If you don't need custom-created graphics, you can get professional quality artwork at very reasonable prices by using copyright-free drawings. Clip art is artwork that is drawn in black ink and printed on one side of a sheet of paper. Usually, one or more images are printed in several sizes on a page. You clip out the one you need (hence the name) and paste it into the work going to the printer. This is the way commercial artists usually got royalty-free art before microcomputers came into widespread use for typesetting and graphic design (desktop publishing).

Because most commercial artists use computers to create ads and other documents for their clients, it has become somewhat difficult to find printed clip art. The best places to look are bookstores and artist supply stores. If you can't find anything suitable, Dover Publishing in Mineola, New York, produces an assortment of inexpensive books containing clip art. You can get a catalog of their products by calling them at 516-294-7000.

Another way to get free artwork to use in your publications is to photocopy images from books of copyright-free graphics available in libraries.

These are typically old woodcuts and other graphic images on which the copyrights have expired. Once you photocopy the images, either you can use the photocopies as camera-ready art (you may have to blacken in the dark areas with a felt-tipped maker) or, if you have a computer and scanner available, you can scan the image into your computer and use the scanned image in art or page layout programs.

If you have a computer with desktop publishing capabilities, you can get royalty-free clip art and royalty-free photographs on computer CD-ROM. These may contain anywhere from a few dozen to hundreds of thousands of images. They range in price from under $30 to over $1,000, depending on the collection and publisher. The actual cost per image for these collec-tions is a tremendous bargain compared to the $300 to $500 you might pay to license one photograph for one-time use and to the cost of $75 an hour and up you might pay to have original work created for you.

One point to note is that although the images in such collections are royalty-free (meaning that you pay only the purchase price and don't have to pay a separate royalty for each image or for multiple uses of a single image), the images are still copyrighted. What you buy isn't ownership of the artwork, but a license to use the artwork in specified ways. Thus you'll find that some clip art and pho-tography collections limit or prohibit certain uses of the graphics on the disk.

> ## Dig Inside the Box
>
> The box that your computer came in, that is. If the computer you bought was sold with pro-grams already loaded on the hard disk, you may have computer clip art already installed on your computer or on CDs that were sup-plied with it. Several Microsoft products ship with clip art included, too. You can locate that, if it is on your computer, by using searching the hard drive for the term *clip art*.

Typical limitations on usage involve use on a Web site and use on arti-cles that you will resell (for instance, a mug or a T-shirt with artwork printed on it). Before using the clip art or photos, be sure to read the licensing agreement carefully.

Some royalty-free art and photograph collections are available from retail stores, but some of the better packages seem to be available by mail order only.

Search and Buy Clip Art and Photos on the Web

Several suppliers of computerized graphics have set up Web sites that allow you to search for and select computer clip art or photos to buy. One of them, ArtToday (http://www.arttoday.com/), offers a yearly subscription service that lets you retrieve as many images as you need to use for your own use. The low subscription cost—$29.95 a year—makes it a very affordable alter-native to purchasing clip art disks. Other services such as Photodisc (http://www.photodisc.com) and Corel (http://www.corel.com/) typically charge by the download.

Get Free Artwork on the Internet

In addition to Web sites that have for-sale artwork, there are numerous sources of free computer clip art on the Internet. Some are sites created by artists who give away a few images as a way of getting customers for paying work. Others are sites that collect free artwork by encouraging visitors to upload copyright-free graphics. In the latter case, you have no guarantee that you really do have the right to use them. One such Web site has a disclaimer that tells you the images on the site have been collected from "a wide variety of sources, all of which indicate that they are free for use." Then the disclaimer goes on to warn that you are responsible for you own use of the images in the event any image you downloaded from the site inadvertently violates copyright law. In addition to copyright violations, you may find that some free artwork on the Internet violates trademarks. Never use artwork for your business that contains the likeness of a popular cartoon character or other well-known designs or symbols without having specific permission to so from the owners of the copyright or trademark. (The same is true for music.)

Keeping that caveat in mind, you can find links to many free as well as commercial clip art sites at Clipart.com (http://www.clipart.com).

Proofread, Proofread, Proofread!

Have several people other than yourself proofread your work before you send it to clients or bring it to a printer. Even if you are a whiz at spelling and grammar, it is very easy to miss mistakes in your own work. Don't rely on computer spell checkers to spot all errors, either. A computer can't tell the difference between *stationery* and *stationary*. One printing company learned this the hard way when they sent out a catalog that included one page extolling the virtues of their line of letterhead stationary. Readers who spotted the error couldn't help wondering whether the company was targeting cave dwellers or graffiti artists.

Other easy-to-miss errors are *your* and *you're; peak* and *peek; they're, their,* and *there;* and *its* and *it's.*

When the printer does the typesetting, proofread the typeset copy carefully before giving the go-ahead to print the job. If possible, have the printer fax a copy of the typeset work to your office so you can ask several people to proofread it before approving the copy for printing. If you spot any typos after you've told the printer to run the job, you'll have to pay all reprinting costs if you want the errors fixed.

Look Inside the Box

Print shops and copy centers generally show you a sample of the finished job when you pick it up. Don't rely on that sample alone to judge the quality of the whole job. Sometimes the quality of what's inside the box will be different from the sample shown you. The ink on part of a print job might look faded or splotchy, for instance, or part of a photocopy job might be too light or too dark.

To be on the safe side, pull out several printed pieces at random from inside the box and look those over carefully. If the work isn't up to standard, ask to have the job rerun. If the error was the printer's fault, you should not have to pay for reprinting.

Cut Printing Costs Without Sacrificing Quality

Careful planning, a little knowledge of how printing costs are determined, and a good relationship with your printer can help you shave dollars off your printing bills without cutting noticeable corners in the quality of your printing. Try some of these tips to keep your printing bills down.

Think Ahead

If you will be using a commerical artist to design your work, give them as many details as you can before they start your job. For instance, is there a particular look you like or don't like? (Give them samples of things you've seen that you like). What about colors? Is it OK for them to use clip art and stock photos when they design your work? Or do you need original graphics? What ways other than the initial job might you reasonable expect to use the work? Will you need to reproduce your logo on coffee mugs and T-shirts in addition to putting it on your letterhead and business card? Will you have a Web site? The more you can tell the designer at the start, the more you'll save in the long run.

▶ Decide on your total budget at the start of the project. Let the designer or printer know in advance what that budget is so he or she can make suggestions that will keep you from spending more than you expect.

▶ If you need design work done, go to a designer and let the designer find the printer. Don't expect the printer to be a graphic designer.

▶ If you are working directly with the printer, ask the print shop if there are certain color inks that they use frequently and if they waive the wash-up fee if your job is printed at the same time other jobs in the same color are being run.

▶ Many small printers can print only one color at a time on one side of paper at a time. They charge you for each side of paper you print, and each color ink they print on each side of the paper. You can keep color printing costs down by planning brochures and other two-sided work so that the second color is printed on only one side of paper.

▶ Use standard color inks and standard papers. Printing charges are based on the price printers have to pay for paper and ink. They get the best prices when they can order in large quantities. If they have to pay a premium price to order a small quantity of paper or special color ink, they'll pass on the costs to you.

▶ Design your work to use standard-size paper. If the printer has to cut the paper to an unusual size or into an unusual shape, your costs will increase.

▶ Get price estimates from several print shops. The difference in costs from one shop to another can be significant. If possible, visit the print shop while you are getting estimates. Look around to see if you can get an impression of the quality work the shop may do. A bargain on printing isn't a bargain if the printing is too light or uneven or if there are ink spots where they don't belong on the paper.

▶ Compare the cost of printing black ink on standard weight paper to the cost of photocopying. Some of the chain office supply stores like Staples and Office Max will photocopy your fliers for less than a quick printer will charge to print them in similar quantities.

▶ Find a service bureau that will print your documents from your computer files. If the printer you normally use doesn't have this capability, look in the ads at the back of computer and desktop publishing magazines.

Use Colored Paper to Look Big

The easiest way to make your fliers look home-grown is to print or photocopy them in black ink on plain white copier paper. Although colored and heavier weight papers cost more, they make your work look more professional and get more attention.

Experiment with different colors and different weight paper. Choose a color and weight that is appropriate for the type of product or service being sold and the way the printed item will be used. For instance, an iridescent orange paper would make a good background to print a flier about a car wash service or a handout to put on your flea market table. Iridescent orange would not be suitable for fliers describing business-to-business services or expensive products.

If you are printing shelf signs or placards for a retail store, or will be folding what you've printed and mailing it without an envelope, look for papers that are heavier than standard photocopier paper.

Be sure the paper color isn't so dark that the words printed on it are difficult to read. A deep blue or deep magenta paper may get attention, but if people can't read the flier or sign at a glance, they won't read it at all. Also check to be sure the paper will work with your printer or photocopier before purchasing a large quantity.

Print Brochures, Letterheads, and More on Demand with Preprinted Specialty Papers

Mail-order companies and office supply stores sell specialty papers that you can use in your computer printer to produce brochures, fliers, labels, letterhead, postcards, and business cards on demand. These specialty papers are preprinted with colorful designs, backgrounds, and borders. To use them, you just print out your text in the appropriate places on top of the colored backgrounds or inside of the colorful borders. The output gives you eye-catching sales literature, fliers, and business stationery at a small fraction of the cost you'd have to pay for custom, multicolored printing.

The preprinted papers come in a wide assortment of designs and colors ranging from ultraconservative to flamboyant. Mail-order companies that specialize in office stationery usually have a much wider selection of styles than the office supply stores do, but sometimes have minimum order requirements.

Scored vs. Unscored Paper

If you will be creating a two-fold brochure and will be folding it by hand, be sure to order paper that is scored for easier folding. If you get the unscored paper you'll find it much harder to make the edges of the brochure line up when you fold it.

Find Out What a Commercial or Quick Print Shop Will Charge to Do the Job

If you have a big job to print, compare the cost and convenience of using specialty paper and printing the work yourself to the cost of having a printer do the job for you. When you calculate the cost of your ink or laser toner, you may find it more economical to have the job done by the printer. If they can't provide colorful papers or brochure blanks, ask what they'll charge to print on paper you supply. If you have more than 200–250 copies of a page to print at one time, you may find it more economical to bring the work to a printer or copy shop than to print it yourself.

Don't Assume Higher Prices Mean Better Quality

Specialty papers cost anywhere from about 11 to 30 cents a sheet for letterhead or brochure paper. The difference in price often has little to do with the difference in design or quality of paper. Instead, the price difference seems to be more dependent on which company you buy the supplies from. This is true for all the paper types and do-it-yourself presentation products sold in specialty paper catalogs. The difference can be significant, too. You'll find the prices for some items in some catalogs are double or triple what the same item sells for in other catalogs. Therefore, it's a good idea to send for catalogs from several companies and compare designs and prices before making your final choice. One other factor that can affect price: whether brochure and other paper is prescored for folding. Some of the economy papers are not prescored. Getting prescored sheets to fold evenly is difficult. To make folding go faster and have the results look good, look for brochure papers that are scored where they will be folded.

Create a Consistent Look

You could do a great job selling a prospect on the need for a product or service, but when the prospect gets around to actually making the purchase, he or she may have forgotten your business name. Help prospects find you in their files and distinguish yourself from your competitors by giving your mailing and stationery a consistent look. One way to create consistency is to use a drawn logo along with your company name on every piece of literature you send out. Another is to be consistent in your choice of typefaces and in the colors you use on letterhead and in fliers and brochures.

Ask for a Sample Before Placing an Order

Not all paper types and weights work with all printers, so be sure to read the specifications in the catalog and compare them to the specifications for your printer. If you have any doubt whether a paper will work with your printer, request a sample and test it before purchasing a large quantity. Most companies will send you a sheet or two at no cost if you have one specific style you want to test. Some companies have sample kits available, but the sample kits usually have to be purchased. In some cases, the purchase price will be deducted from your first purchase.

Use Software Templates to Save Time and Look More Professional

Once you buy preprinted stock, you have to set up your word processor or page layout program so that it prints your headline and text in the right places in an attractive type size and typeface. The easiest way to accomplish this feat is to use software templates that position the text and suggest appropriate type sizes. You can buy standalone programs, such as My Advanced Brochures, that include templates and require no additional software, or you can buy templates that work with specific programs, such as PageMaker. Mail-order companies that sell preprinted papers usually carry templates for their papers as well.

Even when you use the templates, you may have to do a little bit of tin-kering to get the text to line up properly. To avoid wasting expensive paper, print out a test sheet on plain white paper. Position the test sheet on top of the preprinted paper you'll be using, and hold the pages up to a window to allow you to see where your text will fall when printed on the purchased paper.

Hire a Professional When You Don't Have the Skills to Do It Yourself

Owning a computer with desktop publishing software won't make you a designer. Although the many preprinted papers and software templates available are ideal for simple design needs and limited quantities, attempting to do big or complex jobs yourself can be foolish. Walt Thiessen, who works for an ad agency and service bureau in New England, notes that when clients attempt to get jobs ready for the printer themselves, there are often so many changes needed to make the job print properly that they wind up spending more than they would have if they had hired a professional to do the job and gotten it right the first time.

Invest in a Reasonably Priced Color Inkjet Printer

The judicious use of color in reports, proposals, and presentation overheads can make a big impression on your customers. Whether you use color in headlines, for graphs, or artwork on the page, it will not only help get your message across, it will also make your company appear more professional. In fact, it could mean the difference between winning and not winning a contract.

Fortunately, you don't have to spend a fortune to create color docu-ments. You can get good-quality color output from inkjet printers that sell for under $300. The printers will work with many types of paper and with special overhead transparency film.

A special, premium-priced paper made specifically for use in inkjet printers is available as well, but for many jobs, plain paper produces satis-factory results. If you will be printing overheads, you *will* need the special transparency film since inkjet ink blobs up and won't dry on transparency film made to work in laser printers or photocopiers. Shop around for the best price, though. You can save as much as $10 per fifty sheets by buying a "no-name" brand.

Even with the special transparency film, the ink doesn't dry immediately, so don't let printouts stack up in the printer if the film you use doesn't have a paper backing. Even after the printouts are dry, it's a good idea to keep them separated from one another with sheets of paper. This will prevent ink from one transparency from sticking to the one above it and leaving unsightly smudges.

Print out Letterhead and Labels on a Color Printer

If you need only a small quantity of letterhead at a time, consider printing it on demand, in color using a color inkjet printer. Because of the cost of the inkjet inks, the cost per printed sheet will be higher than if you purchased 500 or 1,000 sheets of printed stationery, but you won't have to worry about finding matching paper for multipage letters or reports, and you won't have to buy more paper at a time than you'll use quickly.

One caveat: Although inkjet inks have improved in recent years, they do still tend to smear slightly if they get wet. A strip of wide, clear plastic tape placed over the printed area of a shipping label will prevent the printing from smudging if the package gets rained on during delivery.

> ▶ **Note**
> Plain paper or standard weight ink-jet paper work well for routine reports. Switch to glass or matte-finish ink-jet photo paper for product literature. The difference in quality is dramatic.

Buy Paper from a Wholesaler to Cut Costs

Small offices and home businesses that print or photocopy work in quantity may be able to reduce paper costs by as much as 40 percent by purchasing their paper and envelopes directly from a wholesaler or distributor. To find a paper distributor in your area, look in the yellow pages under the heading "paper." Call ahead to make sure sales aren't restricted to printers and resellers.

Use Color Photocopies When Ink Jet Output Won't Work

Inkjet printers actually spray ink on paper. When you have to print pages that have large inked-in areas such as charts or drawings with solid color, the paper may become wet enough to look rippled even after the ink dries. To avoid this look in work you hand your client, have color photocopies made from your original pages. At the time this book was written, you could get color photocopies made up for less than one dollar a copy at many office supply stores and quick print shops.

Color photocopies are also handy when you have color work to reproduce that wasn't created on your computer or if you have a slow color printer and need multiple copies of pages with a lot of color on them.

Make Color Ink Cartridges Last Longer

When you create a chart with a spreadsheet program or draw a filled-in design with a drawing or paint program, the software you use will normally default to use a solid color. This makes the drawing look bright and colorful, but can use up a tremendous amount of ink and produce the ripple effect mentioned earlier. You can save ink and minimize or eliminate the ripple effect by using a fill pattern with fine lines instead of the solid color fill.

▶ **Tip**
This technique works well for paper printouts, but may not produce vibrant enough colors for use on overhead transparencies. Before designing an entire presentation using fill patterns to replace solid color charts, print out one transparency and see if you are satisfied with the effect.

Make Originals on Your Photocopier

Because of the tendency of the ink to smear when damp, inkjet printouts are not really advisable to use for documents that will need to be stored for long periods. There's an easy way to solve the problem though: Print out the document on the inkjet printer, then photocopy the inkjet printout.

Customize Presentation Folders Without Paying for Custom Printing

Your business looks more established when all the materials you give clients and prospects are customized with your business name and logo. But ordering presentation folders imprinted with your name is expensive and impractical if you need only a handful of folders from time to time.

One good way to solve the problem is to purchase good-quality unprinted presentation folders and customize them yourself with labels bearing your company name and logo. You can order labels printed with your logo and business name from your printer or from the same companies that print business stationery. Or you can make your own using label paper that feeds through your laser or inkjet printer. You'll find a variety of sizes and shapes available in office supply stores and by mail order.

Bind Reports, Proposals, and Capabilities Statements

Staples and paper clips are fine for holding together documents that you retain in your own office. But when you're trying to impress a business prospect, client, or investor with the importance of information you've prepared for them, the lowly staple just doesn't cut it. To make your reports, proposals, capabilities statements, and business plan look important and authoritative, enclose them in some type of binder.

> ▶ **Tip**
>
> Quick printers, copy centers, and large office supply stores often offer binding as a service. If you don't have many documents to bind and seldom have a need for bound copies, look for a quick printer, copy center, or office supply superstore that can do the work for you. Expect to pay about $3 per bound document. That cost is in addition to any charges for having them copy and collate the pages that go inside the covers.

Among the most commonly used binding methods are velum binding, plastic or metal coil bindings, and loose-leaf binders. The best style to use depends on a number of factors such as the number of sheets of paper to be held together, the size of the document, the need to modify or change the document, and how it will be read or displayed. If the proposal is in response to a request for proposal (RFP), any binding requirements described in the RFP should be followed exactly.

Personal preference and stylistic considerations enter into the choice, too. Dudley Glass, a Florida-based consultant to government contractors, prefers loose-leaf binders for most proposals he prepares for his clients. This is due to both the typical length of the proposals and the ability to substitute pages in loose-leaf binders. Furthermore, government RFPs often specify loose-leaf binders, so the format is familiar to those who ultimately will be receiving the proposal.

On the other hand, Jack Groh, owner of Groh Associates, a public relations agency in Warwick, Rhode Island, rarely uses loose-leaf binders for proposals he prepares. He prefers vellum or spiral bindings. Vellum looks neater but doesn't allow the bound document to be opened out flat.

You can buy the binding equipment for punching paper and binding with plastic spines for about $120. Covers and plastic spines are extra. You can purchase blank covers with cutouts that let part of the first inside page show through. You can also purchase covers without cutouts. If you need covers in quantity, you can have them professionally printed. And if your own laser printer will accept heavyweight papers, you may be able to print to the cover stock yourself. (Look in your printer's manual to determine the maximum paper weight it will accept, then compare that weight to the weight of the cover stock you plan to purchase.)

Be Ready to Respond to Inquiries and Requests for Literature

"Send me something."

Those three words can be the beginning of a long and profitable relationship if you actually have "something" ready to send to the prospect the same day he or she makes the request. Although you could just send out a letter, you'll look more professional if your sales letter is accompanied by sales literature or background information about your company. Depending on what you do, the items you keep on hand to mail prospects might include brochures, fact sheets, capability statements, a biography, company history, copies of product reviews, or press mentions.

To save time assembling literature to mail, compile packets containing the information you most frequently mail out and store several of the packets in the same place you store your letterhead. That way, when a prospect says "send me something" you can print up a letter and grab all the information you need to mail quickly without having to hunt through multiple file drawers or stationery boxes to find it.

Shrink-Wrap Your Products

Shrink-wrapping helps protect products from being tampered with, from having important parts stolen (screws, disks, and so on that might be included in a box), and from getting dirty and shopworn. But that's not all shrink-wrapping does. It makes many products more saleable and easier to promote. That's because consumers are so used to seeing shrink-wrapped goods in stores that they tend to distrust products that aren't shrink-

Keep It Simple

Just because your computer or graphic arts program came with a couple of dozen fonts (type styles) doesn't mean you have to use them all, or that all the fonts are appropriate for use by your business. In fact, one of the surest signs of an amateur let loose with a new desktop publishing–capable computer is the use of too many fonts or the poor choice of fonts for headlines and text.

Another sure sign of loving hands at home is overuse and misuse of decorative papers and coordinating designs. Match the design and the amount of coordination to your business.

A party store or a party planner might want multicolored borders printed on every piece of stationery, label, and presentation folder the company handed out. A high-priced consultant targeting large corporations would do better to skip the cookie-cutter look and opt for a more subtle look. For example, the consultant might use cream-colored stationery with a deep navy logo and a strip of deep navy color running vertically or horizontally, and coordinate that with deep navy presentation folders.

wrapped or wonder whether they are purchasing a product that someone else bought and returned. In addition, many magazines will not review products that aren't shrink-wrapped. That's because shrink-wrapping makes it appear a product is actually being manufactured and is actually available to the public.

Therefore, even if your products are safe from theft, tampering, or wear and tear, you may find a machine a good investment if products like yours that are available in retail outlets are shrink-wrapped.

You can purchase shrink-wrapping equipment from large packaging supply companies such as Associated Bag or Chiswick or direct from the manufacturers.

Package Your Products for Success

The way you package your product will affect your customers' perception of its value and of your company. If you are a software developer who sells software to local small business, neither your product nor your company are going to look very professional if you give your customers a disk with a hand-printed label and a "manual" consisting of a few sheets of paper stapled together. But if you take the same disk, put a printed label on it, write good instructions for using the program, and print and bind the instructions, you enhance your image and satisfaction with your work at little cost to you. If you were going to sell that same software through retail outlets, you would need to package everything up in a professionally designed box.

Sometimes the packaging is so important that it is, in effect, part of the product. The main difference between a 1-pound bag of Hershey's Kisses and a 1-pound box of Godiva chocolates is the packaging. Both products contain a pound of chocolate candy, yet people happily spend $29 for the pound of Godiva chocolates even though they can buy a pound of Hershey's Kisses in the supermarket for under $4.

You can find companies that produce packaging by looking in the yellow pages, by searching on the Web for the term *packaging*, or by attending trade shows for your industry or reading industry trade magazines.

Dress Yourself for Success

Whether you are a high-priced financial consultant or run an appliance repair service, the way you and your employees dress when you meet customers is important. A financial consultant who dresses in an expensive suit will inspire a lot more confidence than one of equal ability who wears a cheap suit with slightly frayed cuffs. Similarly, a copier repair technician who dresses in a clean, neatly pressed uniform is going to be considered more professional, knowledgeable, and reliable than one who shows up wearing grease-stained jeans and an old sweatshirt.

Dress is not a substitute for ability, of course. But inappropriate dress will make customers question your ability. Although you may incur some additional costs to dress in a manner that inspires customer confidence, provided you and your employees are skilled, the investment will pay itself back in the form of repeat customers and referral business.

Form Strategic Alliances with Small Businesses That Complement Your Talents

You don't always have to hire a big staff to be able to offer your clients a wide range of services. Instead, form casual alliances with other small businesses in related, but noncompeting, fields. If you are a copywriter, for instance, you establish working relationships with commercial artists and market researchers so you could offer a wide range of marketing services to your clients.

Form Alliances with Trustworthy Direct Competitors

One sure way to look small in your customers eyes is to tell them you can't do their work because you are too busy or that you aren't taking any jobs for the next two weeks because you are going on vacation.

One way around this problem if you are a one-person business is to find trustworthy competitors who can take on your jobs in emergencies or during vacations. They, in turn, send work your way, when they get overloaded or go out of town.

Chapter 5

SHOESTRING

MARKETING SECRETS

Big corporations spend millions of dollars to launch new products and keep their name in front of potential customers. Self-employed individuals and small businesses have the same need, but not the same budget.

Fortunately, there are many inexpensive ways to make customers aware of your products and services. In fact, all it takes to find effective, low-cost marketing opportunities for home-based and small businesses is a little ingenuity and a lot of persistence. Here are some ideas to get you started.

Get Your Act Together

Marketing is like setting out on a trip. To reach your goal, you need to know where you're going and how you are going to get there. In other words, you need a plan.

Your plan doesn't have to be elaborate if your business is small and you plan to keep it that way. But before you embark on any new marketing effort, take the time to consider the answers to these questions:

▶ Who will buy your product or service?
▶ Why do they need it?
▶ How do they hear about and buy this product or service now?
▶ Why should they buy it from you instead of your competitors?
▶ What marketing options are available to you given the time and money you can spend?
▶ How many customers can you reasonably expect to serve?
▶ What do you want to accomplish with this marketing effort?
▶ What will it cost you in time and money to pursue this effort?
▶ How many customers can you realistically expect to bring in from this effort?
▶ How does that compare to other things you could be doing with your time or money?

▶ What will you have to have ready to give prospects who contact you (the product itself or sales letters, fact sheets, photos, press release, free samples)?

▶ What will it cost you to respond to inquiries?

▶ How many interested prospects will buy from you?

▶ How long will it take them to make up their minds to buy from you?

▶ What will it take to deliver the product or service?

▶ Will the results be worth the effort?

Let Everybody Know You're in Business

Most home-based and very small businesses find the best source of business are people they know. When you are starting out, contact family, neighbors, and friends, and let them know you are in business. Ask them for names of their friends you might call, too. As long as the business provides a needed or desirable product or service, most people will be happy to pass on any suggestions they can to help you get started.

Get out into the community and spread the word, too. "Go where clients are," says Jack Slick, a CPA who's built a successful practice in Hagerstown, Maryland. Slick goes on, "See them, talk to them, let them know about you and your business. Chamber of Commerce mixers, business meetings, country club events, social functions all are good places to meet businesspeople. Try to hook up with a good lawyer or insurance agent and do cross-referrals with them. Also develop clients from within by asking your current clients to refer you to others."

If you've left another company to start your own competing business, look for discreet ways to let business contacts you made at that company know you've gone out on your own. Don't copy the company's client list and take it with you—that could get you sued. But do call the contacts you made. Or tell them in person when you see them at conferences or business network meetings. If you signed a noncompete agreement at your former employer, get advice from your attorney before starting the business or soliciting clients.

Avoid Marketing to the Wrong Prospects

A common mistake startup businesses make is to assume products or services will sell because they seem like something many people need.

For instance, many people starting computer consulting businesses expect to build a good business by selling their service to home-based and small businesses. They assume these businesses will need and will pay for consulting services since they can't afford to keep a computer programmer on staff.

Although that line of reasoning seems logical, it isn't. Most low-budget businesses are not a good source of business. Instead of hiring consultants, they look for free advice in books and magazine articles, from salespeople, and by asking computer savvy friends or relatives for help.

To avoid making the wrong assumptions about the desirability of products or services, talk to your potential customers *before* you start a business or introduce a new product. Besides asking prospects if they can use what you plan to sell, ask what they'd pay for it and where they would go to buy it. If the responses you get don't match your original expectations, either research a different market or look for a different product or service to sell.

> ## Don't Go for Broke
>
> If your marketing funds are limited, don't gamble them all on one big ad or one mass mailing. Most one-shot marketing efforts don't work.
>
> Instead, use the low-cost and no-cost marketing techniques discussed to gradually establish a client base and positive cash flow. Wait to spend the big marketing bucks until you have your business infrastructure in place, have tested your marketing ideas on a small scale, and have a cushion of profits and satisfied customers on which you can rely for steady profits.

Target Businesses That Can Afford Your Services

If you *do sell* to home-based and small businesses, focus your efforts on high-income professionals who have been in business for a year or more. Emphasize your experience, professionalism, and ability to deliver quality products and services on time. To close sales, remind top earners that, based on their hourly billing rate, it's cheaper to hire you than to do the work themselves.

Break Down Big Markets into Small, Manageable Segments

Don't try to tackle a large diverse market on a shoestring budget. To build sales and grow your business, you have to get your name in front of prospects repeatedly. If your budget and staff are small, trying to spread your message across a large diverse market will be an exercise in futility. You won't be able to get your message in front of your potential customers often enough to gain recognition.

That doesn't mean you should avoid big markets. The way to profit when there are many customers and many competitors is to break down the big market into small, manageable segments. Concentrate your marketing efforts on one or two of those segments.

William Murrell, owner of Metroserve Computer Corp., is one of many businesspeople who have boosted sales by focusing their marketing efforts. An ad he placed in the *New England Hispanic Yellow Pages* paid for itself in two months. He did equally well selling AfroCentric software in a business directory called the *Black Pages of New England*.

You won't build sales just because you advertise to a niche market, though. Explains Murrell, "Whether the niche is African Americans, Hispanics, desktop publishers, dry cleaning establishments or subnotebook computer buyers, each area has special needs. To succeed you have to become an expert in the niche you want to target."

Dalva Brady, an insurance saleswoman from Long Island, New York, quickly became one of the top salespeople in her office when she began targeting prospects who spoke her native language, Portuguese. Although her clients could speak English, they preferred to discuss insurance with someone who knew their culture and could speak to them in their own language.

Understand What You Are Selling and Market Accordingly

What you sell isn't necessarily what your customers are buying. For example, Ellyn and Norm Ingalls of North Haverhill, New Hampshire, sell specialty foods. Although their company, Poole-Brook Farms, sells relishes and condiments, they don't consider themselves to be in the food business. As Ellyn explains, "We are not marketing food. We are marketing gifts and rewards. If we could produce it incredibly inexpensively and wanted to mass-market through supermarket chains, then it would probably be food."

Get Customers to Ask for Your Product by Name

The Ingalls sell their products predominately to wholesalers, but they drum up interest in the product by doing taste testings and selling them at country fairs, craft shows, and trade fairs.

Although the Ingalls rarely make a profit from sales at the fairs, the fairs generate name recognition among people who are likely to want homemade products when they are ready to give a gift or treat themselves to a luxury. They also find new wholesale buyers for their products this way.

"When you have a brand new product, and it sits on a store shelf, no one knows what it is. Few are brave enough to buy it," says Ellyn. "We do shows to let people sample our products and educate them on the 'story' of the product. Then they go into the stores looking for our products. It is much easier to sell this way."

Become an Active Member of Business Associations and Civic Groups

Personal contact is the least expensive and most reliable way of finding customers for most businesses. One of the easiest ways to make personal contact with potential customers is to join organizations they are likely to join. These include professional associations, civic groups, the Chamber of Commerce, women or minority associations, county or regional business associations, art councils, or even the PTA.

Choose the groups you join with care. Attend a meeting or two as a guest before making a commitment to join the group. Notice how well attended the group is, what type of programs are scheduled for future sessions, and whether members of the group seem open and receptive to newcomers. Note the mix of people who attend, and assess whether the group is the best one for networking for your type of business.

Just joining an organization won't produce customers, though. The key to making contacts that lead to sales is to get to know members of the group personally. The best way to do that is to become a frequent attendee and active member of the organization.

> ▶ **Tip**
> Ease your way gently into groups. If you join an organization and seem overbearing or try too hard to impress members with your expertise, you may make more enemies than business contacts.

Get Listed in Member Directories

Most organizations publish directories of their members. Although it may take five or ten minutes to fill out a form to get your business included in the directory, the time is well spent since other members and nonmembers use these directories to find new suppliers, contacts, and customers.

Cross-Promote Your Business with Others Who Target the Same Market

You can gain valuable new business by linking up with other noncompeting businesses to cross-promote each others' products and services. If you are a resume writer, for instance, you might want to work out a deal with a quick print shop. The quick print shop might give you coupons for twenty-five extra copies printed free with the first order. You, in turn, would give the printer a 10 percent off coupon to hand out to people looking for resume-writing services.

Cross-promotional and cross-referral opportunities are all around if you look. Glenn Oster handles sales and marketing for Gabelli Studio, Inc. in Verona, New Jersey. "Most of our work is weddings, so we have a referral system set up with area florists, travel agencies, caterers, restaurants, and real estate agents." Accountants, bankers, insurance brokers, and attorneys make good networking partners, as do writers, graphic artists and commercial photographers.

Give as Many Referrals as You Hope to Get

Referral networks are two-way streets. To keep referrals flowing, make it a point to refer jobs to other businesses whenever appropriate. An added benefit: customers will be pleased that you care enough to refer them to someone who can solve their problems and may return the favor by referring their friends and acquaintances to your business.

Seek out Subcontracts

Competitors and larger companies in your field may also be a source of subcontracts. Under a subcontracting arrangement, you do the work on the customer's project on behalf of the prime contractor (a prime contractor is the lead contractor on a project). Depending on the arrangements for the job, you may communicate directly with the customer or only with the contractor that gives you the work. In either case, you benefit by getting jobs and establishing a track record for completing them. You can also learn a lot about how an industry works and make contacts that can lead to contracts at some future date.

Subcontracting isn't without its drawbacks, though. You may make less profit on jobs you subcontract than on jobs you win on your own, and you have to rely on the prime contractor (the company that subcontracted the work to you) to get paid.

Furthermore, subcontracting can limit what business you can accept or chase on your own. If you solicit or accept work from businesses you know to be active clients of the prime contractor, you'll develop a reputation for being unethical and untrustworthy.

Sometimes that puts the contractor in a catch-22 situation. "In a number of instances, we have been the subcontractor only to have the primary client ask us to become the main contractor on the project. They wanted to get rid of what they perceived to be the middle

Get Referrals from Competitors

Don't shy away from bigger competitors in your field. They could be the source of new business. Many established businesses will refer customers to a competitor when they don't have time to do the customer's job themselves, or when the customer is too small for them to service profitably. You can get that business often just by staying on a friendly basis with your competitors.

man," says Jack Groh, owner of Groh Associates, a public relations agency located in Warwick, Rhode Island.

Groh always turns down contracts offered under such circumstances. To do otherwise, he says, "would be a betrayal of the agency which hired us to work with the client on their behalf."

Nevertheless, working as a subcontractor has helped Groh Associates and many other microsized businesses land contracts of their own.

Groh traces at least three big clients to subcontracting work. In one case, Groh Associates had worked as a subcontractor on an environmental promotion held at a professional sports organization's national championship. "The following year, when the agency we had worked for turned down the job, we were free to chase the job and get it ourselves," explains Groh.

In another instance, a client left an agency Groh had done work for. The client later came back to have the agency do a special project, but the agency wasn't interested in special projects, so they turned the contract over to Groh.

Yet another time an account executive at a firm Groh subcontracted for left to start his own advertising agency. The account exec took some of his customers with him, and then asked Groh Associates to handle the public relations for one of the accounts. "Once the account had left the original agency, we no longer felt that it was hands off," says Groh.

Pay Bigger Businesses a Commission for Bringing You Work

Instead of seeking subcontracts from larger businesses, consider offering them a commission or finder's fee for locating clients for you. Such an arrangement makes you a revenue-producing asset rather than an expense. For example, Groh works with an advertising agency that has no public relations staff of its own. When the agency locates a customer who could benefit from a public relations campaign, they call in Groh. Groh develops his own proposal, building in a commission for the agency that has found the client. If the client accepts the proposal, Groh does the work, bills the client, and pays the agency its commission.

Consider Joining a Formal Leads Network

Leads networks are groups of businesspeople who meet regularly to exchange business leads. Some such as LaTip, Leads, and Business Networks International (BNI) are national organizations with local chapters. Others are regional or local in scope. Leads groups differ from professional associations or Chambers of Commerce because they are for-profit businesses. The organizers of the group benefit financially by keeping members coming back.

Meetings at local chapters of nationally known leads groups follow similar formats. Typically, they have ten to twenty members and meet for breakfast or lunch once a week. Members introduce themselves and let each other know what kind of leads they are looking for, then pass out leads they have gathered during the week. "Then they all go their own ways until the next week where they do it again," says Curt Kowalski, president of an independent leads group called Team Network Corporation in Washington, D.C.

Membership in each leads group is usually limited to no more than one or two of each type of business to minimize competition among members. Typically, you pay a fee to join the group and to attend meetings. Once you join, you will be expected to attend every meeting and bring leads with you for other members. Depending on the group you join, meetings can be very structured and fast-paced or loose and informal. In Kowalski's Team Network, for instance, members get referrals and develop business as a result of social interaction rather than the formal exchange of leads.

> ## ▶ Tip
> If you don't have time to travel to a leads group meeting, consider forming your own leads group and meeting online. There are numerous services that let you set up your own chat room for free.

Try Before You Buy

The key to benefiting from a leads group is to find the right group to join for your particular type of business. "The chemistry of the group is critical," says Gary LeBlanc, a business owner from New Jersey. "If the chemistry isn't right or the people in the group don't know the prospects you're looking for, you'll be disappointed."

Depending on the leads group you join, you can expect to spend between $300 and $600 a year to be a member. You will also have to foot the bill for breakfasts, lunches, or social functions you attend. Leads groups generally allow prospective members to attend one meeting at no charge, however. To avoid a mismatch, take advantage of this opportunity to see if the group is a good match for your business and personal preferences. While you're there, find out what businesses other members are in. Ask yourself if they know the people you want to know.

Another important consideration is whether the members of the group run their own businesses professionally. "They have to perform to a high enough level when given a referral to keep building on the foundation of trust you are both trying to achieve and maintain for the long run," says Kowalski.

One should also keep in mind that leads groups are profit-making businesses. LeBlanc found that was one thing that turned him off to one of the national organizations. "You're required to bring in a certain number of new members every year or six months. . . . I wish I could force my current customers to bring me additional customers!"

Don't Let Your Business Card Be a Mystery to Your Contacts

Business cards can be a very cost-effective marketing tool. They are easy to carry, unobtrusive, and inexpensive. Better yet, they are the universally accepted way of exchanging contact information at meetings, conferences, networking sessions, trade shows, sales presentations, and service calls.

But many businesspeople don't get the mileage they should from their business cards because their cards don't state what kind of business the company is in. Thus, when a recipient sorts out collected cards and sees one from the president of Lansing Industries, he or she may not remember whether Lansing Industries removes oil tanks or sells landscaping services.

Keep your business from being a mystery by including a very short statement indicating the nature of your business and your capabilities. A line such as "Complete hazardous waste management solutions" or "Professional grounds maintenance services" will remind recipients what you do and can bring in calls weeks, months, and sometimes years after you hand someone your business card.

Include All of Your Contact Information

In addition to your phone number and mailing address, be sure to include a fax number and, if you regularly use electronic mail, your e-mail address. The multiple contact methods make your business seem substantial as well as giving prospects multiple ways to reach you.

Use Every Opportunity to Distribute Your Business Cards

Don't wait to meet contacts in person to give them your business card. Drop your business card in letters to new contacts, include one or two in presentation folders, and attach them to brochures. It's not unusual for contacts to throw away the sales literature, but save the business card for future reference.

If you sell consumer services, tack your business card to cork bulletin boards at beauty parlors, supermarkets, colleges, or other bulletin boards that allow small businesses to tack up contact information.

Help Them Remember You

People you meet are more likely to remember what you look like and what you do than they are to recall your name or the name of your company. To make it easier for them to spot your business card (and your contact information), use your photo on your business card.

Give Out Rolodex-Style Business Cards

Make it easier for contacts to locate your business card a month or two from now by giving them a card that will snap right into their Rolodex. You can have business cards printed on Rolodex card inserts at a print shop, or run them off yourself on perforated paper you can print with your laser or inkjet printer. Look for a heavyweight card stock, and ask for a sample sheet before you order in quantity to be sure the heavy card stock will feed through your printer without smearing the ink or crumpling the edges.

Turn Your Existing Business Card into a Rolodex Card

If you'd rather not spend money on a second, Rolodex-type of business card, consider the tactic that Cindy Mayerich, owner of Mayerich Communications, in Moorhead, Minnesota, uses. She bought a $6 business card paper punch at an office supply store and uses it to put Rolodex-type notches in some of her business cards. She now drops two business cards in mailings—one punched card and one unpunched. (Warning: Be sure the punched holes do not cut out any vital piece of information such as your telephone number.)

Use Your Business Card as a Mini-Capabilities Brochure

Your business card should be a standard size and shape so it can be easily stored in business card files or wallets. But you don't have to restrict printing to one side of a flat card. You can provide more information about your company by using a foldover card that is the same overall size as a standard business card.

Hill Slater, Inc., is one company that makes excellent use of a foldover card. The card stands out initially because the design is vertical rather than horizontal. The company name, a contact name, and the words *Engineering Architectural Support Service* are on the face of the card. When you open the card, you learn the company offers a range of services that include CAD, drafting, design, construction management, construction inspection, energy conservation audits, environmental impact statements, and affirmative action management.

Another good use of a foldover card is to include a small map or directions to your business.

Attract Repeat Business with a Magnet

Have your business card made into a magnet. The flat, flexible type that people can stick to refrigerators or metal file cabinets are a good way to keep your business information and phone number where customers can see it daily. They work particularly well for consumer services where there is a lot of competition such as pizza parlors, insurance agents, drug stores, and appliance repair.

You can order magnets from any advertising specialty company or from your local printer. Depending on the style and the quantity ordered, you'll pay 60 cents to a dollar per magnet, but the repeat calls down the road are worth the investment.

You can also purchase do-it-yourself kits to turn your existing business cards into magnets. These kits are adhesive-backed magnets that you attach to the back of your business card. They are available in office supply stores in packages of twenty-five to fifty and up. You'll pay under 25 cents per magnet this way, but the customer may not keep them around as long since the paper finish on the business card side isn't as durable as the vinyl magnet face you get when you purchase custom-printed magnets.

Store Other People's Contact Information for Future Reference

The time you spend networking today can pay off next month or even next year—if you can still find the names of people you spoke with and remember what they do.

If you store business cards in traditional card files, be sure to cross-reference contacts so you can find them either by name or by industry or profession.

If you have a computer, get in the habit of entering all of your contact names in a database. The database doesn't have to be complicated or difficult to set up. Popular programs such as FileMaker Pro, Microsoft Access, or Microsoft Works, include templates for keeping track of contacts. You can also purchase programs such as ACT that are specifically made for keeping track of contacts.

In addition to the traditional contact information (name, address, business name, phone, and so on) include a field (place to enter data) for electronic mail addresses (e-mail). Sometimes you can reach contacts faster through e-mail than you can by telephone. A field for miscellaneous comments is helpful, too. Use that field to record anything specific about the contact that will help you remember him or her a year from now.

Use a $150 Phonebook CD to Find Customers and Suppliers

Personal contacts make the business world go round. But what can you do when you can't put together a business deal from your personal contact list?

Dig out a CD-ROM phone directory.

Wyndell J. Ferguson uses a CD-ROM phonebook called SelectPhone almost daily to find customers and suppliers for an import–export business.

When he had an overseas client looking for oak veneer, for instance, he searched SelectPhone using the SIC code and found several manufacturers.

"After a few phone calls, we had a bid for the size and quantity requested. I faxed the price bid overseas, and a few hours later had closed the deal! I couldn't have done that fast (if at all) without the CD," he says.

CD-ROM phone directories vary considerably in their capabilities and price. Look at what types of information you can search for, how you can display the information, whether you can export the information (get the information into a form you can use in another program), and whether there's a limitation to the number of names you can look up or print.

Generally speaking, the less you pay, the more limited the capabilities of the directory will be. You can get a good quality CD phonebook for $150 or less. For the best buy, check the prices both in mail-order catalogs and superstores and shopping warehouses. Be sure that you are comparing the same edition of the same phonebook and that both are the most current version before making your purchase decision.

Add a Personal Touch to Your Business Dealings

Here's a simple and inexpensive way to get your name in front of clients: Send a greeting card.

Whether the cards thank the recipients for giving you a referral, wish them a happy birthday, congratulate them on the birth of a child, or even extend sympathy on the loss of a loved one, the cards will remind customers or business acquaintances that you are concerned and interested in them. That helps build relationships that can lead to sales.

Don't wait to buy a card until you need one. Keep a supply in the office so they are on hand to mail out whenever you hear of an event for which a car would be appropriate. Thank-you cards and other standard and humorous business greetings can be purchased from many paper suppliers. Or make a trip to the local card shop and pick up a handful of assorted cards to keep on hand in the office. To make sure they don't look dirty or shopworn when you eventually use them, store them in a clear plastic bag in your supply cabinet or file drawer.

Turn Your Fax Cover Sheets into Sales Tools

The text on most fax cover sheets takes up only about half of the available space on a page. You can get more mileage out of every fax transmission you send by including promotional material on the cover sheet.

For instance, if you run a secretarial service, instead of just including your name and logo on a fax cover sheet, you could list the services you offer in a column down the left side of the paper. Put the body of the fax in a box on the right side of the paper. The new design would remind recipients about all the services you offer. It would also be a good example of your typesetting and design capabilities.

If you sell products, redesign your cover sheets so you can include ads for products you want to feature. Your ad will ride free every time you send an outgoing fax to your existing customers, suppliers, or others with whom you do business.

Cut the Cost of Fax

Get your customers' e-mail addresses and send them e-mail instead of a fax. (Be sure you get their permission in advance.) Include your e-mail address, Web site, fax number, and telephone number along with your signature.

Give a Presentation

One of the best ways to make contacts and bring in new business is to give a presentation to a large group of people. Whether you make jewelry, teach painting, sell insurance products to business, or design Web pages, people who attend the function will view you as an authority on your subject matter because the organization asked you to be a guest speaker. The resulting name recognition can be a significant source of immediate and long-term sales. Be sure to plan your presentation so it is full of useful information. Presentations that are nothing more than a sales pitch for your business will not be well received.

Good targets for presentations are business organizations such as the Chamber of Commerce, Kiwanis, and Rotary; professional and trade associations; regional networks; business women's associations; public libraries; and large bookstores. On a national basis, you may be able to get invited to speak at trade shows and industry conferences. Sometimes, though, those speaking slots are reserved for companies that rent booths for the show or are members of the association.

Often all it takes to be invited to speak is to identify yourself and let the organization know you are available to talk about your area of expertise.

If your target market is a large national audience, contact national associations and trade show promoters, and offer to be a speaker or panelist. Be prepared to pay your own way unless you are an established speaker or sought-after expert in your field.

Remember to plan well ahead. Trade shows are planned as much as a year in advance. Local organizations and retail stores plan their events several months or more in advance. Professional associations often use the summer months to line up speakers for their fall and spring meetings.

Bring Handouts

The best presentation in the world won't do you a bit of good if the people in the audience forget your name or don't know how to contact you at a future date. Help your audience remember who you are and what you do by having handouts available for them to take home.

The handouts that are most likely to get saved are those that contain a summary of the important points of your talk, copies of articles you've had published, or some additional useful facts about the subject matter of your presentation. Be sure every handout has your name and contact information printed on it. Be sure to leave plenty of business cards out, too.

In addition to distributing informational handouts, you may also be able to distribute product literature or actually sell products at the end of your presentation. To be on the safe side, ask the meeting planners in advance if this will be allowed.

Teach a Class on a Subject Related to Your Business

Teachers are expected to be experts, so this is yet another way to gain prestige in the eyes of your targeted customers. Depending on where the class is held and who is sponsoring it, it can also be a good way to sell products related to your subject matter. Many professional artists and crafts designers augment their income considerably by teaching classes and selling the supplies to their students.

Keep Your Name in Front of Customers and Prospects with a Newsletter

Newsletters are one of the most widely used and effective ways of keeping your name in front of existing customers and prospects. They are used to bring in new business as well as to communicate with existing customers. They work equally well for companies involved in international trade, accountants and attorneys, printers, podiatrists, and even one-man bands.

Paul Silva, an entertainer from Hicksville, New York, sends out a monthly newsletter to promote his one-man-band act, A-Band-In-Me. The newsletter is a single, 8 1/2-by-17-inch sheet of paper printed on two sides. It contains a calendar listing of performances for the coming month, a scanned photo of people enjoying his past performances, and a list of events for which he's available. There's a hodge-podge of other tidbits crammed into the newsletter as well. The whole thing is put together in a helter-skelter fashion that might make designers groan, but which, nevertheless, gets across Silva's message that his performances are fun.

The newsletter, which Silva mails to approximately 1,800 people, costs less than $400 an issue to produce and mail at bulk mail rates and brings in three to four new bookings a month. It also attracts people to his club and restaurant appearances. "Before I started the newsletter, " Silva says, "I booked a week in advance. Now I'm booked three months in advance."

Whether your target market is partygoers or top executives of major corporations, the four keys to success for low-budget newsletters are:

▶ Include information in the newsletter that the recipients will want to read.
▶ Present it in a format appropriate for the audience.
▶ Send it to a very targeted mailing list. (Silva takes a notepad to performances and ask people to leave their name and address if they want to get his newsletter.)
▶ Send out a new issue at regular intervals so your name is fresh in the customers' mind when they do need your services.

Make Your Newsletter Work for You

To get the most mileage out of your newseltter, make it relevant to your business and be sure it includes hooks to get customers to call you, stop into your store, or visit your Web site. For instance, include photos of new products that would appeal to your customers, links to a Web page that has key data your customers may require, or a coupon to be redeemed if the reader makes a purchase or visit by a certain date.

Chapter 6

GETTING

PUBLICITY

The more often people hear or see your name, the more likely they'll be to remember it when they want what you sell. And the more confident they'll feel about buying from you.

Companies with big budgets can make themselves known through massive advertising and direct-mail campaigns. Small and home-based businesses usually need to find a more affordable way to accomplish the same goal.

Getting publicity is one cost-effective way your microsized businesses can achieve that goal. In fact, publicity can serve two important functions for your small or home-based business. It makes your name familiar to prospects, and it helps build your credibility. By singling you out, the reporter makes you the expert, and your product one worthy of attention.

But how do you get reporters to talk about you instead of your competitors? Here are a number of strategies to help you get media attention.

Target the Right Media with the Right Message

Don't waste time and money mailing to media contacts who aren't likely to be interested in your story. The features editor at *Family Circle* magazine isn't likely to assign anyone to write a review of your new time management program. But the home business columnist for a computer magazine might consider the program for review. Therefore, instead of blindly sending press releases to editors, create a list of writers and editors who write about your specialty, and send your press releases only to those individuals.

Start with publications with which you are familiar. Look through the publication for a page containing a list of editors. That page usually lists several phone numbers for the publication as well. Call the number listed for the publication's editorial department and ask who would be the right person to receive press releases about your product or service.

For broadcast and cable contacts, listen to or watch radio and TV stations on which you'd like to be featured. Find out which reporters and talk show hosts cover stories about your industry. Then, call the station to find to whom to submit your material for each specific show.

Expand Your Media Contact List

Depending on your industry, there may be hundreds of media outlets you aren't aware of that would make good targets for your publicity. Fortunately, there are a variety of directories and services to help you identify and reach these other contacts.

Among the best known are the publicity services offered by Bacon's Information, Inc. The company publishes several media directories used by public relations professionals, offers publicity mailing services, and also sells media mailing lists. The company's printed directories include *Bacon's Newspaper/Magazine Directory, Bacon's Radio/TV/Cable Directory, Bacon's Media Calendar Directory, Bacon's Business/Media Directory,* and *Bacon's International Media Directory.* The directories include editorial contact names as well as mailing addresses and other information useful to public relations agencies. You'll pay hundreds of dollars for these directories. Thus, if you do only a limited amount of publicity during the year, you may want to look for the directories in a public library, or rent a small list of press contacts at 55 cents per name to keep costs down.

Other media directories include *Editor and Publisher International Yearbook, Gale Directory of Publications and Broadcast Media, Standard Rate & Data Service, Ulrich's International Periodicals Directory,* and *Gebbie's All-In-One Directory.* One or more of these should be available at your public library. Gebbie's is also available on the Web at http:/www.gebbieinc.com/misc/sbn.htm.

Plan to Send Press Releases When Reporters Are Likely to Be Working on Stories About Your Industry

The two most important facts to remember about publicity are (1) reporters, editors, and producers work in advance whenever possible, and (2) they are always pressed for time.

Anything you can do to make your story land on writers' and editors' desks at the time they are most likely to be working on stories related to your product or service is likely to increase your chance of getting publicity.

If you've developed a new Christmas product and don't get your press release about it ready until the end of September, you've missed the boat for magazines. But you still may be able to get publicity in newspapers or on radio or TV.

The best way to find out how far in advance publications and producers work is to contact them and ask. But as a general rule of thumb, special issues of monthly magazines may be planned as much as a year in advance; individual stories in regular issues are usually planned four to six months before they appear in print; newspapers and broadcast media work on general interest features about two to four weeks in advance. Breaking news, naturally, is handled as it occurs.

Ask for an Editorial Calendar

If you know the lead time, it's easy to guess when editors and writers will be planning seasonal issues. But what about articles that aren't seasonal?

You can find out what general subject matter will be covered in which issue of a magazine by calling the magazine and asking for a copy of the editorial calendar. The editorial calendar briefly lists the types of stories that will be covered each month for the calendar year. For instance, the editorial calendar for *Fancy Food* magazine might show the magazine covering snacks in September, baking mixes in October, honey and specialty sugars in November, and cookies and biscuits in December. Once you get the calendar, look it over to see when the magazine plans to run features related to what you sell. Send out your press release far enough in advance of that date so editors and writers can consider your material when planning articles.

Help the Media Find You

Press releases and personal contacts aren't the only way editors and writers find experts. When they need an expert in a hurry, they look them up in reference books. One widely used reference is a yellow pages–type directory of experts called *The Yearbook of Experts, Authorities and Spokespersons*. Approximately 14,000 copies of this directory, which is published by Broadcast Interview Source, are distributed free each year to broadcast journalists, columnists, leading newspapers, and small-town papers. A searchable version of the directory is available at the company's Web site, http://www.yearbook.com. This online version includes links to advertisers'

Reporters Are Human, Too

Remember that reporters often work under worse deadline pressures than you do. If they "never" use any material you send them, or if they should make a mistake, don't rant and rave. Call or send a polite e-mail or fax asking for a correction (if there was an error) and if there is something you can do to help avoid similar problems in the future. On the flip side of the coin, take a moment to send a thank you note when reporters do mention you or use a story you've pitched to them.

Web sites. Fees for being included in the directory start at $375 for a listing of up to fifty words. For information about being listed in *The Yearbook*, contact Broadcast Interview Source, 2233 Wisconsin Ave., NW, Washington, DC 20007 (202-333-4904).

Call Before You Send Releases

When you send a press release, be sure to address it to a specific person's attention. Don't assume the correct person to receive a release is the editor or managing editor of the publication. Call and ask who should get releases about the type of product or service you are publicizing. Ask how they spell their name and what their title is. If you plan to fax the release, ask if the individual has a different fax number than the fax number given out to the general public. Sometimes there is more than one fax machine in the publication's office. You want to make sure the fax machine that receives the press release is the one the person you are trying to reach will check.

Grab the Media with the Headline and First Sentence of Your Press Release

Not surprisingly, the media get bombarded by people seeking publicity. Mitch Wagner, a senior editor at *InternetWeek*, recalls a major publication he once worked for got so many press releases faxed to them that they put a trash basket by the fax machine. "Incoming faxes went straight into the garbage and then got picked up by the cleaning people each night, without any need for other intervention," Wagner says.

That method for handling incoming faxes is the exception rather than the rule. Nevertheless, very few press releases get more than a cursory glance. Reporters, magazine editors, and producers of radio and TV shows get so many releases each day it's impossible to read them all thoroughly. "You have mere seconds to capture a person's attention. They glance at a page, read the first couple of sentences, and if it doesn't grab their attention immediately, they throw it out," says Wagner.

To get the media to sit up and take notice of your press release, relate your product or service to a news event or a holiday, or show how your

▶ Tip
The easier you make it for a reporter to write about you, the more likely they will be to do so.

product or service solves some common problem. Let them know in the headline and the first sentence or two why the information you are promoting is important to *their readers*. Do not start any press release with phrases like "Joe Smith, President of ABC Industries today announced . . ." or "ABC Industries, a leading provider of. . . ."

If you've never written a press release and feel a bit squeamish about trying, look for software or books that offer model press releases. Both normally have tips on how to get publicity as well as how to write press releases. Such products will help you with basic approaches and may help you get local publicity. Since the releases are generic, though, the sample lead paragraphs usually suffer from the "today announced" syndrome, and will need to be reworked to make media sit up and take notice.

Send a Boring Press Release Rather Than Sending No Press Release

A boring press release is less likely to get read than one that makes an editor sit up and take notice. But if you don't send any release, you have no chance of getting publicity. If the release has information that may be of interest to editors, send it even if you can't think of a way to make the release interesting.

Make Frequent Contacts with the Media

Alert the press every time you have a story they would consider newsworthy or of interest to their readers. The more often reporters see your name, the more likely they will be to remember it when they need to interview someone for a story.

Kenneth Sethney, a marketing consultant who is part of businessVISION, a Laguna, California, management consulting firm, used this strategy to publicize a client who was an investment banker specializing in "small" deals ($1–$2 million).

"Every time he did a deal, we put together a one-page newsletter for his [the investment banker's] clients and referral base. We also sent copies to the financial reporters in southern California. Within six months, he was a regular news source—quoted in many articles about 'emerging growth' companies and new business opportunities."

You don't have to put together million-dollar financing deals to find reasons to send out press releases. Remember, a press release is really a "news" release. Thus anything new or different about your products, services, or you is worthy of a press release and might get used if you target your audience and media appropriately. Here are some just a handful of situations that you can use to issue press releases.

Release of a new product

Introduction of a new service

Getting a patent

Introduction of a new or upgraded model or version

Winning an award

Reaching a significant sales or customer milestone

Conducting a survey

Reporting results of a survey

Hosting a well-known guest at your establishment

Opening a new store

Participating in a community service project

Announcing a contest

Announcing the winners of the contest

Unusual use of your product or service by a customer

Release of a product upgrade

Free facts or free booklet giveaways (must be legitimately helpful material to get publicized)

Announcing your upcoming appearance as a speaker

Dare to Be Different

Phone calls, press releases, and personal contacts aren't the only methods you can use to reach the press. In fact, sometimes it pays to be different. Kenneth Sethney attributes part of the success of his client's campaign to the newsletter format used to contact the press. The newsletter drew attention not only because it looked different from a standard press release, but also because it included brief background information about how the deals were put together.

Publicize Your Publicity

Once you get publicity, capitalize on it. The purpose of seeking publicity isn't just to satisfy your ego. (It may well do that, but that isn't going to make you any money.) So, don't just clip the news item and store it in a drawer for future reference. Ask permission to reprint the article and then distribute it every time you mail out product literature to potential customers.

If the article was about only you, consider putting a heading at the top of your reprint saying, "As Featured In [publication name]." If you are just mentioned in a paragraph or two, highlight that section neatly in some way. The printer can do this for you (you'll pay for two-color printing, though). Or you could hand-draw a small arrow pointing to the start of the text. If you have a very steady hand, you could underscore or highlight the text with a highlighter.

If you have a retail store or restaurant, make copies of any articles that praise your product or service or talk about its uniqueness. Put them in a frame and hang them or put them in your front window where customers can see them.

Send a Picture with Your Press Release

Magazines and newspapers frequently use photos and artwork to break up columns of text and make them more readable. Because of time, distance, or budgets, it's not always possible for them to use their own staff to shoot photographs or draw original art.

You can improve your chances of getting media coverage—or make a bigger splash on the page—by sending photos with your press releases.

Photos should be sharp and clear and related to the subject matter of the release. The more interesting the photos would be to the media's audience, the more likely the photo will be used or, for TV, the more likely you'll be invited to make an appearance.

If you don't want to spend a lot of money mailing out photos that may never get used, indicate at the bottom of your press release that photos are available on request.

If you sell software, send the editors screen shots on disk instead of photographs. Or let them know that screen shots are available on request.

> ▶ **Tip**
> Photos of you aren't always appropriate to send. If you are announcing a new product a better choice for most places would be a photo of the product or of someone using it. One exception might be a column in a newspaper that features news about movers and shakers. Attach caption information to your photograph, too. If the picture tells the proverbial thousand words, it (along with the caption) may make it to print even though the press release doesn't.

Have Publicity Photographs Professionally Prepared

If there is a realistic possibility that the press will want to run a photograph of you, have publicity photographs made up professionally. The photos will pay for themselves in publicity value the first time your story gets used or featured more prominently because you were the one person who had a publicity shot the magazine or newspaper could use.

Skip the Photo and Save Money

Don't waste money sending a photograph for reproduction to radio stations or other media that don't use visuals.

Prepare a Backgrounder

A backgrounder is a profile of you or your business and its top executives. It is useful for sending out to the reporters, program directors, business contacts, and anyone who wants a brief overview of what your business is all about.

If you are a one-person business, the backgrounder would summarize your claim to fame. Unless you are looking for investors in your business, keep the backgrounder short but informative. One to two pages summarizing key accomplishments and noting how long you've been in business is usually all that's needed for publicity purposes. Longer backgrounders aren't likely to be read.

The backgrounder should be written as a third-person narrative. If you have trouble writing one, substitute the name Jane Doe for yours, and then write a few paragraphs that would be suitable for introducing Jane to an audience. Use the search and replace feature of your word processor to switch Jane Doe back to your name when you are done.

Have a Press Kit Ready

If your press release piques a reporter's interest, he or she may want more information about you or your business. And she'll probably want it in a hurry. You can get additional information to reporters at the drop of a hat if you make up a press kit in advance. These materials could include a brief overview of your company, fact sheets about your products, a capabilities statement or brochure, and a client list. By making photocopies of these materials and keeping the copies together in a folder near your fax machine, you'll be able to immediately comply with informational requests. That, in turn, will increase your chance for getting free publicity.

You can keep the cost of press kits down by producing them in small quantities as needed. For instance, you could use your own laser printer or photocopier to produce a dozen of each page you want to put in the press kit. Keep a supply of good-quality presentation folders on hand and customize those as described in Chapter 4. That way when an editor—or a potential customer—says send me something, all you have to do is place the inserts in a folder, and drop it in the mail.

Have One Set of Press Kit Materials Ready to Fax

Fax has become so much a part of business life that you may be asked to fax customers (or the press) information about your products and services instead of mailing it. Although you can unstaple product literature, it's more convenient to keep a set of product literature in a file drawer near the fax. If you send faxes from your computer, store all of your good copies of marketing materials in one computer directory so you can find them without searching through your entire hard drive.

Use Light-Colored Paper for Producing Sales and Marketing Literature

Colorful paper stock or inks can make your mailed brochure look attractive and get attention. Unfortunately, the same colored stock or ink can make your brochure unreadable if you have to fax it.

If at all possible, therefore, it's a good idea to use light-colored paper stock for your brochures. If you must use deep color papers, print out one copy of the brochure on white paper (or have your designer print one copy on white paper for you) and use that copy when you are asked to send a fax about your company.

Be Prepared to Respond to Inquiries Generated by Publicity

All of your efforts to get publicity will be for naught if you can't quickly respond to inquiries the publicity generates. Before you send out any publicity, have everything ready you'll need to respond to inquiries. Depending on what you are publicizing, this may be brochures, sales letters, fact sheets, or product samples.

Although you may not want to spend the money to have a large quantity of these items on hand, you should at least have them ready to send to the printer—or to run off on your own equipment.

> ▶ **Tip**
> Seek online publicity as well as publicity in the traditional media. Look for opportunities to be a chat guest or to write articles. Ask the online media to put in a link to your Web site. You'll gain name recognition and sales.

Write an Article or Column About Your Specialty

If you have good communications skills, you can get your name in front of potential customers regularly and set yourself up as an expert by writing about your specialty for newspapers or trade journals.

To get started, contact newspaper or trade magazine editors and tell them how the column you'd like to write will interest their readers. Approach one editor at a time (unless you can write for noncompeting markets) and have a column or two ready to show the editors if they express interest.

If your idea is accepted, you may get paid only a small honorarium for your work. Or you may get paid nothing at all. What you will get is the name recognition and prestige you gain by being published.

"I wrote a weekly column for the *Fort Worth Star-Telegram* for fourteen years starting at $20 an article. Fourteen years later, I was making $40 an article!" says Dr. Ricks Pluenneke, a plant science consultant.

"The reason I wrote wasn't for the money. It was for the exposure. They published the articles under the byline, 'The Plant Pro,' which is my registered U.S. trademark."

Ricks no longer has the time to write the weekly column, but he does still write an occasional article for trade publications for free. The reason? "I'm a consultant," he says. "Writing articles is a heck of a lot cheaper than advertising."

Buy Your Space

If you can't find a publication willing to publish your material with or without pay, consider buying advertising space and using that to write a column. Many (but not all) publications will print the word *Advertorial* at the top of your article to alert readers that the article is not part of the regular editorial content of the publication. Still, advertorials, when well written and informative, do work.

Be sure you get honest opinions on both the value of the content and the quality of writing before you attempt this, however. Better yet, have an ad agency or freelancer write the column for you if you are not a professional writer.

Make Sure Prospects See the Article

Getting an article or column published won't do you much good if no one knows about it. Be sure to refer to your column or article in sales literature. Make copies of your published works and distribute those with your sales literature.

Get on Radio and TV Talk Shows

Being a guest on radio or a TV show is a wonderful way to build sales. The fact that the show has invited you to talk about your business or demonstrate your products gives you instant recognition and, in most cases, instant credibility. As a result, you can often gain more sales from a single radio or talk show appearance than you can with a paid ad on the same station.

Getting on radio and TV shows can be surprisingly easy. Shirley Frazier, a gift basket designer and consultant from Paterson, New Jersey, has rung up thousands of dollars in sales as a result of appearances she made on CNBC's *America's Talking* and Fox's *The Television Food Network*.

Her "trick" for getting on the shows is to send out a press release about a month or so before major holidays, describing the unique gift basket specialties she has for the occasion. The release includes a reminder to contact her for booking or further information.

"Sometimes they bite, sometimes not," Frazier says, "but I keep on sending the best-written releases I can to all the television stations in my area. Like a true entrepreneur, I never give up. There will always be a market for lively guests with unique products that viewers want to see."

▶ **Tip**
Look for contests and award programs you can enter. If you win, or even if you are a finalist and don't win, you may get valuable free publicity.

Publicize Your Appearances After the Fact

Get more mileage from your radio or TV appearance by mentioning it in publicity you distribute about yourself or your business. Phrases such as "a featured guest on . . ." or "as seen on . . ." lend instant credibility to you and your business.

Chapter 7

ADVERTISING TIPS

AND TRICKS

No matter where you turn, there seems to be some avenue where you can advertise.

There are newspapers, phonebooks, magazines, radio, billboards, bus benches, cable television, coupon books, weekly shoppers, the Internet—so many choices, so many markets. Which, if any, should you use?

Ask a group of microsized business owners that question, and each is likely to give you a different response. The owner of a small software publishing company may tell you she spent thousands of dollars for an ad in a major computer magazine and got almost no response. The guy who runs the lawn care service you use may tell you he advertises regularly in the spring, but thinks he gets most of his customers by word-of-mouth. A management consultant may tell you that advertising in the yellow pages is a waste of money, whereas your friend who's been running a secretarial service for a few years may tell you she gets a lot of new business from her ads in the yellow pages.

Who's right? Does it pay to advertise? How can you get the most mileage from your ad dollars if you do advertise?

Here are some tips to help you make better decisions about when, where, and how to advertise your microsized business.

Know Your Customer

A man who had been operating a game and hobby center for a year complained at a marketing workshop that advertising wasn't working for him.

Someone in the room asked where his store was located. When he mentioned the location, another person in the room said, "That's only a couple of blocks from my house. My kids would love your shop, but I've never heard of it!"

The shop owner, it turned out, had never made any attempt to advertise locally to attract teenagers from nearby neighborhoods. Instead, he had assumed most of his customers would be men in their early twenties and had placed ads sporadically in a daily newspaper that circulated in two counties and also in a small national gaming magazine that he, himself, enjoyed reading.

To avoid this pitfall, create a profile of your most likely prospects. Include age, income, education, sex, geographic location, and any other criteria that will help you identify likely prospects. Don't guess at the information you use to fill in the profile. Do enough research so you are working with facts. Look for information in trade magazines; talk to people you think will buy; and ask friends, relatives, and business acquaintances whom they think would be interested in the product or service.

▶ **Tip**

If you have a Web site, create a short survey and put it on the site to gather data from your visitors. If you have a lot of visitors, hire a programmer to set up the survey so that all responses are entered directly into a database.

Know What Your Customer Expects

Knowing demographic information about your customer is only half of the battle. The other half is to determine how to reach them and how to get them to make a purchase.

Once you've identified likely prospects, probe further to gather information about their buying habits.

Among the factors to ask about are:

Do paid ads influence their buying decisions?
If so, where would they expect to find an ad for this type of product or service? In a daily paper or a weekly shopper? In a magazine? In the yellow pages?
Do they ask friends for referrals?
Do they ask business associates, doctors, or other professionals for referrals?
Do product reviews influence their decisions?
Do they buy this product from a catalog?
Do they look for discount coupons before they buy?
Do they look for a brand name?
Do they look for a convenient location to buy the product?
Do they need to see a demo before buying?
Do they buy as a result of getting an ad in the mail?
Do they respond to telephone solicitations?
Do they listen for ads about the product on radio or TV?
Are there specific features they look for when they buy the product?
What else influences them to buy the product or service?

Use the answers to these questions to help you determine where and how you should advertise.

> ▶ **Warning**
> To avoid being sued under privacy laws, state the purpose of your survey and use the data you gather *only* for that purpose.

Set Goals for Your Ads

Advertising is no different from anything else in business: To be successful, it has to be planned.

Start by setting specific marketing goals and listing the ways you can reach those objectives. Don't use "increase sales" as your goal; that's too vague. Instead, list "attract 25 orders," or "get 100 new sales leads," or "double sales of widgets next month." Set realistic goals based on both the response rate of the medium you will be advertising in and on your own ability to produce the work or deliver the product you sell.

If you haven't advertised before, call a few noncompeting businesses that advertise regularly and ask what kind of response they have gotten from their ads in the media you are considering. If you have a computer and modem, look for an online forum that has people in your industry or trade. Post a message asking what advertising media works best for this type of business. People share that type of advice online more readily than they do in person.

Match the Media to Your Market

Advertising costs are linked to audience size. The bigger the circulation or audience, the more you pay. If only 10 percent of the media's audience are likely customers for what you sell, 90 percent of your advertising dollars spent with that publication will be wasted. Save money and get better results by putting your advertising dollars into media that will deliver the highest concentration of people who match your typical customer profile.

Before you place an ad, ask advertising sales representatives to give you a profile of their audience. Calculate what percentage of the media's audience matches the profile of your typical customer. Spend your advertising money with the media that can give you the highest concentration of likely customers at the lowest price. Remember, if 90 percent of the media's audience lives too far from your establishment to shop there, you've wasted 90 percent of the advertising dollars you spent.

Advertise Where Your Competitors Advertise

If your competitors have been advertising for many months in a specific media, their ads are probably working. Ride the coattails of their media research to increased visibility by placing your ads in the same media. Doing so will reduce some of the trial and error associated with finding the right advertising media. It will also put your product's benefits and features where your competitors' prospects will see them before they make a purchase decision.

Choose the Appropriate Media to Reach Your Customers

The right place to advertise one product or service isn't necessarily the right place to advertise another. For instance, consumer and business-to-business products generally require different advertising approaches.

Rik Rasmussen spent ten years as a regional sales manager for Cellular One before leaving to manage his own business, Direct Call Inc., in Raleigh, North Carolina.

As a regional sales manager for Cellular One, a company that targets the consumer market, Rik bought $150,000 worth of print and broadcast ads each month. But as general manager and part owner of Direct Call, a company that provides a cellular alternative to business owners, Rasmussen never places ads in the mass media.

The reason? Direct Call's customers never look in the mass media to find the services they offer.

To reach its market, Direct Call relies on traditional cold-call selling; a small yellow pages ad telling readers they have an alternative to high-priced cellular service; an ad in a local builders' trade magazine; and small, monthly direct mailings to targeted customers.

Decide on the Purpose of Your Ad

The purpose of any ad is to sell. But there are different things you can "sell" in an ad. An ad may be used to get orders, to get sales leads, to provide information, to get people to visit your store, or just to get name recognition. To get the most mileage out of your ads, make sure you know what your objective is before you write and place them.

Write with the Prospects' Interests in Mind, Not Your Own

Eliminate from your copy all phrases such as "We are proud to announce." Most of your customers won't really care what you are proud about. They want to know how you can make them feel proud about something, or how you can help them solve a problem or fill a need.

Dave Millman, of TACTICS, has run two different business-to-business advertising agencies. Looking at his own experiences he notes, "We were relatively unsuccessful with our first agency when we tried to put together big programs and promotions, showing how clever we were and how much experience we had. But when we buckled down and started building personal relationships with prospects, they started explaining their problems to us. Soon they were paying us to solve them."

His advice to all small businesses: "You'll start making more money when you stop trying to sell some brilliant idea of your own, and start to listen to what your prospect thinks his problem is, and what he really wants."

▶ **Tip**

If there is more than one publication or station or Web site that reaches your target audience try advertising in each. The same ad may get very different results from similar media. If there are two weekly newspapers, for instance, one may bring far more inquiries to your classified advertisement than the other. Be sure you have a way to identify which sales or leads came from which source.

Get Personal

Don't talk *at* your customers; talk *with* them. Use pronouns like "we" and "you" instead of cold nouns to draw readers into the copy by making them feel as though they are listening to a friend or business associate.

Instead of saying, "A business can reduce costs with . . ." try, "Lower your costs with. . . ."

Don't Sacrifice Sales for Creativity

A brightly colored mailer with a clever headline may catch the eye, but if it doesn't make your message clear, you may not get the response you should.

According to a story in *Direct,* a magazine for the direct mail industry, Network General mailed a four-color direct-mail offer to 100,000 carefully targeted prospects. The mailer offered a free booklet, but the headline talked about putting out fires (troubleshooting), rather than focusing on the free offer. The ad drew a 3.8 percent response. In several subsequent mailings to lists of the same size, the company cut production costs 35 percent and got a 6 percent response rate by using two-color brochures with headlines that made their offer clear.

Use a Picture

Your ad won't be effective unless it gets seen and read. If it consists only of words, there's a chance your headline and text will blend in with all the other text on the page and not really be noticed.

An easy way to make it stand out on the page and catch your prospect's eye is to illustrate the ad with an image. The image should be something that matters to the customer. If your ad is big enough, photos that tell a story related to your product (before and after photos, for instance) do a good job of catching the reader's eye.

If your budget won't allow you to hire a professional photographer to shoot the photo or if your ad is too small to use a photo, use illustrations.

If you sell name-brand products, ask the sales reps if they have ad slicks you can use for creating your own ads. Ad slicks are sheets of logos, artwork, or complete ad layouts with space for your own ad copy. They are called "slicks" because they are printed on shiny slick paper. With the slicks and your words, you can create your own personalized ad.

"Vendors hire expensive graphic artists to generate ad slicks," says Rik Rasmussen. "They work really well because they give your ad the kind of finished, substantial look you don't get with a homemade ad. If I'm the customer and I'm going to spend a lot of money, I don't want to deal with someone who looks like they're working on their kitchen table. I want to deal with a company that looks like it has substance behind it."

Get Free Help Creating Your Ad

If you don't know how to produce your own ad, and don't want to hire someone to do the work, ask the newspaper or magazine in which you plan to advertise if it offers help preparing the ad. Many will produce an ad for you to use in their publication at no charge. For best results, have some idea of what you want the ad to look like and say. Even a rough sketch would help. And, of course, proofread the copy to make sure your name, address, and phone number are correct.

Don't Pass Up Any Good Opportunity to Advertise for Free

If you keep your eyes open, you'll find many opportunities to advertise your business for little or no cost. One Halloween we ran a contest in the Business Know-How forum on America Online asking members to suggest ways to "scare up" business. Several people replied that along with candy, they drop samples, brochures, or coupons into kids' trick or treat bags on Halloween. The kids get the candy, the samples or coupons goes home as a treat for the mom or dad who inspects the goodies before letting the kids eat them.

Create Your Ad on Your Own Computer

If you have a computer and appropriate graphics, word processing, or desktop publishing software, you may want to create your own ads.

You don't have to be able to draw to create your own ads. If you need artwork or borders, you can purchase CD-ROMs containing thousands of drawings and photographs. Most also include a variety of fonts to make headlines stand out on the page. Good-quality computer clip art starts as low as $30 or $40.

You will have to know how to use your software reasonably well, however, and have a sharp eye for what will look good in print. Your best bet is to keep things simple, using only one graphic and one or two fonts.

"It's a skill well worth learning . . . since they can use the same skill to make in-store flyers, signage, direct-mail postcards, and more," says Kate Holmes, of Sarasota, Florida. Holmes is editor of *Too Good to be Threw, The Resale Industry Newsletter* (http://www.tgtbt.com). She owned a consignment shop before starting the newsletter.

Hire a Freelancer

If you want more help designing your ad than the media can give you for free, but aren't ready for an advertising agency (or can't get one interested in working with you because your business is too small), hire one or more freelancers to do the work. You'll find them at local business networking groups such as the Chamber of Commerce, through ads in weekly newspapers or business papers, and by asking other business acquaintances who they use to write and design their ads. If you use online services, you'll also find that many freelancers are regular contributors to the Business Know-How Forum and Web site (http://www.businessknowhow.com) and other communities on the Web that provide advertising, sales, and marketing help to business owners.

> ▶ **Worth Noting**
> Advertising, marketing, and public relations agencies often hire freelance help, too. You could wind up with the same writer and artist you'd get if you dealt with a graphics design agency, but at much lower cost.

Ask for references before hiring anyone. Ask to see the freelancer's portfolio, and look it over closely to see if his or her style appeals to you. If your ads, production costs, or marketing materials are going to be expensive (a relative amount you set based on your circumstances), look for freelancers whose primary business is preparing advertising and marketing materials.

Get References and Check Them

Whether you use a full-service agency, freelancer, or broker, don't make a judgment on a portfolio of samples alone. Ask for references and check them out.

Robert Schiesel is a direct-marketing consultant who was general manager of the business mail-order division at The Stationery House, Williamhouse-Regency before starting his own business in 1996.

"Don't deal with anyone who won't supply you with a client reference list," advises Schiesel. "Call the references. After the references check out OK, ask for list and media recommendations from more than one agency (three—if you can find three that check out). Then compare, contrast, and evaluate how each one plans to spend your money."

Use Position to Make Your Ad Stand Out

The same ad can have different impact depending on where it appears in a publication. Ads on a right-hand page of a publication get more visibility (because of the way people turn pages) than ads on left-hand pages. Ads in the center or outer edges of the right-hand page are more visible than those on the inner edge.

Ads near the front pages of a publication and in the back pages get seen more often than ads in the middle. Ads targeted at particular groups of people (computer users, for instance) are more likely to be noticed by potential customers if they appear on the same or opposite page as articles of interest to that group of people (a computer industry column, for instance.)

Use Design Elements to Make Your Ad Stand Out

Once you've got the text of the ad set, look for ways to make the ad stand out on the page. Some inexpensive design tricks:

▶ Add a border around the ad
▶ Include a coupon in the ad
▶ Use inexpensive clip art (pictures) in the ad
▶ "Reverse out" the type—use white type on a black background

If you use reverse type, use it sparingly and use it for headlines only since it's difficult to read if the type is small or extensive.

Calculate Your Break-Even Point on Ads

The break-even point on an ad is the point at which the ad would pay for itself. To determine that figure, divide the cost of the ad by your profit margin. For instance, if you spend $4,800 for an ad and your profit margin is 15 percent, you would have to sell $32,000 worth of products to break even on the ad ($4,800/.15 = $32,000). It's a good idea to calculate the number of customers you'll need to reach that dollar amount, too. To do that, divide the dollar value of sales needed to break even by the average amount a single customer spends with you. For instance, if the typical customer spends $50, you would need 640 (32,000/50) customers to pay for the ad. If you convert half the people who respond to your ad to customers, you'd need a total of 1,280 inquiries to break even on the cost of the ad.

The higher your profit margin, of course, the fewer inquiries and customers you'd need to pay for the ad.

> ▶ **Tip**
> In calculating your break-even point for ads, be sure to allow for credit card processing fees, per-inquiries fees, toll-free costs, and other expenses you may incur.

Buy Leftover Space

If you're flexible, you can save considerable money on the cost of advertising by buying remnant space (advertising space that hasn't been sold as deadline approaches.) Space (or air time) that hasn't been sold is space and time that isn't producing any income. As a result, it may be sold at 50 percent or more off the going rate.

Use Classified Ads To Reach Ready-to-Buy Prospects

Like yellow pages users, people who read classified ads sections of newspapers or magazines or in weekly "shoppers" (publications that are almost all ads and no editorial content) tend to be ready-to-buy prospects. They don't have to be convinced that they need a product or service. They just want to find a source for that product or service.

To tap into this pool of ready-to-buy customers, study the classified ads in various publications to see what types of businesses are advertising and what advertising headings are in place. If one or more headings are appropriate for your type of product or service, and a number of businesses are advertising under that heading, the publication is probably a good place for you to be. To be sure, get back copies of the publication. Compare the ads to determine if the same businesses that were advertising then are advertising now.

Check These Elements Before Finalizing Your Ad

Before you send your ad to the media, be sure it does these things:

- Tells readers what you are selling (you'd be surprised how many ads never really do that!)
- Tells readers why the product or service is important to them
- Is easy to read and understand
- Tells readers what action you want them to take (for instance, call you, visit your store, send money)
- Tells people how to contact you
- Includes your complete business name, address, and phone number

Keep Classified Ads Short, but Meaningful

Your classified ads should be short and to the point.

It must tell, in just a few words, what you are selling, who you are, why the reader should choose you over others in the section, and how to reach you.

The first two or three words in the ad serve the same function a headline does in a display ad: They should stop the reader's eye and encourage him or her to scan the rest of the copy. Words that promise a benefit such as "free," "fast," and "reliable" work well to drag the reader's eye into the rest of the ad.

Although you pay by the word for classified ads, don't cut so many words out of the text that the ad becomes meaningless. To make sure your ad is clear, have a few friends and family members read the ad before you submit it to the publication. If your neighbors (or their ten-year-old) don't understand what you're selling and why someone should call you, rewrite the ad.

Use Classified Ads to Generate Sales Leads

Many successful mail-order businesses were built on classified ads, but few of them have flourished by selling merchandise directly from the ad. That's because classified ads usually are too short to contain enough information to convince readers to part with their money.

That's why successful mail-order businesses use a two-step approach. The first step is to use classified ads to get likely prospects to identify themselves by responding to an offer for free information or by a low-cost for-sale item. The second step is to include additional advertisements or a catalog with the information or low-cost item the customer requested.

Start Small and Work Your Way Up

Don't go for broke with your first ads. When you are just starting out, you will need to test which markets and which offers and which headlines and which media work best for your business. When you think you have found

---

* Statistical Research, Inc. *Yellow Pages Industry Usage Study,* 1994. Depending on the heading being referenced, 53 to 90 percent of yellow pages users are undecided about where to make a purchase.

a winning combination, try a slightly bigger ad or a publication with wider circulation or a different type of media. Test only one element at a time, however.

Advertise in the Yellow Pages

If you rely on walk-in trade or if you sell products or services that can be easily categorized, plan to advertise in the yellow pages.

Having an ad in the yellow pages can mean the difference between getting business and giving it to one of your competitors. Unlike radio, TV, newspapers, and magazines, yellow pages users are people who have already decided to make a purchase. The majority,˙ however, are undecided about where to make their purchase.

These people turn to the yellow pages to find telephone numbers and facts to help them decide where to make their purchase. About 90 percent of these references actually result in a purchase or intended purchase.

Know When Not to Advertise in the Yellow Pages

Not all businesses benefit from yellow pages advertising. If you can't find an appropriate heading for what you do, or if there is a heading but very few listings under it, then yellow pages advertising may not be right for you.

Among those who often report gaining no benefit from yellow pages advertising are independent consultants, computer programmers, and writers (unless they list under public relations or advertising agency headings).

Get in the Right Yellow Pages Books

Once you decide to advertise in the yellow pages, you still have to decide in which book or books to place your ads.

With more than 250 companies publishing more than 6,000 yellow pages directories in the United States today, that's not an easy choice to make.

One tool to help make that decision is a rating system developed by the National Yellow Pages Monitor (NYPM). This rating system compares frequency of use of the directory rather than on the number of copies distributed. It can give you a clearer picture of which of two competing books to advertise in.

Unless you know that an alternative yellow pages is used heavily by your target customer base, call some of the businesses listed in it and ask what kind of response their ads have gotten.

Plan to Advertise Consistently

No matter what type of advertising you use, plan to advertise frequently. Advertising repeatedly makes your name familiar to your prospects and helps ensure they will find you (instead of your competitor) when they are ready to make a purchase.

Snare the Price-Shoppers

Most people like to get a bargain and yellow pages users are no exception. Many will call several companies listed under a heading to find out what they charge for a product or service.

Some small businesses find this objectionable and complain that they get more shoppers than real customers from their yellow pages ads. Others accept the inquiries as a fact of business life. Still others, like Paul Mayer, capitalize on their customers' penchant for price shopping.

Mayer is a software developer and a professional photographer. In 1971, he bought Marshall Photographer, Inc., a studio in downtown Chicago. "The studio had been in existence since 1906, and the old fellow we bought it from knew his customers," Mayer says. "The studio was one of ten portrait studios located in the Loop, or so I thought at first."

"The studio had a large display ad in the yellow pages, but there were also three other studios at the same address. I only knew of one other photo studio in our building. The other two ads—one for DeGore Studio and one for Baker Studio—were businesses once run by the owner of Marshall Photographer, Inc. He had kept the names and phone numbers because he knew that people shopped on the phone before making a decision. We'd get calls on all three of the phones from the same people, as they'd call studio after studio to get the best price. Since we were close to the Federal Building, we'd get calls for prices on passport photos and immigration photos. We'd get calls for pricing on business portraits, light commercial, and just about anything you can think of."

"By being our own competition, we'd generally end up with the business. After a few years, I even added another studio name to our list of names in the yellow pages. A. Aaron Studio was born to give me position at the top of the list."*

Mayer sold the business in 1991 when the profits from his software business outpaced the profits from the photograph studio.

"When I sold the studio," he says, "there was only one other studio left downtown who did black-and-white portraits, so we had that locked up. And there were only a few doing color. Rent is very high in the Loop and

Work Your Way Up

If your budget is limited, keep your ad small the first year you advertise in the yellow pages. Ask everyone who calls how they located you and keep track of the number who found you through the yellow pages. The following year, increase the size of your ad and keep track again. Keep increasing the size of your ad each year until it doing so no longer brings additional business. Stop advertising in the yellow pages when you get too few responses to pay for the cost of the ad.

---

* If you use multiple business names, be sure to register each with the appropriate authorities.

by maintaining the downtown customers, we were able to see all the others close down or move out of the downtown area."

So the truly enterprising business owners do more than accept whatever calls come to them from price-shoppers; they play to this known customer preference.

Use Color in Your Yellow Pages Ad

If all your competitors run their ads in black type, run yours in color. The ad will jump off the page compared to ads in all black type. If there are many businesses running their ads with colored ink, consider using a white background and colored ink for your ad.

Note that each color (and a white background on yellow pages would be a color) adds to the cost of your advertisement. It's therefore advisable to test your ad in black first to be sure the copy and classification heading bring in business. When you are ready to add color, don't change anything else about the ad except the color. The only way to tell what really affects response is to change one element at a time and compare the results after the change to results before the change. If you change the headline and the color or the copy and the color, you'll never know which change really made the difference.

Budget for At Least a 1-Inch Ad

A one- or two-line listing in the yellow pages isn't likely to do you much good. To bring in business, plan on having at least a 1-inch, in-column ad. Although the cost of that small ad can run to thousands of dollars a year in many parts of the country, the ad should more than pay for itself provided you offer products or services that consumers tend to look for in the yellow pages.

Advertise Under Multiple Headings

If your business might be found under more than one heading in the yellow pages or in the classifieds, it's a good idea to take out ads under each of them. For instance, someone who does word processing should consider taking out ads under the headings of "word processing, "secretarial service," "resumes," and "typing." Similarly, your cleaning service might be listed under "house cleaning," "office cleaning," and "janitor service."

To be sure you have chosen the most applicable headings (and found all of them), ask friends and potential customers to tell you what heading they'd look under to find your type of product or service. If you can't afford to list under all the headings, choose the one that's mentioned most often.

Fill Yellow Pages Ads with Buying Cues

Yellow pages readers don't need to be convinced of the need to purchase a product. They just need to know you can solve their problem now.

You can help them decide in your favor by including some of these key factors:

1. Products and services
   - Brand-name products
   - Authorized sales and service center
   - Replacement parts available
   - Niche markets served
   - Hard-to-find products or services
   - Company or product slogans
2. Reliability
   - Years in business
   - Association memberships
   - Licenses and bonding
   - Degrees (for professionals) or certification
   - Customer satisfaction guaranteed
3. Convenience
   - Twenty-four-hour service or extended shopping hours
   - Delivery services
   - Parking
   - Free estimates
   - Availability of credit
   - Proximity to major highways or public transportation

Don't Bring This Page with You

The one place not to use discount coupons is within your yellow pages ad. If you put a coupon in the ad and your prospects rip or cut out the coupon or the page, they won't have your name and address the next time they look in the yellow pages to find what you sell.

Worse, if the customer has clipped out your ad to use a coupon, the next time he or she looks in the yellow pages only your competitors' ads will be there to see. So guess who he or she will call.

If you think a yellow pages coupon would help generate business, ask your sales representative if the book has a special coupon section. If so, place your coupon in the special

---

Give Visual Buying Cues

Make your ad as visually appealing as possible. Graphic elements such as logo and pictures of products, and boxes around the ad, can make your ad stand out on a page. There should be enough white space around text to make it readable. If the ad looks crowded or difficult to read, potential customers will skip on down to your competitors' ads.

section to gain extra exposure and help prevent your main ad from being ripped out of the book.

Watch Out for Phony Yellow Pages Invoices

There are con artists out there who send out bogus yellow pages invoices on a billing cycle similar to the legitimate ones that advertisers receive.

Be sure to check your invoice carefully to ensure it really is going to the book that has your advertising in it. Don't be fooled by symbols like the traditional walking-fingers yellow pages logo.

Con artists will do everything they can to make the bills look real.

Choose Classified and Yellow Pages Headings with Care

Ask everyone you know to tell you where they look for your type of product or service. If you are thinking of advertising in the yellow pages or in classified ads, ask as many people as you can what headings they'd look under to find what you sell. Write their answers down so you can look for recurring responses when you are ready to choose your means of advertising. You may discover that customers for your secretarial service, for instance, turn to the "typing" or "word processing" headings because they need a typist or word processor, not a secretary.

While you're at it, ask what might make them choose one vendor over another.

Get Students to Conduct a Study

For a more scientific study, see if there is a college or university in your area that offers marketing as a course. If there is, ask the professor if he or she is looking for research projects that students can conduct. If so, you may get a more unbiased and scientific survey than you'd have if you conducted it on your own.

Don't Pay for Exposure You Don't Need

The more widely distributed the yellow pages book you list in, the more you'll pay for your ad.

If your business serves an entire county, or if most people look at the county book to find even local vendors, then the place to be is in the county book. But if you can service only local customers and if those customers would look there to find what you sell, advertise only in the local book. You'll save time and money.

Ask Customers What Directory They Use Most Frequently

The telephone company's yellow pages isn't the only game in town. Private businesses and organizations publish yellow pages directories, too. In 1995, there were more than 250 yellow pages publishers in the United States.

The best way to find out which directory your customers are most likely to reach for when they need your product or service is to ask them. Ask every caller how they got your name, too, and keep track of the answers. Any easy-to-use computer database or spreadsheet could handle this task. A word processing program would do in a pinch, too.

Lower Advertising Costs with Manufacturers' Cooperative Advertising Programs

Look for manufacturers to share some of your advertising costs. Many have cooperative (co-op) plans in place that will help you recoup some of your advertising expense.

Every cooperative advertising plan is different, but often a manufacturer will put a small percent of the money received from you into an advertising fund. Once you accumulate enough money in the fund, the manufacturer will draw from the fund to pay you back as much as 50 percent of the money you've spent to purchase advertising.

"Co-op money is not 'free money,'" notes Alan J. Zell. "It's given out only with proof of advertising—tear sheets or broadcast receipts. What all co-op plans do not allow for is production of the ad. It can only be used for media buys."

Zell, who ran a jewelry business for many years, now runs a seminar business teaching sales and marketing skills to other small businesses.

Cash back isn't the only type of co-op advertising plan offered by manufacturers. Depending on the manufacturer or other business you are working with, you may be offered merchandise or merchandise allowances instead of cash.

Ask about the Co-op Advertising Arrangements Before You Choose a Vendor

Manufacturers and sales reps don't necessarily publicize their cooperative advertising program. So be sure to ask if they have one. Experienced buyers will ask sales reps about their co-op advertising programs before they make any purchases. You can do the same thing. If you're not sure which manufacturers offer co-op advertising plans, ask your media contacts for information. Newspaper and radio stations often know which manufacturers have cooperative advertising programs.

Look for Media Buying Services

If you have the type of product or service that could be advertised nationally, consider using a media buying service to place your ads once initial small-scale tests prove successful. The service should be able to get you discounts on advertising and should be able to help you locate media that matches demographics already shown to be successful for you.

Media buying services are listed in the *Standard Directory of Advertising Agencies* (the *Agency Red Book*). You can find the *Red Book* in the reference section of many public libraries.

Pump the Advertising Sales Rep for Information

Don't rely on blind faith to make your ads pay off. Get as much information as you can to help you place the ads wisely and to make them stand out from ads placed by your competitors.

One of your best resources to gather the information you need to make informative decisions is the advertising sales reps you work with. Ask them to send you a media kit, and carefully read over the demographic information that comes with it. This will tell you who the media's target market is, what their income is, what occupations or interests they share, and other valuable information. But don't stop there. Ask the sales rep to tell you what you need to do to make your ad stand out from those of your competitors. Do you need a bigger size ad than you are running now? Your sales rep's answers will not only help you plan your own advertising, but also may give you some clue about what your competition has planned, suggests media consultant Steve Yankee of Yankee Communications in Grand Haven, Michigan.

Choose Your Business Name for Good Ad Placement

If you are just starting a business, consider making your business name start with a letter near the beginning of the alphabet. Shoppers often don't browse through all the listings under a particular heading.

If your business name begins with an A and you plan to advertise in the yellow pages, be ready to provide a business license or other official proof of your business name. Businesses in some parts of the country have found that yellow pages publishers or their sales reps have insisted on seeing such proof because so many businesses want their listing to show up near the beginning of listings.

Seek CoMarketing Agreements

Find companies that sell related products and work out arrangements where each of you advertise and sell the other company's products. Both products get added advertsing at no extra cost and each gets added revenue from both the extra sales that result and from any commissions they get on the sale of each other's products.

Let Restaurants Serve Up New Customers for You

Restaurants won't pay for your advertising, but they can help make your business known in the community at relatively little cost to you. How? Give them place mats featuring your ad.

Advertise Once, Benefit Many Times

A single ad in a large publication isn't likely to bring in a lot of business on its own. Yet, as mail-order sellers learned years ago, you can capitalize on a single ad for years if running the ad is part of a long-term advertising and marketing plan. How? Include reprints of the ad marked "As seen in . . ." in subsequent direct-mail campaign literature.

Capitalize on the Manufacturer's Advertising Dollars

Are you selling a product in your store that's recently gotten a good review in a well-known publication? Or that's currently being advertised in a major publication? Put that in a display and say, "As seen in . . ."

Offer a Discount for Advance Orders

The customer gets a bargain, and you can plan inventory and staffing needs for busy seasons.

Include Confidence-Building Credentials

When consumers have to choose among several unknown service providers, they'll choose the business whose ad inspires the most confidence that the job will be done properly.

Your ad should conjure up images of stability and professionalism by including words and phrases such as "board certified," "licensed," "insured," and "serving the community for 20 years."

Place the 20-Cent Ad That Gets Repeat Sales for Years

You spend considerable time or money to get new customers, and you bend over backwards to make sure those new customers are satisfied with your products or services. But what happens next time they need what you sell?

If they don't remember your name, they will be as likely to call one of your competitors as you.

Make sure your name and phone number are easy to remember and find by placing a heavy-duty label containing your name, address, and phone number on an inconspicuous place on the products you sell or service. These labels, available from companies such as Nebs, Avery-Dennison, 3M, and many others, are typically chrome or gold and very durable. They are usually placed inside the door of appliances or inside panels the user would normally open or close for routine procedures such as changing toner cartridges.

> **Be Predictable**
>
> Recency and frequency are the keys to advertising success. The more your ad is seen and the more recently it's been seen, the more likely your prospect will be to buy from you when they are ready to make a purchase.

Run Advertising Campaigns to Celebrate Special Events

The greeting card industry probably invented the special event, and you can capitalize on it, too.

There's a great reference book listing special events, celebrations, and momentous occasions throughout the world. It's called *Chase's Guide to Special Events* and usually can be found in your library. It contains ideas on holidays to celebrate and would be useful to gift-related businesses.

Honor Coupons After the Expiration Date

Here's an easy way to build good will: If you use coupons to promote products and services you sell all the time, think of the expiration date on those coupons as a way to encourage shoppers to come into your store now, rather than as a "limited" time offer.

Kate Holmes, editor of *Too Good to be Threw*, and of *ShopTalk*, a newsletter published by the National Association of Resale & Thrift Shops, says, "I started doing this one day after I had an epiphany while ordering pizza." She realized after she went to get the pizza that a coupon she had was outdated. "I [was told], 'sure, we'll honor that expired coupon,' which made me feel so good that I figured my customers deserved to feel as good, too!"

Although you may not want to publicize a policy of accepting coupons after the expiration date, if the merchandise or service is still available, doing so for an occasional customer who presents an expired coupon can help build customer loyalty, repeat visits, and most important, repeat sales.

Turn Your Car or Truck into a Mobile Billboard

If you're in a service business, you can bring in business by having your company name and phone number professionally lettered on the side of your truck or van. The sign works in several ways; it makes your business look professional and permanent; it builds name recognition in areas you travel frequently, and it lets you make confidence-building statements such as, "You may have seen our truck in your neighborhood." (Whether they have seen your truck or not, they may think they've seen it, and therefore identify with it.)

Negotiate Rates

Don't pay the advertising rate listed on the rate card. Think of those rates as the media's starting point for negotiations.

Familiarize Yourself with Advertising Laws

Just because you are small doesn't mean you can ignore or avoid complying with laws regulating advertising. Whether you've just started a small, home-based business or have millions in sales, you must be aware of and comply with advertising laws. Failure to do so can result in steep fines and high legal fees. FTC actions in the late 1990s, for instance, have resulted in small businesses being fined anywhere from $1,000 to as much as $16 million.

Although a wide range of advertising laws may potentially apply to your business, these are some of the areas that most frequently trip up small and big businesses alike.

MISREPRESENTATION OF THE PRODUCT

All descriptive text and photos must give consumers an accurate representation of what they will get. If you are selling frozen ice cream bars, for instance, you can't show a picture of five bars on the box if the box contains only four. Nor can you touch up photos to make a product look better or bigger than it is.

No facts about the product can be misrepresented either. Two Seattle business owners learned that the hard way in 1996 when they were fined $20,000 each for claiming Native American style artwork they sold was made by Native Americans when, in fact, it wasn't.

UNSUBSTANTIATED CLAIMS

You must be able to substantiate factual claims with proof that there is a reasonable basis for each one. A New Jersey talent agency, for instance, was fined more than $175,000 over several years for misrepresenting its ability to place children in high-paying modeling and acting jobs. The substantiation must exist before you make the claims.

The fact that someone might be able to realize the benefits you state in your ads, or that one or two individuals have achieved the advertised results won't suffice when claims lead people to believe that the average purchaser could achieve the touted benefits.

In recent years, the Federal Trade Commission has won multimillion-dollar settlements from a number of business-opportunity companies that could not substantiate the income claims made in their advertising were achieved by the typical purchaser of the plans.

If you make claims such as "recommended by doctors" or "tests prove" or "leading experts say," you must have proof that will stand up to scrutiny by experts.

The same is true if you imply expert approval by the setting and garments worn by actors in your commercial. If someone is dressed in a lab coat and holding up a test tube as an example of the superiority of your product, you will need scientific proof that the product is superior even if you never say the person wearing the lab coat is a scientist.

You need a high level of substantiation if you are making health, nutrition, or safety claims. In such cases, you need reliable scientific evidence. To provide that, you should have at least one independent double-blind study to support your claim. The study group also should be of sufficient size to provide reliable data.

The Federal Trade Commission publishes guidelines that can help businesses avoid the pitfalls. One of them is a guide to advertising laws covering dietary supplements, which is available on their Web site at http://www.ftc.gov/bcp/conline/pubs/buspubs/dietsupp.htm.

The other covers endorsements and testimonials in advertising. That is available from http://www.ftc.gov/bcp/guides/endorse.htm. The FTC has many other publications available to help businesses understand the laws. Many are available on their Web site at http:/www.ftc.gov. Many FTC publications are available in print as well. If you do not have a computer or Internet service available to you, you can contact the FTC at 202-326-2222.

FAKE TESTIMONIALS

If you use testimonials in your advertising, the people making the testimonial must actually use your product or service. If you pay them for their testimonial, that fact has to be disclosed unless the person giving the endorsement is a well-known person or an expert.

> ▶ Tip
>
> Exaggerated claims are not only illegal, they're counterproductive. Customers won't buy from you if your ads aren't believable.

SIMULATIONS OF REAL SITUATIONS

If you retouch before-and-after photos, such as showing someone cleaning a floor with one swipe of a mop when it really would have taken five, or use something other than what is stated to demonstrate your product, the facts must be disclosed.

In a classic case, the Colgate Palmolive Company was sued for a commercial "demonstrating" that its shaving cream could soften sandpaper. Since the sandpaper didn't appear coarse through the camera lens, the company used glass sprinkled with sand to sweeten the look, but this resulted in the suit for false advertising.

PRICE AND MERCHANDISE COMPARISONS

If you use words like "sale," "reduced," and "$150 value," you must have actually offered the product at that price for a reasonable period.

Similarly, if you say a product you are selling is "Sold elsewhere for $30 more," you must be able to prove that the item actually has been sold at that price. Terms like "special purchase" or "inventory clearance" should be reserved for times when you actually have bought merchandise at a special purchase price or are actually clearing out your inventory.

Neither can you advertise something as a one-day sale or being on sale for a limited time unless the pricing actually is for only a limited time.

WARRANTIES AND GUARANTEES

You don't have to advertise a warranty or guarantee, but if you do, you must state the terms and any limitations that apply. If you sell by mail, and will refund the purchase price if a customer is unsatisfied, but not the shipping and handling costs, your guarantee must make that clear, too.

Include Testimonials from Your Customers in Your Sales Literature and on Your Packaging

Testimonials are almost as powerful as personal recommendations for selling your product. They give you credibility and help assure prospects that others who have bought what you sell have been happy with their purchase.

If you've been in business for a while, you may already have a file of letters praising your product or service. If so, contact each customer who has praised you and ask for permission to include their comments in advertisements and sales literature.

If you don't have any testimonials, ask your customers for them. Encourage your employees to ask for testimonials, too, by offering them some type of incentive for each testimonial they bring in on customer letterhead. Be sure your rules include getting the customer to agree to let you use the testimonial in your advertising.

Send out an Ad Every Time You Fill an Order

The easiest sale to make is to a new, happy customer. To boost your profits at minimal cost, be sure that ads for one or more related products that you sell are included in every order you ship. The ads can be tucked in an order when it is wrapped for shipping, or they can be packaged inserts added at time of manufacture.

Include an Ad with Every Invoice or Payment

Take a cue from credit card companies. Don't let any opportunity go by to ring up an extra sale. Slip a coupon or special offer into the invoices and payments you mail. You'll benefit from the extra advertising exposure without having to spend anything extra on postage.

Trade Inserts with Other Businesses

Swap package inserts with other small businesses that sell to the same market but don't compete with you.

If you sell pottery, for instance, you might trade inserts with someone who makes hand-crafted jewelry; if you sell contact management software, you could swap inserts with a software developer who sells small business accounting software.

If the inserts are discount coupons, you and the business with whom you trade inserts benefit in two ways:

1. You get the opportunity to put an ad under prospects' noses at almost no cost.
2. The value of the coupons adds to the perceived value of your product. In fact, the inclusion of discount coupons for other products could mean the difference between getting a sale and losing it to a competitor.

Put Free Ads in Coupon Books

Advertising in coupon books sold by charities and other nonprofit organizations is another good way to bring in business. Since consumers buy the coupon books, they don't throw them out; they refer to them throughout the year.

Some organizations charge you for inserting your coupon in their book, but some cost you nothing. You can get free ads, for instance in coupon books published in many communities across the United States by

Fraud Hotline

As the number of SOHO businesses grows, so, too, does the incidence of fraud. To help spot trends in fraud and to identify wrongdoers, the U.S. Federal Trade Commission has set up a fraud hotline. Complaints can be registered by calling 1-877-FTC-HELP, or by filling out an online complaint form at http://www.ftc.gov/ftc/complaint.htm. The information is stored in a database that is accessed by law enforcement agencies in the United States and Canada.

Entertainment Publications (810-637-8400). The company not only gives you a free ad, they'll also lay out and typeset the coupon at no charge. "Coupon books have brought us the most new customers," says Anne Hopkins, who owns a pizzeria in Waretown, New Jersey. Such coupon books are well worth considering since they can deliver new customers to your door. Hopkins and her husband keep computerized records to show what advertising methods work, and have found that the coupon books have brought them the most new customers.

"The book comes out in October and is valid through the following year. That's a year's worth of free advertising," she notes. "I don't think a week has gone by when we don't get at least a few coupons."

Give Away Products or Services to Individuals Likely to Send Business Your Way

One of the best sources of new business is word-of-mouth advertising. A prospect who comes to you because he or she has been referred by a friend or because he or she has heard your name repeatedly is one who expects to make a purchase and expects to be satisfied with that purchase. In fact, surveys of small and home businesses have repeatedly shown that word-of-mouth advertising is one of the leading sources of new customers for small and home businesses that don't sell retail products.

Word-of-mouth advertising can take years to develop. You can speed up the process, however, by giving away your product or services to individuals who are in a position to recommend them to many other people. A New Jersey photo studio, for instance, gives holiday photos, photo cards, and occasionally, a complete wedding photography package to florists, travel agencies, caterers, restaurants, and real estate agents in their area. The giveaways serve as samples of their work and as incentives to encourage those businesses to refer photography clients to them.

Understand the Dynamics of Broadcast Advertising

Radio and TV ads must run frequently to be effective. Unlike printed ads that remain available until the publication in which they appear is thrown away, radio and TV ads are transient. They are heard or seen only by those individuals tuned into a station at the time an ad runs. The transient nature of broadcast advertising also makes it more difficult for the audience to remember important details such as your address or phone number. Larry Hryb, promotion director at WKSS radio in Hartford, Connecticut, suggests that to get results, a business should plan on doing one spot each hour of the evening drive-time for a week. That's four spots a day for five days.

Whether or not a business can afford to advertise that frequently depends partly on where it is located.

"Single-location, mom-and-pop shops aren't likely to gain enough business to benefit from paid radio advertising in higher-priced markets," notes Hryb. "One sixty-second spot on a New York City radio station can cost hundreds of dollars. That same money might buy a week's worth of ads in less populated parts of the country, though."

Run Vertical Ads

If you could benefit from radio advertising, but aren't ready to invest in it every day, Hryb suggests running a vertical ad campaign. This is a campaign that groups all of your ads over a brief period, say ten spots on a Thursday or Friday afternoon before a special sale you want to promote.

Be sure to plan ahead, though. Place the ads at least a month ahead. "Radio stations sell out toward the end of the week," says Hryb.

Give the Impression of Being a Major Advertiser on a Shoestring Budget

If you aren't advertising a specific sale or event, you can give the impression of being a steady advertiser by running one ad at the same time on the same show every week over a period of months. The people who always listen to that show will get so used to hearing your name after a while that they will remember your name and think of you as a big advertiser, notes Art Millman, who owned a radio station before he retired.

Bargain the Price Down

If you've tested radio or TV and found that it works for you, ask stations what discounts they give for placing ads on a regular basis. Depending on how much advertising you plan to place with the station, you may be able to get a 25 to 30 percent discount on the cost of air time.

Trade Products or Services for Radio Ads

If you can't afford to buy radio advertising, consider bartering (trading) your goods and services for ads.

Making such trades is common in radio; it's one way stations get products and services they need for themselves or to give to big advertisers or as contest prizes.

Treat these trades as you would any negotiation, trying to get the best deal you can. A typical arrangement is that the radio station will give you $2 worth of advertising for each $1 of the retail cost of what you are bartering. Thus, if you were to supply the radio station with 100 sweatshirts that you'd normally sell for $12 ($1,200 value), you could expect to get $2,400 in advertising in return.

Another option: Don't talk about the dollar value of the trade at all. Instead, suggests Millman, trade a product or service for a specific amount of advertising at a specific time.

Ray Baldwin, owner of Baldwin Electronics in Odessa, Texas, frequently makes such trades to advertise his business, which sells car radios and other mobile electronic products.

"Most TV stations do very little trade," Baldwin has found. But radio stations "always need prizes to give away, and they need sound systems for their demo and remote location vehicles."

Among the prizes Baldwin has given away are alarms and sound systems. "We donate the equipment in exchange for being a sponsor of the event or contest. In this way, we're able to tie our name to a big event without a large cash expense."

As a typical example, Baldwin worked with a local concert/car show promoter to provide the prize for a stereo contest at the annual car show. "This is a very big event," he says, "with a large draw, and it's a bull's eye to our target demographic (male, automotive enthusiast, eighteen to thirty-five years old)."

"For an actual out-of-pocket expense of approximately $1,500, we're getting an advertising package that they're selling for $4,500. Of course, this doesn't take into consideration the time and employee costs involved, but I consider this more PR time than cost time."

Be Picky About When Your Bartered Ads Run

Barter ads may be offered as "run of schedule" (aired when no paid advertising is scheduled), but as part of your barter deal, try to get the station to agree to run a certain percentage of your ads during times you select. If all of your ads run in the middle of the night, the ad response may not make up for the value of the goods or services you've bartered. If the station won't agree to give you times that are beneficial for you, try another radio station, suggest Millman.

Get the Sales Rep to Tell You the Best Times of Day to Advertise

Every advertising sales rep will tell you about his or her station's demographics and ratings. These figures may not tell you the whole story, though, says Millman.

A station may have women from twenty-five to forty as their primary audience, but those women may not be listening all day long.

"If your primary market tunes in at 3 p.m. each day and the station puts you on the air at 1 p.m., you've missed your market," Millman says.

To find out the best time of the day to advertise, Millman suggests telling the ad sales rep the profile of your typical customer and asking what time the largest number of customers like that are listening. "That is the only time you want to advertise," Millman says.

Use Radio's Unique Characteristic to Your Advantage

Radio is different from every other medium because there are no visual clues to help you form an impression of the product or service being advertised.

"Radio works on the imagination," explains Millman, who has forty years of experience in advertising.

"One of the tricks to successful radio advertising is to make a suggestion and let the listener's imagination fill in the details. On radio you can talk about a 'beautiful dress,' and each person listening will *see* a different dress in their mind's eye. You can't do that on TV."

Consider Cable TV

Price tags that can run tens of thousands of dollars (or more!) put national television advertising out of the reach of most small businesses. But cable TV, which can cost as little as $20 to $50 a spot, can be a surprisingly affordable alternative to radio advertising and can work well for consumer goods or services that can be photographed. Like radio, cable ads should run frequently over a short period. But with cable, more than radio, the demographics can change significantly from show to show on the same channel. Be careful, therefore, in placing your ads so that they all run to audiences made up of your typical customer.

Remember, too, that TV works best for selling products or services that can be demonstrated visually. Before and after examples of cleaning services, shots of furniture on sale, or demonstrations of how easy a product is to use would all be suitable for TV.

Using the Net As Testing Ground

Use the Web to test your ads before you run them in more expensive print media. Start by running the same ads that you run in conventional media. Track those ads long enough to get an accurate measurement of the response rate. Then, replace the Web ad with the ad you plan to introduce in print. Compare the resonse rate of the new Web ad to the first one. If the new offer produces better results on the Web than the first one did, there's a good chance it will do comparatively well in print. If the new offer is a dud on the Web, it's likely to be a dud in print, too.

One other advantage to testing on the Web: you find out in days how well an offer will work instead of having to wait weeks or months for your ad to appear in conventional media.

Look Good Without Paying a Lot for Production

A low-budget cable TV ad could be produced for as little as $200, but often a low-budget ad looks low budget. If you sell brand-name products, ask the manufacturer if they have canned (ready-made) TV spots you can use. If they do, you'll get a professionally created ad at virtually no cost other than what it may cost you to have your logo dropped into the ad.

Bring in Customers with Special Offers and Giveaways

Advertising specialties (items you give away without a purchase) and premiums (items you give away in exchange for a purchase) are a good way to keep your name in front of customers and prospects. A study of business executives reported by the Promotional Products Association International showed that 68 percent of the recipients could recall the name and message of advertisers who had given them promotional items, and that 34 percent of the executives used the items weekly.

Choose Items for Their Quality and Usefulness

Remember that the advertising specialty or premium you give away represents you to customers and prospects. If you want recipients to think highly of you, the item should be of good quality. If you want them to remember you the next time they need your product or service, the item needs to be something that is useful and that has a place for including your name, logo, and contact information.

▶ **Tip**

Nothing sells like the word "free." Look for premiums that would be desirable to your customers. Offer the premium if they make a purchase, or free if they make a certain number of purchases.

Use Multiple Forms of Media Advertising for Added Impact

Don't rely on one form of advertising to bring in all of your customers. The more places customers see and hear your name, the more likely they will be to make a purchase. As your business grows and your budget allows, consider using several forms of advertising to reach your customers.

Research conducted by Statistical Research, Inc., for the Yellow Pages Publishers Association showed, for instance, that when yellow pages advertising was used in addition to newspaper advertising, the percentage of purchasers influence by the ads increased by one half. When yellow pages ads were combined with television advertising, the percentage of purchasers influenced doubled. And when yellow pages ads were combined with radio, the percentage of purchasers influenced tripled.

Add the Web to Your Advertising Mix

A Web site can be yet another advertising medium for your company. If you can create your own Web pages, you can even put up a Web site as part of your subscription price to several commercial online services. If you need something more sophisticated, you can have a large, full-featured Web site for a whole year for about $1,000 (see Chapter 14).

Make It Easy for the Customer to Buy from You

Display your 800-number or regular phone number, your fax number, and your street address prominently in your ads. The easier you make it for the customer to contact you, the more sales you'll make.

Track Your Advertising Results

You won't derive any benefit from advertising if your ads don't bring in customers. Find out which ads are bringing in the most customers by keeping track of responses. Use your records to eliminate unprofitable advertising and replace it with more of the type that brings in customers and sales.

One common way to track ads is to code coupons so you know what publication or mailing they came from. Be sure you or your staff records the information from the collected coupons.

Record the number on each coupon that is returned, and you'll be able to quickly see which publication drew the most responses.

If there is a significant difference in response, consider dropping the publication with the lowest response rate and substituting another in its place.

"We have here in Columbus eight neighborhood papers all published by the same company. I tracked a coupon that appeared in all of them and discovered that the closer neighborhoods pulled most, but I was surprised by the figures on further neighborhoods. Tracking the coupons helped me decide to add (or) subtract some of these areas from future ads," says Kate Holmes, who owned a consignment shop for twenty years. Holmes now edits a newsletter for the resale industry.

If customers call your business rather than sending in coupons, you can track advertising results by telling people to call special extension numbers or to ask for a specific individual. For instance, your radio ad might say to call Jack for details. Your print ad might say to dial your phone number and ask for extension 25. Whoever answers your phone would keep a list of all incoming calls, noting what extension or name was asked for.

You could train yourself or your salespeople to ask where customers heard of you and record that information. That is the least accurate way to get information if you have walk-in traffic. In many cases, the customer won't remember where he or she heard of you. For example, I once ran a survey for one of my online forums and included a question asking people how they had found the forum. One of the possible responses was an "advertisement in a print publication." A fair number of people chose that option, but I had never placed any ads for the forum in any publication.

▶ **Tip**

Your existing customers will always be your most profitable customers. Here's why: There's a hidden cost factor in every sale you make: the cost of acquiring the customer. If a customer buys from you only once, the profit you make on the sale may not even cover the cost of acquiring the sale. For instance, if you spend $100 for an ad and get 2 customers from that ad, your cost to acquire each customer is $50. If each customer buys a $75 item that cost you $30, you'll lose $5. ($30 cost of item) + $50 (cost of acquiring the customer) on each sale.

Keep Them Coming Back

Whether you have a handful of clients for a small consultancy or run a retail business with thousands of customers, the key to long-term success in business is to turn one-time customers into regulars. To accomplish that goal, plan to keep in touch with your customers often. Depending on the type of business you run, plan on frequent advertising, regular mailings, special "preferred customer" mailings and discounts, phone calls, or even occasional lunch invitations. Doing so will make your business name rather than a competitors' leap into your customers' minds when they need what you sell.

Chapter 8

USING THE MAIL TO BUILD BUSINESS

The U.S. Postal Service, which delivers 182 billion pieces of mail annually, estimates that one type of business mail alone—bulk business mail—accounts for 55 to 60 percent of its revenue.

Much of that bulk mail is made up of catalogs, advertising circulars, and direct-mail campaigns sent out by experienced direct mailers who know from years of experience that direct mail gives them the best bang for their advertising bucks.

Small businesses that attempt to do bulk mailings are often disappointed, however. Despite the relatively low cost-per-contact associated with direct mail, small and home businesses often get dismal results when they attempt to do large mailings. If you find yourself in that position, these strategies will help you get maximum mileage from the money you spend on mailings.

Don't Do a Large Mass Mailing if You Have a Microsized Budget

Don't assume a single mass mailing will bring a flood of business to your door. Usually, it won't.

A chiropractor located near Chicago learned that the hard way. He wanted to jump-start his new practice, so he spent several thousand dollars to create, print, and mail a brochure extolling the benefits of chiropractic and offering a free spinal examination. The flier was mailed to 5,000 homeowners within driving distance of his office. To his dismay, he got only five inquiries from the mailing, and only one of those actually came in for the free examination.

The chiropractor's experience is unfortunately common. Loosely targeted bulk mailings simply don't work for most small businesses. Residential mailings often bring only one tenth of a percent response rate (1 in 1,000). Work out the numbers before you do a mailing. If your total cost for the mailing (list rental, postage, printing) comes to $1 per name, and if your mailing produces five new customers, each customer will need to spend $1,000 before you break even. If you get 5 inquiries and only one becomes a customer, that one customer would need to spend $5,000 just for you to break even on the cost of the mailing.

Focus on the Three Ms When Using the Mail to Market Your Product or Service

A wide range of factors ultimately affect the response you get from mailings. But underlying them all are the three Ms of successful mail marketing:

The market—the number of identifiable people who need or desire the product or service enough to be willing to make a purchase

The message—the words and images and special offers used to get attention and get customers to take action now

The mailing list—the actual people who receive a mailing and how closely those people match up to the types of people who are known to have a need or desire for the product or service

Where small businesses usually go wrong is by failing to get those three Ms in sync. To get good results from a mailing, you need to send a compelling message to a carefully selected list of people who are likely to need or desire your product or service and have the means to acquire it now.

Test Every Element of Your Mailing Before Doing a Large Mailing

Don't even consider sending bulk mail until you have done a series of smaller mailings to determine the effectiveness of your mailing piece and your mailing list.

Test a mailing list before you send out a large mailing to determine how current the names on the list are and how responsive the list will be. To test a list, ask the list broker for an *n*th name selection. This is the term used in the mailing list industry to indicate names are selected on a fractional basis (every *n*th name in the master list is selected). This gives you a random

▶ **Tip**
Test only one thing at a time. If you make two or more changes and there is a difference in results, you won't know which change caused the difference.

selection of names that will most accurately reflect what the response rate will be if you mail to the entire list.

If the mailing doesn't get much response and the addresses were deliverable, change your headline or your offer and do another small mailing. See how the response compares. Keep testing with small samples until you have a good handle on what copy, offers, and lists work best for you.

Build Your Business with Small Mailings to a Hand-Picked List of Prospects

Instead of a mass mailing, send very small mailings to a list of hand-chosen individuals who are likely to have an interest in what you sell. These individuals may be promising new prospects or existing customers whom you expect to make additional purchases. The more closely your sales offer matches their specific interests, the better your response rate will be. For instance, if you own a pet store, a mailing announcing a sale on scratching posts for cats will get a much higher response rate if you send it only to cat owners than it will if you send it to all pet owners. In fact, highly targeted mailings often have a response rate of 2 to 3 percent (or higher for mailing to existing satisfied customers).

> ▶ **Tip**
> You can buy small, targeted mailing lists on the Web. One Web site that lets you select a list of names by SIC code, zip code and other criteria is MySoftware company's www.myprospects.com site. Prices vary depending on the list, selection criteria and number of names. Prices for business lists of fewer than 100 names start at 50 cents per name.

Create Your Mailing with a Specific Objective in Mind

Many mailings fail because the mailing doesn't make it clear what the recipient should do after reading the mailing piece. Either the mailing doesn't tell the reader to take action or it suggests too many different things for the reader to do. To make your mailing profitable, have one specific objective in mind and build the mailing piece around that one objective. Some examples are:

▶ Get the customer to place an order.
▶ Get the customer to visit your store or office.
▶ Promote an inventory clearance sale.
▶ Get leads for a sales staff to pursue.

▶ Get customers to call for information about consulting or other services.

▶ Get the customer or patient to make an appointment for routine maintenance or annual checkup.

▶ Create name recognition.

▶ Ask the customer for referrals.

▶ Ask for testimonials.

▶ Announce the relocation of an office or a phone number change.

Before you send the mailing to be printed, give the text to several people who will be totally honest and ask them to tell you what action the mailing piece is asking them to take.

Plan on Repeated Mailings to Prospects

Don't stop at one mailing. Send mailings at monthly intervals to the same list of prospects even if they don't respond initially. The repetition will help build name recognition for you and increase the chances that your marketing materials will be on hand when the customer or prospect develops a need for what you sell.

Mail Often to Existing Customers

One of the easiest ways to build your business is by selling more products to your existing customers. Satisfied customers will be more receptive to your sales messages than strangers because they already think of you as a reliable, honest source for goods or services. And if you've taken the time to listen to them, you already know what kinds of goods and services they want to buy.

Capitalize on this combination of circumstances and turn your existing customers into repeat customers by sending them frequent mailings to remind them to order consumables or to get them to buy new products. If you haven't already done so, collect address information from customers by getting them to sign up for a preferred newsletter.

Don't Use Mass Mailings to Sell a Single, Low-Cost Product

Mail-order profits come from back-end sales. (A back-end sale is a sale of additional products to a customer who has responded to a direct marketing offer.) A single mailing with an offer for a low- or moderately priced item rarely pays for itself.

If you think that your one product is an exception, work out the math before you commit to doing a mass mailing. Price the mailing list you plan to rent, the cost of writing and printing your mailer, the postage, and any labor needed to get the mailing ready to drop at the post office. Add in your costs for the product and the labor costs to process the order, track inventory, and restock inventory. Add in merchant card processing fees and shipping costs (though those can usually be assessed separately as a shipping and handling charge). Total up all the costs and compare the total to the price you hope to sell the item for. Then make realistic estimates about the number of responses you'll get to your mailing. (The average response rate for a targeted mailing list is only 1 to 2 percent. If you can't closely target your mailing, response rates drop considerably.)

Get the Mailing Read by Appealing to the Customer's Interest

Many mailings fail to achieve their objectives because they talk about facts that are of interest to the business sending the mailing instead of talking about what interests the person getting the mailing. For instance, you may be proud of your newly expanded office facility or the new computer system you've installed, but your customers couldn't care less. What customers need to know is how you are going to save them money, help them make a profit, or solve some real or imagined need.

Convert Features to Benefits

You'll get the best response rate to mailings if you focus on the benefits of your product or service rather than on the features.

Features describe the size, shape, color, speed, availability, or other details about a product or service. Although they are important, what actually sells a product or service is usually the benefits the customer will derive by owning those features. For instance, no one really wants to purchase a resume. What people want to purchase is something that will make them look good on paper and help them get a new job. Similarly, few people really want nutritional supplements. What they want is to be healthy and strong. And no one really wants to buy a computer. Instead, first-time computer buyers want the benefits a computer promises such as increased productivity, the ability to make more money or to make money at home, or the chance to acquire new work skills or to give their kids an educational advantage. Second-time computer buyers

What a Teaser!

The first "sale" you have to make, is to sell the recipient on the idea of opening the envelope instead of dumping it in the trash. One way to do that is to use teaser copy on the envelope. For instance, if you are introducing an upgrade to a product, you can get your customers to open the envelope by placing a line of copy like this on your envelope: "Upgrade offer. Act now to save $75."

don't want to buy a computer either. What they really want is more power, faster access to the Internet, or more room to store important files and programs.

Don't Ignore Features Completely

Benefits are what get your prospect's attention and make him or her want the product. Features help nail down the sale by providing the solid facts today's consumer looks for to justify his or her purchase decision.

One good way to determine what kind of information to put in mailings that ask for an order is to ask friends and acquaintances what they'd want to know before buying the type of product or service you sell. Be sure that your mailing includes facts that would answer their questions as well as basic information such as size, color, availability, and operational details.

Write Short, Punchy Sentences

Whether you use a short letter and brochure for your mailing or a long sales letter, make your sentences short and to the point. Pepper them with active verbs, and play up key sales benefits in bulleted copy. Doing so will make it easy for prospects to quickly determine what benefits your products offer and what action you expect them to take.

▶ **Tip**

If you *are* a sales and marketing expert, get involved with an online forum. Help answer questions, write articles, or volunteer to be a chat host. It's a good way to promote your own services.

Get Help from Experts for Free

The Business Know-How Forum on America Online and the Business Know-How Web site include many articles from advertising sales and marketing experts. These articles are an excellent source of ideas for improving your direct-mail results. In addition, many of the experts answer visitor questions in the message boards online. If you haven't tried these resources, they are worth your while to investigate. Each article includes contact information for the person who wrote it, making it easy for you to contact the expert to ask about pricing and other matters if you decide to have someone write your sales letters or brochures for you.

Include a Call to Action

To get good results from a mailing, be sure it includes explicit directions about what customers should do after reading the piece. Do you want them to call? Write? Make a visit? Make the response you desire clear, and when possible, offer the customer an incentive for taking the action you want within a specific time frame.

For instance, if you've opened a new gift shop and want to attract customers, don't mail a flier that merely tells people there is a new gift shop in town. Mail a flier with a tear-off coupon good for a gift if the recipient visits your shop by a designated date. If you are trying to get existing customers to make a new purchase, send them a mailing thanking them for their business and giving them a special discount coupon good toward their next purchase.

Don't Forget the Clinchers

If your mailing is intended to get customers to place an order (rather than to get sales leads), be sure to include all those statements that give people a feeling of security about the order they are about to place. These include statements such as "money back guarantee," "in stock," "immediate shipment," and "name you can trust."

Be Careful with Mail Merges

If you maintain your own mailing lists and use them to send "personalized" letters, be sure that whoever does the data entry pays attention when they enter the names. If they don't, your mailing is likely to get laughed at rather than acted upon.

Typical of the types of letters that result when data is entered incorrectly is this one received by Ross Greenberg, a computer virus expert who lives in the Catskill area in New York on a farm called Virus Acres:

```
Dear Virus:
Our computer has selected you since you have two
little Acres running around your legs, sitting in your
lap and . . .
```

Use Local Newspapers to Build Your Own Mailing Lists

If you haven't discovered it yet, there's gold buried inside the newspapers you are stacking up in the garage for recycling. Feature articles and columns in the business section will give you the names of businesspeople in the area who have been promoted or have some other momentary claim to fame.

Large circulation daily newspapers and regional magazines often can yield insight into who's who at big corporations in your area. Small-town weekly newspapers can clue you in on the names of new businesses, organizers of fund-raising events, heads of local nonprofit organizations, and names of local shop owners and service providers. They are also a good source for names of people getting engaged, winning sports awards, and so forth.

Once you have these names, it's usually a simple matter to get an address and phone number from the local telephone book or from a CD-ROM phone book. You can often get an executive's phone extension by calling the company he or she works for and asking for it.

Henrik (Rik) Rasmussen, general manager of Direct Call Inc., in Raleigh, North Carolina, used to rent mailing lists to generate business for his radio communications service. But he wasn't satisfied with the quality and responsiveness of the list. Looking for an alternative, he began compiling his own list by scanning local publications for names of business executives that could use his service. Now he uses that method exclusively to prospect for new business. Each time he finds a name of a person who seems a likely prospect, he jots it down. Then at the end of each month, he sends a mailing to each name he has collected on his list. "It's low cost and it works well for us," Rasmussen says.

Create a Mailing List from Trade Show Attendees

When you attend small industry trade shows, you may be given a list of attendees. Use such lists to prospect when you get home from the show. If you are an exhibitor, be sure to have a means for collecting names of visitors.

Get Nearly Free Mailing Lists from Business Organizations

When you join the Chamber of Commerce or other business organizations, you are often given a member directory that contains the names, addresses, and phone numbers of all the members. Type or scan the directory into a database and you'll have a mailing list of local businesses that you can use indefinitely without additional payment.

Use High-End Marketing Databases to Choose Your List

If you know your market very well, high-end software can be used to build hand-picked mailing lists.

Brian D. Wannan of Retail Automation Systems, Inc. in Dallas, Texas, uses a marketing database system called Marketplace to build mailing lists. The software, published by iMarket (800-532-3775) includes the entire Dun & Bradstreet database on a CD. It allows users to target businesses by region and then narrow down that selection by zip code, company size, number of employees, and SIC code.

"If you were selling chop sticks, you could target only Chinese, Japanese, and Taiwanese restaurants that had three or more employees, had been in business more than two years, and had sales greater than $500K," Wannan notes. He estimates that he's had a 50 percent or more improvement in cost–benefit ratio since he started using this software to compile his mailing lists.

Share Mailings to Keep Costs Down

If you belong to an organization such as the Chamber of Commerce, ask if they have a program that would let you insert your flier or brochure in their mailing at a lower cost than you'd pay to mail it on your own. Alternatively, look for noncompeting businesses willing to share the cost of a mailing or to buy space in a mailing you send out.

Adding to Your Mailing List

Use your Web site to build your mailing list. Put a guest book on your site and ask visitors to leave you their e-mail address and their postal mailing address if they would like to be notified about new products or special offers. If you have trouble getting people to include their names and addresses, make registration on your Web site a requirement for some special feature like a bulletin board. Giveaways, contests, coupons, and downloads can all be used as incentives to get your Web visitors to leave their contact information.

Include a check box that asks people if they would like to receive e-mail or conventional mailings from you. Only send mail to those who indicate they are willing to receive mail from you.

Get Other Businesses to Help Foot Your Mailing Costs

Dale Kroll publishes *Pharmacy Purchasing Outlook*, a subscription newsletter for pharmacy purchasing agents. The newsletter carries no advertising. However, he has developed a program whereby drug companies can include their brochures in the envelope in which the newsletter is mailed. He charges them by the weight of their brochure, and by the number of subscribers getting the newsletter. The fee he gets for the inserts generally covers the cost of his mailing.

Consider Placing an Ad in a Card Deck

Card decks are stacks of index-sized cards with advertising messages from many different companies. Typically, they are mailed to a niche market such as people known to buy business books by mail, or readers of an industry trade magazine, or known opportunity seekers.

Since the cards from many companies are sent out in one mailing package, the cost to each company for each card in the deck is less than the cost of mailing an individual postcard to the same number of people.

Cards in a card deck generally have an advertising message printed on one side with space for the prospect to write in his or her name, address, and phone number. The flip side of the card often contains the address of the company placing the ad, along with either a business reply postage imprint or a place for the recipient to place a stamp. Thus the card serves two purposes: it is both an ad and a postcard that can be used to reply to the ad.

▶ **Tip**

Companies with only one moderately priced product to sell usually don't benefit from being in a card deck. The reason is simple math: If a card deck goes out to 80,000 people and 1 in 1,000 responds, you'll get 80 responses. If you make $15 profit on each sale and your total costs for being in the card deck come to $1,500, you'll lose money.

Although card decks let individual businesses mail a message to a large number of prospects at a low rate per card, they are not the low-cost answer to all of your marketing prayers. If there are many individual cards in the card deck and yours is buried in the middle, people may tire of going through the cards before they ever find yours. "You need to be in the top twenty or bottom twenty cards in the deck or your card may never get read," says Stan Cohen. Cohen often uses card decks to gather names for his company, Mar-Cohen Publishing, which is located in Boca Raton, Florida.

Companies that benefit from card deck advertising are those that use the media to attract customers who are likely to make a series of purchases over time and those who use the card decks to bring in sales leads for big-ticket items. In the latter case, the product and the card deck need to target a very specific niche market such as quick printers or chemical engineers.

Card decks targeted at specialized industry groups are often published by trade magazines. Look in a public library for reference publications such as *SRDS Card Pack Rates & Data Directory* for other card deck publishers.

Create Your Own Card Deck

Consider getting together with noncompeting businesses and creating your own card deck. A mailing of 30 black-and-white cards to 10,000 names could cost as little as $3,200 to have printed from camera-ready copy and packaged. If you get enough other businesses to chip in, you should be able to let your card ride free in the deck.

Give Yourself an Easy Way to Know How Much Product Literature to Reorder

If you have order forms and brochures that you send out on an as-needed basis, you'll want to avoid overordering or underordering the items. An easy way to accomplish that goal, says printer Roger Snyder of Smithtown, New York, is to print the date of printing and the print quantity in very small type in the document. This identifies the revision and helps you determine the quantity of brochures you will need to order.

Make Packing List Slips Do Double Duty

A packing list tells your customer what to expect in the package he or she has received from you. But if that's all it does, you're losing out on an almost free way to build sales. Instead of leaving the bottom or the back side of the packing list blank, use the space for an ad or discount coupon for one of your products. Since you are including the packing list anyway, the ad travels free. Your only cost would be any extra printing expense you incur for printing (if you put the ad on the back of the packing slip) or toner if you use your own laser printer to print the ads onto your packing list.

Take Orders Twenty-Four Hours a Day

Large mail-order companies have discovered it pays to be able to take orders in the wee hours of the night. As a result, they keep their 800-number order lines open twenty-four hours a day. You can do that by using a fulfillment service or by call-forwarding your calls to an answering service when you aren't available to take calls. Or set up a Web site to take orders and include your Web site URL in your mailing.

Save Money with Postcard Mailings

If you sell to small businesses or consumers, one good way to stretch your advertising budget is to send postcard mailings. At only 20 cents apiece to mail, postcards save you 12 cents for each person you mail to. What's more, since the recipient doesn't have to take them out of an envelope, your message may have more of a chance of getting read.

Among the ways you could use a postcard mailing is to:
Announce new products
Offer discounts
Send a reminder to schedule periodic maintenance or checkup services
Send a coupon
Announce a special sale
Acknowledge an order
Send monthly follow-ups to an initial sales call or mailing

Save on Printing with Postcards

Lower cost isn't the only benefit of a postcard mailing. Printing postcards costs less than printing brochures of similar weight. That's because you can print up to four postcards on a single sheet of stock, rather than just one flier. Thus if you needed 4,000 postcards, you'd be paying only for printing 1,000 sheets of stock, not 4,000.

Print Your Own Postcards

For small mailings, save money on printing costs by printing the postcards on your own laser printer using preprinted paper that is made to be separated into postcards. If you plan to print more than 300 to 500 identical postcards at one time, bring the job to a quick printer. Most laser printers and photocopiers made for home office use are not built to withstand volume printing jobs. Printing many sheets of heavyweight paper at one time could cause the equipment to break down.

Use Bold Colors and Sturdy Card Stock to Make Your Postcard Mailing Stand Out

The only disadvantage to a postcard mailing is that it can get buried in with other junk mail. You can make sure it stands out by printing your message against a bright, bold-colored background. Bright yellow, bright light green, or bright orange make good backgrounds. Deep blue, red, rose, or other dark colors are unsuitable because they make the type too difficult to read.

To speed your mailing through the U.S. Postal Service, use the bright color only on the message side of the postcard or use a white, barcoded label.

▶ **Tip**

Use the data you collect about your customers buying habits to generate minimailings. For instance, if you have an overstock of size 5 skirts, use your database to produce a list of people who have previously ordered size 5 clothing. Send them each a notice of a special clearance on those size 5 skirts. You'll turn your inventory over faster, and save on mailing costs because you'll only be mailing your offer to those people most likely to be interested in it.

Watch Out for Peak Mail Periods

Christmas isn't the only time of the year when the volume of mail handled by the postal service soars. Certain other holidays and events such as Valentine's Day, Easter, back-to-school time, and election day result in heavier-than-usual mail volume. To keep your mail from being lost, delayed, or ignored, avoid such peak mail periods if you don't sell seasonal products or services. If your business is seasonal, allow enough time in advance of a special event for your mailing to hit. The money spent on a mailing offering customers a 20 percent discount if they make a purchase on Columbus Day will be wasted if the mailing arrives the day after Columbus Day.

Use Preprinted Brochure Forms for Small Mailings

If you're mailing only a couple hundred pieces and want a colorful design to make your piece stand out, consider using preprinted brochure paper and your own laser printer to create the brochures. Your costs will be less than having a printer do the work. Choose your stock carefully and use a software template to guide you in layout and choice of typefaces and sizes.

If you will be printing more than a couple hundred pieces, you'll usually save money by working with a commercial or quick printer.

Track Responses to Mailings

Track the results of every mailing you send out. Keep a record of when you sent a mailing, who the mailing was sent to, and what the mailing said. Then, make notes when people begin to respond to the mailing. Note what product or service each buys and any other information you'll find helpful in the future. To help you gather this data, try to include a response mechanism in your mailings. For instance, don't just send a newsletter to your customers. Include a discount coupon in it so you can tell whether it's being read. Kate Holmes, publisher of *Too Good to be Threw*, a newsletter for the resale industry, did mailings frequently to her customers when she ran her own resale shop. "Everything I sent out had a reason to return a card," Homes says. "A free pair of earrings, a discount, whatever. In the case of the newsletter, the 'clip-out coupon' was printed back-to-back with the address label space. We made notes in our database about which customers returned coupons. Thus we could note who were the most active customers. (It was simply a counting field, so I could tell, for example, that Mrs. Jones had returned three of eight mailings, etc.) As the mailing list grew too large (based on how much I wanted to spend in printing and postage), I would delete those names who had responded the least."

Chapter 9

MAILING AND

SHIPPING STRATEGIES

Depending on the nature of your business, mailing and shipping costs can be a major expense. Besides the actual cost of postage or shipping, there's the cost of the packaging and the labor to get orders and mailings out the door. Unfortunately, there's no simple way to deal with all the costs and hassles. But there are a number of strategies you should consider to reduce costs or the headaches associated with mailings and order fulfillment. Consider each in light of your own business needs, budget, and goals.

Account for Shipping and Handling in Your Pricing Structure

You will incur significant costs to package and ship orders. These will include labor costs; packaging materials such as boxes, filler, shrink-wrap; and as your operation grows, space and additional equipment. To allow for these costs, either add them into the price of your item or do what most big mailers do: State them separately to make the cost of your product appear competitive.

Your out-of-pocket costs for fees and packaging materials will be relatively easy to calculate. But where many small businesses go wrong is in failing to accurately calculate the cost of the labor to enter orders and get the orders ready for shipping.

To calculate this cost, time how long it takes to enter an average order; print the shipping label, packing slip, and invoice; transfer the order information to customer and accounting files; and wrap the item or otherwise prepare it for mailing. If those processes take a total of ten minutes per order, your staff will be able to fill only six orders per hour. Assuming time off for lunch and breaks and interruptions, each person could probably fill no more than 35 orders per day, or

175 orders per week. If the salary and payroll expenses for that person cost $420 a week, your cost per order for labor will be $2.40. That's a significant amount of money and will siphon off profits if you don't include that cost when calculating your shipping and handling charges.

Nearly Free Shipping "Insurance"

If products you ship arrive damaged, your customers will return them and expect a full refund. Therefore, before you stuff your product in a shipping envelope, consider whether the envelope will give the product enough protection. If the product could be damaged if the soft-sided shipping bag were bent or stepped on, consider shipping the item in a box. Some sturdy, white cardboard boxes cost no more than padded shipping envelopes or bags, and offer better protection.

Get Free Boxes and Envelopes

The U.S. Postal Service (USPS) and some other shippers provide some priority and overnight mail envelopes, labels, and boxes at no cost. If you will be shipping using these methods, stock up on and use the free supplies. Put your materials directly into the mailer's envelope, too. Don't waste money by putting your materials into one of your own envelopes before putting it in the shipper's envelope. Besides the cost of the envelope, the added weight of your envelope might put your mailing into the next rate class.

Compare Third-Class Rate to the Priority Mail Rate

Depending on the shipping location and the weight of what you are mailing, there may be very little difference between the third-class mailing rate and the priority rate. When that's the case, choose priority mail instead of third class. Your shipment will reach its destination more quickly. An added benefit: The "priority" status will leave a favorable impression on your customers.

Consider Box Sizes When Designing Products or Choosing Gifts

If you expect to use priority mail to ship products and if you have control over the final size of the product, be sure it will fit in one of the boxes the post office gives away for free. Sturdy boxes are often priced at 50 cents or more each; thus any time you can use a free box, you save money.

Get Discounts on UPS, Airborne, and Other Shipping Services

If you expect to ship items regularly via UPS, Airborne, or another commercial shipper, don't accept their quoted rates as gospel. Bargain the rates down. One Chicago business owner, for instance, called the marketing division of UPS and told them that he expected his mail-order business to be making more than 100 shipments a week of approximately 1 pound each. He said he'd like to use UPS instead of Airborne or Federal Express and asked if they'd be willing to work out a deal on shipping fees. The result? A 35 percent discount off standard rates. Even though the actual number of packages didn't reach the anticipated 100 per week, the shipper never changed his discount.

Use a Fulfillment Service to Take Orders and Ship Orders

Your business isn't going to look professional—and you'll lose sales and customers—if you don't handle orders properly. An experienced fulfillment service will have the experience to handle incoming calls properly and to make sure the orders are packaged, shipped, and mailed promptly.

The fulfillment company should have a twenty-four-hour 800-number service and be able to clearly explain its charges. Expect to pay some type of initial setup charge. This will cover the cost of a script the company has to write so their inbound telemarketers (the people who answer the calls) will be able to answer all the questions your customers are likely to ask before placing an order. As a small business, you may also have to pay a monthly minimum in advance.

Compare the costs and benefits of using a fulfillment company to the cost of setting up and managing fulfillment in-house. If your average order is at least $15 and your volume isn't sufficient to allow you to automate and streamline order-taking procedures, you may come out ahead by using an experienced fulfillment service. You can find them in the yellow pages of your phonebook or in back of the book advertising in trade magazines.

► **Tip**
Be sure to ask how the company transfers the names of your customers to you. The best method is to have them send them to you in e-mail or on disk in a format that can be imported into your database. If they only fax or mail printouts, you'll have to pay someone to enter the customer data so you have it available for future mailings.

Familiarize Yourself with Postal Regulations

The more you know about how the post office works, the faster your mail and packages will be delivered, and if you mail in bulk, the less you'll pay for the service. The U.S. Postal Service will help you learn what you need to know, too. They have Business Centers throughout the country that offer booklets and training seminars to help you learn the ropes. Your local post office will give you the phone number of the nearest Business Center if you can't locate it.

Use an Addressing Company to Prepare Your Direct-Mail Offers

If you've tested your mailing list and offer, and are ready to do large mailings, get price quotes from companies that specialize in preparing mailing. These companies can be found in the yellow pages under the heading "mailing services." Compare the lettershop's per-piece cost to your actual costs for preparing mailings. If they are highly automated and you're not, their charges may be less than your cost for staff time to do the mailing. They may also be able to reduce your postage costs by properly addressing and bundling the mail for delivery.

Get Your Children or Family to Help with Your Mailings

Mail preparation—particularly stuffing envelopes, labeling, and stamping them—is one activity that children as young as seven or so can do. Pay them for the work and deduct their salary as a business expense or bribe them with some special favor (movie tickets, those fancy new sneakers they want, a party for their friends). Be sure to supervise their work to make sure they don't stuff anything into the envelopes that they shouldn't and make sure they do firmly affix stamps. Otherwise, the money you spend on the mailing will be wasted. If you don't have kids, or they aren't willing to do the work, try to enlist your spouse to help out.

Speed Mail with ZIP+4 Codes

You will get faster delivery and better bulk mail discounts by adding ZIP+4 codes to your mailings. If you don't have the ZIP+4 code for the names on your list, if you can provide the list in a standardized format, the postal service will add them free of charge as a one-time service. For information about this service, contact the National Customer Support Center at 800-238-3150

If your list is small or you need to add ZIP+4 information on to a few names on your list, you can look up the ZIP+4 codes online at the USPS Web site (http://www.usps.gov/). Click on the word *ZIP Codes* at the top of the page to get to the ZIPcode locator and other related services. You'll find a wealth of other information for business mailers on the site as well.

Buy U.S. Postage Stamps at Less Than Their Face Value

Believe it or not, there is a legitimate way to get postage at a discount. The trick: Buy your new stamps from a stamp dealer rather than the post office. Stamp dealers often buy stamps in quantity hoping they will go up in value. When the stamps don't go up, or when the demand for them stops, dealers mark down their inventory just as any other retailer would to bring in cash and clear out what isn't selling.

The stamps will usually be in small denominations, so you may have to apply several individual stamps instead of one 33-cent stamp. But even that has an added bonus: Most people can't resist opening a letter that arrives bearing five or six colorful stamps.

Bar Code Your Mail for Faster Delivery

If you've ever had a piece of mail take several days to get from one part of town to another, you know how frustrating mail delays can be. Although you can't prevent all delays, there is one step you can take to minimize them: Add bar codes to the addresses you print on labels and envelopes. If you have a current version of Microsoft Word on your computer, the chore is quite easy. Just click the options button when you are using the envelope wizard, and then put a check mark in the box that says Use Delivery Point Bar Codes.

Get Noticed with Priority Mail

Recipients usually regard overnight mail as urgent or very important. Therefore, it usually gets opened as soon as it arrives.

If you want your letters or packages to get opened immediately, but don't need to send them via overnight mail, send them using the U.S. Postal Service's priority mail. The envelopes for priority mail are so similar in appearance to the post office's express mail (overnight) envelopes and packages, recipients often confuse the two. Your budget won't though. The cost of sending a letter priority mail is only $3.20. The cost of sending the same letter via overnight mail is $11.75.

> ▶ **Note**
>
> Priority mail isn't likely to arrive overnight. Unless you are mailing to a nearby community, it usually takes two days or more. But if it's the impression of urgency you want to convey, rather than a real need to get something to its destination overnight, priority mail is the way to go.

Avoid Overnight Mail or Use Cheaper Alternatives

Make an effort to reduce the number of overnight letters you and your staff send. Remind yourself and your staff that every overnight letter you send costs a whopping thirty to forty-five times the cost of sending the same document via regular first-class mail.

When possible, schedule work so it's completed early enough to put in regular mail. When that's not possible, look for reasonable alternatives. You might send a document via fax or electronic mail to get the information there in a hurry, and then follow up by sending the original document in regular mail.

Use a Delivery Service Instead of Overnight Mail

If you're shipping something heavy to a neighboring community, compare the cost of using a messenger service to the post office fee. You may find the courier service is cheaper.

▶ **Tip**

Missed the last overnight mail dropoff time? Consider using a same-day air-delivery service if you must get your package to its destination on time. Sky Courier (1-800-336-3344) charges a $155 base rate plus mileage to and from the airport for next flight out delivery services for packages under 25 pounds. While the cost is steep, it's likely to be less than taking a roundtrip flight to deliver a package yourself and less than the cost of your time to drive to a distant location.

Fold Up Mail Savings

Whenever possible, fold letter-sized sheets of paper to fit into a standard business envelope instead of mailing them flat in a 9-by-12-inch envelope. If you are mailing first class, you'll save 11 cents for each piece of unsorted first-class mail you send. Another advantage: The letter-sized envelope may look less like an advertisement and get opened more quickly than the 9-by-12-inch envelope.

Send a Double Postcard

A single postcard doesn't give you much space to put advertising copy and an order blank. To get around that problem, consider sending a double postcard (two postcards folded over in the middle). This will allow you to put your advertising message on one side of the fold (one card, when separated). The other side of the fold (the part of the card that will get returned to you) can give recipients space to answer questions that will help your marketing efforts. This double card can be mailed for the low postcard rate provided that there is no advertising copy on the mail-back side of the postcard.

If you do put advertising on more than one card, the postage fees go up to 40 cents per card, which is a little more than the cost of a first-class letter. Before going that route, consider using a two-fold card (three postcards folded over each other like a brochure). Mail that at the regular first-class rate to save 7 cents per mailing piece.

Clean Your Mailing Lists Regularly

Take the time to clean your mailing list of incorrect addresses and duplicate names. Doing so will cut your costs in two ways: You'll reduce your overall postage cost and may save money on printing as well.

To keep costs down, take advantage of the U.S. Postal Service's free mailing list service. On a one-time basis, it will clean up a mailing list at no charge to you.

Watch Out for Address Correction Costs

Your out-of-pocket costs for address corrections depend on the number of undeliverable pieces of mail returned to you and the size and shape of your mailing package. Therefore, before you stamp Address Correction Requested on your mailings, bring a sample of the mailing to the post office and ask them what you would be charged for address corrections on undeliverable mail. If your list is old, 15 percent or more of the addresses might be undeliverable.

Use Postcard Mailings to Clean Your List

Save the 40-cents fee on address corrections by using a postcard mailing to clean your list. Put the words *Address Correction Requested* and *Do Not Forward* on the stamp side of the card, and a promotional offer or ad on the message side. Since a postcard is first-class mail, all address corrections will be returned to you free of charge. Added bonus: The business that comes in as a result of the advertising on the message side of the postcard could make cleaning your mailing list a profit-making activity.

Size Counts

Be sure mailing pieces you plan to have printed conform to U.S. Postal Service size standards. If they don't, you'll pay a surcharge for each piece in your mailing.

Don't Wait in Line to Buy Stamps

You don't have to go to the post office to buy stamps. You can order them by mail by calling Stamps by Mail (816-455-0970).

Or print out postage from your computer. Thanks to a new service offered by several vendors you can connect to the Internet, choose the amount of postage you want and print it on envelopes and labels in your office. Among the vendors who will be selling postage through the Internet are Stamps.com (http://www.stamps.com), the E-Stamp Corporation (http://www.estamp.com), and NeoPost (http://www. simplypostage.com/.

Mail Early in the Day

Your local post office usually moves mail on its way several times a day. Because most people wait until the end of the day to send their mail, your letter may reach its destination a full day earlier if you mail it before noon.

Check up on Those Important Packages

Most shipping companies now have capabilities to let you check the whereabouts of your parcels. To determine whether a shipment has been delivered, check the appropriate site from this list:

Airborne Express
http://www.airborne.com/trace/

Airnet Systems
http://www.airnet.com/tracking.html

BAX Global—Baxtrax
http://www.baxworld.com/tracking/track4.html

DHL Worldwide Express
http://www.dhl.com/track/track.html

UPS
http://www.ups.com/tracking/tracking.html

United States Postal Service
http://www.usps.gov/cttgate/

Roadway Express
http://www.roadway.com/tools/quiktrak.html

Purolator
http://www.purolator.com/cgi-bin/pt1005e.pl

OCS America
http://www.shipocs.com/track_dir/default.htm

Nippon Express
http://www3.nittsu.co.jp/EDOC/HOWTOE.HTM

GeoLogistics
http://www.geo-logistics.com/ue/tracking/index.html

Consider Using a Postage Meter as Your Mail Volume Increases

If you send out more than ten pieces of mail per day from your office, a postage meter and scale can save you time, and perhaps money by avoiding the need to put more postage on a letter or parcel than is needed. But if you consider a postage meter compare costs carefully. Be sure to get the figures on all costs. Remember you have to pay for the ink to imprint the indicia and labels you'll use. Postage meters have to be rented, but the scales that go with them can be purchased. The following companies are authorized by the post office to rent meters:

Ascom Hasler
800-243-6275

Neopost
800-624-7892

Pitney Bowes
800-322-8000

Postalia
800-341-6052

Telemailing?

Get mail to the post office without leaving your office. No, it's not an exercise in telepathy, and it's not the U.S. Post Office jumping on the e-mail bandwagon. Instead, it's a new service called NetPost that the postal service has been testing. It will let you send a document file and a mailing list to the USPS for processing. The postal service will print, address, and deliver your letter without you leaving the comfort of your small office. The cost per letter will be close to or just a few pennies more than printing the letter on paper and putting it in an envelope yourself.

Chapter 10

TRADE SHOW
SAVVY

Trade shows attract more than 1.25 million vendors and 100 million attendees each year.* They offer buyers a single location to view new products, compare products, talk to current suppliers, and find new suppliers. Sellers gain a single location to showcase their products to large numbers of prospects, many of whom are ready to buy.

In fact, trade shows, when carefully chosen, can be one of the most cost-effective methods for getting new orders. Results of studies conducted by the Center for Exhibition Industry Research indicate that approximately 75 percent of show attendees buy one or more products as a result of a trade show.

Buying and selling isn't all that businesses do at trade shows either. Beyond the frenzy of the selling floor, businesspeople make important contacts with key industry leaders, develop relationships with new distributors, form strategic alliances, and work out new comarketing deals.

Although many trade show exhibitors are big corporations with massive eye-catching displays, you don't have to be big to profit from trade shows. Whether you're ready to fast-forward your small company into the big leagues or just want to make a few contacts, you can profit by exhibiting at or attending trade shows.

Decide What You Want to Accomplish at the Show

Before you decide to exhibit at any trade show, know exactly why you want to be there. Don't settle for a hazy objective like "to boost sales." Be specific. List each objective you expect to attain. Among the objectives to consider:

---

* Center for Exhibition Industry Research (CEIR), 2301 South Lake Shore Drive, Suite E1002, Chicago, IL 60616. Phone: 312-808-2347; fax: 312-949-3472; http://www.ceir.org/.

▶ Introduce new products
▶ Get new orders for existing products
▶ Find new distributors
▶ Find sales representatives
▶ Sell to the end user
▶ Gather sales leads for future follow-up by your sales force
▶ Build name recognition
▶ Meet with current customers
▶ Reach hard-to-get prospects
▶ Test market products, services, and promotional material
▶ Find strategic partners
▶ Learn new skills and industry information
▶ Keep tabs on your competition

Compare Costs to Expected Benefits

To determine whether exhibiting at a trade show is worthwhile, add up all the costs you expect to incur if you exhibit at a show and compare them to the benefits you hope to derive. Be sure to account for booth space, signs, artwork, product literature, press kits, shipping, and for transportation, hotel, and meals for the booth staff. Consider whether you could gain the same benefits for less money through sales calls, direct-mail campaigns, and other marketing efforts.

Bennett Engineering, an engineering firm that targets small industrial firms with its services, spends an average of $800 to $1,400 for booth space plus lodging and meals for each show at which it exhibits. The company, which is based in Huntsville, Alabama, spends approximately $300 more for preshow promotional materials, including the postage to mail them. Shipping and setup costs can tack on significant sums to the show costs, too. The investment pays off for Bennett Engineering, however, because the company needs only one client to make enough money to pay back the company's yearly cost of exhibiting in trade shows.

Bigger and more expensive shows come with bigger price tags for booth space. The Lightstone Group, a Mineola, New York, company that produces RIMMS scheduling and routing software for the transportation industry, spends an average of $800 to $4,000 for booth space at each of the shows at which it exhibits. For that money, the company hopes to get twenty to thirty solid leads from each show.

On top of those costs are one-time costs such as the cost of having a reusable, portable display created for your booth if you decide to exhibit regularly. Those costs can run anywhere from about $500 (for a very basic tabletop display unit) to tens of thousands of dollars for elaborate, free-standing display booths.

Choose Shows Carefully

One of the keys to profiting from trade shows is picking the right shows to attend. Your hand-crafted wooden mailboxes won't sell to buyers looking for cheap metal mailboxes to be sold through a national discount chain. And if your goal is to meet corporate bigwigs, you may not find them at small regional shows. To avoid such unpleasant surprises, get as much information about a show as possible before you agree to exhibit. Among the questions you should ask:

▶ What segment of your industry will the show target?
▶ What percentage of attendees are like your typical customer?
▶ How many times has the show been held?
▶ How many times has it been held at this location?
▶ How many people attended in the past?
▶ How many exhibitors were at the last show?
▶ How many exhibitors are expected this year?
▶ Is your competition exhibiting?
▶ What other businesses will be participating?
▶ How and where will the trade show be publicized?

> ▶ **Tip**
> Sometimes one of the biggest benefits of a trade show is the opportunity it gives you to network with other vendors in your industry. That senior vice president who hasn't returned your calls may be more receptive if you introduce yourself briefly before the show opens to the public, or in the evening at a party or reception. When you follow-up after the show, be sure to mention the circumstances under which you met.

Don't Be a Guinea Pig

Steer clear of shows that are being held for the first time. Promoters often talk a better show than they put on. To get you to sign up, they'll talk about promotion efforts they have planned, publicity in the works, support from major backers, and offer discounts on space at a single show or for booking several regional shows at one time. But the talk is meaningless if they don't actually deliver the audiences they promise or if they run out of money before paying for promotion or even rental for the hall.

Locate Trade Shows That Target Your Market

Thousands of shows are held across the country each year. Ads and editorial content in industry trade magazines are a good source of information about major industry shows. So are networking contacts you make through trade and professional associations. Such contacts can alert you to the good shows—and the disasters in the industry.

To learn about local and regional business-to-business and industrial trade shows, read local business newspapers and stay in touch with local business organizations (such as the Chamber of Commerce or local chapters of national professional organizations) and local offices of government agencies (Small Business Administration branch offices, economic development offices, Small Business Development Centers).

If you will be traveling to a distant city and want to know what shows are held there, the visitors' bureau or city convention center often can provide information.

Other resources for identifying shows include printed trade show directories available in the reference sections of public libraries and searchable trade show directories available on the World Wide Web. Among those you may find useful:

Trade Shows World Wide
Comprehensive directory of major
    trade shows.
Gale Research
835 Penobscot, Bldg. 1
Detroit, MI 48226-4094

Trade Shows USA
Pamphlet-sized directory of general
    merchandise trade shows held
    throughout the United States.
Sumner Communications
24 Grassy Plain St.
Bethel, CT 06801-1725
203-748-2050, 800-999-8281
http://www.wholesalecentral.com

Trade Show Week Data Book
Comprehensive directory of con-
    sumer and industry trade shows.
Tradeshow Week, Inc.
Subscription Department
P.O. Box 6340
Torrance, CA 90504
http://www.tradeshowweek.com/

Trade Show Central
Searchable directory of trade shows
    on the World Wide Web.
http://www.tscentral.com

Trade Show News Network
Searchable directories of trade
    shows, suppliers, and exhibitors.
    http://www.tsnn.com/news/

Exhibitor Magazine
Exhibitor Publications
206 South Broadway, Suite 745
Rochester, MN 55904
507-289-6556, 888-235-6155

The Exhibitor Network
ExhibitorNet is *Exhibitor* magazine's
    online resource for trade show
    and event marketing informa-
    tion. Sources include *Exhibitor*
    magazine, trade show and sup-
    plier directories, conferences
    and workshops, and weekly
    exhibiting tips.
    http://www.exhibitornet.com

Consider Exhibiting at Lower-Priced Shows

Fees for trade shows and business-to-business expos vary greatly. Individuals selling professional services often report spending between $400 and $1,500 for booth space at a one-day show; some local and regional shows charge less. Kenneth Bob, CEO of the Lightstone Group, says his company has spent as little as $250 to exhibit at some small regional industry shows.

If you can find low-cost trade shows that target the same audience you do, exhibit at them before you exhibit at larger shows. Doing so will help you gain firsthand knowledge and sales floor experience that can spell the difference between succeeding and failing at bigger, more costly shows. Talking to vendors at smaller shows can also help you identify which of the more costly shows are the best for exhibitors like you.

Don't choose a show solely on price of booth space, however. A $250 show that doesn't attract the types of individuals or businesses who would buy from you is a waste of $250 plus your costs for literature, food, and accommodations, if needed.

Have Someone Else Display Your Wares at a Trade Show

Instead of renting your own booth at trade shows, let a sales rep display them for you. Your products will have to share the booth with other products the rep handles, but you'll get wider exposure for far less money. David Whalen, a West Coast manufacturer and screen printer, sold seasonal decor for many years. Working with sales reps made it possible for him to get his merchandise displayed at 150 to 180 shows a year across the country.

"The reps took care of show displays, did the selling, and chose the shows they thought my products would be best in," Whalen says. Since the reps split show costs between several manufacturers, Whalen was represented at some shows for less than $100. Had he exhibited by himself, booth fees, transportation, display costs, hotel accommodations, and staff salaries would have amounted to thousands of dollars.

One disadvantage of this strategy is that your products will be one of many on shelves in the rep's booth and may not get promoted as much as you'd like. Still, if you have no other way to get products into trade shows, this is worth considering.

Start by Exhibiting Locally

Exhibit at small, local shows. Software industry associations, manufacturing associations, and local business associations are some of the places that often have thriving business communities and low-cost trade shows. Besides saving on the cost of a booth, you'll save on transportation costs and hotel costs. You'll also start to get known as a member and supporter of the local business community.

Be a Volunteer

Can't afford your own booth? Watch for requests for booth volunteers from industry associations to which you belong. Organizations often let volunteers hand out their own information while they are volunteering at the organization's booth. Although you won't be able to spread out over the whole booth, you will get an opportunity to distribute some material about your company and may also make useful contacts just by being in the booth.

Share Booth Space with Another Vendor

If you don't need a lot of space to sell your product or service, consider sharing booth space with a vendor in a related but noncompeting field. If you are a human resources consultant, you might team up with a commercial insurance broker or a payroll company at a show, for instance. You'll save money and have one or more other individuals with whom you can share booth duties.

Display and Sell Other Vendors' Products

Act as a sales representative or consignment shop for other noncompeting businesses in your industry. Long-time crafter April Millican (http://www.auntie.com) suggests assigning ID numbers to each vendor. Make sure each item is securely tagged and numbered. The system she uses combines the vendor number with an item number, as in A234-001 for the first item from vendor A234, A234-002 for the second item and so on. "Have each vendor prepare an inventory sheet with the item number, description, and selling price. When you make a sale, write down each item number and description on a sales ticket. At the end of the day, check sales tickets against inventory sheets," Millican explains.

Millican suggests charging a minimal commission (10 to 15 percent) on sales plus a fee for table space. "Make sure everyone signs a disclaimer freeing you of responsibility for theft or damage by customers," she advises.

Be sure the show allows such arrangements before signing agreements with other vendors, however.

Attend as a Visitor

Before taking a booth at a trade show, attend as a visitor. Find out what segment of your industry the show targets and make sure it attracts the kinds of customers and networking contacts you seek.

Look around to see if there are small companies like yours displaying their products and, if so, whether people stop at their booths. Note whether they are actually selling from the booth, taking orders, or just getting sales leads.

Look at your competitors' displays, sales literature, press kits, and give-aways. What seems to attract passersby the most? Check out the kinds of clothes booth personnel and visitors are wearing, too. Are East Coast business suits par for the course, or do exhibitors and attendees dress more as though they were ready to head to the golf course?

Keep notes on what you see. They will help you later on when you are ready to decide which shows to attend or when you are looking for new ways to attract customers to your own booth.

Ask Noncompeting Businesses About the Value of a Show

To get a feel for the show, ask noncompeting businesses to tell you how they are doing (or did) at a particular show. Ask if the show attracted the size crowd they expected, and how much sales literature you should expect to bring with you. If their booth is busy, don't expect them to spend time chatting with you. They won't, and they'll resent the intrusion. Instead, ask if there's someone you could contact for information when the show is over.

> ▶ **Tip**
> You don't have to be an exhibitor to make deals at a show. Find out in advance what key prospects will have exhibits and make an appointment ahead of time to meet them. If you can't get an appointment, visit their booth and look for the opportunity to introduce yourself. If the person you want to contact will be a speaker, attend their talk and position yourself so you approach them as they are leaving the room. You won't have much time to get their attention, so rehearse what you want to say to them in advance. Make sure your pitch focuses on a need or problem they want solved—not your desire to get work.

Get a List of Last Year's Exhibitors

If you can't attend a show in person, ask for a list of exhibitors from the previous show. Call businesses that you believe to be small like yours and ask how they did at the show last year. Ask if they encountered any unexpected problems or costs, and if they plan to exhibit again this year.

Reserve Your Booth Space Far in Advance for Popular Shows

Some shows book space as much as a year in advance, so don't wait until the last minute to book space at a show. The earlier you book, the better your chance of getting the location you want. And, if you wait too long, you may not be able to get space at all.

Choose a Good Location for Your Booth

The location of your booth on the trade show floor will influence the amount of traffic you get. If you must choose a booth without having attended a show as a visitor, get a map of the trade show and try to determine how attendees will enter the room and how they are likely to work their way through booths.

Harvey Bennett, owner of Bennett Engineering, exhibits at trade shows frequently because he has found them an effective way to bring in business for his engineering firm. He suggests avoiding booths against the walls of the room unless the entrance is such that the wall aisle is where people are forced to start. "Try to avoid being to the back or end of the show because some people will get tired and not go back that far." Bennett notes, "I have had by far the best traffic on a near center aisle somewhere in the front third of the show. You catch people who start from both sides before they give up three-quarters of the way through."

Other considerations include:

▶ Poles, walls, or other obstacles that might block your booth from sight
▶ Lighting
▶ Availability and proximity of electric and telephone lines
▶ Location of competitors' booths
▶ Location of lunch facilities and bathrooms
▶ Location of seminar rooms

Tailgate the Big Boys

If possible, find out where major industry players will have their booths and grab a booth nearby. You'll benefit from the crowd the big company attracts and by making it easier for people you've arranged to meet at the show find you. One office furniture manufacturer, for instance, always gets a booth near the Microsoft booth at PC Expo in New York City. The reason: Most customers and prospects have no trouble locating the company's booth when they are told it's across the aisle from the Microsoft exhibit.

If you try this strategy, be sure that your location is in the direction traffic will flow. You don't want the big exhibitor's booth to box you into a corner where few people will go.

Promptly Read All the Material the Promoters Send You

You don't want any unhappy surprises when you go to set up your booth the day of the show. Therefore take the time to read everything the show promoters send well ahead of the show. Note what you'll be able to do yourself and what you'll have to use help available at the site for. Pay attention to the time of the shows, setup and tear-down dates and times (and whether they fall on weekends or legal holidays when you'll have to pay extra for labor costs), union jurisdictions, and drayage (moving exhibits into and out of a hall and also between storage warehouses and truck). At some shows, you may not be able to plug in an electrical cord on your own, for instance. If you don't have your own display booth, find out whether tables and backdrops are provided. If there's anything you don't understand or aren't sure of, call the promoters and ask.

> ## Save—Try a Hospitality Suite
>
> Here's a way some companies avoid the high cost of exhibiting at trade shows: They take a hotel room near the exhibit hall and set up a hospitality suite—and their product demos—in the room. Then they invite key customers to visit the hospitality suite. If you try this, you won't get a big crowd visiting. But if all you need is to sell a couple of top brass on the merits of your product, this strategy may be worth trying.

Get Your Hotel Rooms Early

Many businesses like to stay in a show's headquarters hotel because of the networking opportunities doing so provides. "I've seen a lot of selling and networking take place at the hotel bar," says Bob Peters of the Trade Show Group, which is based in Las Vegas, Nevada. "It's a great place to say, 'Hi, what does your company do' and 'Stop by my booth, I think I can help you out.'"

If you plan to stay in the headquarters hotel, be sure to book your rooms at least six to eight weeks ahead. The number of rooms offered at the show discount is generally limited, and if other functions are going on (or if it's a large trade show) the hotel—and all surrounding hotels—may be completely booked (see Chapter 18 for more tips on travel and hotel accommodations).

Sleep in Your Truck

That is exactly what one entrepreneur with a mission did so she could afford to be at key industry trade shows when she was launching a line of versatile book and document holders. Safety, proximity of campgrounds or other facilities for bathing, and personal comfort make this an option few will follow. Nevertheless, it has been done.

Make Your Booth Look Professional

First impressions are as important at trade shows as they are any place else. If your booth looks as if it was haphazardly thrown together, your company will look haphazard and unprofessional to passersby.

A professionally created display booth can solve that problem, but what can you do if you can't afford to spend hundreds or thousands of dollars to have a display created?

If the show promoters will be providing tables and drapes (to separate booths), ask if you will be able to hang things from walls or the pole structure. If you can, consider hanging up professionally printed signs and photos of your product in use. Or have a large plastic or fabric backdrop of your own created and hang that from the pole structure. Still another option: Look in the office supply superstores for folding foam boards that are sold for use for classroom displays. If done carefully, you could turn one of those display boards into a tabletop display.

Never use hand-drawn signs unless you want to convey a bargain-basement image. Hand-drawn signs or banners printed on continuous form paper will make your company appear small, disorganized, and too cash-strapped to deliver quality products and services on time.

If the show promoters won't be providing drapes as backdrops, consider using inexpensive portable folding screens to set off your space. Test ahead of time to be sure they'll hold up any signs you plan to hang from them. And, make sure they will comply with fire regulations. The material the show promoters send when you register should outline fire regulations and other rules with which you must comply.

Rent a Display

If you can't afford to purchase your own display or aren't sure if you will exhibit regularly at trade shows, consider renting a display. The rental fee won't be cheap. It may be as much as one-third the cost of a new booth. However, if the display is rented from a company that designs display booths, the company may credit some of your rental price toward the purchase of a new booth should you decide to have one created.

If you purchase a display and don't plan to use it frequently, consider renting it out to other businesses.

In either case, be sure written agreements spell out who is responsible for shipping costs and damages in case something happens to the display at the show or in-transit.

Make Your Booth Inviting

Many small trade show exhibitors set up a table at the front of their booths. Although there are instances where that may be appropriate, more often than not the table at the front of the booth acts like a fence to keep the prospect out of your booth. A better strategy is to put the table or tables along the side or back walls of the booth. Doing so removes the physical and mental barriers to entering your booth.

Know When Not to Cheapskate It

Decide who must see your product to make it successful, and what it will take to interest those people in what you sell. If you must look like a serious player in a competitive industry, a small, do-it-yourself booth at a low-priced show won't accomplish your objective.

Make Your Booth Stand Out from the Crowd

You have approximately five seconds to interest passersby to stop at your booth. If your booth consists of just a table, a sign with the name of your company, and a stack of brochures, nobody will know what you do, and very few will stop to ask.

Try to have something in your booth to help grab attention of those walking by. Engineer Harvey Bennett uses a toy train to attract attention to his firm's booth. The Lightstone Group, which sells software for the transportation industry, grabs attention by displaying a digital map on a very large computer monitor.

Ideally, the attraction should be related to your product or be the product itself. "You don't want a lot of people who aren't interested in your product hanging around and taking up your time," says Kenneth Bob, Lightstone's CEO.

A self-running multimedia computer presentation highlighting your product, a video, boxes of your products stacked up high in the booth, and even balloons can help attract attention, too.

Make Your Signs Speak for You

If you want people to stop at your booth, your signs should do more than state the name of your company. Make sure at least one sign tells people what the product or service does and how they will benefit buying it from you. A passerby isn't going to know whether Johnson & Smith Industries sells nuts and bolts or plastic tubing or whether FastJet is a new kind of ink for inkjet printers or a new brand of inkjet printer. On the other hand, people will know immediately what you do and why they should be interested if your sign reads:

FastJet Color Printers

- Fastest inkjet printers on the market
- Ink won't smear when wet
- Perfect for budget-conscious home businesses

In addition to a sign that tells what you do, consider hanging up customer testimonials where everyone can see them.

Make Small Signs on Your Laser Printer

Every large sign in your booth should be professionally printed. Small signs are another matter, however. A good laser printer and tabletop presentation supplies from a company like Paper Direct work well for small signs.

Send Out Preshow Mailings

Don't assume prospects and customers will see your booth and stop at it. They won't. According to the Center for Exhibition Industry Research (CEIR), almost 76 percent of attendees make a list of "must see" exhibits before they arrive at a trade show.

To get on those must see lists, use every opportunity you can to promote your exhibit to customers and prospects before the show. Among the steps you can take are to send out a special mailing before the show and to include promotional literature with every order you fill and every bill, payment, and brochure you send out. According to CEIR, preshow promotion can increase attendance at your exhibit by up to 33 percent.

Don't wait until the last minute to send your preshow promotional literature, either. If you do, your announcements may find your way to prospects' desks after the show is over.

Give Attendees a Reason to Visit Your Booth

Getting customers and prospects to attend a show is only half the battle. To be effective, your preshow promotion should give recipients a good reason to stop by your booth. Among the reasons people will put you on their must see list are:

To see a new product demonstrated
To learn about an upgrade of an existing product
To enter a contest
To retrieve a coupon for a gift
To get a sample of a product

▶ **Tip**
A colorful or unusually shaped pen makes a great tradeshow giveway.

Make Press Contacts Before the Show

Members of the press make must see lists, too. If you are introducing a new product or have made changes to your existing products, let the press know several weeks before the show so they can schedule a visit to your booth or make an appointment to interview you. Be sure to have background information available about the new product, existing products, the company, and principal employees. The more quickly you can get this information to reporters if you are asked for it, the better your chances for publicity.

Make Appointments Before You Get to the Show

Don't wait until you get to the trade show to schedule appointments with important customers or suppliers. If you do, you may not be able to find the people you want to meet, or their schedules may be filled. Call before the show and set up a specific time for a meeting. If you don't have a booth in which to hold the meeting, or if the booth is too busy, scout out a suitable alternative well before the time the meeting is to take place.

Confirm Appointments a Few Days Before the Show

It's not unusual for people's plans to change or for people to simply forget appointments they've scheduled for a trade show. If you have your secretary confirm appointments a few days before the show, you are less likely to waste time waiting for no-shows.

Make Sure You're Waiting in the Right Place

Finding people at a show is difficult—especially if you've never met them before. If you won't be holding meetings at your own booth and don't have a hospitality suite, make sure you have all the details you need to find the people with whom you've set up appointments. Be sure you get a description of the person you are meeting in addition to the location for the meeting. Both things will help prevent incidents where you are waiting impatiently on one side of a hotel lobby while your contact, equally impatient, is pacing up and down within your viewing range on the other side of the lobby.

Put Product Literature in the Press Room

Major trade shows have special areas set aside where reporters can retreat to work, retrieve messages, eat lunch, and relax. Known as the press room, this area usually includes tables where companies can leave product literature and press kits for reporters to pick up. If the show you are attending has a press room, make sure to put product literature there, even if you've previously notified the press about new products or upgrades you'll be introducing. Doing so will make information about your products available to members of the press who weren't on your mailing list.

The show promoters will be able to tell you if there is a press room and where it will be located at the show. They should be able to tell you approximately how many press attendees they expect, and they should be able to give you a list containing their names and addresses.

If a reporter picks up your literature in the press room but can't easily locate your booth, they won't hunt you down. So be sure the literature you put in the press room prominently mentions your booth location.

Don't Print Special Brochures or Product Sheets for the Show

Heavyweight papers, multisided, multicolored printing and folding costs make brochures expensive to produce—especially in small quantities. If you have special versions of such promotional literature prepared for a trade show and can't use it all, or get it back from the printer too late to mail, the money will be wasted.

To keep costs down, try any of these less expensive alternatives:

▶ Slip an insert or discount coupon for the show inside your regular product brochures.
▶ Attach a coupon-sized announcement to existing product literature.
▶ Have the show date and your booth number printed on brightly colored stickers and attach the stickers to mailings and literature you send out prior to the show and to literature you put in the press room.

Plan Your Sales Literature Strategy Before the Show

Check your supplies of sales literature well before the show. If you wait until the last minute, you may find you are running short and have to pay rush charges to get it printed on time.

A good way to estimate how much literature to bring is to plan on bringing enough for 10 or 15 percent of the attendees for small, niche market shows. For bigger shows or shows that attract a diverse audience, make the percentage considerably smaller.

Some exhibitors prefer not to distribute much literature at shows, however. As Kenneth Bob of the Lightstone Group explains, "You see people walking around trade shows with bulging shopping bags. Do you really want your best sales literature stuffed into those bags or mixed in with the piles of things they bring home?" Bob's approach is to get contacts' names and send them product information after the show is over.

Bring Two Sets of Literature to the Show

Have an inexpensive, one-page piece to hand out to individuals with a casual interest in what you sell. Keep more extensive, better-quality brochures or capability statements under the table or at the back of the booth. Hand those out only to people who are qualified leads.

Hand-Carry a Small Supply of Product Literature with You to the Show

Product literature is heavy to carry, so you'll want to ship most of it. But if it gets lost or misplaced, you won't have anything to hand out. To avoid that problem, carry a small amount of product literature with you and find out in advance where the nearest copy centers (such as Kinko's) are located in case your materials should get lost before the show or run out during it.

> ▶ **Tip**
> Can't afford a nice table-top display? If you're exhibiting at a small, local show, you can create a presentable display using a good color printer and inexpensive folding presentation board (available for under $10.00 at office supply superstores like Office Max, Staples, and Office Depot). In a pinch, you could make do with nothing more than literature holders to lift your sales literature off the table top and make it more visible. Literature holders are also available in the big office supply stores for very reasonable prices.

Bring Plenty of Business Cards

Business cards cost 10 cents a card or less. They are an effective marketing tool since they get your name and company name into the hands of prospects.

Make the most of your business cards by bringing a healthy stack of them with you to trade shows. Leave them on your booth table and offer one to any prospects you talk to. Business cards are often saved for months or years, and could lead to a sale long after the trade show is over.

Wear Clothes with Pockets

Be sure clothing that you are planning to wear to the trade show has pockets. That will make it easier for you to get at your business cards when you want to give them out. A good strategy to use during the show is to keep your business cards in one pocket and the cards you receive in the other. That keeps you from mixing up your cards with those you've received from your prospects.

Bring a Trade Show "Tool Box"

There are a variety of office supplies and small tools you may need at trade shows. These include everything from paper clips and staplers to pens, tape, scissors, and screwdrivers. Make a list of all the items you might possibly need and pack them up in one container to take with you. A large plastic shoebox or sweater box with a tight-fitting lid is useful for this purpose.

You might also want to pack a "first aid" box for yourself and your booth helpers. Bandages, change for coffee and phone calls, aspirin, tissues, and even spare pantyhose might come in very handy.

Have Enough Knowledgeable People Staffing the Booth

Your purpose for being at a show is to sell. If you keep people waiting too long, they'll just move on to your competitor. Be sure each person working in your booth is knowledgeable about the product and the industry. If your staff can't answer inquiries knowledgeably, visitors will move on to the next booth.

Set Goals

If you like talking to people, it's easy to get sidetracked at trade shows. An interesting conversation with a booth visitor, a fishbowl full of business cards from unknown visitors, or an armload of sales literature won't do your business much good.

To make sure you stay focused during the show, decide what you want to accomplish before you leave your office. Set specific, measurable goals. How many sales do you want to make during the show? How many leads do you want to acquire? What new products do you want to look at? What sales agents do you want to meet with? Write the goals out on paper and bring them to the show. Periodically throughout the show, compare your progress to your stated goals.

Make Your Goals Realistic

If your product appeals to a very small, focused market or is high priced, you aren't likely to make hundreds of sales at the show. Kenneth Bob sets his goal for small shows at twenty to thirty solid leads; Harvey Bennett, owner of Bennett Engineering, a small industrial engineering company, sets his goal at five good leads and one contract for each show he attends. "I only need one contract to pay for all the shows for a year," he says.

Offer an Incentive to Order at the Show

The order that someone puts off until next week is the order you probably will never get. To secure more sales, plan to offer an incentive for making a purchase or an appointment at the show. This might be a gift, a percentage discount, a buy-one, get-one-free offer, or other sales incentive that works well for your company.

Collect Names of Booth Visitors

You may meet and talk to hundreds of people during the course of a trade show. The only way to keep them all straight is to make notes about each important contact immediately after talking to them.

At bigger shows, attendees are given badges that have their names and addresses imprinted in raised type. At such shows, use an imprinter to make an impression of each qualified prospect's badge. Jot down notes about the prospect's needs or print them on the same form on which you imprint the name and address.

If you don't have an imprinter available (or if the show doesn't issue badges with raised print) write a brief notation on the back of the contact's business card. Or if your customers are consumers, have lead forms you can fill out by hand.

When you have a free moment at the show or that same evening after the show, transfer the notes you've made to a notebook or to a notebook computer, expanding on them as necessary so you will remember which contacts to call when you get home and why you wanted to call them. If you use a notebook computer, keep the original lead slips until you return to your office—just in case you have trouble with the computer or it gets stolen.

If anyone seems particularly interested in what you sell, try to make an appointment to meet again in the contact's own office (or yours) after the show is over. A good way to do that is to offer to stop by the contact's office with more information in a week or two.

Attend Relevant Seminars

Attending seminars is an excellent way to learn about new trends, techniques, and products that could boost—or harm—your business. If you ask knowledgeable questions and aren't afraid to walk up and introduce yourself to a speaker after a talk, it can be a good way to make new contacts. Remember, though, the speaker may have appointments to keep or have a booth to get back to. So, plan to be brief. Use your thirty-second commercial to tell the speaker who you are and what you do. Then state your question or reason for stopping the speaker. Make it short and to the point. If you have something you want to discuss at length, ask for the

Giveways Make an Impression

Bright colored pens or pencils in unusual shapes make great giveaways at trade shows. Stand a few of them up in your literature display to attract attention. It will help people spot your booth who otherwise might have passed it by. Besides attracting attention, the unusual giveaway is likely to get saved and help the person who picked it up to remember you. One warning: If you have giveaways that do get a lot of attention, don't leave them out during a luncheon or any other time when your table is unattended. If you do, they may all disappear while the booth is unattended.

speaker's business card and when would be the best time to call once he or she returns to the office. Briefly state why a follow-up contact will be beneficial. Be sure to follow up when you get home. If you reach a secretary or administrative assistant, state your name and that your contact asked you to call. When you get the contact on the phone, reintroduce yourself and mention the conversation you had at the show.

Be Sure Your Product Is Ready to Display

Big corporations can get by with announcing products that are still in development. Small companies can't. If your product doesn't work or doesn't do what you claim it will do, you'll lose sales at the show. You'll also make customers leery of dealing with you in the future.

Provide for Adequate Security

Theft and damage can be a problem at trade shows, just as it can in retailing. Goods and equipment are most prone to disappear during setup and tear down periods, so be sure to have plenty of security available during those times. When possible, ship items in unlabeled containers and keep expensive items covered until show time.

During the show, protect valuable merchandise and equipment by locking it to tables or by equipping it with some type of alarm mechanism. If you make cash sales at shows, keep the money on your body or under constant surveillance. Don't keep it in a box that could easily be stolen if you turn your back.

Learn Good Booth Manners

The impression you and your staff make on visitors to your booth is likely to be lasting. If they, or you, act or look unprofessional, few people will buy from you. Though that principle ought to be common sense, a stroll through any big trade show will prove it's not. Among the scenes I've personally encountered are:

▶ Booth personnel picking their noses.
▶ A demonstrator who looked as though he needed his hair washed and a good night's sleep.
▶ Booth personnel reeking of smoke, garlic, alcohol (or sometimes all three).
▶ A salesperson at a trade show in New York City telling me how shoddy products made in the United States were.
▶ Salespeople who speak English so poorly that they can be neither understood in a noisy room nor understand the client.

▶ Sales staff talking to each other rather than the customers.

▶ Salespeople who knock the competitors rather than explaining the benefits of their own products.

▶ Salespeople who sit behind their table reading a paper or watch people walk by without greeting them.

▶ Booth personnel who look and sound bored when they describe their products.

▶ Booths that are unmanned.

▶ Signs that indicate the staff is temporarily gone, but no definite time when they will return. (A sign that reads "Will return in fifteen minutes," is useless to the person who walks by and doesn't know whether the person who left the sign has just left or left ten minutes ago and will return in five minutes.)

Be Stingy with Your Time

It's easy to get caught up in lengthy conversations about your industry, the trade show, or product. But if the conversations don't lead to sales or to appointments, you've wasted precious trade show selling time. To avoid the problem, determine in advance how long you will spend with each prospect. Rehearse what you will say to customers and how you will move them toward whatever action you want them to take (see a demo, buy a product, agree to have a sales rep visit). At the show, stick to the time frame and scripts you have planned. If you have trouble doing that, calculate what it costs you per minute to be at the show.

Qualify Prospects Before Spending Too Much Time with Them

Not everyone who asks about your products will be qualified buyers. Some will be tire-kickers, and some may have a sincere interest in the product but not have the authority to make purchases. A few may be sent to your booth by your competitors to try to get your sales staff to divulge information they can use to undermine you.

To get the most benefit from your trade show participation, qualify prospects before spending much of your time with them. Learn to question the client to find out if he or she has a real need for your product or service, if

Don't Lose Touch

Just as you would with other sales leads, keep in touch with your trade show contacts regularly. Put them on your mailing list and drop them an invitation to stop by your booth or hospitality suite at future trade shows. Even if they don't become customers now, they may change jobs or develop a need in the future for what you sell.

he or she is the decision maker, if he or she has the budget to make a purchase, and by what date he or she plans to purchase.

If the answers to those questions satisfy you that the prospect is indeed a likely customer, then proceed with your demonstration and sales pitch. If the prospect isn't a good prospect, suggest he or she look around your booth. Then move on to the next prospect.

Make Demos Viewable to Multiple Onlookers

If you or your staff are demonstrating your product to one or two people and passersby see nothing but your backs, they will quickly move on to your competitors. Learn to demonstrate standing behind your product and facing the aisle (audience). When appropriate, use movie screens, projections screens, or very large computer screens to make a demonstration visible to many people at one time.

Follow up, Follow up, Follow up!

It costs you plenty to gather all those sales leads at a trade show. Plan to follow up on them immediately. If you will be too busy to follow up yourself, assign someone else to follow up on the notes you made on the backs of cards. Don't wait weeks or months. By then, the hot lead will be someone else's customer.

Ask for Lists of Attendees and Exhibitors for This Year's Show

Not everyone who attends a show will leave you contact information or stop at your booth. Get more mileage out of the show, suggests Kenneth Bob, by asking show promoters for a list of attendees. Look for likely prospects (purchasing agents in industries your company targets, for instance). Send them a note telling them you're sorry you didn't have a chance to meet at the show, and let them know how your product or service can help them meet their goals.

Give Something Away

Giveaways help attract people to your booth. Something as simple as a bowl full of hard candy or Hershey's Kisses may get customers to stop at your booth momentarily. Catch their eye and ear as they reach for the candy, and you could win new business.

Bigger giveaways such as samples of your products, a night out on the town, or even a trip to Hawaii, make people go out of their way to find your booth if you promote the contest both before the show and during it.

Maximize the exposure you get by giving away small prizes periodically during the show. If there's a PA system, ask to have each contest announced shortly before the drawing will be held. Each time you award a prize, ring a bell, sound a horn, or have the winner announced on the show PA system.

On the downside, contests can attract a large number of people who have no interest in your product and visit your booth only to enter the contest. To minimize this effect, try to make the prize related to the type of product or service you sell, and ask all entrants who can't use your product for referrals to individuals or businesses that can.

To help your follow-up efforts after the show, have contest entrants fill out an entry blank to be eligible to win. In addition to spaces for name, address, type of business, and phone number include a checkbox on the form to let contest entrants indicate whether or not they'd like to receive more information

Upcoming Highligts
Tell people where you'll be next.
If you frequently do craft shows, have a flier printed up announcing the list of shows you plan to attend. Have it available (along with other contact information) at each show. Encourage customers to take a flier home with them. If your phone number is on the handout, they'll be able to reach you when they get home and regret not having made a purchase at the show. One caveat: if you sell hand-crafted jewelry or any expensive item from home, giving out a business card with your phone number and address on it could lead to a robbery. To minimize the possibility, use an 800 phone number and a post office box number located in a different town on your business card and handouts.

about your product. This will make it easier for your staff to sort out the names that should be added to your mailing list from those that shouldn't. It also gives you an opportunity to contact entrants after the show to give them "the information they requested."

Run Multiple Contests to Gain Maximum Exposure

Instead of running just one big contest for the duration of the show, consider awarding prize at regular intervals. When you announce the winner of each contest on the show's PA system, let show attendees know you are now collecting names for your next giveaway.

Don't Overlook Country Fairs and Flea Markets

These are of particular interest for people who sell crafts, specialty foods, jewelry, or low to moderately priced clothing and variety merchandise. They provide a way of selling to the public without having to commit to high rents or long leases, and they offer a low-cost method for test marketing new products and business ideas. Look for festivals, craft shows, and flea markets that are well established. They'll bring the largest number of people past your table or booth.

Protect Your Merchandise from the Weather

If you do exhibit at outdoor craft shows, flea markets, or country festivals, plan to protect your merchandise from rain, sun, dirt, and wind. Keep in mind that even a cool, breezy summer day can be a problem if you have breakable merchandise or lightweight merchandise that would be soiled if it blew off the table. Other problems you may have to contend with include rain damage; fading colors from merchandise being exposed to the sun repeatedly; bleeding colors; wrinkling if merchandise or packaging gets wet; and condensation if merchandise is encased in plastic.

To avoid the problems, devise ways to protect your merchandise from dampness and rain, and if at all possible from direct exposure to the sun. Investigate the practicality, and show rules for using overhead canopies to keep sun and rain off. Use picnic tablecloth clips or some other reliable method to secure tablecloths to tables and to keep the edges from blowing up and knocking merchandise over.

For quick coverups in sudden downpours, bring sturdy, clear plastic and something heavy to weight the plastic down so it won't blow off or over on top of the merchandise it's supposed to be protecting. If you'll be storing or displaying merchandise on the ground, plan on ways to keep that dry on the bottom in case of bad weather or mud, too.

Sell Inexpensive Novelties to Pay Your Table Space

No one likes to go home empty-handed from a craft show or flea market. You can help pay for your booth space and help visitors satisfy their need to bring something home (and silence their offspring who are whining "Buy me something!") by having a supply of low-cost, desirable items to sell.

Be an Early Bird

Arrive at the trade show hotel the day before the trade show starts so you can familiarize yourself with the area and start off the day relaxed. Plan on getting to the trade show floor well before the show opens each day, too. This lets you pull your booth and yourself together before the crowds pour in and gives you a chance to meet other vendors and key contacts who can lead to partnering deals or new sales.

Be a Speaker

Long before the show, contact the show promoters and find out if they plan seminars and panels. If so, offer to be a speaker. If your bid to speak is successful, you'll benefit from the name recognition and prestige attached to being a "featured speaker."

To gain the most mileage from your appearance, be sure to post signs during the show giving the time and location of your seminar or panel. If you are allowed to do so, bring literature about your products or services to the conference area and place it on tables. Mention it during your talk so that the audience knows to look for the material. And bring plenty of business cards.

If you are given a special speaker's badge, wear it all during the show. After the show is over, use your appearance to gain credibility and prestige by including a brief mention of it in biographical material you hand out to customers, prospects, or the press.

Get a Seminar Attendance List

Show promoters may or may not be able to give you a list of people who attend the seminars you give. To make sure you get a list, give a small prize away. This will give you a reason to collect business cards from the audience (so you can choose one out of a hat for a winner).

Plan to Introduce Yourself to Someone Important

Don't wait for business to show up at your booth. Target specific prospects, specific reporters, or key industry players that you haven't been able to make appointments with in advance and look for opportunities to introduce yourself. Praise their product, presentation, or articles they have written. (Do your homework! Get the name of their product or magazine right.) Briefly mention a specific way your product can help them achieve their goals. Then state what you'd like them to do and why it will benefit *them*. (For instance, how your product or service will build their sales or how your product benefits their readers.)

Keep a Journal

Write down your observations about trade shows you attend as soon as you get home (or back to your hotel room in the evening). Note how well-attended the show seemed, what displays got the most traffic, and what pattern the foot traffic seemed to follow. Was the best spot at the show the one nearest the food booth? Did the side aisles seem to get as much traffic as the middle? What would be the best location for you if you attend next year? Your notes will come in handy next year when you plan your trade show attendance.

If the person doesn't have time to talk to you or doesn't want to talk to you then, ask what would be a good day to contact him or her after the trade show is over. Get a business card and call on the day indicated. If your call gets intercepted by a secretary or other gatekeeper, respond by saying, "Joe asked me to call today. Is he in?"

Talk to Strangers

Opportunity is all around you at a trade show. Don't let it pass you by. Instead of silently waiting your turn at the lunch counter or quietly browsing through literature before a seminar starts, introduce yourself to the people around you and find out what they do. Such chance meetings can help you discover new prospects, suppliers, and media contacts.

Work the Parties

Stop into parties and hospitality suites your prospects sponsor or may attend. These are often important sources of leads and contacts. Don't be shy about introducing yourself. Keep alcoholic consumption to a minimum, though. Although the event may be called a party, you're there to network and convince contacts of your professionalism. Indiscretions could cause you to lose business now and for years to come.

Get a List of Exhibitors and Attendees from the Trade Show Promoters

The other vendors at a trade show are often as important as the attendees. Be sure to save any vendor contact list you are given by the trade show promoters. Ask for a list of show attendees, too. Use the list for a mailing after the show.

Chapter 11

SELLING TO THE
GOVERNMENT

U.S. government agencies, large corporations, and public utilities buy billions of goods and services from small businesses every year. Their purchases not only provide the organizations with needed goods and services, they also help keep the nation's small businesses humming along. They could be pumping orders and profits into your business, too.

Discover the Federal Marketplace

Despite budgetary cutbacks in the 1990s, the U.S. government is still the largest market on earth. Each year its 2,000 purchasing offices buy more than 6 million different items costing a total of nearly $200 billion. Some $40 billion of that total is awarded to small businesses. The Department of Defense, which alone dishes out some $140 billion in federal funds each year, estimates that 98 percent of all its purchases are for dollar amounts of less than $25,000.

Contrary to what you may think, you don't have to sell missile parts or carry million-dollar inventories to tap into the federal marketplace. The government buys everything from commercial art and typesetting services to clothing, light bulbs, waste water analysis, computer training services, and carpentry. Contracts for these small purchases are often awarded to small businesses. Your business could be one of them.

Dig for Gold Closer to Home

The federal government isn't the only big spender. State, city, and county government agencies collectively buy billions of dollars worth of goods and services, too. Although you won't get far hawking battleship parts to state and local agencies, you may find them to be good sales prospects for asbestos removal, desktop publishing, toilet paper, filing cabinets, cookie mixes, fencing, and most other products or services the federal government buys. In fact, you may find selling to local government agencies more advantageous than selling to the federal government. Among the reasons: lower marketing and delivery costs because of your proximity to the local office, possibly fewer competitors, policies or preferences that give local businesses an edge in finding and bidding on work.

Understand the Process

Many small businesses and self-employed persons lose out on government contracts because they don't understand what it takes to break into this market. Typically, they'll submit an application to get on a bidders' mailing list and then sit back and wait for solicitation notices to arrive. Or they'll spot a notice in the *Commerce Business Daily* (CBD), and spit out a proposal on their computer without fully understanding or addressing all the ramifications of the project. When they don't get the contract, they'll complain that it must have been "wired" for a favorite vendor long before it appeared in the CBD. Or that it's useless to try to win a government contract if you aren't a minority-owned business.

Where they go wrong is in assuming marketing to the government is fundamentally different from marketing to any other organization. It isn't.

The key to success is to follow these basic marketing principles:

▶ Determine whether there is a market for what you sell.
▶ Identify the potential user of your product or service.
▶ Understand their needs.
▶ Make them aware of your capabilities.
▶ Identify the buyer (often this is not the user).
▶ Price your offerings competitively.
▶ Deliver a quality product on time and within budget.

Plot Your Attack

To turn those marketing principles into sales, Dudley Glass, a procurement consultant and former government procurement attorney, suggests the following strategies:

1. Establish whether your product is a GSA schedule item* (GSA Federal Schedules). Items such as stationery supplies almost always are. If so, the sales path is hellacious and possibly not worth the bother.

2. Find the user (not the buyer). For the smaller players, this will usually mean canvassing local agencies. And it's got to be done

---

* Certain products that federal offices want to buy must be chosen from a list of approved products and vendors maintained by the General Services Administration (GSA). This list is known as "the schedule."

with some understanding that there's always a dislike of "cold call" sales efforts. (This is *not* a "sales" effort, but a "marketing" one; the distinction's critical.)

If the user gets the item from a stocking location, that's the next stop, and the stocking location should be thought of as the "user."

3. Having identified the user, find out which agency will do the purchasing of the particular commodity or service in question. In some organizations, there may be three or four different sources for acquisition support, depending on the type of commodity and dollar value of the requirement.

4. Approach the small business specialists at the purchasing shop. Get "mentored." Become a "pet." Win contracts.

Let Your Fingers Do the Walking Through the Blue Pages

The place to start your search for government customers is right under your nose: the phonebook. Get out a county phonebook (or the largest regional phonebook you have) and turn to the blue pages. This is where government listings are grouped. If you are located in a large, metropolitan area, you will find listings for hundreds of city, county, state, and federal offices. Look for these key offices to start your search:

▶ Small Business Administration (federal listings)
▶ General Services (look in county, state, and federal listings; each is likely to have a General Services office or administration)
▶ Economic Development (county or state listings)
▶ Department of Defense (federal listings)
▶ Small Business Development Center (state listings)

Get Free Help from Small Business Specialists

Call the number listed for each office and ask how you can locate government offices that would be interested in your products or services. Ask if there are small business specialists or advisors who can help you learn how to do business with the government. If there are, the advisors may help you locate the buyers of

Do Your Homework

Nothing turns buyers and small business specialists off faster than would-be vendors who want everything handed to them on a silver spoon. Don't ask them to tell you everything you need to know to get a contract. Instead, ask if they have information available for small businesses that want to sell to their office. (Most government agencies have handouts that explain what they have to do to be considered for contracts. Usually the titles of these hand-outs start with the words "Selling To.")

your products and services; determine the appropriate Standard Industrial Classification (SIC), North American Industry Classification System (NAICS) Standards, or Federal Supply Class (FSC) numbers to use; and alert you to conferences or contacts that will help you succeed in government sales.

Don't Forget the Web!

Yes, even your government—and their buying offices—are online these days. In most cases their government Web sites contain considerable information to help you get started in contracting. In many cases they also contain current and upcoming bid opportunities. For instance, you can search for all current bids from the Department of Defense at http://www.dodbusopps.com/.

Don't Rest Your Hopes on 129s

Small businesses traditionally have been told to fill out standard form 129 to request placement on bidders lists. Yet submitting a 129 has never meant that you get mailed copies of every solicitation notice sent out. When many potential vendors are interested in bid opportunities, names are rotated for each mailing in an attempt to be fair to all interested vendors.

"Filling out the good old 129 guarantees nothing except frustration," says consultant Glass. "Literally dozens of purchases of the commodity could go by before your 129 bubbles into the list of offerees. And, that is assuming that there was a SIC-code 'hit,' which assumes that both you and the clerks picked the same code. On the other hand, if a requesting user suggests that you be included as a possible source, you will be."

Getting your name to bubble up also assumes that the data you submitted on form 129 gets transferred to an active bidders' list. Although form 129 has not been officially discontinued, some government procurement offices tell vendors not to submit them.

Get on Multiple Bidders Lists

Some purchasing offices do maintain and use bidders' lists. If small business specialists or your contacts at government offices suggest you complete an application to be placed on a bidders' list, by all means do so. You may have to fill out applications for multiple agencies.

Listing with one government buying office does not make your information available to other offices. "If you are on the Department of Transportation's bid list, you still wouldn't know anything about solicitations from the Department of Parks and Wildlife, state universities, the Department of Health, or the Department of Agriculture," explains Dr. Ricks Pluenneke, a plant science consultant based in Fort Worth, Texas. Pluenneke calls the whole process of finding bids "rather haphazard," but adds that taking time to get on multiple bidders' lists can help bring in business.

Don't Sit Back and Wait

Don't wait for bid opportunities to come to you.

Seek them out. Read state, city, or trade publications that list projects coming up for bid in your field. If you don't know of such publications, contact a nearby Procurement Technical Assistance, SBA, SBDC, or SCORE office, and ask if any government agency or private organization publishes such listings in your region. If they do, get the name and send for a sample copy to see if it would be worth subscribing to.

Don't forget about daily and weekly newspapers. Government agencies and public utilities may be required to publish bid notices in one or more newspapers. Find out which papers those notices are published in and read them regularly.

Be a Joiner

Join at least one active trade association or regional business organization and attend their meetings. These groups are often among the first to know about new businesses coming into a community or major new projects that will be coming up to bid. Since businesspeople attend such groups as much to network with one another as to hear the featured speaker, these groups can also be an excellent way to make and maintain personal contacts that can lead to contracting or subcontracting opportunities.

Read Publications That List Bid Opportunities

Another way to find government offices that buy your products is to read publications that list bid opportunities. The best known of these is the *Commerce Business Daily* (CBD). The CBD lists federal contracts coming up for bid that are expected to exceed $25,000. Although the publication announces contracts coming up for bid, experienced contractors often find that waiting for bid opportunities to be listed in the CBD is not an effective way to win contracts.

"The CBD bid notices have limited value," says Jerie Powell, program manager at INTECS International, Inc., a contractor that is part of the U.S. government's 8(a) program. Before joining INTECS, Powell worked in business development for another government contractor. "I never depended on CBDs for bid notices," she says. "By the time an announcement is made in the CBD, most of the experienced contractors would have developed a proposal strategy after extensive go/no-go consideration. Not only that, prime contractors would have identified their preferred subcontractors. I would have had no chance if I had waited for CBD announcements to be published."

Finding bid notices isn't the only thing contractors use the CBD for, however. Powell found it helpful for making sure the contracts she was targeting were announced and for getting a list of bidders (potential competitors) from contacts listed in the announcements. She and others in contracting use the "sources sought" announcements to identify buyers they should get to know, and they read the awards section to keep tabs on competitors and to find potential subcontracting opportunities.

State and Local Bid Listings

State and city bid opportunities are published in other publications. To locate publications you should consider, ask the purchasing agents you contact if there are publications you should be reading to locate bid opportunities.

Look for publications listing state and local bid opportunities as well. These may be published by government agencies, as is New York City's *The City Record*, which lists contracting opportunities expected to be valued at more than $10,000 ($15,000 for construction). Or they may be privately published like the *Daily Pacific Builder*, which is published by a division of McGraw-Hill.

Don't overlook notices published in weekly or daily newspapers, either. Government agencies and public utilities may announce contracts coming up for bid under the public notices section of local or regional newspapers.

Try Before You Buy

Subscriptions to publications that list bid opportunities can cost as much as $400 a year. Before you subscribe to a publication, read several back issues to determine whether or not you want to subscribe. Large public libraries are likely to have the *Commerce Business Daily* and state publications. Procurement assistance offices and other agencies set up to offer free help to small businesses are also likely to have a copy of such publications that could be read in their office.

Search Online

If you own a computer and modem, numerous Web sites have free versions of the *Commerce Business Daily* online. One is the U.S. Air Force's Office of Small and Disadvantaged Business Utilization (http://www.selltoairforce.org).

You can also search for state and local bid opportunities on the Web. Merx Bidline, a fee-based bid search service, offers access to federal, state, and local bid opportunities. It's available at http://www.merxbidline.com/ or at keyword bidline on AOL.

Learn the Lingo

When you start investigating the government marketplace, you may hear many new terms and acronyms tossed around. Though some of the terms and acronyms are of little real consequence (the use of the word *procurement* instead of purchasing, for instance), others could be critically important. Be sure to ask your contacts for explanations if they use any terms you don't understand. If you don't understand the terms of your contract, you could be locking yourself into a deal that will be unprofitable, or worse, for your company.

Get Your Ducks Lined Up

Or to be more exact, get your numbers lined up. Several numerical classifications systems are used to group businesses by industry and types of products they sell. Here are some of the numbers that are most frequently asked for:

SIC code. The U.S. government has developed a set of Standard Industrial Classification (SIC) codes that categorize and label products and services by industry. Purchasing agents look for these codes when they search databases for vendors. SIC codes are also of importance in the 8(a) program, which is discussed later.

NAICS. The North American Industry Classification System (NAICS) is replacing the U.S. Standard Industrial Classification (SIC) system. A printed manual showing the two sets of codes and how they correspond is available from NTIS in either print form or CD-ROM. Each costs under $50. For current pricing, call NTIS at 800-553-6847 or 703-605-6000.

If you have a computer and modem, you can find the comparisons on the Web at http://www.census.gov/epcd/www/naicstab.htm#download

FSC code. The federal government groups products into broad categories called Federal Supply Classification (FSC) groups. Each group is assigned a code that starts with either a single letter or a two-digit number. Many federal purchasing offices maintain source lists by FSCs instead of SIC codes. Furthermore, some federal procurement offices specialize in buying in certain FSCs. You can reduce marketing costs by targeting your efforts at those offices that do regularly buy what you sell.

Another advantage to knowing your FSC group: The *Commerce Business Daily* arranges the solicitation notices it publishes into sections by FSC group. Thus, if you know your FSC number, you can quickly find solicitation notices that are of interest to your business.

CAGE code. The Commercial and Government Entity (CAGE) code is an alphanumeric code used to identify individual contractor plants or establishments. The codes are used by many buying activities to identify vendors

▶ **Tip**
If you have trouble identifying the right SIC, NAICS, or FSC codes for your business, ask a small business advisor at a government agency or a Procurement Technical Assistance Center (PTAC) to help.

and are required for all government EDI transactions. You can get a CAGE code by completing DD form 2051, Request for Assignment of a Commercial and Government Entity Code. The form is available at all federal buying offices or by calling the Defense Logistics Service Center at 888-352-9333.

DUNS number. The Data Universal Numbering System (DUNS) is another identification number you'll need if you use EDI. Dun & Bradstreet will issue you a DUNS number if you call them at 800-333-0505.

EIN. This is the Employer Identification Number. If you don't have one, call the Internal Revenue Service at 800-829-1040.

Never Pass Up the Opportunity for a Free Directory Listing

Many government agencies and industry associations publish business directories. Often, the only cost for being listed in such directories is the time it takes to complete a survey form with contact information and a description of your company. These directories are typically distributed to purchasing agents, small business liaisons, and others in a position to buy or recommend products and services for purchase. Surprisingly, only a small percentage of businesses that are offered the opportunity for a free listing bother to complete and return the forms.

Since purchasing agents and end users of products and services do look in directories when they need to locate vendors, spending the fifteen minutes or so it typically takes to complete and return directory survey forms is a worthwhile effort. Even if you never can trace a sale to a specific free directory listing, having your business included in such directories helps establish name recognition and an industry presence, both of which can indirectly build sales. Your listing sometimes brings an added bonus too: Information from one printed or electronic directory might get reprinted in other directories, causing your one listing to have a snowball effect.

Here are directories to consider listing yourself in:

Listings in trade association directories. Some associations and local industry groups offer members a free directory listing as part of their membership benefits. These listings are then sold, given away free, or even distributed electronically. To find out about this type of listing, contact your trade association.

Central Contractors' Registration database. There are numerous databases in which you can register your business to get found by government buyers and by prime contractors who want to subcontract work to small businesses. But if you want to sell to the Department of Defense (DoD), you must register your business in the Central Contractors' Registration

(CCR) database. The DoD won't award contracts to any business unless it is listed in the CCR. You can register online at http://www.ccr2000.com/.

If you don't have a modem and computer, you may fax or mail in your registration to the CCR Registration Assistance Center (RAC). Call 888-227-2423 to obtain a form and instructions for registering by fax or mail.

Despite the name, the "Central" Contractors' Registration database isn't central to all government agencies. It is required only by the Department of Defense. So you may need to register using other forms with other federal agencies with which you want to do business.

Pro-Net. Pro-Net (http://pro-net.sba.gov/) has been developed by the Small Business Administration (SBA). The SBA calls it "a search engine for contracting officers, a marketing tool for small firms and a 'link' to procurement opportunities and important information."

Others include the U.S. Air Force Virtual Teaming Center (http://www.suppliernet.net), WobLink for women-owned businesses (WOBs), (http://www.supplierlink.com/woblink/), and the National Small Business Network Directory (http://www.businessknowhow.net).

Develop a Thirty-Second Commercial

First impressions count! You'll appear to be well organized and in control by having a thirty-second commercial ready to describe your business, says Karen Nance, director of Business Programs at Barksdale Air Force Base, in Los Angeles, California. Your commercial should be simple and straightforward, summing up your capabilities and key benefits in a nutshell. For example, if you service photocopiers and facsimile machines, you might introduce yourself with this thirty-second commercial:

```
I'm Bill Roberts, president of Electronic Maintenance
Services. We specialize in providing fast, professional,
economical repair and maintenance for all brands of photo-
copiers and fax machines. We've been serving businesses in
the area for more than fifteen years.
```

Market to the Right People

Once you've found one or more agencies to target, make them aware of the products or services you sell. Make the first move by sending a brochure or a line card.

Don't send your brochure or sales literature to the highest-ranking person you can find, though. Instead, send your literature to the people who actually will use the product and will specify* it to the purchasing agent. If you don't know who that person is (the one who will decide on the specifications), ask a small business officer to help you locate the right individual.

Get in Face Time

"Face time" is a slang term for face-to-face contact. It's important in government contracting because government contracts are awarded to the lowest responsive and responsible bidder. *Responsible* means able to perform the contract. Your potential customers will be more apt to believe you are capable of performing a contract if they have met you (or someone from your organization). Therefore, follow up mailings with phone calls to make appointments for in-person visits.

"Don't wait weeks to follow up, either," says former purchasing agent Mercia Bailey. Bailey, who is the owner of Interior Solutions, a facilities consulting firm located in Titusville, Florida, adds, "The people responsible for selecting products are usually inundated with phone calls, sales literature, and personal visits from vendors. Make your initial phone call within a week while your mailing is still fresh in your prospect's mind."

Be Reliable and Trustworthy

Remember that making a sale is only the first step in selling. You've got to be sure the product is delivered on time and meets the purchaser's expectations. If you don't, you'll miss out on repeat sales and referrals.

When Mercia Bailey worked for her former employer, she was usually the person who decided whom the company would buy office furniture from. "I was pretty tough in my position, as my job and reputation was on the line," she recalls. "Furniture, interior design, and executive offices can be very political. So, I found vendors that I could count on. If someone promised me something they couldn't deliver (more than once) or didn't return phone calls, they were removed from my list. Time was so crucial there wasn't much of it to waste on vendors who didn't perform. There were too many out there willing to go that extra mile."

Trying to do an end run around the person responsible for making purchasing decisions isn't advisable, either, says Bailey. "I had a situation one time where a vendor was constantly going around me. They would call my boss or various other people. Once they even called the general manager of the facility complaining that I wasn't specifying their furniture for his office. I warned them more than once that I was the person they were going to deal with or they weren't going to do business with us anymore. They ignored me. . . . In the end, they lost hundreds of thousands of dollars because we pulled their contract and gave it to another vendor. They just weren't playing

---

* In contracting, to "specify" a product or service means to write the specifications to which the purchase must conform.

by the rules. Bottom line is you do tend to do business with people you trust, who will get the job done, and who will be around for the long term."

If the purchasing agent mentions their bad experience with you to others in the industry, or changes jobs and works for another company in the same industry, your poor performance on the one job could cost you sales elsewhere, too.

> ▶ **Tip**
>
> If you need to hire help but don't want to take on a regular employee, or can't find an employee who meets your criteria, check your local employment directories to see if there are any independent contractors and small business suppliers who can do the work you need done. If you need a traditional employee (someone to work in your office) do your hunting at online employment Web sites such as Monster.com.

Attend Free and Low-Cost Procurement Conferences and Training Sessions

Besides making occasional personal visits and phone calls to government users and buyers of your products, make it a point to attend conferences hosted by the organizations you want as customers. These conferences may be set up to alert businesses to sales opportunities or to training sessions. They are an excellent way to meet the people with whom you hope to do business.

Typically, such conferences are one to two days long and cost between $25 and $100 (not including hotel or plane reservations) to attend. Some focus on how to get started in government contracting. Others key in on a specific phase of contracting such as writing proposals or handling paperwork. Still others focus on particular opportunities in specific fields such as environmental remediation.

No matter what the focus, you are likely to come away with an armload of handouts and a wealth of useful tips about selling to the government. However, if that's all you come away with, you're missing the boat. These conferences are fertile grounds for developing subcontracting leads and finding other businesses to team with for projects that may be too big to handle on your own. Therefore, lots of plain, old-fashioned handshaking, back-thumping, call-me-in-the-morning networking goes on. Attend armed with a stack of business cards and be ready to deal them like playing cards from a deck. Keep product literature handy as well in case anyone asks for it.

Attendance is also a good way to show prospects you are interested in learning about *their needs*. When you make follow-up calls after the conference, start them off by giving your name and saying, "I met you at the conference on. . . ." The reference to the meeting will give you a hook to

Snoop Out Bid Opportunities Before They Are Published

Keep in touch with individuals who are likely to hear about projects before they are announced. "Getting to know the people in the permit department at city hall is a good idea since they know about all the construction projects coming up in the city limits," says construction contractor Larry Williams.* "The same is true for county people," he adds. Other sources of prebid information include architects, engineers, and bankers. Banks often know what's going to be happening before anyone else does because they are putting up the money for projects, Williams notes.

He adds, "When you get to know these people well, you sometimes get to help them write the bid package—to your benefit, of course!" That can happen, the contractor adds, when "they believe you can provide the best service and feel comfortable working with you."

This strategy can backfire, however, particularly in federal government contracting. Procurement consultant Dudley Glass warns, "it is easy as part of the 'marketing' to provide draft descriptions, statements of work, and other descriptive information to ease the troubles of the user in expressing his needs . . . but it is also fatal. In federal contracting, those who do that are excluded from benefiting from the resulting contract. Does this prohibit a typical commercial 'slip sheet' flyer being provided? Probably not. But it might be worth asking the purchasing agency's small business specialist for advice first."

---

* The name of this contractor has been changed to protect his identity.

peg your call on and help remind the contact that you are serious about doing business with his or her firm.

Get Free Procurement Assistance

Another source of invaluable free help is Procurement Technical Assistance Centers (PTACs). These centers are funded partially by the Defense Logistics Agency and partly by state or local funding sources. Their goal is to help small businesses find contracting opportunities with federal, state, and local agencies.

Some PTACs are small, consisting of just two or three people. Others are much larger and may be affiliated with state or local agencies that serve small businesses. The larger procurement centers are generally able to provide more extensive help than the smaller centers. New York City's Procurement Outreach Program, for instance, offers businesses help in identifying, locating, bidding on, and completing city, state, and federal government contracts. The program has enabled New York City firms to win more than $225 million in new business in industries that run the gamut from metal fabrication to medical supplies, apparel, furniture, electronics, food, and handbags.

The specific services offered by PTACs vary somewhat with the size of the office, but many provide a range of free help that includes searching the CBD and forwarding announcements to small businesses that would be interested; maintaining a mil-spec library (a library of military specifications); researching past procurement history for items with National Stock Numbers (NSNs); assistance with bid packages; and help understanding acquisition regulations. You can locate the nearest PTAC center to you through the state listings on the Internet at http://www.dla.mil/ddas/procurem.htm. Or contact your local SCORE or SBDC office and ask for the phone number of the nearest PTAC.

Take Advantage of Free Bid-Match Services

State and local small business outreach services as well as PTACs often offer free bid-match services. As the name implies, these services will look for contracts going up for bid and notify a business when they find opportunities that match the business's capabilities. Some of the services will search only the CBD and any similar state services. Others also search small purchase notices for contracting opportunities. Some conduct their search and matching functions electronically; others still eyeball published sources, and when they spot something they think might be of interest to a client, they photocopy it and fax it to the client.

It's important to note that most bid-match services make use of SIC codes. If you aren't sure what SIC codes your products or services fall under, ask for help making that determination.

Remember Your Manners

After you've gotten help from a procurement assistance center or any other government source, remember to send a thank you note. Be sure to highlight any positive outcomes of your visit. These notes not only make the person who helped you feel good, they also have a much more important function: They attest to the usefulness of the center and can help the office get the funding it needs to remain open in future years.

Attend Bid Openings

When contracts are awarded through a sealed bidding process, bids are opened in public and read aloud. You can find out how your competitors bid by attending bid openings and writing down the information as it is read aloud. Seeing how the competition bids can help you decide whether you need to adjust your prices up or down.

Study Your Competitors' Bidding Strategies

Your competitors may have fallen into the habit of ending all of their bid prices with a certain number. One contractor noticed that one of his competitors ended all of his prices with a 900. He began changing their bids so the last part of the number was an 800. The next time they bid on a project, they made the last part of their bid 800. The strategy worked. Their bid was $100 less than their competitor, and they won the contract, which was worth several hundred thousand dollars.

Understand the Difference Between Sealed Bids and Proposals

Sealed bids are legally binding. They are firm offers by you to do work at a stated price. Once bids are opened, you can't withdraw your bid and you can't change the amount you charge unless your customer issues a change order authorizing additional payment.

Include a Deadline in Your Bids

This is particularly important in dealing with local government agencies, bidding on projects that depend on the acquisition of grant funding, and private companies. Plant scientist Ricks Pluenneke tells of the time when he bid on a job that required him to be able to determine which trees were dead and which alive. He bid on the job in the summer when it was clearly evident which trees were alive, but the contract was awarded in December when he could no longer tell by the foliage which trees were alive. His bids now include clauses saying how long offers are valid.

Ask for a Debriefing

When contracts are awarded on the basis of competitive proposals instead of sealed bids, proposals are not read in public. If you aren't awarded the contract and want to know why, submit a written request for a debriefing after the contract is awarded. This debriefing session will let you know what criteria the contracting office used to make the award and will let you gain a general overview of your own proposal's strengths and weaknesses. The contracting office cannot, by law, give you specific details about your competitors' offers or point-by-point comparisons to yours. However, what you learn about your own proposal should help you in preparing future proposals.

Think Small

The easiest way for small businesses to break into government contracting has always been by winning contracts for small purchases. These are easier to get than bigger contracts, and federal small purchases generally have less paperwork associated with them. Since federal purchases under $25,000 do not have to be listed in the CBD, the best way to learn about these is often through personal visits to local offices.

Follow Instructions Exactly

You could be the low bidder on an RFP and still lose the bid if you don't follow the instructions to offerors carefully. If the instructions say to double-space your bid, and you use a one-and-one-half-space setting, you will be found to be a nonresponsive bidder. Similarly, if the RFP says proposals should be no longer than thirty pages, only the first thirty pages will be considered. If you submit a proposal with more than thirty pages, only the information appearing in the first thirty pages will be considered.

Accept Credit Cards

Some federal and state buying offices make some of their small purchases via credit card to cut down on paperwork. The types of products that may be purchased this way are office products, computer items, tools, building supplies, magazine subscriptions, and other items that are priced under $2,500 and aren't on a mandatory source list.* Small business specialists at government offices should be able to tell you what goods are purchased this way and whom to contact to let them know about your business. You will need a merchant account to take advantage of this sales opportunity. Since you will incur some expense to set up the merchant account, don't do so until you are sure you have people interested in your product who would be likely to use credit cards to pay for the merchandise.

Be a Subcontractor

Contractors come in two flavors: prime contractors and subcontractors. The prime contractor is the one who is normally responsible for managing the project, putting up bid bonds, and making sure the work is done on schedule and within budget. A prime contractor doesn't necessarily do all the work on a project, however. Often, especially in government contracting, work is subcontracted out to specialists or smaller companies.

In fact, prime contractors working on government projects may have to subcontract out a percentage of the work to small, disadvantaged, minority-owned, or women-owned businesses. If you meet the size or classification standards and if you are qualified and "responsible" (financially capable of handling the work), subcontracting to prime federal or state contractors can bring in significant business for your small company.

Functioning as a subcontractor is a good way to get your feet wet in federal contracting. It can help you learn procedures and reporting requirements, and possibly help you make contacts that will be invaluable should your company later win a contract on its own.

Be an 8(a) Contractor

Section 8(a) of the Small Business Act sets up a program known as the 8(a) program to assist small companies owned and operated by socially and economically disadvantaged persons.

Under the 8(a) program, the Small Business Administration (SBA) can act as a prime contractor and enters into contracts with other federal government departments and agencies. In its role as a prime contractor, SBA

---

* By law, certain items such as brooms, mops, and cleaning rags must be purchased from Skillcraft, an organization that provides jobs for the handicapped.

then awards subcontracts for the performance of those contracts with small companies in the 8(a) program.

To participate in the 8(a) program, businesses must be at least 51 percent owned, controlled, and managed by either a socially and economically disadvantaged citizen of the United States or an economically disadvantaged Indian tribe, including an Alaskan Native Corporation or an economically disadvantaged native Hawaiian organization.

If you believe you fit into one of those categories, contact the SBA for details of the program.

Fight Back

Contracts are generally awarded to the lowest responsive, *responsible* bidder. That means you must be seen as being financially and technically capable of performing the work or delivering the product ordered.

If you are denied a federal contract because a contracting officer deems your company incapable to perform the contract, you can ask the SBA to evaluate your business's ability to perform. If SBA finds your business is capable of performing the contract, they will issue a Certificate of Competency (COC). The COC will reverse the contracting officer's decision, resulting in your business being awarded the contract. During fiscal year 1990, the SBA's certificate of competency program issued more than 700 certificates of competency valued at more than $470 million to small businesses.

Don't Get in over Your Head

Although you can appeal to the SBA if you lose a bid solely because you are considered financially or technically incapable of performing the contract, don't do so until you carefully consider whether an appeal is a wise decision. If you win a contract and then don't do the work or don't complete it satisfactorily, your contract can be terminated for default. If that happens, you will have to pay the difference between the original contract price (the price for which you agreed to do the job) and what it actually costs to have someone else complete the work you didn't do. The result can be devastating.

"More than once, I've watched a company go belly up because it was adamant it could handle a job that was patently beyond its capabilities," says procurement consultant Dudley Glass. If you haven't clearly understood all the technical terminology or researched all the references in a contract, it's possible to make an "offer that is superficially acceptable, but has too low a price or grossly overreaches your capabilities." In one case Glass remembers, a company bid on a contract to produce remote control vehicles used to simulate tanks in war games. The company had no facilities except a garage and some tools. "The award was forced," Glass says. "The buggies were issued months late and did not work. Contract litigation followed."

Be Sure You Understand All the Terms of Your Contract

Under some circumstances, you may be awarded a contract that will require you to produce a "first article" before being given the go ahead to proceed with the contract. In other cases, your contract may give the customer the right to buy from you at a certain price, but not specify any minimum number of items or time frame in which the purchase must be made. In either case, you could lose your shirt (and whatever collateral you've put up for loans) if you go out and order all the materials to produce the item called for in the contract and the customer rejects the first article or doesn't buy all the items you manufacture.

If You've Got It, Flaunt It

If you are female and have been thinking about selling to the government this is the time to strike. That's because the U.S. government took a look at who it was buying from and discovered that although 40 percent of the businesses in the United States are women-owned, less than 2 percent of the products and services it was buying came from women-owned businesses. The upshot: there's now a concerted effort underway to increase the number of government contracts awarded to women-owned businesses

Chapter 12

BRINGING

IN SALES

Like it or not, if you are in business, you have to be a salesperson. If you work alone or have one or two people working for you, one of your primary functions will be bringing in business. No matter how good your products or services, customers aren't likely to find you. You have to find them and convince them to buy from you.

As your business grows, you will find that you need to sell to a different group of people. You will need to sell that first real employee on the benefits of working for a business as small as yours. You may have to sell suppliers on the value of extending you credit, sell the banker or investors on the soundness of your business plan, and sell strategic partners on the benefits of working with you. In fact, for as long as you are the head honcho of your company, you will also be the chief drumbeater. The better you learn to beat that drum, the better you'll succeed.

Get Your Name Widely Known

Use the tactics mentioned in the looking big, shoe string marketing, publicity, and mail chapters of this book (Chapters 4, 5, 6, and 8) to get your name widely known in your community and industry. Join associations and attend their meetings, and learn to work the rooms. Get to know everyone, and get them to know what you do. Your goal is to be the first name that rolls of anyone's tongue whenever anyone thinks about your type of product or service. If you learn how to play this game right, you'll find that people who have never dealt with you or seen your work will recommend you to friends and business associates. (When they do, don't forget to send them a nice thank you note!)

Sell by the Numbers

For many types of products and services, selling is a numbers game. If you make and track enough calls, you will begin to see a pattern emerging that allows you to determine what percentage of calls will result in a sale and what you need to do to increase sales. If you determine that 1 in 20 people you call makes a purchase, then you know you have to call 100 people to make 5 sales. If you want to double sales next week, you'd have to make 200 calls. Tracking results in this way can help keep you (or your sales staff) from feeling depressed by a string of rejections. It can also help you determine the effectiveness of changes in your sales presentations, evaluate the success of sales training, and serve as a target you strive constantly to exceed.

Change Techniques for Big Business-to-Business Sales

Landing those big business-to-business sales requires a different approach.

When you are selling big-ticket products or services, there's a lot more at stake than just the final dollar amount of the contract. On the customer's side, your product or service will in some way affect their business and profitability. And because of that, the decision to buy your product will ulti-mately reflect on, and perhaps have an effect on, the career and reputation of the people who make the buying decision.

On your side, there are considerations such as the time and cost of get-ting the sale, and the effect the terms of the deal will have on your business operations, profitability, and ultimately, reputation.

With so much at stake, making big sales requires significantly more work and a more structured and professional approach. "Trying to short-circuit the process will damage your chances for success," says Dan Wasserman, president & CEO of Thorne, West, an Internet marketing con-sultancy located in Ontario, Canada. Wasserman, who has more than twenty-five years of experience negotiating big sales and strategic alliances for major advertising agencies and traditional and Internet media compa-nies, recommends this ten-step approach to landing big deals:

1. Determine your commercial targets and why they make sense to approach.
2. Find the correct contact.
3. Develop your opening pitch and "advance" materials.
4. Book your meeting(s).
5. Prepare your presentation and leave-behind(s).
6. Conduct your meeting, anticipating questions and answering truthfully.
7. Follow up on initial issues raised at the meeting.

8. Negotiate based on expressed need and appropriate deliverables.
9. Develop the final sales proposal.
10. Re-present and close the deal.

"All too often," says Wasserman, "clients think they can short-circuit the process. What they fail to recognize is whether they do the work themselves or use a specialist, to be successful the process is always the same."

Use a Structured Approach for Smaller Sales

A sale doesn't have to be worth tens of thousands of dollars or more to warrant an organized "attack" on the customers. Sales for any type of product or service that requires one-on-one selling can benefit from some structure and preparation. If you are trying to get an appointment to sell something that won't require a major commitment on the part of the buyer, try this approach:

1. Prepare a simple brochure or one-page product sheet describing what you sell. Write a simple sales letter to go with it.
2. Choose a list of key prospects.
3. Call the prospects and tell them that you will be sending them information about your product and how it will help them.
4. Send the information immediately.
5. Call a week after you've sent the material, ask if the prospect got it, and make your pitch to get an appointment to meet the client. (Or if you can sell the product over the phone, be ready to take orders.)
6. If they aren't interested now, tell them you'll stay in touch, and do so on a regular basis until you determine they are no longer a qualified prospect for what you sell.

Hold Free Seminars

If your products or services require a significant outlay of cash, your customers will want to gather as much information as possible about the product before they make a purchase. You can help them get that information and, in the process, help them learn to think of you as a trusted resource by giving free seminars about your industry. Be sure the seminars are truly informative and do a lot more than just promote your business. Give your attendees a good understanding of what

Offer a Free Consultation

Free consultations benefit you as much as the customers. They give you the chance to talk to the customer and discover what their real problems are and sometimes what their budgets are to solve those problems. Once you have this information you can determine if you can help them, and if so, tailor your sales presentation and service to match their needs.

the entire buying process will involve. Tell them what to do first, what next, and what to expect at each step along the way. Give them names of key contacts who don't compete with you, and finally give them checklists or planning sheets and other material to take home that they'll want to hang onto and use. Make sure your name and contact information is on every page of those handouts. If you have a Web site, be sure that it and your e-mail address are on the handouts, too. Every time the prospect uses those handouts, he or she will see your name again and remember how helpful you've been. That name recognition and credibility—along with following up after the seminar—will help you win sales and get referrals.

Go to Seminars and Conferences

Find out what seminars your target customers are likely to attend. Try to meet them at breaks. If they are speakers, sit near the front of the room and ask the conference coordinators whether there will be an opportunity to talk to the speakers immediately following their speech. If not, position yourself near a door where you may have a chance of following them out of the room and catching up with them.

Look for likely prospects to seat yourself with at lunch or dinner. If you don't see specific individuals you want to talk with, try to read name tags or look for company logos as you stroll through the tables looking for a place to sit. Try not to position yourself with a group of people who appear to be friends unless they are from a company you want make contacts with. And never sit with your own friends at a conference. Your reason for being at the conference is to make new contacts as well as to gain information.

Keep Hours That No One Else Does

Small and home-based businesses are often advised to keep normal "business hours" to show they are professional and to separate home life from the business. Normal business hours, however, are often the worst hours for customers of many businesses to shop or to arrange for services. Most consumers work during business hours. Follow the lead of shopping malls

▶ **Tip**

If you moonlight, don't apologize to potential customers for your inability to do their work during the day. Turn it into an advantage. For instance, instead of saying, "I'm sorry, but we can only do installations at night or on Saturdays," say "We'll be able to do that installation for you after hours so it doesn't interfere with your normal workday." Or, "Mrs. Jones, you'll be pleased to know we can accommodate your busy schedule by dropping by one evening. What time would be convenient for you and your husband?"

and make yourself available after traditional 9-to-5 workday hours if you want to grow your business. To capture customers who can't reach you during the times you are normally open, set up a Web site (see Chapter 14) that offers information about your services or the opportunity to place an order. When you're not available at night or on weekends, have your answering machine or voice mail point customers to your Web site to get information or place an order.

Start at the Top

When you attend association meetings, you may get a chance to meet executives in companies you hope to target. Introduce yourself and ask who in the company is responsible for buying your type of product. Write down any names and phone numbers they give you, and follow up with a phone call. Refer to the executive you met at the meeting and the fact they suggested that you call.

Make Sure You're Talking to the Right Person

Call the company and ask who buys your types of products. Ask for the name and phone extension, and then call that person. Ask if he or she is the right person to talk to. If he or she says yes, try to get enough details to determine if this person's a likely prospect for you.

Once you get someone to answer the phone and talk to you, take the time to qualify the prospect. Find out if he or she needs and uses the product and if he or she has the budget to buy in the quantities you sell. As you describe what you do, ask questions that will tell you whether or not you will be able to meet the prospect's needs, too. If you work alone and your Web development skills are limited to what you can do in FrontPage and the prospect needs an ecommerce solution for the firm's Web site, you'll be out of your league. Similarly, if you charge $150 an hour to build database-driven Web sites for corporations, you'll probably waste your time trying to sell Web site development to World Global Enterprises, Inc. if World Global is a small chemical laboratory with cash flow problems.

Find out, also, if he or she is the only person involved in the decision. If there are others, whenever possible make arrangements to have them present when you make your initial presentation.

If you sell big-ticket items to consumers, determine who it is who will make the buying decision. Decisions about home improvements such as new siding, roofing, revamping a kitchen or bathroom, or building a swimming pool are likely to be joint decisions. To limit the number of times you have to visit the home to make the sale (and to avoid making a presentation to one partner when the other will nix the project), plan to call on prospects only when both the husband and wife will be present. Time is money, after all, and traveling to and pitching a potential customer on a big-ticket item can take several hours. Be sure you spend those hours in the most productive ways.

If a big-ticket item isn't necessarily a family purchase, listen carefully to your prospects to determine who the real decision maker is. Be sure you make your pitch to that person.

Get to Know Buyers Personally

Sales are built on personal relationships. Get to know the people who are responsible for choosing and placing orders for your products or services. In large companies, there may be several people. In a small company, the person is likely to be the owner or an office manager. Find out more than just their names. Find out what their personal interests are, if they're married, if they have children, what sports teams they route for, or anything else that will help you personalize your relationship with the buyer. Keep track of all the information in a database (or in a card file if you don't have a computer), and use it to personalize calls and visits to the buyer. Questions like "How's Monica's soccer team doing this year?" or "How was you trip to Mexico?" are the kind of specific comments that make good relationship builders.

Be Resourceful

If you can't get that kind of information from your prospects, be resourceful. Talk to their gatekeepers, talk to people at association meetings, read local newspapers, and even "Who's Who" directories. The information you can glean can be the ticket to sales success. Tracy Kornfeld, a Nike district sales manager tells of the time he was trying to land a major corporation as a client. "We couldn't get to first base. No one could get past the secretary," he recalls. "Then a salesman did some research and found out the buyer loves tennis. I acquired four tickets to a U.S. Open. It was amazing how quickly I got in the door then." Getting in the door paid off, Kornfeld notes. "Those four tickets turned into a $6 million sale. Find out what the person's passion is and you'll do it every time!"

Don't make the mistake of thinking friendship is a substitute for product and industry knowledge or product belief, however. "You have to believe that your product is the best thing in the world since white bread and you

Buying Seasons

Clothing isn't the only thing that is seasonal. Find out if your customers buy your type of product only at certain times of the year. If so, plan future sales calls accordingly. If there is no set buying season, contact the customer a month or two before the end of their fiscal year. They may have money to burn before the end of the fiscal year. If not, you may be able to get them to budget an amount to buy your product or services in the coming fiscal year have to make your customer believe that. Eat it, drink it, breathe it, live it. Then you can go out and push it. Believe in yourself and believe in your product, and you will be successful," Kornfeld adds.

Befriend the Gatekeeper to Get to the Customer

Purchasing agents and others who deal with salespeople frequently have "gatekeepers" in place who screen their calls and decide who will get to talk to them on the phone or meet with them in person. One way or another, you will have to get past this gatekeeper to talk to the boss.

Often the best way to get past the gatekeeper is to simply to get the gatekeeper on your side. A good gatekeeper may know nearly as much about the business and what's important as the boss does. In fact, if the person is a longstanding employee and highly trusted, he or she is likely to be making recommendations to the boss in addition to screening out people he or she thinks will waste the boss's time.

"An effective executive makes sure to have a gatekeeper who understands what kinds of calls she wants and what kinds she doesn't have time for," says Mary Ann Chapman. Chapman, who owns Fanfare House, Inc., an Internet marketing service, ran one business in which she frequently got calls from salespeople.

"Court the gatekeeper, don't view her as an immovable obstacle. An effective gatekeeper will ask exactly what it is that you want to discuss with the contact person and suggest the most effective way of getting your message across. If she doesn't, you should ask her to suggest a method or to refer you to another staff person who can."

Follow the Procedures Suggested to You

Sometimes all it takes to get through to a buyer is to do what you are told to do. The instructions may come from the buyer, or from the buyer's gatekeeper. In either case, you have a much better chance of getting heard if you do exactly what you are told to do.

"Everyone is different," says Maryann Chapman. "Some contact people will talk with salespeople any time. Some will return calls if the message has sufficient information to ensure that the time spent will be worthwhile. Some will take calls on slow days—ask the gatekeeper if there will be a day later in the week that is more appropriate."

Chapman herself never took calls from salespeople unless she had requested they call her. But what she would respond to personally was e-mail. "I will respond to virtually any e-mail that appears to be personalized. I can do it at any slack moment when I feel like it, even if it's at 2 in the morning. With many salespeople, my office manager repeatedly told them to e-mail me and instead, they just kept calling."

Don't Alienate the Gatekeeper

Repeated phone calls trying to get the gatekeeper or the prospect to listen to a sales pitch can backfire. If you don't respect the prospect's time and follow his or her requests, you may be thought of as pushy or annoying.

"I have been both the gatekeeper and the contact," says Jennifer L. Morey. "I have had tons of cold calls from salespersons trying to reach 'the person in charge of whatever.' They all start the conversation with the same line: 'Hello, Jennifer, how are you today?' Then they wait for me to answer before introducing themselves. This tactic instantly puts me on the defensive because I know they are going to try to sell me something."

Morey also advises salespeople to follow instructions they are given.

"I usually don't have time to listen to a long spiel about the benefits of your product, and would rather receive material in the mail that I can peruse while hastily gulping my lunch. And, when I tell you that, please gracefully accept it and then follow through with my request instead of calling me again tomorrow, or asking me when would be a good time to call back. There is no such thing as 'a good time to call back.' My work day is frantic and I have constant deadlines. If you keep yakking at me I will just tune you out, and then when I finally do get your info in the mail it will go straight into the round file because you have left a negative impression. I will forever associate your name or your business name with 'pushy and obnoxious.'"

Call When the Gatekeeper Isn't There

One way to get past the gatekeeper is to call when he or she isn't there. If you call fifteen minutes or more before normal working hours or a half hour after the day's end, the person who picks up the phone may be the boss. And sometimes the boss will pick up the phone himself or herself when the gatekeeper is out to lunch. Be brief and have something important to say if you do get through. This isn't the time for a lengthy explanation of who you are or what you do. Use a fifteen- to thirty-second introduction for yourself and your company, and then say something important. Not something important about your company, but something the prospect is going to realize is important to his business. For instance, if you sell recycled ink cartridges, don't ask the customer if the company has ever considered using recycled ink cartridges. Instead tell him or her you'd like to meet on Monday to discuss a way your product can help his or her firm save thousands of dollars a year on office supplies.

Make the Five-Minute Promise

If you can't connect when the gatekeeper isn't there, explain your reason for calling. If you've been referred by someone, be sure to let the gatekeeper know. Promise you'll be brief, that you need only five minutes of the boss's time, and then stick to it. Be sure to thank the gatekeeper when you do get through, too.

Use Nonreferral "Referrals"

Any time someone gives you the name of someone to contact, technically, they are referring you to that person. Thus if you get through to the VP of marketing, and she suggests you call the purchasing agent, do so. When you get the purchasing agent or his or her gatekeeper on the phone, you can truthfully tell him or her that the VP said to call. Refer to the vice president by her full name, as in "Hello. Kathy Marsh suggested I call you."

Consider Leaving Voice Mail If You Don't Get Through

Don't leave a sales pitch in voice mail, but if you have qualified your prospect carefully and know he or she has both a need for what you sell and the means to make the purchase, leave a brief message saying who you are and why you are calling. Make the message brief. Clearly state your name and phone number, and say them slowly enough so that someone can understand them and write them down. A good tactic to use is to state your name and phone number at the beginning of the voice mail message and then state it again at the end of it. That way, if the listener caught part of the number the first time, he or she may be able to get the last part without replaying the voice mail.

Don't Take No for an Answer

Be politely persistent. Remember, needs may change, the current supplier may screw up giving you a chance to get your foot in the door, there may be personnel changes at the company, or any other set of circumstances may occur that will help you make a sale in the future.

Do Follow-Up

If you've followed instructions, don't sit back and wait forever for a response. Call within a week of sending information to be sure the gatekeeper or the prospect has it and that it hasn't settled to the bottom of a pile of things to do. Ask for an appointment or if there's more information you can provide. If the contact says to call back in a month, mark it on your calendar and be sure you make the call. If you see the contact at business gatherings before the month is up, say hello, ask if he or she got your information, and remind him or her you'll be calling. Then chat briefly about the event you are both attending, the association's goals, or whatever it is that put you both in the same room at the same time.

Stay in Touch Regularly

Don't stop at one follow-up call, either. "Sometimes it takes months, even years, to establish a business relationship with someone," says Morey. "A monthly call is the best way to keep in touch. Eventually, I'll stop thinking of you as a cold-calling salesperson and begin to see you as a business resource. *That's* when you can start asking me, 'How are you today?' and 'How's business?'"

Don't limit your contacts with your customers to just a couple a year. Keep in touch regularly. Sales trainer, Jim Ziegler, suggests making "phone touches"—quick calls averaging two minutes or less. Every "touch" ends in a selling question such as, "Say, Bob, do you have any new managers who haven't been to the seminar yet? I have one coming up in Denver that's pretty close to you."

Get the Buyer's Home Address

If you keep track of only your contacts' business addresses and phone numbers, you could be losing out on sales. Since most people change jobs several times during their careers, Ziegler suggests getting the home address as well as the business address for each of your contacts. Each time you do a mailing, mail to the home address as well as the business address. That way, if your contact has moved on to a new position, he or she will still get your mailing and may be instrumental in helping you add his or her new company to your list of clients.

Focus on the Customer

Have you ever tried to offer help to a friend or relative only to be told, "But you don't *understand*!"

Selling products and services to customers isn't much different from offering advice to a friend. Before you can get anyone to buy your help (or what you sell), you have to get them to believe you understand *them* and what *they* want to accomplish. Only then will they buy into the concept that you can solve their problems or fulfill their dreams.

Don't try to convince customers that you understand them by repeating pat phrases or well-rehearsed scripts. Instead, get to know them. Ask questions. Find out where they are in the buying process. Do they buy what you sell now? Are they satisfied with their current vendor? If not, why not? If you get to know your customers, ask the right questions, and listen to the answers, you really *will* understand their needs, expectations, goals, and concerns. Focus your sales efforts on showing how your product meets their specific needs and address their specific concerns, and you'll be in a good position to close the sale.

Remember, the Customer in Front of You Is the Most Important Customer

That's what they want to think, and it's your job to make them believe that. You may have three more people to see before the end of the day and may be expecting a call about that big contract you've been trying to land. But none of that matters to that customer sitting across the desk from you. That customer's only concern is what you and your product can do for him or her.

Get Them to Say Yes

One way to get customers to make a decision in your favor is to get them to say yes to a series of questions about their needs. The dialog might go like this for instance:

> "George, I hear you will have a booth at the trade show in June."
> "Yes."
> "I guess you'll be mailing your clients in advance to let them know you'll be there?"
> "Yes, we expect to do that."
> And you'll need that mailing to get out on time and get their attention, right?
> "Yes."

Enthusiasm Sells?

If you have trouble convincing customers to buy from you the problem may not be your sales presentation. It could be your delilvery. Susan Berkley, who is a speech coach and president of Berkley Productions (http://www.voiceover-training.com) says that sales people often aren't convincing because they don't sound enthusiastic. "You can increase your vocal energy level by up to 40 percent by standing while you speak," she says. Other tricks she suggests to add energy to your presentations are speaking with your hands and putting a smile on your face while you talk.

Assuming you've qualified the your customer in advance, each small yes answer you get helps move the client gently toward the close. By the time he or she has said yes a half dozen or more times to your questions, he or she will find it difficult to say no when you ask for an order.

Find Out How Many People Will Be Involved in the Purchase Decision

If you are making big sales, often numerous people are involved. The first person you may need to convince may be the department that will actually use your products or services. That person may have the primary say in recommending vendors, but may not be the one who negotiates the contract or signs the purchase order. If that is the case, be prepared to make a presentation that will make it easy for your initial contact to sell you to the other people who will be involved in making the decision.

Reduce the Risk

If you are a small business, one of the unspoken questions your prospects may have about buying from you is likely to be whether or not you can do the work you say you can. This is especially true if you are trying to get your first customers. One way to overcome the newbie objection is to do some small part of the job for free. You won't want to do this often, but if you are breaking into a new field and have no established credentials, or if there is a customer who could produce significant sales over time, it's worth a shot. If you are as good as you think at what you do and are careful about when and to whom you give free services you could bring in tens of thousands of dollars (or more) in sales using this technique.

"Look upon every presentation as one before a committee . . . be it a formal or informal committee," says Alan Zell, a sales trainer and former jewelry store owner." A presentation will work best when the customer or client can take that presentation and carry the message forward to others. "A presentation is a teaching process that allows the customer/client to see that without making any big changes, they can take the offer to their FFAACCC's—family, friends, associates, acquaintances, customers/clients, or their own conscience—as this is where selling takes place. If the customer/client and/or their FFAACCCs do not believe they can talk with confidence and intelligence, and without the fear of embarrassment, they most likely will not buy or buy into what is under consideration."

What specifically they will need to carry forward the sale will depend on the situation. Past history, samples of work, testimonials from other customers, news clippings about your company, fact sheets or product reviews, and comparative analysis with your competitors products are among the types of materials that may be useful.

Get Your Foot in the Door with a Small Sale

Businesses and consumers alike often consider that the risk of dealing with a new, small business far outweighs any benefits they may derive, particularly when a lot of money is involved. One of the ways to overcome that resistance to dealing with you is to take small steps toward getting your customer familiar with you and the quality of your products and services.

One of the simplest ways to do that is to give key prospects a free sample. Software programmers who sell their programs on the Web often make available demo versions of their programs that will work for a limited time. People interested in the program can download it and try it for short period to determine whether it meets their needs. Other programmers give away simple versions of their products to get people to purchase the versions that have highly desirable add-on features.

If you worry that free samples will result in more tire-kickers than real customers, develop a low-cost, but desirable product or service to sell to your target market. Be sure the product or service is top quality. Once you've gained the customer's confidence on a small sale, it will be easier to reduce concerns about placing big orders with you.

If the client doesn't bite on the first attempt to trade up to bigger and better sales, don't forget about him or her. If you have qualified the customer in advance and know there are good possibilities for additional sales, stay in touch on a regular basis. Send the client news clippings, press releases, product announcements, and anything that will help build your case for being a qualified and reliable supplier to his or her company.

Offer a Guarantee

Consumers and business buyers want to be sure products they buy will live up to their expectations. To overcome such concerns, offer buyers a money-back guarantee or a free trial period.

Don't Let Contract Negotiations Throw You

Getting a company to agree to use your products or services may be only half of your job. Once you have convinced them you can do the job they want done, you may still have to negotiate the deal. And that chore may be more difficult than convincing the company in the first place that they need what you are selling. Conflicts may arise over price, delivery terms, quantities, or even the length of the contract. Depending on the company, the size of the contract, and the negotiator, tactics that may be used may include anything from low balling you on prices, to insulting you, to taking weeks to respond to your inquiries or counteroffers on price, to demanding control or rights you don't want to give up.

To avoid coming out on the short end of the deal, or losing it altogether, determine in advance exactly what you want out of the deal. How much money do you want? What's the minimum you could accept and make it profitable? What's the most you think they might pay? What do others get for similar work? If intellectual property is involved—copyrights, trademarks, or patents—which rights, if any, are you willing to give up? How long are you willing to license those rights for? Are there benefits you'll get from the deal other than money?

When you get an initial offer, look it over carefully. If you are presented with an offer in-person, or one is faxed to you while the client is on the phone, don't be pressured into making any kind of decision or definitive answer. Tell the client you will have to read the offer carefully and will get back to him or her.

If the customer is a large corporation or a company that regularly buys goods or services through negotiated contracts, the contract you are initially shown is likely to be a boilerplate contract. Prices and terms are likely to be negotiable. The initial price offer may be just that—a first, low price, made in expectation that no matter what price is offered, you'll try to bargain it up.

Take the time to carefully look at all the terms, not just the price, and consider them in comparison to your objectives for the deal. There may be some terms included that are unacceptable, and some that you don't like but that you could live with if you had to. Have your attorney look over the offer and alert you to issues he or she thinks are important that you may have missed, too. Then, go back to the client. Go over all the issues you have with the offer and settle what you can. Focus on the most important issues to you. If the price is too low, try to negotiate the highest price you think the company's budget will allow. Remember that the minimum amount you will find acceptable is just that—a minimum! Don't be too quick to lower your fees to that level. Don't be greedy, but do expect to make a fair profit for your work. And do keep your overall objective in mind.

When necessary trade off the less important issues to win concessions on the items that are more important. If you sense tempers are beginning to wear thin (either yours or the customer's), hand off negotiations to your attorney to distance yourself from the negotiations. (Be sure the attorney knows which issues you insist on and which to trade off so your legal bill doesn't get run up unnecessarily.)

While all this is going on, stay in touch with any people in the company you will actually be interacting with after the contract is settled. If they recommended you, they have a strong interest in seeing your contract settled and, whether they admit to it or not, are likely to be doing what they can behind the scenes to speed things along.

Learn to Overcome Objections

One of the most difficult aspects of selling for most people is dealing with objections. Business owners who aren't used to sales situations assume the client's initial no means they aren't interested at all in the product or service. Experienced salespeople think of the initial no as a first objection. Instead of giving up and going away, they probe to find out why the prospect said no and work to resolve any questions the customer has.

Typical of the unspoken objections are concerns about the risk of a purchase (risk to the buyer's business, career, or budget if your product or service doesn't do what you claim), the difficulty in implementing the decision (will they have to make changes in the procedures they now use to accomplish some task), the true value of your product or service (will it really save or make the money you claim), your ability as a small business to deliver on time (or to deliver at all!), and your ability to provide service after the sale.

You will win more sales if you learn to probe for these underlying objections and develop strategies for dealing with them. Don't present your response to objections as a defense of your company or product. Structure your responses to show the benefits to the customer. Is the customer's real worry that your business is too small and he or she will look bad to the boss if you don't deliver on time? Don't say your small size doesn't matter. Instead, assure the customer that you have extensive resources at your command and can pull together exactly the right team to get his or her project done on time and within budget. Or remind the customer of the cost savings his or her company will enjoy because you can keep your overhead costs low. Is price the real concern? If so, go over what it is that the client expects you to deliver and ask, what price point would get the sale? If the client comes back with a lower figure, work at negotiating a price you can both agree on.

Practice your responses in advance. Have a spouse or friend play the role of the client and throw objections your way until you can answer them with ease.

> ## What Sales Reps Look For
>
> Getting a good sales rep can be as difficult as landing a big customer. A sales rep's reputation—and income—depend on the quality and reliability of the goods they sell to their customers and, of course, on the size of the commission they make. Thus, they are likely to base their decision about representing your line of products on these factors:
>
> - Amount of commission
> - How well they understand your products
> - How much advertising you'll be doing
> - Related products they could sell
> - How much support you provide the end user after the sale

Study Sales Techniques

Although selling something you know has value ought to come easily, often it doesn't. Invest the time to read one or two books on the subject or take a course on selling. The money and time you invest will pay off in the long run.

Find and Work with Sales Reps

There are only a limited number of people you can reach on your own. If you don't want to hire your own staff, you may find it advantageous to use one or more independent sales representatives to bring in new business. Depending on what you sell, a sales rep will show your products in their show room, bring them to trade shows, and promote them to their existing customers.

Finding really good sales reps is sometimes easier said than done, however. One way to find them is to work backwards. Go to the stores you think would sell your product and ask what sales reps they buy from. Contact those reps about selling your products as well.

Jacques Werth, chairman of High Probability, Inc., a sales training company that conducts open sales training workshops for individuals in several cities, recommends calling manufacturers of noncompeting products that sell to the same market and asking for their list of sales reps. "Some companies print up such lists. Others treat it as top secret information," Werth says. But sometimes a call to a top executive produces results. "I called the VP of sales of those companies and just asked for their list. Very often they would fax it to me. Sometimes I would have one of my people call the sales department of a company and ask for the name and phone number of their rep in the area that I was looking to fill, i.e., Phoenix."

If neither of these methods work, see if your public library has directories that list sales reps.

Be prepared to explain to the sales rep how you will meet the demand for your product, and to prove you'll be able to handle the paperwork, fill orders, ship on time, deliver quality merchandise, and provide service after the sale.

Find out all you can about the rep, too. Why does he or she want to rep your product line? What other products is he or she a sales rep for? Nail down contract terms and commission rate, and be sure to have it all in writing.

Sell on Consignment

Still another way of letting other people sell your merchandise for you is to sell it on consignment. When you sell on consignment, what you do, in effect, is lend inventory to retail stores. The retail stores display your merchandise for sale to their customers. If the merchandise sells, the retailer pays you for it but keeps a percentage of each sale for themselves. Depending on the store and the type of merchandise, that percentage can be anywhere from 25 to 50 percent.

Selling on consignment in some ways benefits both you and the retail outlet. The retail outlet gets inventory to sell without having to tie up a lot of cash. You get a place to sell your products without having to pay for rent, overhead, or the salaries of people to staff the store. You can also spread your work around to many different locations, giving you multiple sales outlets and a way to get your name widely known.

There are a number of pitfalls to be aware of though.

One of the biggest problems is that your work is tied up until it's sold or you retrieve it from the consignment shops. If a shop doesn't get a lot of traffic, or puts your work in an out-of-the-way area, it can be months before your merchandise sells—if it sells at all. If the shop is located at a distance from you, retrieving your merchandise if it doesn't sell can be costly or impossible, too.

"I had one place that had my work for over a year, never sold a thing, and I have called to have my pieces returned and have never gotten them back," says Joy Reside, a jewelry designer from Springfield, Illinois. "Artist beware."

Choose Consignment Shops Carefully

To improve your chances for sales, look for consignment shops that sell the same general type of merchandise you are offering. For instance, if your work is contemporary, a shop that focuses on a country look isn't likely to bring you many customers. Similarly, if you do primitive art, it's not likely to fit in with Victorian-era merchandise.

Eyeball the shop and try to determine how many customers come in and how carefully the goods are treated and protected. Ask what type of insurance they have, too. Joy Reside recalls one shop that wanted to display her work, but didn't have insurance against the theft of artwork, and didn't have locked cases to put the jewelry in. "She was just going to put the pieces on tables. I refused!"

Finally ask how inventory is tracked and when goods are paid for. Marlo Miyashiro designs sterling silver jewelry, sells on consignment, and at one time ran a consignment shop. She recommends spelling out the details of your agreement with a shop in a written contract and getting the owner or buyer to sign and agree to your terms regarding when payments should be made and the responsibility for lost or stolen goods and display and upkeep of the merchandise.

Satisfy the Customer After the Sale

Making the sale is only half of the battle. To build your business, you want to get repeat sales from your customers and you want them to refer you to other consumers or businesses who can use your products. Within reason, do everything you can to satisfy a customer. If you don't, the customer is likely to tell friends and business associates about the terrible experience they had with your company.

Follow up After the Sale

Show your customers you care by calling a few days after you've delivered their work to make sure they are satisfied. Customers will appreciate the concern you show and be more likely to call you the next time they need work done. Feedback you get from follow-up calls can also help you monitor quality.

Keep Selling After the Sale

If you sell consumable products (foods or products that get used up and need to be replenished), don't assume the customer is in the bag after you've made the first sale. Let them know you are still there and still interested in helping them by sending them tidbits of information on an ongoing basis that will validate their purchase and help them remember to reorder from you. Send a postcard a few weeks after they've received the product to remind them of the product benefits or to suggest additional uses for the product. Follow up a month or so later with a news clipping related to the product or some other brief contact.

Sell More Products and Services to Your Existing Customers

Don't stop selling once you've gotten a new customer to buy from you. Since the hottest prospects for new sales are recent satisfied customers, you can profit by selling additional products or services to your customers. These "back end" sales can be additional products suggested to the customer at the time a purchase is made, repeat sales of the same product at a future date, or sales of related products or services. For instance, if you sell cosmetics, you might suggest a new eye shadow to the person ordering a new lipstick. A month later, you might call that person and suggest a new nail polish that has come in. The month after that, you might suggest a perfume or sunscreen product. If you sell desktop publishing services, you might also want to expand into offering Web design to your customers.

Ask for Referrals

Among the easiest leads to convert to sales are people who have been referred to you by their friends, family, or business associates. Such leads are generally prequalified—they know they want your product or service—and generally don't have to be convinced of your ability to satisfy that need. After all, their trusted friend sent them to you, so you must be good!

Some of your customers will refer new business to you on their own. But that's a slow, undependable process. You can hurry that process along and win even more approval from your current customers by asking them to refer customers to you. Here are some of the ways other small businesses do that:

▶ Call customers and tell them you're expanding your business. Ask them for the names of specific people you could call in their organization.

▶ Offer your customers cash for referrals. Decide whether you'll pay out money for all referrals or only for those referrals that actually become customers. The actual amount you offer should be determined by the size of the sale or expected profitability.

▶ Give businesses customers a discount on their bill if they'll send out literature for your company in their mailings.

▶ Give customers gift certificates to give to their friends. As a thank you for passing the gift certificate on, give the customer a small gift certificate for their personal use as well.

▶ Offer spiffs to telemarketers or in-store salespeople for selling your products. A "spiff" is an added incentive for selling a product. You might give salespeople \$5 for every product they sell. If they know they'll earn extra commissions on a specific item, they're likely to recommend the product to as many customers as they can.

▶ Ask people who don't buy from you to give you referrals. Just because they can't use your product now, doesn't mean they don't know someone who could use it now.

Don't Ignore Complaints

No matter how good your product or service is, there will be people who don't like it, who want a refund, or who want some other concessions from you.

When confronted with a complaint, don't go on the defensive. Instead, make your response start with these two magic words: "I'm sorry!" If you sound sincere, and then ask the customer to explain exactly what the problem is, you will immediately ease the tension.

Always try to solve the customer's problem. If you have a customer who insists on a refund even though he or she has damaged the merchandise or taken some action that caused the problem, weigh the cost of refunding the money against the time and trouble that will be involved in "proving" he or she is wrong and refusing to give a refund.

Remember, irate customers are bad for business. They can make anyone overhearing their complaint skeptical about doing business with you. Worse, they can influence the buying decisions of dozens of people (or more!) that you'll never see. They also make work unpleasant for you or your employees who have to deal with them.

Make Good Use of Mirrors

People who train telemarketers have long claimed that putting a mirror by the telephone and using it to make sure you are smiling when talking to prospects will boost sales. But Jim Ziegler has a different approach to using mirrors. Get a big mirror and put it in the customer service area of your store or shop. Put it behind your customer service manager. Customers who have a problem with a product are less likely to rant and rave if they see what they look like when they are angry.

Call On Former Customers

Past customers don't have to be lost customers! Very often customers stop buying from a vendor because someone else got their attention first when it was time to reorder. All it may take to win them back is a phone call or visit. Be ready to tell the person about new products you have, price reductions, or about enhancements to your service.

Part 3

Operating in the Internet Age

Chapters

▶ 13   **Increase Productivity and Profits on the Web**

▶ 14   **Build and Promote Your Web Site Without Going Broke**

▶ 15   **Creating and Working in Your Home Office**

▶ 16   **Choosing and Using Office Equipment**

▶ 17   **Making More Profitable Connections**

Chapter 13

INCREASE PRODUCTIVITY

AND PROFITS ON THE WEB

When I started my first online forum in 1988, few people knew what an online service was. Fewer still cared. Trying to explain what I did usually produced puzzled looks, and if I could corner anyone long enough to give a demonstration, the usual response was a polite, "That's nice, but who will use it?"

No one asks that question anymore. Hundreds of thousands of individuals a month use either the Business Know-How Forum on America Online or my company's Web site at http://www.businessknowhow.com. Big and small businesses alike have flocked to the Internet and to online services because that's where their customers are. And that's where their suppliers are. Researchers expect there will be 100 million Americans online* in the year 2000.

Every type of product you can imagine is being sold on the Web, too. In 1999, 76 percent of retailers and 43 percent of manufacturers were selling online or planned to sell online.† Besides computers, books, and CDs, you'll find leather jackets, soda pop, lingerie, and clothing. You'll find some rather inconceivable offerings, as well. One enterprising college student set up a Web site to sell horse manure. Her target wasn't farmers or gardeners. It was any individual who wanted to "get even" for being laid off, dumped by a love one, and so on. For $19.99, the site would giftwrap a clump of horse manure and ship it to the sender's least favorite people.

---

* Throughout this chapter, and throughout the book, I've used the terms *online*, *Internet*, and *Web* interchangeably. Each meant something slightly different when the terms were first coined, but today most people use any of those three words to describe that kaleidoscopic world that has also become known as cyberspace. Where I refer to "online service," I mean a service that provides both access to the Internet and its own content. References to ISPs (independent service providers) indicate services that offer access lines to the Internet and e-mail accounts but no content or very little content of their own. Host or hosting services are companies that provide a place to put your Web site and the means to connect it to the Internet and make it available to Internet users.

† Source: The Second Annual Ernst & Young Internet Shopping Study, sponsored by the National Retail Federation.

Name Games

AOL and Compuserve (without the .com endings) are fee-based services. AOL.COM and Compuserve.com can be accessed without charge from the Web.

You don't have to be a retailer to benefit from the Web, however. Small and home-based businesses throughout the world are discovering that the Internet reduces costs and improves efficiency. In fact, the improvements are so significant that you will be at a competitive disadvantage if you don't learn to put the Web to work in your business.

Before You Go On...

Don't let the savings and productivity enhancements described in the following pages make you rush out and spend thousands of dollars overnight to have someone set you up with your own Web server, hosted Web site, or intranet. Take the time to learn about the Web firsthand before you make any major investment in it.

Learn the Inexpensive Way

If you have no experience using the Internet, the easiest way to learn about it is to use a personal computer hooked up to a standard telephone line and sign up for an online service such as America Online, Compuserve, or Microsoft Network. Or pay an Internet service provider (ISP), such as AT&T Worldnet or BellSouth, by the month for an e-mail address and a connection to the Internet.

The reason to start with one of these services is they simplify the process of getting connected to the Internet. Some offer their own content (news, feature articles, and so on) as well as just the connection to the Internet. Once you have an Internet connection with access to the Web, you can also use any of the popular Web "portals" (Web sites that categorize sites according to their content and give you links to them) to look around the Internet for Web sites in your industry.

Here are some of the most popular portals. Each offers links to various categories of information as well as powerful search engines that search the entire Web for keywords you choose:

AOL.COM
http://www.aol.com

Yahoo!
http://www.yahoo.com

Netscape Netcenter
http://www.netcenter.com/

Lycos
http://www.lycos.com/

AltaVista
http://www.altavista.com

MSN
http://www.msn.com

Excite
http://www.excite.com

Snap
http://www.snap.com

Infoseek
http://infoseek.go.com/

AT&T WorldNet
http://www.worldnet.com

Get in the Habit of Using E-mail

Having an e-mail address is just about as important these days as having a business card or a sales tax number. Millions of businesspeople are using e-mail to send routine business correspondence, requests for proposals, contracts, instructions, price lists, spreadsheets, and sometimes orders. If you don't have an e-mail account you won't appear professional, and in some cases, you may not be able to do business at all.

Set Goals and Focus on Them

The Web offers so many ways to inform, do research, entertain, and sell that it's easy to lose site of your business reason for being on the Web. The "wow" factor attached to it all can cause you to waste countless amounts of time and money doing little more than playing around on the Web.

To avoid that pitfall, make a list of your goals before you make any decisions about what to put on your Web site or how to present the material. Don't include things like "set up a Web site" or "set up a bulletin board." List only the results you want to accomplish, not the tools you'll use to get those results. Your list might include some of the following goals:

Send and receive business correspondence
Keep tabs on your competitors
Generate sales
Generate advertising revenue
Reduce support calls
Enhance customer communications
Reduce costs
Provide product information to customers
Give demos

Assign priorities and a value to each goal. Weigh every decision you make about your use of the Web against these priorities and values.

For instance, suppose you have decided a Web site would help build your business and you are thinking about putting a video on the site showing you demonstrating your product. Consider whether that demo will really enhance sales. Do people understand what the product does? Or does it really require a demo to sell it? Will the video really build sales or just stroke your ego? Any feature that doesn't help you reach your goal should be eliminated—at least at startup. You can always add capabilities once you see how customers actually use your site.

Find It Faster on the Web

Most of the stories you read in the press these days focus on the use of the Web for ecommerce—buying and selling goods and services. The Web, in one sense, is the world's biggest mail-order catalog.

But ecommerce isn't all the Web is used for. In fact, the biggest advantage of the Web for many businesses is that it offers near instantaneous access to a vast array of information. It gives them access to research data and opinions that would be impossible for many small businesses to get in any other way. Whether you want to know what options are available on the new van you are planning to purchase, what percentage of women work outside the home, or how to market your business on a shoestring, there's a good chance the information you seek is out there somewhere on the Web.

And that fact quickly leads most people to discover the leading *disadvantage* of the Web: how difficult and time consuming it can be to find exactly the right information. A recent search of the Web for my own full name, Janet Attard, produced 469,105 "hits" (Web pages the search engines found to contain references to my name).

To minimize the time you spend searching for information, and to minimize the time you spend trying to find your way back to information that was valuable to you, read the help files available on search sites and learn to use the advanced search capabilities for each site. When you get to a Web site that you'd like to return to (such as http://www.businessknowhow.com) use the bookmark or favorites capability of your browser to save the URL (the Web site address) for future reference.

▶ **Tip**

If you know how to create databases, set up a simple database to store Web site URLs and descriptions of the Web sites. Once you collect a lot of favorite sites, it's a lot quicker to find a Web site that way than it is to try to scroll through dozens of bookmarked listings to find the one you want.

Ferret Out the Information Fast

A program called WebFerret can help you find information on the Web much faster. The program, which installs in your Find menu on PCs running Windows 95 or Windows 98, is a search agent that simultaneously searches several portals for the search terms you choose. There's a freeware version that performs simple searches. A "pro" version is available for $26.95. That version offers Boolean search capabilities, searches more portals, and adds other enhancements for e-mail addresses and other capabilities. A PowerPack version includes a number of other add-ons such as the ability to search for e-mail addresses, and search news items. One software developer used the e-mail search capability to find the e-mail address of a customer who had made a typo when entering his e-mail address in the programmer's online database.

The freeware and pro versions of the program are available at http://www.ferretsoft.com/.

Talk to Your Peers, Listen to Your Customers

There are thousands of industry-specific discussion groups on the Web and on commercial online services. Some of these discussions are located in areas called message boards, bulletin boards, or newsgroups, which you'll find located in the forums on the commercial online services or through various access providers and Web portals. Others, called mailing lists or listservers, are carried out through e-mail. Some are moderated (controlled to keep out unwanted messages such as insults, foul language, and unwanted ads), and others are unmoderated. Finding discussion areas of interest to you can take a little digging, but once you do locate them, they can be an invaluable source of industry information and contacts. Among the discussion topics you may find are how to price your services, where to find good suppliers, what software can help you work more productively, or how to market your product or services more successfully. Industry issues, financing, and legal matters all may be discussed as well.

If you sell products or services to a particular industry, monitoring bulletin boards and newsgroups related to that industry is a good way to find out what your customers like or don't like about your products and your competitors' products.

You can locate discussion groups through commercial online services and Web portals. Association trade magazines, popular magazines, and computer magazines sometimes list such resources as well. If you have an America Online account, that service's WorkPlace channel is a good place to start your search. It offers about 100 special interest industry forums containing thousands of discussion topics. Among them are some of the busiest and most informative message boards you'll find anyplace online.[*]

There are thousands of individual mailing lists on the Web. Some such as the Online Advertising list and eTailers list are active and very useful.

***

[*] Business Know-How message boards are included in the WorkPlace channel.

Others get few messages, and some have nothing but opportunity advertising and arguments.

Watch What You Say

Participating in message board or mailing list discussions can make you feel as if you are part of a closed community. You will usually see the same handful of people posting messages every day, and others who post messages occasionally. There's often a feeling of camaraderie that evolves. In fact, the sense of sharing of ideas and experiences can make you feel as though you are sitting in your living room discussing issues with a small group of close friends.

Don't be fooled! If the list or board is big, there may be thousands of people reading even though you see only a few people post messages. Thus, you should be extremely careful about what you say. If you make disparaging remarks about a person or company, you could be sued for what you say. Or if you talk about a new project you are working on you run a risk of giving away confidential information to your competitors.

Other risks: Your customers, your employees, or your employer (depending on circumstances) may be reading every message you post.

Even messages that are supposed to be private, such as e-mail, may be copied on purpose (by someone who wants to get you in trouble) or accidentally to a public area. So, the bottom line is never say anything in a newsgroup or message board or e-mail that you wouldn't be willing to say if you were giving a speech to a large audience.

Get the Low Down on Products Before You Buy Them

In the past, the only way to find out how well a new product worked was to wait for magazine reviews to come out in print, wait for a friend to buy it, or buy it yourself. If you're hooked up to the Internet and an online service, your wait should be significantly shorter. You can usually find out the first reactions to the product by looking for computing forums and for the new product reviews sections of Web sites run by computer magazines. Some places to look include computing forums on America Online, Compuserve, or MSN or the message boards at Yahoo, Lycos, Excite, the Mining Company, ZDNet, and CMPnet.

As you read messages, keep in mind that some information posted to a newsgroup or message board may not be true. Some people may just have a bone to pick with a manufacturer or may not have followed directions, and some people hear rumors and spread them without bothering to check on the facts. But if you see a pattern in the messages (say, many people indicating they have a similar problem), consider carefully whether such a problem would interfere with your use of the product if you encountered it, too.

Finally, some manufacturers have product support Web sites. If there is a product support message board for a product you are considering, read the questions and problems that are raised there. Write to some of the customers to see if his or her issues were satisfactorily addressed. Doing so can alert you to problems the manufacturer might be ignoring.

Save Money on Conference Calls

If you frequently use telephone conference calls to communicate with people who use the Web or online services, consider conducting your conferences in an online chat room rather than on the telephone. You can test online chatting for free using the chat option at sites such as Yahoo, Lycos, Parachat, or AOL, Compuserve, and Netcenter. Several of the chat programs such as the AOL Instant Messenger and America Online proprietary service buddy chat, let you create your own private chat rooms and allow access to only those people you want to join you.

If you have your own Web site and are willing to pay a fee, you may also be able to install a chat room on your site. You will need to contact your Web administrator or company that hosts your Web site to find out if this capability is available and what it will cost. Some hosting services charge about $1 per simultaneous user per month to add chat to your Web site. However, when you consider that one ten-minute telephone conference call with ten people could cost you $50, it may be worthwhile.

▶ **Tip**
If you just have to deliver information and don't need to have people talking live back and forth, send the information out in e-mail instead.

Discover Your Customers' Real Needs and Gripes

The Internet is a communications tool as much as it is a marketing tool. One of the leading attractions of the Internet is that it opens channels of communication that were never possible before. Users of various products or services can, and do, get together in public message boards, newsgroups, and chat rooms to talk about products, services, and vendors they like or don't like. Listening in on these groups can help you spot trends, determine what product features customers like most, what they would like to have but can't find, and what they are saying about you and about your competitors. That knowledge can be used to help you develop new products, determine what changes need to be made to existing products, and spot competitor weaknesses you can exploit (by doing what they aren't doing). It can also help you increase advertising response rates by zeroing in on your customers' real problems and the way your product solves those problems.

Use an Intranet to Hold and Update Presentations and Training Programs

If you have a sales staff, consultants, or trainers who travel and rely on company-generated presentations, you can be sure they have the latest materials if you set them up on an intranet.* The presentations can actually be loaded to run as presentations from a Web site (if your people will have live access to the Web during their presentation or training sessions), or they can be set up so your traveling staff can download the new versions of the presentations. Training and product demos can be done in the same way. You'll save on mailing and printing costs.

Save on Intranet Programming and Hardware Costs

The cost of hardware and software doesn't have to prevent you from setting up your own intranet. Instead of investing in equipment or programming, look for ready-made solutions. Any company that hosts Web sites can provide you space for an intranet. You can then use programs like FrontPage to set up a communications areas for your business. A better solution—but slightly more costly—is to use one of the turnkey virtual office packages like Hot Office (http://www.hotoffice.com) to set up an intranet for your office or associates. Hot Office gives you electronic bulletin board capabilities, document sharing and retrieval, bulletin online conferences, e-mail, calendars, and more in one central location that can be shared with your colleagues. There is a monthly fee for each person using your virtual office, but if you have only four or five people working for you and none of them are skilled programmers, it's more practical to pay this fee than to pay someone to set up a system just for you.

Save Time and Money on Press Releases

Instead of renting a press list and stuffing press releases into envelopes or tying up your fax machine, send your press releases via e-mail. You'll save on postage and get your releases to editors faster than you would by mail. E-mail will cut the phone costs if you normally fax releases. And added benefit: Some editors and reporters prefer e-mail and read it before they look at faxes or printed releases.

The best way to get the e-mail addresses of writers and editors is to look at the publications you want to target with your release. Look in the masthead and look at the tops and bottoms of articles in the publication. If you can't find the e-mail addresses you want, try calling the publication and asking to speak to the individual writer or editor you'd like to add to your list. Don't hang up if you get voice mail. Some reporters are easiest to con-

---

* The term *intranet* is used in this book to describe any Web site set up for use only by a company's employees.

tact by e-mail and include their e-mail address in their outgoing voice mail. If you get through to the writer or editor, ask if he or she is the right person to receive releases for your industry or topic. If he or she says yes, ask what his or her preference for releases is: e-mail, fax, or mail.

If you don't want to compile your own e-mail list, you can buy e-mail press lists or use a service that sends the e-mail for you.

Among the companies that will e-mail your press releases or rent you a list of names of the press are:

http://www.gapent.com/pr/prices.htm
http://www.gebbieinc.com/misc/sbn.htm
http://www.owt.com/dircon/
http://www.newsbureau.com/
http://www.editpros.com/media.html

For additional sources of press lists (e-mail and traditional), see http://www.prWeb.com/mediapress.htm. See Chapter 6 for additional information about getting publicity and for sources of conventional press lists.

> ▶ Tip
> If your business is hard to find and is not located at home, put directions and a map showng how to reach you on your Web site. It will help customers find you, cut down on the number of times someone at your company has to give out directions, and save on phone costs if you'd be faxing directions.

Slash the Cost of Communicating with Distant Branch Offices or Associates Without an Intranet

If you have offices in distant cities or distant countries and are not using the Internet to communicate, you could be throwing away thousands of dollars a month on communications costs. Mike O'Neil is a San Francisco Bay Area banker and financial consultant who has been involved with several businesses. Among them is a fern farm located in Costa Rica. To keep costs down, the company's Costa Rica office sends weekly accounts, price quotes, and other paperwork to the United States using e-mail or efax. Most of the sales deals with European buyers are done either directly through the Internet or using efax technology. And the company has also sourced suppliers and technical information over the Internet. O'Neil says, "I would expect a company our size with 100 percent exports to be spending several thousand dollars a month at least on communications. The tea company I ran in Kenya spent $40,000 per month. However, our total cost for all communications is around $300 a month and that includes the server charges on both ends."

Use One Service to Manage Voice Mail, E-mail and Internet Fax

If you travel frequently, or if you have to communicate with someone who travels frequently, look into the services that let you use the Internet to access and manage all the ways you communicate. With these services, you can send faxes to e-mail, e-mail to a fax machine, voice mail to e-mail, and e-mail to voice mail.

You'll need software or a service provider to get the process rolling. Before deciding whether the services will be beneficial, consider how often you will need the capability and what the cost per outgoing or incoming fax will be. Will you incur extra fees for sending faxes overseas? Will you be charged by the page or by the amount of time it takes to send the fax? How will those sending you a fax reach you? Will they need to call a long-distance phone number?

Compare the prices, services, and way several services work before signing up with any one. You can locate Internet fax and e-mail services from this URL: http://www.savetz.com/fax-faq.html.

Shorten the Selling Cycle

Sales—and payments—happen faster for many companies that do business on the Internet. One reason is that the Internet makes it possible to give demonstrations and provide fact sheets, brochures, and other information on demand and at low cost. Instead of setting up an appointment to visit a client when it's convenient for both of you, you can put graphic images, text, slide presentations, video, or audio on your Web site and let the customers read about the product whenever it is convenient for them. You save on the cost of travel, on the cost of your staff time, and on the cost of color printing. The only costs are the costs for creating the Web site and materials—costs that can be small over the course of a year compared to the traditional ways of accomplishing these goals.

Marcelino Sanmiguel operates a credit bureau for the Dominican Republic market. His company has gained customers worldwide because of their Web presence. The company saves time and money by not making in-person presentations to customers. "We don't have to spend money to present ourselves over and over to customers," Sanmiguel says. Instead, they refer customers to their Web site to read about what they do.

Another way the Internet can shorten the cycle and improve productivity is by automating the entire sales process. If you have an order form or shopping cart on your Web site, the customer types in the name, address, credit card number, and other details of the order. If you set the order entry system up to work with the rest of your procedures, you may be able to process the credit card charge, print a statement, print a pick list, print a shipping label, and print a thank you letter all from the information the customer typed in.

Take Orders on the Web to Cut 800-Number Phone Costs

If you are taking orders on an 800-line, you may be able to reduce your expenses by setting up a Web site and encouraging customers to place their orders there instead of calling them in. If a significant number of customers use the Web for order entry, you'll save on labor costs as well as phone charges since your employees won't have to spend as much time talking to customers on the phone. If your system is set up to generate the paperwork you need or to collect customer information in database format, you'll also be able to reduce the amount of time your staff spends entering data.

Reduce Overnight Shipping Costs by Using the Internet

If you frequently use overnight mail to send letters or documents to associates, clients, or prospects, you may be able to save hundreds or thousand of dollars a year by sending the documents in e-mail or transferring them through a private Web site.

If you need only to convey the text of a message and don't need an official letterhead or special formatting, the easiest way to get that text to another person is to type it into the body of an e-mail message. (Or if you have written the message in a word processor first, copy the text and then paste it into the body of the e-mail message.)

If you need to send a formatted file, use the "attach mail" or "insert file" function of your e-mail software to send your document. Documents will need to be under 2 megabytes in size (some e-mail systems may have smaller size limitations), and the person receiving the document will need to have a software program that will read the file you are sending. (Send text e-mail in advance to find out what software the other person uses, then if possible, save a copy of your document in that format using the Save As option in your software.)

The attached mail function is particularly handy for working on projects where several people may have to review and approve a document. For

▶ **Note**
Be sure that everyone keeps their virus software up-to-date to avoid transferring viruses along with the files.

instance, if you are negotiating a contract, don't send the contract in overnight mail to the people who have to review it. Send it in e-mail as an attached document. Each person who receives the contract can review it and make changes, using tracking functions in the software to mark the changes. When all parties have agreed on a final version, the contract can be printed (without having to retype the entire document) and mailed. Thus the number of times you have to pay overnight mail fees is reduced to one.

Recipients can see documents within minutes of the time changes are made, rather than having to wait until overnight mail arrives.

You can save considerable money on the cost of color printing and photographs if you normally send pictures through the mail. Instead of printing these items out at high cost, you can realize significant savings by digitizing them and posting them on a Web site or sending them as e-mail attachments.

> ## Tip
>
> If you frequently exchange documents with people who don't use the same software you use, or if you want to send them documents to view that they can't change, consider purchasing Adobe Acrobat software. This program converts your documents to a format that looks identical to your original document and can be read, but not altered, by anyone who has a copy of a free Acrobat Reader program Adobe publishes. The program also lets you publish documents to the Web.

Cut Color Printing, Paper and Mail Costs

When Chad Wold finished law school and joined his father's law firm, Wold Law Firm, P.C., in Montana, he was "shocked" to discover how much money the firm was spending on color copies that were being sent in traditional mail. "We were working on a case involving a death that occurred on a tractor," he recalls. "We were defending with three other law firms and dealing with two insurance companies. Every time we wanted to discuss any issues with the other law firms and insurance companies, we would have to send out an enormous amount of color copies to describe our theories of what happened." To reduce those costs, he started a secured Netmeeting page, scanned the photos and relevant photos, and put them on the site. Doing so not only cut costs, but also allowed them to animate the sequence of events to get a better idea of how the accident most likely occurred.

Wold also used the Internet to speed up communications between the attorneys and their clients by having secretaries type phone messages into e-mail and forwarding the e-mail to a pager system. Each attorney could then return calls in a more timely fashion. Next, he added document scanning, so secretaries could immediately send documents to an attorney who wasn't in the office. This allowed the attorneys to get the information sooner and the secretaries to be able to file the originals without having to wait for the attorney to return to the office to see them.

Reduce or Eliminate Print Advertising Costs

If the majority of users of your product or service are likely to be Internet users, you may be able to eliminate or greatly reduce print advertising costs by using the Internet. Marketing consultant Aruna Aysola helped Panelight Display Systems, Inc. save more than $300,000 in advertising costs by replacing traditional magazine advertising with online ads. The company saw no reduction in sales or customer base after making the switch.

Replacing print advertising with online ads can work for businesses that sell products to consumers, too. Beth Ellyn Rosenthal, of Dallas, Texas, has substituted two Web sites (http://www.meltdown.com and http://www.stophairloss.com) for advertising she used to run in newspapers and magazines. "Before the Web, I paid for newspaper and magazine advertising in the Dallas area. It was very, very expensive. Now I pay $55 a month for both sites and advertise to the world. I have customers in thirty different countries," Rosenthal says. The business, which is a sideline business for Rosenthal, has annual revenues of $40,000 to $60,000.

Identify Revenue Streams

In addition to cutting costs and facilitating communications, most small businesses can use the Web to generate income in one way or another. In fact, some successful small business Web sites bring in revenue from multiple sources. Depending on what you sell, here are several to consider:

▶ Selling your own line of products
▶ Publishing original books, records, or software
▶ Selling other companies' products through drop-ship deals
▶ Selling other companies products through affiliate programs
▶ Getting leads or orders for services
▶ Selling or reselling Web site space
▶ Creating Web sites for other companies
▶ Creating database solutions for Web site owners
▶ Selling banner and pop-up advertising on your own site
▶ Selling sponsorships of your site
▶ Selling classified advertising on your site
▶ Selling advertising space in a newsletter or mailing list you send your site visitors
▶ Teaching classes
▶ Consulting through e-mail or an online chat
▶ Licensing your content to other Web sites

Decide on the most likely revenue streams for your business and then plan your site's content and budget around those revenue streams.

Put Your Existing Store or Mail-Order Business on the Web

If you already have a line of products you sell that you are selling successfully, adding an Internet storefront can be a good way to increase your profits without significantly increasing your bottom line. That's because overhead and labor costs for running a retail Web site are often considerably less than the overhead and labor for a retail outlet.

Barry Gainer is president of The Indian River Gift Fruit Company in Titusville, Florida. The company is a family-owned business that ships oranges, grapefruit, and other fruits and gift food items around the world.

"It is very cost effective for a small business to market this way," Gainer explains. "We have retail stores and the associated costs that go with them. Mortgages, taxes, water, electricity, phone, workmen's comp, insurance, payroll. That adds up to $6,000 dollars a month for our smallest Indian River Fruit store. On the Web, however, my Internet access for taking care of my store is $21.95 a month. My phone line is $42.95. My computer with all the bells and whistles is $1,500.00 (one-time cost only). Labor at forty hours per week answering questions, submitting the store to search engines and cross linking to other sites is $300.00."

But lower costs aren't the only advantage. Gainer's sales are higher on the Web than from his smallest retail outlets. In 1998, sales at his two online sites http://www.giftfruit.com and http://www.indianriver.com totaled $1.5 million. Retail sales at the company's smallest Indian River Fruit Store were $365,000.

Not all businesses are able to keep their Web costs as low as Gainer has. Gainer has been successful at keeping his costs down because the company makes only relatively few of its products available on the Web, thereby avoiding the necessity of a store front or expensive custom programming.

Harness the Web to Build a New Business

If you have developed a new product or service, you may be able to use the Web to fast-forward the process of building a customer base. To make this work, you will need to start off with these ingredients:

A superior product that would appeal to people who use the Web
Professional packaging
A Web site set up to display the product and take orders
Samples to send to reviewers and people who are in a position to promote the product
The ability to produce and deliver the product in a timely fashion
The time and patience to find and participate in discussion groups that would include likely prospects for your product

One company that got its start this way is Espirit Development Corporation, the inventors of Wipe Out! CD Repair Kit (http://www.cdrepair.com). The product, which was invented by one of the founders of the company, repairs scratches and eliminates skipping on CDs and CD-ROMs making them work like new.

As a small company, Espirit didn't have the funding to do a major media campaign to launch Wipe Out! Instead, they put up a Web site and sent out press releases and samples of the product to the media.

"The Web gives us credibility and the ability to provide information whenever people want it," explains Marc Howard Guest, the company's CEO. "It lets us show customers a demo, lets them know we have been awarded a patent on the product, and it lets them get information without worrying about being pestered by salespeople."

Guest believes the Web site also helped establish the startup's credibility to the press. Reviews of Wipe Out! appeared in forty publications, and *PC World* featured the product on the front cover of their October 1998 issue.

Guest and his partners spent "thousands of hours" over a period of eighteen months getting their Web site registered in Web search engines, posting to online newsgroups related to CDs and CD-ROMs, making contacts, and getting listed in import–export trade directories. "People who tried the product raved about it and recommended it to friends and relatives," says Guest. "The customers became our best salespeople. We grew from nothing to almost $200,000 in sales in our first year on the Web."

Guest had also tried banner advertising, but found it was only marginally effective. "Word of mouth is better than anything."

> ▶ **Tip**
> Use your Web site to explain difficult to understand concepts. Michael Fox, director of Internet sales and marketing for Promo-T.Com reduced operating costs and increased sales leads by using the Web to demonstrate their line of compressed T-shirts. The shirts are used as promotional giveaways by large and small companies, but were difficult to explain on the telephone. Sales increased 100 percent after the company put up their Web site, and the company eliminated the need to send out samples of the product to nonqualified leads. One other benefit: the sales cycle was reduced from 6 to 8 weeks down to 2.

Make Income Projections and Timelines Realistic

Just like a conventional business, your Internet business is likely to take time to get established. You have to find ways to attract attention, get people to look at your offerings, and find ways to capture their names and get repeat customers. (See Chapter 14 for more details on how to accomplish these goals on the Internet.)

Plan on no more than 1 in 1,000 visitors making a purchase until you build a steady stream of repeat customers. If you have a unique product that has gotten top product reviews and good word of mouth advertising, or if you have a wide range of products and a unique market, your percentage may be higher. WipeOut! converts about 5 percent of its visitors to sales. But that conversion rate is highly unusual for new small businesses. WipeOut! had few competitors when it was introduced and got great reviews from computer magazines; further, reviews usually ran with their Web site address included. Most new products don't get off to that kind of a start.

Don't Plan on Advertising Revenue to Sustain a Startup

Unless you reach a very targeted market, you aren't likely to sell advertising directly to big companies or their media buyers. Big companies—companies that are willing to pay $20 or more CPM (cost per thousand impressions)— generally don't want to buy advertising unless they can be guaranteed at least a million impressions. (When a Web page loads and displays an ad, it's counted as an impression. You can estimate your total number of impressions by looking at the number of page views your Web site statistics shows per month.) There are exceptions, however, such as when a Web site targets a very specific niche market that the advertiser wants to reach.

Use an Advertising Network or Broker to Get Ads for You

You may be able to sell advertising space on your pages through a media firm that pools together all the available advertising space from small Web sites and sells the space to big advertisers. Don't expect to make much money this way, however. Chances are you won't make more than $1 to $2 CPM ($50 to $100 a month for 50,000 impressions) until you can attract a lot of traffic to your site.

Several media-buying companies set up these pools of Web sites. Each has its own spe-

Don't Expect Miracles

Although there are people who build Web stores into successful businesses, you can't count on opening a storefront and having it become an immediate hit. In fact, there's no guarantee you'll ever make a profit. Those businesses that are most successful on the Web are similar in many ways to businesses that are successful off the Web. They are started by someone with knowledge and a deep interest in a product line; they are run by someone with the drive and focus to make the business successful; and they offer products or services that focus on a specific niche market.

People who buy turnkey business opportunities without any experience in a field and those who are selling the same mail-order products as thousands of others who buy a particular opportunity offering, or fall for the same old 900-number "opportunities," envelope stuffing schemes, and other get-rich-quick scams aren't likely to make much, if any, money.

cific method for sharing revenue with the Web sites for which they sell advertising. Usually, however, there is some specific percentage of the total advertising revenue designated to go to the pool of participating Web sites and some percent that the agency keeps for itself. Each Web site within the pool gets some percent of the amount set aside for the pool. For example, the media company may have a plan whereby they get 50 percent of all advertising revenues, and the other 50 percent goes to the pool of Web sites. If the total advertising revenues collected is $5,000, the media company would get $2,500, and the Web site pool would get $2,500. If there were three Web sites in the pool, and 10 percent of the ads were actually placed on site A, site A would get 10 percent of the Web site pool's $2,500, or $250. If 40 percent of the ads sold were placed on site B, site B would get $1,000, and if the remaining 50 percent of the ads sold were placed on site C, that site would get $1,250. If there are more Web sites participating in the pool, the actual percentages and dollar amounts would be proportionately lower.

> ## Save Time by Multitasking
>
> If you are self-employed, you've probably already learned how to do many things at one time. But did you know you can do that on the Internet, too? You can get your mail while your Web browser is loading up a screen. Or if you have several places you want to check into, you can open up multiple copies of your Web browser. Then you can switch between windows to read each site. This is extremely useful if you're comparing prices of products listed on competing companies' Web sites.

Though a number of media companies pool advertising from several Web sites in this way, some work only with the Web sites that are getting hundreds of thousands of page views a month. There are a few that work with smaller sites, however. Here are two:

24/7 Media	Burst Media
http://www.247media.com/	http://www.burstmedia.com/

For a long list of advertising networks, brokers, and reps, see http://www.adbility.com/WPAG/baf_network.htm or http://www.markwelch.com/bannerad/baf_network.htm.

Sell Ads for a Flat Rate

Instead of selling ads by the CPM, price them at a flat rate. If your market is very focused, offer ad space on an exclusive basis to companies that serve your market. For instance, if your Web site features content about gardening, you might allow only one company that sells fertilizer to advertise on your pages, and only one company that sells seeds. The ads would run for a set period (say, six months) on every page that was related to the products. You benefit because you don't have to keep track of impressions. The advertiser benefits since they will be the sole advertiser of their type of product on your Web site.

Make Money Through Affiliate Programs

Affiliate programs are about the closest thing you'll find to a free lunch. These programs pay you for referring customers to them. Typically, once you sign up to be an affiliate, you'll be given a tracking code that will be used to identify purchases made by people clicking on the link from your Web site. When people entering the store using your link make a purchase, you earn from 5 to 15 percent of the purchase price.

Some of the more widely known affiliate programs are those offered by Barnesandnoble.com, Amazon.com, OutPost.com, OfficeMax.com, 1-800-Flowers.com.

You can find extensive information about affiliate programs, including what to look for and which work best at http://www.associateprograms.com/.

You can find a directory of ad resources such as affiliate programs and media buying and selling at http://www.ad-guide.com/.

Learn to Manage E-mail Efficiently

E-mail gives you a quick and efficient way to communicate with customers, suppliers, competitors, employees, and others in your field. But if you're not careful, it can become a big time drain instead of a productivity tool. Notes from customers, friends, mailing lists you join, news reports, as well as ads from vendors you deal with and spam from people (unsolicited advertising) can quickly fill your mailbox. Sorting through it all can eat up hours of your time each day.

Dealing with the problem often requires resolve and changing your habits.

If much of your mail has similar questions, set up a database of boiler-plate responses. Copy and paste the responses into the e-mail, making only those changes absolutely necessary for the circumstances. Another possible solution is to get someone else to read your e-mail. Let them filter out the junk from the important mail.

If your e-mail program will let you, set it up to highlight mail from important contacts and customers. I have Microsoft Outlook set up so that incoming mail from an important client is highlighted in red. Even if I have

▶ **Tip**

Be sure to copy the e-mail address from business cards when you enter their contact information into your database. If you can't get through to the person in follow-up phone calls, try e-mail.

twenty or thirty messages all show up at once, I can immediately pick out the messages from this client without stopping to read the from and subject lines on all the other mail.

Set up a folder system and e-mail filters that let you automatically assign nonurgent mail (such as mailing lists) to particular folders based on a subject line or from line. Doing so lets you read that mail at leisure, thereby helping you avoid the temptation to "just take a peek" and blow half the morning on some unimportant mail.

> ### ▶ Caution
>
> Don't delete mail just because you don't recognize the e-mail address. You might delete something important that way. I almost deleted mail one time that had details I needed for a $25,000 contract. I knew the mail would be sent to me, but it came from a different e-mail address than I was used to seeing for this contact. Fortunately, something in the subject line made me hesitate for a moment before I hit delete.

If you use AOL, set up mail controls to block mail from individuals or domains that regularly send spam.

Read the from line and the subject line of mail, and use those to determine whether to read mail or delete it sight unseen.

Set up autoresponders on your Web site to handle functions like providing routine information. These can be made to work something like fax-back systems where anyone sending an e-mail to a particular e-mail address will receive an automated reply. Most Web-hosting companies can set these up for you or will give you the tools to set them up yourself for little or no additional money.

Store e-mail addresses along with other contact information. It's a lot quicker to find an e-mail address by searching a database or a contact manager than it is to hunt through old mail or even a long list of names in an address book.

Sign up for the digest version of mailing lists. Internet mailing lists can provide a wealth of information. Unfortunately, though, the better lists can generate dozens of messages a day. Opening and closing each message as it arrives can be time consuming at best. But most mailing lists give you an alternative. They let you sign up for a "digest" version of the list. Then instead of getting a message every time someone replies to the newsgroup, you'll get a single digest periodically that has been edited to include only the most pertinent "posts" to the list.

Sign off lists you don't have time to read regularly.

Set your mail program to get your mail automatically at periodic intervals.

E-mail Aliases

Set up a "play" e-mail address to use for reading newsgroups or for reading and responding to message boards on Web sites and online services. Doing so should help separate spam and nonurgent mail from your more important business mail. An added advantage: If you use an e-mail address from a domain name that can't be associated directly with you, you can snoop on your competitors and get feedback from customers without anyone knowing who you are.

Make Your Business Look Bigger with Alias E-mail Accounts

Big corporations have one person who gets all inquiries on a Web site for sales, someone else who gets press inquiries, someone else who handles billing, and so on. You can look bigger by doing the same thing. Instead of having all mail go to you, set up aliases for key "departments" in the company. For example, you might have e-mail aliases set up for sales@yourname.com, support@yourname.com, and investorrelations@yourname.com. The mail can all be forwarded to you, but the people who sent the mail will never know unless you tell them. An added benefit: When someone leaves your company mail and their e-mail address is erased, mail won't get sent back unread to the reader. It will go to whoever is assigned to read the mail coming from the e-mail alias account.

Protect Your Home Business

If you work from home and worry that including an address and phone number will cause thieves or other unsavory types to show up on your doorstep, rent a mailbox at the post office or a mailbox acceptance center such as Mailboxes, Etc. Choose a post office or mail acceptance center that is in a different town from the one in which you live. Use an 800-number for your incoming calls instead of your regular exchange, and your real location won't be readily detectable. (See Chapter 16 for ideas on working with new clients you must see in person.)

Chapter 14

BUILD AND PROMOTE

YOUR WEB SITE*

* Without Going Broke

W hen I was writing this chapter, I posted a message on the Online Advertising (http://www.o-a.com) mailing list asking people to tell me about how they made or saved money on the Web. One individual wrote to me saying that small businesses lose money more often than they make it on the Web because of the high cost of creating and running a Web site.

Unfortunately, there is some truth in what that individual had to say. Many small businesses have spent more money on the Web than they will ever make or save.

But the good news is that doesn't have to happen. You can profit from the Web if you plan carefully and use your ingenuity.

Decide What the Purpose of Your Web Site Will Be

If you go to business meetings or look in the local papers, you will find numerous service providers who offer Web site design, hosting, and marketing services. Among them are advertising agencies and marketing firms, desktop publishers, office support services, commercial artists, computer programmers, computer consulting firms, and companies that also sell Web site hosting and Internet connectivity services.

Some of them will have experience setting up huge corporate sites, some will have limited experience building Web sites, and some may be people claiming to be Internet consultants or Web site developers because they have just purchased a Web page creation program and assume that owning the program gives them the expertise to design Web sites.

Many will try to convince you to buy their services now, whether or not you know anything about the Web—or about them. Don't be pressured by their solicitations. Don't sign any agreements to buy Web site space or to have a Web site created until you have a clear vision of what you want the Web site to accomplish.

Every decision you make about your Web site should be focused on what you want to achieve by having a Web site. Do you want to use the Web site primarily as a capabilities statement or online version of your press kit or promotional materials? Will you be selling products to consumers directly from your Web site? Or will your primary purpose be communicating with customers, employees, or suppliers?

To avoid spinning your wheels or spending money on services you don't need, make a list of all the capabilities you need and put them in priority order.

Determine Your Needs

To save time, money (and possibly your sanity), plan out the Web site carefully before you sign any contracts or spend any money on developing it. You can determine what capabilities you'll need and gather the information you need to get accurate pricing estimates by answering these questions:

▶ Who do you want to use the Web site?
▶ How many people do you expect to use the site?
▶ How will you let them know about the site (how will you market it)?
▶ Who will do the marketing?
▶ What capabilities (ordering, database, audio, video, and so on) will you need?
▶ How often will you have to update the Web site?
▶ Who will do the updates?
▶ What will it cost to host the site (or for your own server and Internet connection)?
▶ What will it cost to design the Web site?
▶ What it will cost to market the Web site?
▶ What will it cost to update the site?
▶ How much will you have to spend on inventory?
▶ What will fulfillment costs be?
▶ Will you need warehouse space?
▶ Will you have to hire employees?
▶ How many sales or leads will you need to break even on costs?
▶ What sales volume do you want to attain?
▶ How much, if anything, do you expect to make in advertising revenues?
▶ How soon do you need to reach your sales goals?

Use the answers to these questions to determine what it will cost you to build the site and maintain it. Then compare your costs to the results you hope to achieve and determine if the cost will justify the results.

If the results will justify the cost, set specific goals and timelines for achieving the goals and start the project. At each step along the way, compare your progress to your needs to keep it on target.

If the results won't justify the costs, look for ways to cut expenses or increase revenues. Or don't build the site at all. You can reap many of the benefits of the Internet without having your own domain name and Web site.

Don't Purchase Your Own Internet Server

You don't have to have your own Internet server (computer dedicated to serving pages to the Internet) and Internet access lines to put your business on the Web. The most cost-effective way for most small businesses to launch and maintain a Web site is to rent server space from a Web-hosting company.

Similarly, if you don't have the time, skill, and interest to do a good job of designing a Web site, farm out the chore to a reputable contractor or Web design company. The reason is simple: The time you would have to invest to learn to create Web pages could be put to better use selling your products and services and running your own business.

> ▶ **Tip**
>
> If you are having someone design your Web site for you, be sure you have them assign all rights to the Web site to you. Under copyright laws, a designer owns all copyright to their designs. If you don't get a written agreement about ownership of the site upfront, the designer could prevent you from using your Web site if you decided to choose another designer.

Know What to Expect

With Web design, like other services, you don't always get what you pay for. High price is no assurance of good design or a result suited to the intended use for your site. One organization paid more than $9,000 to have their Web site designed and hosted for a year. The Web site consisted of only a few pages of text and one graphic image. There were no databases and no order forms. The only interactive feature was a function to send mail to the owners of the site. The entire job, including creating the graphic image, shouldn't have taken more than a day or two to create.

You could get ripped off like this, too, if you don't know what you are buying. Launching a Web site is a process that involves several types of activities. Depending on the nature of your site, those services will include some or all of the following:

▶ Setting up the Web site on a hosting service
▶ Hosting the Web site on an ongoing basis (storing the Web site on a computer, connecting it to the Internet)
▶ Registering a domain name (giving yourself a unique "address" on the Web, such as yourbusiness.com)

▶ Designing Web pages (similar to typesetting and laying out a newsletter)

▶ Designing artwork (creating original artwork for the Web site)

▶ Writing the editorial content for the Web site

▶ Programming a database to work on the Web (for mailing lists, surveys, catalogs, customer sales data, and so on)

▶ Registering the site with Internet search engines

▶ Marketing and promoting the site (on the Web and offline)

▶ Advertising (on the Web and offline)

▶ Scanning your graphics and text to make them usable on the Web

▶ Maintaining the site on an ongoing basis

Few companies offer all these services. Many, however, offer "complete" packages that include setting up and hosting the site along with design and limited maintenance. Although using a single source to do all the work sounds convenient, it isn't necessarily a good idea. The person who is a whiz at computer programming may have no artistic abilities and no eye for graphic design. Someone who is capable of putting text into html format may not know anything about creating the editorial content for the site or about Internet marketing. (Don't assume they can type well or spell words correctly either!) And the company that hosts the Web site may charge a small fortune to "design" your Web site, when all they do is plug your material into a cookie-cutter template that they use to "design" every Web site they create.

Furthermore, if you are charged a flat fee, you may wind up paying for services you don't need, or overpaying for the ones you do need.

To make sure the price you are quoted is fair, ask the provider to give you an itemized list of services they provide and to specify the fee they are charging for each service.

Get quotes from several vendors and compare them. Look at how much disk space you get, how much bandwidth you are allowed (how much data can be transferred monthly for the fee), and what extra charges you'll incur if you go over these amounts. If you plan to sell online, see if there are extra charges for a storefront, too. Ask whether you will have access to update the files yourself if you decide to; how many e-mail accounts you will be given; and whether there are extra charges for autoresponders, mailing lists, and other services you may want.

Don't Overbuy!

Even if you have big plans for your Web site, you aren't likely to need a tremendous amount of disk storage space or bandwidth right away. Getting a Web site up and running can take time. Decide which features of the site you want to set up first and purchase only the services you need for the initial launch. You can add on more pages, more bandwidth, more disk space, or even that storefront later on when you need them. That way you won't have to pay for them until you are ready to use them.

Know the Going Rates

Be wary of deals that offer you a set number of pages unless you have no plans to add anything to your site after it is set up. A page requires very little space on a computer. If you need to have only a few pages on the Internet, you shouldn't have to pay more than $10 or $15 a month for hosting them, plus a reasonable hourly fee for taking your material and converting it into html Web pages.

In 1999, Web-hosting prices for people who could build their own Web sites ranged from as little as $15 a month to $50 a month or more depending on the amount of computer (server) space needed and whether the Web site would require database, audio or video capabilities. A site costing $15 per month in hosting fees is adequate for most small businesses whose primarily goal is to put sales literature on the Web to get sales leads. Some hosting companies included shopping cart software (software for setting up a retail site) at no extra charge with host plans costing about $25 a month. Graphic artists and programmers typically charge $75 an hour and up. Conversion of documents to simple html pages costs between $15 and $25 an hour.

Find Affordable Web Hosting

If you will be creating your own Web pages or if you want to compare the prices your service provider quotes to price elsewhere, be sure to visit BudgetWeb.com   http://www.budgetWeb.com/budgetWeb/index.html. This Web site contains a directory of companies that offer Web-hosting services and a primer that explains some of the terms you may encounter in setting up your Web site. There is also a list of questions you should ask a Web-hosting company.

Ask for References and Check Them

Before you agree to have anyone design your Web site, ask for references. Get the names and URLs of Web sites they have designed for other companies. Look at those sites and see if you like them. Is the design of the pages attractive? Do they load quickly? Do they all look the same? Look around the sites for the e-mail address of the owners and send them e-mail. Ask if they were satisfied with the work that was done for them and if it was done in a timely fashion.

Use Ready-Made Shopping Cart Software

If you are selling products on the Web, look for Web-hosting companies that offer shopping cart or storefronts as part of their services. Many host sites offer this capability at no extra charge.

Do It on the Cheap

If you are a low-budget or no-budget operation and want to experiment with building your own Web site, several online services and Web portals allow you to create one or more pages as a feature of your membership. America Online subscribers are given up to 2 megabytes of disk space for each screen name on each master account. By using each of the five screen names that can be set up for one account, that adds up to a total of 10 megabytes of space, more than enough for most simple Web sites. GeoCities and Yahoo give you 11 megabytes of space. They offer a store-front setup option for $24.95 a month.

Although it is preferable to have your own URL, these types of free and low-cost sites make it possible for do-it-yourselfers and skin-of-the teeth startups to test the waters and launch their businesses at relatively little cost.

Don't Hide What You Sell

In many instances, the "content" that visitors want is information about the product they want to buy. If you make it difficult to find your shopping area, if your pages take a long time to load, or if visitors can't find your order form, they will either give up or go shop in your competitor's online store.

To improve the shopping experience for the customer, try to keep each page to no more than 40 kilobytes. If you use graphics, use thumbnails with the descriptive text. The thumbnail-sized photos can be set up as clickable links to larger versions of the photo for anyone who wants to see them enlarged.

If you sell a lot of different items, try to classify them in some way to make them easier to find. For instance, if you were selling office supplies, you might have one category called paper and stationery, another called writing instruments, and another called software.

Make It Look Professional

It wasn't long ago that just having a Web site was enough to make a small, home-based business look more professional. It didn't much matter what the Web site actually looked like. But that's changing. Though there are still some pretty ugly Web sites that are relatively successful, customers for the most part expect a company's Web site to be as neat and professional looking as their printed sales literature and marketing materials. Anything less than a professional façade for your online shop will make your business look small and unreliable.

Make Your Site Easy to Navigate

Businesses and consumers today have little time to waste. If they can't find what they want quickly on your site, they'll move on. To help them find their way around, put a table of contents (often called a navigational bar or navbar) on your home page. Include a search function for the Web site as well.

Encourage Browsing and Impulse Buys

Retail stores get you to purchase more merchandise by putting sale merchandise at some distance from the cash register (so you have to walk through the store and see more things you may want to buy). They also increase sales by putting items that make good impulse buys in places that you pass through to get out of the store. Fast-food stores and supermarkets often have candy and magazines near the checkout counter. Clothing stores may have socks, jewelry, or perfume near the cash register.

You can use similar tactics on your Web site to increase product sales. For instance, if you have an article on how to choose digital cameras, create a small ad for digital cameras if you sell them and put it in the margin of the article. If you sell books, write short book reviews and put a link in each book review to a place on your site where the reader can buy the book you are reviewing. Another tactic: Run banner ads for your own products on editorial pages on your Web site. These ads will work like ads on the window of your favorite supermarket. They'll remind visitors of goodies you have in other parts of your Web site.

Tell Them How to Reach You

Customers want to know who you are and how they can contact you after they've made a purchase. And they want that information to be easy to find. If it isn't, they may question your honesty or credibility and move on to a competitor's Web site to make their purchase.

You can avoid that trap by having a "Contact us" button on every page of your Web site. The Contact us button can lead to a Web page that lists your business name, business e-mail address, telephone, fax, and other information customers may need to know. If you don't want to take the calls yourself, have an answering service take them for you.

Give Them Ordering Choices

Not everyone is comfortable giving out credit card information over the Internet, and not everyone likes to shop with a credit card. To maximize your sales, be sure you give customers alternative methods for making a purchase. In addition to your online order form, provide a way for people to order by telephone, fax, and mail. Make those options easy to find, too. If your customer has to hunt for ways to make a purchase, you'll lose sales.

If you find too many customers call in, fax, or mail their order, consider adding a surcharge for orders that aren't placed electronically. Or increase your prices slightly and then offer a discount for ordering online.

Include a Feedback Form

A feedback form serves three purposes. First, it gives your customers another way to reach you. Second, it lets you know what customers think about your products and services and what they wanted but can't find. Finally, the feedback form is good for public relations. Having it on your site will help customers form an impression of your company as one that cares what its customers have to say.

Put the feedback form where people can find it easily on your Web site. This might be on a navigational menu or as a text link.

▶ **Tip**

Remember the Internet is "on" twenty-four hours a day, seven days a week. People can and do use it all night long. If you don't have someone answering phones twenty-four hours a day, be sure to indicate your hours of operation and your time zone with your contact information.

Read and Answer E-mail At Least Once a Day

One of the leading attractions of the Internet is its immediacy. You can find information, shop for products, send and receive letters, place orders, send invoices, view pictures, and access documents twenty-four hours a day, seven days a week. But that's also one of the leading disadvantages of the Web, at least for Web site owners. Because the Web and online services are available twenty-four hours a day, visitors expect them to be staffed around the clock, too. If they have a question, they expect to get a response in hours, rather than days, as they might if they sent a question to your company using traditional mail.

To keep customers happy, therefore, plan to answer all e-mail within twenty-four hours or less. If you don't answer your e-mail in a timely fashion, your customers are likely to have little difficulty finding one of your competitors on the Web who will answer quickly.

Help People Who Stumble into Your Web Site Find Their Way Back

When visitors find your Web site, they may save or print some of your information to read at a later time. When they find that information later on, they may want to return to your site. To make sure they can find their way back, be sure that every page on your site includes the name of your Web site, your phone number, and your URL on the bottom of the page. To avoid typing that information in manually on every page, include it on the bottom of whatever template you use to create Web pages.

Shop Around for a Merchant Account

In order to accept credit cards, you'll need to get something called a merchant account. Banks offer merchant accounts to retail and service establishments that meet their customers face to face. But most traditional banks don't want to offer merchant account to home businesses, mail-order companies, and companies that sell on the Internet. That doesn't mean you can't get a merchant account though. There are third-party providers, called independent service organizations (ISOs), that do offer home-based businesses merchant accounts. These companies usually sell their services through sales representatives. To get an account through these companies, you have to pay an application fee. If your application is approved, you will need to purchase some type of software or some device to process your charge card orders.

Talk to several sales representatives before deciding where to apply for your account. Get a list of all the fees you will be charged. Ask how much the application fee is, how much the discount rate is (the percent of sales you pay on each transaction), and if there are any per-transaction fees you'll have to pay. (Those are flat fees you pay on top of the percent of sales. Usually the amount is about 25 cents per transaction.) Find out if there are monthly minimums or if there is any charge for sending you a monthly statement.

Finally, find out what the software or terminal will cost to process your charges.

If you can't locate a company that offers merchant accounts to Web businesses, contact your host site to see if they have a source they recommend. Or see the list posted on Business Know-How at http://www.businessknowhow.com/money/tips6.htm.

Don't Overpay for Credit Processing Software and Equipment

You don't always have to purchase the software or equipment for your merchant account from the merchant account provider. In fact, you may save money purchasing the software elsewhere. One company that sells terminals and software for processing credit card charges is:

Merchant Warehouse
72 Railroad Ave.
Norwood, MA 02062
800-941-6557
http://www.merchantwarehouse.com/

They also will refer you to banks that accept most businesses, even those that may have trouble getting merchant accounts from other sources.

Beware of Fraud

One of the drawbacks of selling on the Internet is the high incidence of credit card fraud. When you accept transactions over the Internet, you have no card to swipe, no photo ID to look at, and few other clues of whether the person presenting a credit card number is the owner of that credit card or authorized to use it. As a result, banks hold you 100 percent liable for all fraudulent transactions—even if they have been approved by the bank.

Thieves have a variety of ways of getting credit card numbers. Sometimes they use computer software to generate numbers at random until they find one that matches. Sometimes they retrieve charge card carbons from the trash at small retail stores, or they call consumers or send them e-mail telling them that due to a technical problem they need to confirm their credit card information (by telling the credit card number to the person who called or typing the number into e-mail or a form if it's on the Web).

There are several steps you can take to help minimize the potential for fraud. One is to use address verification and refuse to ship product to any place other than the address of the credit card holder. But sometimes thieves are able to get the address of the credit card holder, too, so address verification alone isn't enough. Be on guard for unusually high dollar amounts of sales, an unusual number of sales in a short time, and anything else that might signal a problem. Ask for a phone number as well as the shipping address. Before processing any sizable order, call the credit card holder to verify that the purchase was made. Have a field for e-mail address on your order forms and make it a required field. Be sure the address comes from a valid domain. (You can do that by opening a browser while you're connected to the Internet and typing http://www.domainname.com (where domainname.com is the name of the domain you are checking up on.) Another option: Send a "thank you for your order" message before you process the order. If the message comes back to you as undeliverable, don't send the order.

A couple of resources have sprung up to attempt to address the problem. The least expensive option is to become a member of AntiFraud.com (http://www.antifraud.com) and compare e-mail addresses and IP information against their lists of known fraudulent sources. More expensive resources that may help are offered by Cybercash and Cybersource. These services are expensive to set up, but if your sales volume is high and you are experiencing a high rate of fraud, they are worth investigating.

Automate

The Internet has the unique ability to turn your spare bedroom office into a high-traffic Web site. Although that probably won't happen overnight, when traffic does develop, you will run yourself ragged unless you've devised ways to automate routine tasks. As you grow your business, take the time to analyze every step of the work you and your staff do. Make sure there is nothing you are doing just because it has always been done that way. Be on the lookout for routine jobs that take a substantial amount of time to complete. If there are such jobs being done, consider whether you could streamline the process by using off-the-shelf software to perform some of the work or by paying someone to write a program for you.

Although you may need to spend a considerable amount of money to automate your procedures, there's a good chance you'll quickly recover your cost in the form of increased staff productivity.

For example, we run about seventy chats a week in the Business Know-How Forum on America Online. These chats are scheduled across several different chat rooms, and are usually held between about 8 P.M. and midnight Sunday through Friday. Each chat has a host, and each host has a general subject area he or she is supposed to cover. Each week each host chooses a specific topic related to their subject to discuss.

One of my staff members has to get the topic descriptions for all of the chats and compile them into one weekly listing of live chats. Before we automated the procedure, getting and tracking those changes took my staff person four days a month.

We cut that time down to four *hours* a month by automating the process. That allowed my staff person to use her time in ways that were more rewarding both to her and to the company.

Do It, Dammit!

Don't spend months agonizing over every little detail of your Web site. One of the most important things to remember about a Web site is that it's fluid. It doesn't have to be perfect the first time. Or the second. Or the third.

"Test and learn, test and learn," says Dan Wasserman, CEO of Thorne, West, a consultancy that specializes in Internet and hi-tech marketing. "The beauty of the Web is its immediacy. Unlike traditional media, you don't have to wait months to get a reaction."

Unlike traditional media, it won't cost you a fortune to make changes if something is not just right. All you will have to pay for is the time it takes to actually make the change. So, be brave. Put the Web site up. Let your customers tell you by their purchases or their feedback what is working and what isn't

Make Your Computer Work for You

Ask your Web site provider about setting up an autoresponder to answer product inquiries. An autoresponder an e-mail address works like a fax-back system. Whenever an autoresponder receives e-mail, it automatically sends a reply containing a form letter. You might set up an autoresponder to answer inquiries customers might have about a new service. Be sure the letter sent out by the autoresponder includes an e-mail address and a telephone number for further inquiries.

working to their satisfaction. You might even set up a survey to solicit feedback from your visitors. Remember, your site doesn't have to be a work of art. It just has to be functional.

Plan to Promote the Web Site

People won't find your Web site just because it's there. Although your Web site serves as an advertisement for your products or services, there's one big difference between the Web site and print advertising: There's no publisher or broadcast media putting a unique collection of articles, shows, and advertisements into your audience's hands on a regular basis. You have to find affordable ways to do that yourself or to get others to do it for you.

Keep It up to Date

Nobody likes to read yesterday's news. And few people like to read old Web pages. Even if the main purpose of your Web site is to serve as a corporate brochure, try to update your site periodically with new information. New articles, fact sheets, handouts from seminars you give, new information about your business are all appropriate. Check periodically, too, to see if the overall look of your Web site is in tune with what most of the Web is doing. Web site design has style trends just as fashion design does. Having a Web site that sports yesterday's look leaves the same kind of negative impression that a frayed or seedy-looking business suit would make.

Shy Away from High-Priced Banner Advertising

Banner advertising is a numbers game. Like other forms of advertising, the more your banner is seen, the more likely it is that some sales will result. But those sales don't come cheap. Most high-traffic sites charge by the number of impressions (number of times your ad is displayed, no matter how briefly the page it is on is left open). If your ad is placed on a page that has a very similar audience to yours, no more than 1 or 2 percent of the people will click on your banner. If placement is random, that click-through rate may be as low as or lower than 1/10 of a percent.

Click-throughs don't equate to sales, either. They are more like sales leads. Once someone clicks into your site, you have to "convert" them to customers by getting them to make a purchase, sign up for a mailing list, browse through your site, or take whatever other action you want them to take.

So, before you purchase a banner ad, work out the numbers. For example, assume you have a product with a proven need and few competitors. You might be able to convert 5 percent of the people who clicked on the ad to become customers. If you buy 100,000 advertising impressions at $20 CPM, your cost for purchasing the advertising space will be $2,000. If

1,000 people (1 percent of the 100,000 impressions) click through the banner and get to your Web site, and you have a 5 percent conversion rate, you could expect fifty people to become customers. Each customer would have to spend at least $40 just to allow you to break even on the cost of the advertising. If the click-through rate for the ad were 2/10ths of a percent, you'd get only 200 click-throughs. Assuming the same 5 percent conversion rate, you could expect only ten individuals to become customers. Those ten individuals would then have to account for $200 in sales or advertising revenues just to cover the cost of the ad. Factor in the cost of your inventory, labor, and overhead, and the amount of revenue each click-through would have to generate to be profitable is even higher.

Big businesses with multiple products and multiple retail outlets benefit long term from repeat sales and back-end sales (sales of additional products to the customer). If they have other retail outlets, they benefit from the name recognition a banner ad campaign creates as well. Small businesses usually don't have deep enough product lines or pockets to wait for such long-term benefits.

> ### ▶ Note
> Banner ads can be effective if you can find Web sites that attract the market you want to reach. Since small Web sites are often looking for interesting information to pass along to their visitors, consider sending the Web site owner tips about your product they can e-mail to their visitors. Or, make a special offer avaiable for their visitors. Give the Webmaster all the code they may need to put the ad online, too. The easier you make it for a Web site to promote what you do, the more likely it will be that they will not only be an advertiser, but an active supporter of your product or service.

Get a Little Help from Your Friends

Networking is just as useful in the online world as it is in traditional businesses. Contact friends, business associates, and noncompeting businesses in your industry and ask them about exchanging Web links. To get others to help promote your site, look for ways you can help them accomplish their goals.

Anders Brownworth and "Lizi" Obolensky used this strategy to attract attention when they started Evantide Graphical, a Web development business. They launched the business in 1995 when relatively few people used the Web and even fewer understood its potential. As a result, Brownworth and Obolensky spent most of their time trying to educate their customers. "We found ourselves repeatedly doing Web 101 as the first phase of our sales pitch, just to lay the groundwork," says Obolensky. "We realized we needed to design a sample of our Web services so people could better grasp our visual concept for this new marketing tool."

For their sample, they created a Web site to celebrate the heritage and local culture of the Hamptons, the ritzy resort community on Long Island, New York, that has long attracted the rich and famous. "Our goal in designing *the*Hamptons.com (http://www.thehamptons.com) was to build a marketplace that would promote the Hamptons, sell local products, and attract high-end advertisers who could benefit from the cobranding affiliation of the community Web site."

The strategy worked. The Web site won several awards for design excellence, was featured in newspapers, on Internet sites, and in David Siegel's book *Secrets of Successful Web Sites.* The critical acclaim focused positive attention on the community. And the community lavished attention on its namesake Web site. The Rogers Memorial Library made the Internet and *the*Hamptons.com the theme of its annual Summer Gala Event, which commands a pricey $350 per ticket. American Express promoted *the*Hamptons.com in their *Hamptons Tour Guide*, which was distributed to 15,000 targeted people. The Hampton Classic Horse show, which attracts more than 60,000 spectators, made *the*Hamptons.com their official Web site for several years and included the site in their press kits and sponsor kits. Local establishments that advertised on the site benefited from all that publicity, as did the site's creators.

Establish Link Relationships with Noncompeting Businesses in Your Industry

You don't have to know famous people or win design awards to capitalize on cross-promotional opportunities. If you keep your eyes open, you'll find cross-promotional opportunities all around you. Look for businesses on the Web that target a similar audience to yours, but that don't directly compete with you. Exchange Web site links, ads, and plugs. For instance, we have a link to the publisher of Business PlanPro on our business startup page, (http://www.businessknowhow.com/bkhstartup.htm) since people starting businesses can benefit from business planning software. The publisher (Palo Alto Software) has a link to my Web site in their list of business information Web sites. You'll also find links back and forth between the Business Know-How Web site and Adams Media's BusinessTown.com and CareerCity.com.

Exchange Links with Your Competitors

That's done surprisingly often, particularly among Web sites whose primary focus is providing information. When there's more than enough market share to go around and you and your competitors may each benefit from added exposure, it's worth testing joint links. Watch your site statistics to see whether you benefit from the arrangement.

Get Found by Search Engines

Imagine walking into a large public library and trying to find this book if there were no catalog system in use. Finding anything on the Internet would be equally difficult without some method of cataloging Web sites. Fortunately, a number of companies have developed huge, searchable databases of Web sites on the Internet. These databases are called search engines, and there are hundreds of them. The more of these search engines that list your site, the better chance you have of being found.

Because so many Web sites are cataloged by each search engine, you have one additional hurdle to face after you get your site listed. Any search for a common word can result in thousands of matches for the search terms. If a search engine finds 25,000 pages, few people are going to find your Web site if it shows up as number 19,347 in the list of sites found. So, your challenge is to get your Web site to show up near the top of the lists of sites displayed when someone searches on keywords that relate to your site.

Among the ways to help ensure your Web site comes up near the top in search engines are these:

▶ Update pages frequently.

▶ Use text containing words people are likely to search for on the pages you register with search engines. Use those keywords several times on the page if appropriate, and try to get at least some of the words up close to the top of the page.

▶ Register more than one page with search engines if appropriate.

▶ Stay up-to-date on what the search engines look for by reading articles at http://www.searchenginewatch.com.

▶ Learn as much as you can about the criteria search engines use to rank pages, then adjust your pages to optimize them for various search engines. You might want to optimize your home page for one search engine, and a table of contents page for another search engine.

▶ Learn to use the metatag function of html to write brief descriptions of your pages and to enter keywords that people may search for. Not all search engines use these; carefully chosen metatags will help get your page found on those search engines that do use them.

▶ **Warning**

Don't use your competitor's trademark in your metatags. You could be sued if you do.

▶ Make the title of your page relevant to the subject matter and typical keywords people will search for.

▶ Choose a Web site name that contains keywords people will look for.

▶ Use your own name as a domain name or in a page name and on pages of text if people are likely to search for you by name.

▶ Be sure that each of your Web pages has links to other pages on your site to make it easy for visitors to wander through.

Study Pages That Come Up Near the Top of Search Engine Lists

Look at the text on the pages, and then look at the source code (go to the View menu in your Web browser and then look for something that says "source"). Look at the page description and the keywords used in the metatags. Consider using those words in your own text and metatags.

Find Out What Sites Link to Your Competitors

Links bring you traffic. The more sites that link to yours, the more ways there will be for Web users to find you. An easy way to determine what Web sites might be interested in linking to your Web site is to find out what Web sites are linking to your competitors. You can do that quickly by using the Alta Vista search engine at http://www.altavista.com. Once there, put your cursor in the search box and type, http://www.competitorurl.com, but replace the "competitorurl.com" with the name of your competitor's domain. For instance, if your competitor's domain name is greatgifts.com, you'd type in http://www.greatgift.com.

Save the pages or print them out.

Next, if you've had your Web site up for a while, do the same search, but enter your domain name. Print out that listing and compare it to the listing for your competitor. Contact sites that link to your competitor but don't link to you and ask if they'd consider adding a link to your site.

Hire Someone to Do the Grunt Work

Promoting your business inexpensively on the Web requires considerable time—time that you might use more profitably working on other aspects of your business. If you find the time to do the promotional work becoming a burden, consider hiring someone else to do the grunt work. A family member, teenager, or anyone who offers typing or office support services could easily do the work if you provide a description of your Web site, a letter to send Web masters to request a link, and other instructions you want followed. If no one you know can do the job, search the National Small Business Network Directory at http://www.businessknowhow.net for at-home workers with your zip code or one nearby.

Put Links in Your E-mail Messages, Newsgroup and Message Board Postings

One of the best ways to get the name of your Web site known is to make sure people see it frequently. If you participate in online newsgroups or bulletin boards, be sure every message posted to the groups includes your business name and URL. And be sure to include your URL in every e-mail message you send. If people are interested in what you say and think of you as an expert on the subject matter, they will often go to your Web site out of curiosity or because they want more information about the subject or what you sell.

▶ **Tip**

Some newsgroups let you include a promotional slogan with your URL and others don't. Read the newsgroup for a few days to get a feeling for what is acceptable.

Link Your Free Web Site to Your Domain or Storefront

Look around the Web for communities that give members free Web sites. Set up a home page and one or two pages that seem to get a lot of traffic. Include links in the free Web site to your complete Web site. That way people looking through the Web sites in the free area may find yours and click through to your domain.

Setting up a Web site makes information about your products, services, or company available to millions of people around the world. But making the information available to customers and prospects doesn't mean any of them will ever see it.

Get Added Traffic Through Link Exchange Services

If you have unused advertising inventory, consider signing up with a service like LinkExchange (http://www.linkexchange.com). There are several companies that let you trade your advertising space (called advertising inventory) for free banners on other people's Web sites. These programs may bring you some traffic, but if your Web site doesn't bring in a lot of traffic on its own, you can't count on these programs to support your Web site or make a profit.

The reason goes back to the "numbers game" concept. Most banner exchange programs are on a two-to-one basis. You get one banner impression for every two banners displayed on your site. If you don't have a lot of traffic to begin with, you usually are not going to be able to have enough page views to generate much revenue or barter credits. But if you aren't using the ad inventory for any other reason, and you can get an advertising barter exchange or outsourcing service to include your space on a nonexclusive basis, there's no harm in trying. If it doesn't work out you can just discontinue the relationship. You can find a list of companies that have banner exchange programs by searching with any search engine for the words *link exchange* or *banner exchange*. One that has a long list of companies that have banner exchange programs is http://dir.yahoo.com/Computers_and_Internet/Internet/World_Wide_Web/ Announcement_Services/Banner_Exchanges/

▶ **Warning**

Don't use phony names to post false testimonials for your product or service. Such messages might be construed as false and deceptive advertising, which is a violation of advertising law and is potentially punishable by fines of $10,000 per incident.

Send Your Ads in E-mail Without Spamming

Not surprisingly, the way to make e-mail marketing work for you isn't much different from the way to make mailings sent through the postal service work: targeting. The more closely the list of people who see your ad match your ideal customer, the more likely you'll get response.

But how do you target e-mail? And how do you send it without getting accused of sending spam? The answer is to buy advertising space on e-mail newsletters and ezines (online magazines) that are sent out from Web sites that target your target audience. You can locate these Web sites by searching the Internet for Web sites that appeal to your target market, and writing to the Web master to see if he or she has a mailing list and if he or she accepts advertising. Or you can visit one of several sites that maintain lists of mailing lists. Look for appropriate matches, and contact the people responsible to see if they would be interested in running your ads. Be sure you read the list first, though, to be sure the list content is appropriate for your ads and that it attracts the type of audience you want as customers.

Here are places to find opt-in mailing lists, newsletters that sell advertising, and more:

http://www.copywriter.com/lists/

http://www.postmasterdirect.com/welcome.mhtml

The List Exchange

    http://www.listex.com/category.html

Liszt

    http://www.liszt.com/

CataList (catalog of L-Soft lists)

    http://www.lsoft.com/lists/listref.html

Oaknet publishing

    http://www.oaknetpublishing.com/services/welcome.cgi?269

OneList

    http://www.onelist.com

> ▶ **Tip**
>
> To get subscribers to your newsletter, put a button banner on your home page labeled "Free Newsletter" and link it to a subscription form. Be sure the button can be seen without using the scroll bar.

Develop Ways to Get People to Come Back to Your Site

Web site visitors have short memories. Once they've discovered your Web site, they are likely to forget it exists unless you remind them to come back. Constant advertising may remind some of your visitors to return, but a more effective way of capturing their attention in the future is to capture their e-mail addresses (with their permission) the first time they visit your site and then send them periodic reminders to visit or announcements of special sales.

Internet pioneer 1-800-FLOWERS.com (http://www.1800flowers.com) gets repeat Web business and provides a needed service to its customers with an online reminder system they've developed. The system lets customers enter the names and dates they would like to be reminded of. When the date nears, 1-800-FLOWERS.com sends the customer a reminder in e-mail far enough in advance so they can order a gift and have it arrive on time.

The company's Web site, which has won widespread recognition for design, features a mix of how-to information, flower-related trivia, and care and handling tips as well as special arrangements and gifts for various holidays during the year. The combination of these promotional elements with ongoing advertising has proved highly successful. As a result of these strategies, online and Internet sales now account for more than 10 percent of the company's total annual sales, which exceed $300 million.

Start Your Own Mailing List or Newsletter

One of the best ways to get visitors to return to your Web site is to correspond with them on a regular basis. Your "correspondence" can take one of two forms. It can be a one-way communication such as a newsletter or ezine sent to their e-mail address at regular intervals, or it can be a two-way mailing list (like some LISTSERV and majordomo lists), which allows those on the mailing list to send (post) messages to one another through the list.

If your goal is to get people back to your Web site, a one-way newsletter works best. It should contain teaser copy telling readers what's new on the Web site. The teaser copy works very much like a classified ad. Its purpose is to "sell" people on the idea of clicking on a link to get more information. The link then takes them to your Web site where they can see advertisers' ads or buy products you sell in addition to getting the information described in the teaser copy in your newsletter.

Here is an example of how the teaser copy might written:

Cleaner Keyboards

Your keyboard is the grungiest place in your office. But it doesn't have to be. Learn three simple ways to get the pretzel salt and hairs out from between the keys. Read about them in the "Bottoms Up" article on our Web site http://www.anywhere.com/features.htm.

To be useful a mailing list needs to be moderated. That means you or one of your staff will have to read all the messages that are submitted to it and choose the ones that will be allowed to get sent through to all members. This can be quite time consuming if many people join the list. But an unmoderated list quickly fills up with off-topic messages or unwanted ads. You'll also want to have a digested version of the list for those who don't want to read messages one by one. The companies that offer mailing list services will have instructions for creating the digest.

Include Paid Advertising in Your Newsletter or Mailing List

Once your list grows to about 2,000 names, you may be able to convince advertisers to run small ads in it. Until the majority of Internet users can receive html mail, these ads would be text ads that are very much like classified ads.

Promote Your Web Site Offline

Don't limit your promotional efforts to the Web. Be sure you promote your Web site in every way you can. Add the URL and your e-mail address to your business cards; include it in brochures, print advertisements, radio and TV advertising. Add the URL and e-mail address to your letterhead, too.

Hire Experts When You Are Ready

Once you are sure you have an income model that works for the Web, consider hiring professional help to promote your site. You can find a list of Internet-savvy marketers at http://www.markwelch.com/bannerad/baf_agency.htm

Keep up with the Industry

The Web changes daily. So do trends and marketing methods. Make an effort to keep up with what's happening by reading the information available at these sites and signing up for newsletters of interest.

> http://www.webpedia.com/
> http://www.larrychase.com
> Tenagra
>   http://marketing.tenagra.com/
> ClickZ Network
>   http://www.clickz.com/index.shtml

Chapter 15

CREATING AND WORKING
IN YOUR HOME OFFICE

Years ago, it seemed as though the only people who ever worked at home were novelists, babysitters, and artists. Today, business owners and telecommuting employees in a wide range of professions work from home some or all of the time. And with them at home are many of the same types of business equipment they would have in a corporate office. In fact, some home offices are better equipped than the employers for whom they work. Still, working at home isn't all a bed of roses. Here are tips and hints to make your home office work harder for you.

Let Necessity Dictate What Equipment and Supplies to Buy

There's never any shortage of cool new things to buy when you're in business or starting one. New tools, supplies, furniture, equipment, software, training materials and books are all appealing and potentially useful. But they all add to your cost of doing business. Before you buy new supplies, equipment, inventory, books, or software, make sure you really need them. Although that sounds like common sense, overbuying and buying on impulse are common mistakes and sometimes put small businesses into a big financial hole.

Newcomers to business are most often tempted to overbuy, but established business owners aren't immune to the practice either. To control your own spending, carefully consider how you will use what you want to buy and when you will need it. Are you managing now without the product you want to buy? Is there a specific contract you will be able to get if you have the piece of equipment you want to buy? Are you sure the contract would go to you and not to a competitor? Can you subcontract out a part of a job until you see whether there will be enough orders to pay back your investment in a reasonable amount of time? Or is your productivity and ability to compete being impaired because you don't have the item you want? Will the item you want to purchase be something you will use every day or only occasionally? Can you afford to buy the item and pay the credit card bill when it arrives?

Use All Available Space

If you are running out of space in your home office, chances are you have used all available table and cabinet tops for equipment, supplies, or inventory. But what about the walls and the floor? Could you be more productive if there were cabinets on the walls or storage space under your tabletops? The office superstores have a wide variety of hutches, shelving, and roll-away furniture that can give you the space you need.

> ▶ Tip
>
> Save time by organizing your work area so that things you need often are close at hand. Printer stands, telephone stands, and other home office desk accessories can give you the extra storage space you need to make your office more efficient.

Make Space in a Closet

One way to make more space if you work in a small room is to build your office into the closet. Remove the door, add bookshelves, and install a tabletop for the computer. Purchase a low, roll away file cabinet to fit under the table top.

Turn File Cabinets and a Door into a Desk

It's an old trick, but one that works: Get two, two-drawer file cabinets that are the same height, and then top them with an inexpensive door. You'll get a desk that's wide enough to hold a monitor and hard drive and keyboard at a small fraction of the cost of regular office furniture.

If the height of the file cabinet/desk is to high to be comfortable to work at, get a chair with a pneumatic seat and a foot rest. Then raise your seat up to a comfortable work height.

Buy Furniture and Equipment at Garage Sales and Auctions

If you are looking for items you can use in a home office, garage sales can be a good place to find used bargains. You're best bet: Look in weekly shoppers or newspapers for garage sales being held in high-income neighborhoods. Pay particular attention to those that indicate the sale is being held because the family is moving out of the area. Plan to get to those sales at the very earliest date and time indicated in the ad. If there's a phone number, call ahead and find out if they are selling what you want and if you can look before the sale starts.

Find Treasures in the Trash

Office furniture and equipment doesn't have to be new to be serviceable. You can often find what you want at considerable savings or even free if you are willing to accept merchandise that isn't brand new. My son once got me a commercial four-drawer filing cabinet for free because his employer was throwing it out. My son asked if he could have it, the employer said yes, and I've been using it ever since. Savings? About $125–$150.

Home offices aren't the only ones to find other businesses' castoffs useful. Paul Cimino, CEO of Snickelways Interactive, a multimillion-dollar ecommerce solution provider, furnished the company's first office with a combination of used furniture and castoffs he found by skateboarding at night through New York City streets.

Finding sources of used goods is easier than you may think, too. One way to find used merchandise is to look in the yellow pages. Search for the category of goods you want to buy and look for the word *used* or *remanufactured* in ads. Or look in the classified advertising section of newspapers and trade magazines for used items for sale and auction notices. Keep your ears open for news of companies leaving down, closing divisions, or closing down, too. They may be willing to sell you furniture or equipment for pennies on the dollar. The owner of a chemical laboratory once got all the lab tables and a hood he needed for expansion for a few hundred dollars by purchasing them from a company that was closing its laboratory division.

> ► **Important**
> Don't skimp on your chair. Buy a brand name chair that is ergonomically designed and sturdy. You'll save in the long run by avoiding backaches and other medical problems that inferior seating can cause.

Trade up!

One enterprising woman spotted a slightly outdated computer when she was shopping for office furniture at a garage sale. She bought the computer for $65 and then took it to a computer shop that gave her $500 for it as a trade-in on the purchase of a new computer she wanted.

The same person bought some office furnishings she didn't need herself at an auction, and then resold them for a profit at a yard sale. She used those profits to buy office supplies.

Match Your Work Surface to the Job It Has to Do

If you are going to be sitting or standing at your work area for more than a few minutes at a time, be sure it is comfortable and adequate for your needs. Measure any equipment you plan to put on a desk or table to be sure that it fits and that there is adequate space around it to work. A conventional 17-inch computer monitor is about 20 inches deep. If your desk is only 26 inches deep (as many desks sold for home use are), the keyboard is going to come right up to the monitor base, and you'll be sitting so close to the monitor that you'll develop a headache or eye strain.

Check Your Insurance Coverage

Don't assume all that expensive equipment you've purchased for your home office is covered by your home insurance policy. Call your insurance broker and ask! Many home insurance policies limit coverage for computer equipment, and don't cover computer systems used in a home business unless you've purchased an add-on policy called an endorsement or rider.

Be sure to tell your agent or broker exactly what you need covered and what the value of the equipment is. If your computer is a notebook computer and you take it with you when you visit clients or travel, be sure your agent knows. You may need a special policy to cover you for this purpose. Many riders that cover home office equipment don't cover equipment that leaves your office. Plan ahead and get the right protection for your needs.

Be sure to tell the agent if there is more than one computer in use in your home, too, and ask him or her to find out whether the policy or endorsement you are buying covers everything. Some riders will cover only one computer system in a home office. Double-check and read the policy once you get it.

While you're asking about equipment coverage, ask about liability coverage for injury to business contacts coming to your home. Again, you may require an inexpensive endorsement to give you adequate coverage.

Repetitive Stress Injury

Minimize your risk of repetitive stress injury by using a wrist rest. They do help! If your wrist aches after using a mouse all day, try replacing the mouse with a touch pad. Seek medical help if the condition doesn't improve in a few days.

Get More Coverage Than Endorsements to Homeowners' Policies Offer

If you need more insurance coverage for equipment or inventory than your homeowner's policy provides with an endorsement, you will need to purchase a businessowner's policy. These have been difficult to get in the past for home businesses, but several companies, including the Hartford and RLI offer them now. The policies typically offer a package of risk and general liability protection. Endorsements are available for your computer equipment, and an off-premises option provides insurance coverage for notebook computers if you travel. Insurance is available for specific business categories such as crafts, graphic arts, and publishing.

Trade associations or your insurance broker can provide additional leads to good policies. Expect to pay $200 to $700 or more for a business-owner's policy for your home business. Although that may sound like a significant expense, the amount is reasonable compared to what you could stand to lose without such insurance. Take the time to compare prices and coverage, too.

> ► **Important**
>
> If you have employees you may be required to carry workers' compensation for them even though your office is at home. Check with your accountant or state department of labor to determine what the laws are in your state.

Don't Forget About Professional Liability Insurance

No one likes to think about lawsuits when they start a business, and most home businesses think the only ones whoever get involved with lawsuits are big businesses and scam artists. Nothing could be further from the truth. If your home business causes individuals or businesses harm, you can be sued for their losses. If you are sued, your house and personal assets could be at risk.

Don't believe those who tell you incorporating will protect your assets if you should be sued. If you run a one-person business, you could be found personally liable for your own actions. If the company has employees, incorporation might protect your personal assets if one of your employees caused your corporation to be sued. But without insurance, the legal fees to defend the corporation might force you out of business. Without a business to support yourself and your family, how long are your assets likely to last?

To protect your savings, home, and other assets, you will need to purchase professional liability insurance. The insurance, which is often available through trade associations, may cost hundreds or even thousand of dollars a year. But considering what's at stake if you do get sued, insurance is not something to do without.

Get Rid of What You Don't Need
That old computer sitting on the corner of your desk may have sentimental value, but are you actually using it? If not, toss it out. If it has programs and data you might need sometime in the future, retrieve the data first, or store the computer in the basement or another room.

Clean your file cabinets out before you buy another file cabinet, too. If you have been in business long, you'll be surprised at what you will find. If there are records you think you may need, but don't need to access regularly, put them in a plastic storage container and move them to a basement or garage or other out-of-the-way area. Make copies of important documents such as your business license, certificate of incorporation, long-term contracts, or other essential information. Put the originals in a safe deposit bank and keep the photocopies with your other stored records.

Shop for Office Supplies and Equipment at Midnight

Or shop any time of the day or night that it's convenient without ever leaving home. All the major office supply stores and several computer manufacturers have set up stores on the Internet. You can search for products, compare prices between stores, and place your order all in the middle of the night if it's convenient.

One added benefit: Since you don't see as much in an online store as you would if you walked in the doors of the retail outlets, you are less likely to see and purchase items you don't really need.

Buy for the Future

Buying a laptop computer? Look for one that includes a built-in CD ROM and floppy disk drive, and lets you use both at the same time as the battery. A big hard drive and lots of RAM are just as important on a notebook computer as they are on a desktop, too.

Recycle Paper

Chances are you print out a lot of information that you don't need to keep. To keep costs down, don't throw out the sheets of paper after you've read them. Recycle them. Either feed them back through your printer and use the blank sides for rough drafts of your work, or do what Marilyn Strong, of Strong Communications Group in Castlegar, British Columbia, Canada, does. She cuts up the paper into notepaper size and staples it together in small notepads.

Eliminate the Word *Home* When Discussing Your Business

When you introduce yourself or present your products and services to clients, don't tell them you work from home. Although millions of men and women work from home, there are still many businesses that won't buy from you because they consider home business owners to be less reliable and less professional than businesses owners who operate from traditional commercial locations. Others may buy from you but not be willing to pay you as much as they'd pay someone who has a "real" office.

You should never lie about any aspect of your business. But neither do you have to volunteer unimportant information. If you rented an office suite in the Smith Building, you wouldn't be likely to introduce yourself by saying, "Hello, I'm John Wolff. I run a Smith Building business producing newsletters." Similarly, there's no reason to introduce yourself by telling prospects that you run a home business producing newsletters. Remember, your business is the work you do, not where you do it.

▶ **Tip**
Don't hang out your shingle! Putting a sign with your business name in your window or on your door could cause neighbors to complain and force you to stop working from home.

Roll with the Punches

Despite your best efforts to keep your home out of your office when customers are on the phone (or visiting), there will always be times when something happens to blow your cover. The mailman may ring your doorbell while you are on the phone, or your cat may decide you're spending entirely too much time talking on the telephone and leap onto your lap, landing claws out on your shorts-clad, sunburned legs. Or one of your toddlers may start screaming.

If the interruption is momentary, sometimes a clever line will save the day. One entrepreneur I was speaking to on the telephone quipped that someone was testing his burglar alarm system when his two dogs started barking furiously during our conversation.

If the interruption isn't momentary, the best thing to do is to say there seems to be an emergency in progress. Ask for the customer's phone number if you don't know it, and say you'll call him or her right back. Take care of the emergency and then immediately make the call back.

Get Rid of the Kids

Well, for a little while each day or week, at least. Send them to nursery school, or to daycare or to a relative's house so you can work undisturbed or make calls to clients. If they are in school all day, work while they are away. Don't use that time to do errands or do the wash or clean the house. You can do those chores after the kids get home or during the time you would have to spend commuting to and from a job in the outside world.

Use Templates for Documents You Prepare Often

Formatting documents so they look attractive and professional can be time consuming. You have to choose appropriate typefaces for headlines, the body of the text, and other elements, and figure out how to position those elements in the location on the page where you want them.

Save time by using templates to create your documents. Templates are the computer equivalent of blank forms. They are created with a word processor, database, spreadsheet, or page layout program, and contain stylistic elements and standardized text that you use over and over again. They are typically used for memos, invoices, letters, fliers, brochures, and other documents you create frequently.

Many software programs come with a set of templates for commonly used documents. Microsoft Word, for example, comes with templates for faxes, memos, labels, and other documents. Excel, Access, PowerPoint, and FileMakerPro (a much easier-to-use database than Access) and most other top-of-the-line software come with templates for doing common tasks.

But you can also make your own templates. If your logo is scanned into your computer, for instance, you can make a template for your letterhead and call it up whenever you need to write a letter. Or you can put your logo on a template for fax cover sheets and other frequently used documents. Estimate forms, statements, proposals, and any document you use often can be set up as templates. To use them, you just call up the appropriate template and add the nonstandard information.

Don't Be Too Available

Just because you work at home doesn't mean you have to be available to your customers round the clock. If you don't want customers to call or visit after a certain hour, make that plain. If they insist on calling anyway, don't pick up the phone. Corporate executives aren't the only ones entitled to screen their calls. If people knock on your door late at night, don't answer. They won't be happy, but do you really want to be bothered late at night?

Don't Look as Though You're Alone

If you do meet clients in your home, you should take some safety precautions. Try to keep all expensive equipment out of site. Try to get to know customers before inviting them to meet you at your home. When a new customer does arrive, look out the window before you open the door, and if you have any uneasy feeling about letting him or her in, go with your gut. Don't let the customer in. Your personal safety is more important than having a new client.

If you are alone, leave a radio or TV on in another part of the house so that it sounds as though there might be someone else around. Leave lights on throughout the house, too.

Chapter 16

CHOOSING AND USING

OFFICE EQUIPMENT

Many of today's small and home-based businesses are possible only because of the advances in office equipment in recent years. Low-cost computers, printers, fax machines, and photocopiers make the small office boost productivity; look professional; and get connected to customers, suppliers, and information. But the widespread availability of office electronic equipment combined with the speed with which such equipment becomes obsolete makes equipment a recurring expense for many small offices. Here are some time- and money-saving tips and hints for choosing and using small office electronic equipment.

Don't Buy the First Model of a New Product

Manufacturers work very hard to make brand new products work flawlessly. After all, they want rave reviews to help make the product a success. The very newness of the product, however, usually means that as it goes into widespread use, purchasers will either find minor flaws the manufacturer missed or have suggestions to enhance the performance or usability of the product. In fact, by the time the first model hits the retail stores, the new improved versions may already be in design or production.

Unless the product is likely to make or save enough money to at least pay back its cost before the new model hits the streets, wait a few months to make your purchase. Read reviews in online and print publications, and look for others who have purchased the product to see how they like it. Doing so can save you hundreds of dollars in upgrade costs and dozens of hours of frustration if first-time users discover the new model or new program doesn't operate quite as advertised.

List the Features You Need Before You Shop

Take the time to do your homework before you start shopping for new equipment. The computer magazines and trade magazines frequently publish articles that mention important features to look for in products. They also publish charts from time to time showing how various brands and models of various types of equipment compare. A digital camera, for instance, might be rated by price, zoom capability, resolution of photos, ease of use, availability of lenses, and other features. These feature charts are invaluable for helping you select the best product for your needs. Even if you can't find the exact models the magazines reviewed when you do your own shopping, you can at least compare the features of models in the stores to your top choice from the magazine charts.

If you can't quickly find a magazine with guidelines for buying the type of product you are looking for, get on the Web and visit BuyersZone (http://www.buyerszone.com) There you'll find information on purchasing a wide range of products and services for your business. A section called Learn! tells you what key criteria to look for when purchasing anything from postage meters and scales to photocopiers and payroll services. There are comparisons of some products and links to purchase various types of products as well.

Save Money on Your Equipment Purchases

Chances are you will be buying a lot of equipment in the course of a year. And so will your friends. You can save money off every purchase by signing up for appropriate Internet store affiliate programs (see Chapter 13 for more information). Once you are approved for the program, put the link to it on your Web site and click through the link to make your purchase. You'll get the advertised percent off your purchase. Encourage visitors to your Web site to buy through your affiliate programs, too.

▶ Note

Many of the best affiliate programs require you to have a minimum of 500 visitors to your Web site a day. Sign up for an affiliate program, put the icon up on your Web site, and buy your own merchandise through the program. You'll reap a savings of 5 to 20 percent off the selling price (whatever percent you get back as an affiliate, but minus the tax you'll have to pay as earnings).

Buy Peripherals and Add-ons at the Time You Buy the Device

Manufacturers often tout the expandability of their products, citing various add-ons that you can purchase to meet your individual needs. Although those add-ons are usually available at the time they are advertised, they may not be available if you need them six months or a year after the computer or other device was originally purchased. Therefore, if you are sure you will need an add-on, plan on purchasing it at the time you buy the system.

Buy from Reputable Sources

When you pay hundreds or thousands of dollars for office equipment and software, it's tempting to look for bargains. But be on your guard! Prices that sound too good to be true are usually come-ons to sell inferior products or pirated software. In some cases, merchandise may not be delivered at all.

Don't Pay for Add-ons You Don't Need

Retail stores and discounters often sell computers as package deals. Instead of just getting a computer, you get the computer, some software programs, or a printer as part of the deal. Although these may be good deals for people buying their first computer or buying a computer for a second person in the office or household, they may not be a bargain if the computer you are buying will replace an existing computer.

That's because all those "free" goodies that come with the computer actually cost the manufacturer money, and their costs are factored into your purchase price. If you already have the programs loaded on the computer, or already have other software you use for the same function, the software is likely to be useless. Printers that typically are offered free in package deals may not be adequate for your needs, either.

Sometimes the package deals really are bargains even if you throw out the software. Before you make your purchase, make a list of all the key features on the computer: CPU type and speed, memory, hard disk space, DVD or CD drive, speakers, monitor size and pitch, network cards, modem manufacturer and speed. Check for serial ports, USB ports, and midi ports, and find out how many open "slots" there are in the computer for add-ons at a later date.

Then, compare the prices and features of the special offer computers to a computer that you can have custom built for you by the manufacturer. Dell, Compaq, and Gateway are among the manufacturers that let you choose what you want in the computer.

Low-Cost Computers

You can buy a name-brand computer for less than $900. But how good are they? Pretty good if you don't have a lot of programs and don't require a lot of memory to run them. Low-cost computers usually provide the minimum memory and hard drive space necessary to run business programs efficiently. However, if you do a lot of work with DTP software or graphics or have filled up the hard drive on an existing computer, you'll want a model with more memory and hard drive space than the low-cost computers offer.

Ask About the Return Policy and Warranty Before You Buy

Not all equipment or software can be returned. When it can be returned, the time frame and method of return may have changed since the last time you made a purchase from the same store. Find out how long you have to return the item and whether or not they charge a restocking fee to take the merchandise back. (A restocking fee is usually a percentage of the original purchase price, and sometimes as high as 15 percent). If you purchased the item through the Internet or mail order, find out when the return period begins. Is it when you receive the item or when it was shipped from their factory? Check, too, on whether a returned item has to reach them before the cutoff date for returns, or just be shipped by you before that date. And don't forget to find out what kind of warranty comes with the equipment.

Decide in Advance What You'll Do About Add-on Warranties

Most product manufacturers will try to sell you an add-on warranty. This warranty usually extends the time frame for the existing warranty and may add some additional protection—for a fee, of course. The fee is often about 10 percent of the original purchase price. Whether or not to get the additional warranty can be a tough choice. Most of the time, if a product is going to break down due to manufacturing defects, it does so within the first few months of use and is covered by the manufacturer's warranty. So, any extended warranty could be a waste of money. But if something does break down outside the warranty period and you don't have the extended coverage, the cost of getting it repaired may far exceed any additional warranty cost. As a good example, one of the few pieces of equipment I bought for which I didn't buy an extended warranty was a $700 multifunction printer. The printer failed one month after the manufacturer's warranty had expired. I had the printer repaired at a cost of more than $300, got it home, used it for another month and a different part broke down. Rather than spend the estimated $100 to fix it the second time, I bought a new multifunction printer from a different manufacturer. But I've also had other equipment for which I did buy the extended warranty and never had to use it.

▶ Tip

One of the benefits some credit card companies offer is a free extension of the manufacturer's original guarantee period. If your card offers that benefit it can save you hundreds of dollars on service contracts.

Watch out for Equipment Leases

If you are running a very small business and financing it from your own funds, equipment leases are generally not a good idea. Such leases are likely to have higher interest rates than you could get by borrowing money as a personal loan from the bank, and may add hundreds of dollars to your purchase price over the life of the lease. If you have a reasonably good credit record, but don't want to lay out cash for the computer, buy it on a credit card. Then, the next time you get one of those credit card offers that gives you a special low, introductory rate for transferring balances, apply for it and transfer the balance of the computer purchase to it. If you pay off the computer in the time frame during which you get the special low interest rate, you'll save a considerable amount over what you'd have paid for the lease.

Always Use a Credit Card if You Don't Know the Vendor

Whether or not you plan to use your credit cards to finance your business equipment purchase, you should always use your credit card to make purchases by mail order, over the Internet, or from any vendor that is not well known. The reason is that if there is a problem with your order and the vendor doesn't work with you to solve it, or if the order never shows up, you can charge the purchase back (force a reversal of the charge) through the credit card company. If the vendor doesn't accept credit cards, choose a different vendor, no matter how good their prices sound.

> ### Add Shipping Costs
>
> If you are comparing the cost of purchasing equipment from a retail outlet to the cost of buying it through the Web or traditional mail-order catalog, be sure to add in the shipping charges.

To avoid finance charges on purchases, just pay off the credit card bill when it arrives.

Don't Rip Open the Carton

When you get your merchandise shipped to you, open the carton very, very carefully. Some equipment manufacturers don't give you a refund if you return the equipment in a damaged carton.

Wait Until After the Trip or the Project is Done to Install New Software

Trust me on this. Even the simplest upgrade to your existing computer system will either crash your computer, freeze your keyboard, or cause your network to go down if you try to install it before your finish your project or before you leave for that important trip. The same is true of adding any new peripherals (you have to add software with most peripherals), or with buying and setting up a new computer. No matter what the task is, no matter how experienced a computer user you are, if you do it before the project is finished or before your trip, you'll waste at least four to eight hours completing a chore that will take only ten to twenty minutes after the project is done or after you return home from the trip.

Go with the Leader

If you're buying a can of beans, you can save money by purchasing an unknown or a private label brand. But when you are buying high technology products, it pays to stick with brand names that are known for being the leader in the field for the particular type of technology you are purchasing.

Use Removable Disk Labels When You Plan to Reuse Floppy Disks

Disk labels that are included with floppy disks you purchase are usually almost impossible to remove once you apply them firmly to a disk. As a result, computer users tend to apply a second label over the first or stick a Post-it note to the disk to indicate what files are stored on the disk. But both the Post-it notes and the second label can easily loosen from a diskette and get jammed inside the computer disk drive, causing an expensive repair. You can avoid that risk and have neatly labeled disks, however, by purchasing removable disk labels from an office supply store.

Clean Your Keyboard the Easy Way

Dust, cat hair, crumbs, and other debris invariably find their way into computer keyboards. You can clean the dirt out of your keyboard easily by following these three steps:

1. Turn the keyboard upside down and shake gently. (You'll be amazed at what falls out if you've never done this before.)
2. Put the keyboard back on your desk and then take a Post-it note and run the sticky part between each row of keys. (Use only removable note paper. Labels, even removable labels, are too sticky and could get stuck to the keys or under them.)
3. If your keyboard is really grimy, consider taking it apart and cleaning it. Start by disconnecting the keyboard from the computer. Then separate the metal casing or plastic casing surrounding the keys from the keyboard. (You will probably have to remove a couple of screws from the underside of the keyboard to accomplish this.) Once you remove these screws, you can lift the casing off the keys. You can then take the caps off each key and

clean them with soap and water in a sink. Dry them thoroughly before replacing the caps on the keyboard. (Note: It's a good idea to take only a couple of caps off the keys at a time so you can remember where they go when you are ready to put them back on.)

Capture the Order Details

Find out how long it will be before the product will arrive, and ask for an order confirmation number. If your merchandise doesn't arrive on time, the confirmation number will help track down what happened to it.

Watch for Special Offers on Software

Computer software manufacturers are always interested in getting you to switch from a competitor's software package to theirs. Thus, they often have special pricing offers called competitive upgrades. To take advantage of the special low price, all you have to do is show proof of purchase of the competitor's product, or sometimes just have it on your machine when you install their product.

Watch for discounts from publishers of software you own, too. When they launch significant upgrades of the product, they frequently offer the upgrade version to existing customers at a bargain price for a few months.

Virus Software

Be sure your computer has virus software and that you check for updates at least once a month. The fastest way to get those updates is (you guessed it) online at the Web sites of the companies that created the virus protection software.

Discover Low-Cost Shareware

Shareware is try-before-you-buy software. It was developed as a way for small software publishers to get their product to market. It gets around the problems small software publishers have in getting into the traditional distribution systems. The way it works is that you download it from an online service like America Online or ZDNet or from the software developer's site. You try it for the time specified in the product, and if you like the way it works, you pay the author for the program to keep on using it. If it's not suitable for your needs, you stop using the software

Paper Makes a Big Difference

If you plan to use your color inkjet printer to make sales literature to hand out, spend the extra money to buy specially coated paper made specifically for imaging and for printing photos. The special finish makes the colors more vibrant and the heavier weight of imaging paper makes your brochures or product sheets look and feel more like traditional, professionally printed materials.

and don't pay for it. (Some shareware programs have controls built in to prevent you from using it after the trial period is up.)

The purchase price of the shareware is usually considerably less than what you'd pay for similar commercial programs. And some of it is as good as packaged products that you'd pay hundreds of dollars for. Check the shareware libraries of popular sites such as AOL, Compuserve, and MSN, or look on ZDNet, Download.com or PaulsPicks.com, or BusinessKnowHow.com for recommendations for good shareware.

Buy a Multifunction Printer

If your small office is like most, space is almost as tight as your budget. Conserve both money and space by purchasing one device that does the work of three or four. You can get a top-notch Hewlett-Packard black-and-white printer/fax/photocopier/scanner for under $700. The quality of the laser printouts is good enough to produce your own brochures, fliers, and letterhead.

> ▶ **Note**
> There are many other laser and inkjet multi-function devices on the market, but none that I've used to date have equaled the quality of the Hewlett Packard laser multifunction printer.

Allow Enough Time to Print

High-resolution color inkjet printers can take an excruciatingly long time to print in best mode. Depending on which printer you use and the capabilities of your computer, you may also find that printing at high-resolution prevents you from doing anything else on your computer until the printing is complete. Therefore, if you expect to print out high-resolution color pages often, consider spending the extra money to purchase a fast color printer. If you can't get a high-speed printer, leave yourself plenty of time for printing. Printers rated at four pages per minute may actually take several minutes per page to print if there are large photographs or drawings on the page.

Another alternative: Make one color printout and then have color photocopies made of the printout. The copies may not look as good as your original and will cost more than printing the copies out yourself on good paper, but if time is a factor, they are worth considering.

Test Printout Samples

Be sure you look at sample printouts from any printer that you are planning to purchase. But don't stop there. Test them to make sure the ink doesn't rub off. With some laser printers, the ink doesn't fuse well onto all papers.

As a result, when the paper is folded or rubbed, the ink breaks off or imprints onto touching surfaces. To make sure that won't happen with the printer you plan to buy, bring some of your own letterhead to the store and test the printer using that. Then fold the paper and unfold it a few times. Finally, take a second piece of paper and rub it across the printed page. If the ink rubs off or breaks off the surface of the page, don't buy it. Your letters will look awful when they arrive in the mail at your prospects' offices.

Don't Refill Inkjet Cartridges

You may see ads that say you can refill inkjet cartridges up to ten times. Don't be tempted. Although the ink is cheaper than the cartridge and it may work most of the time, it takes only one accidental spill to ruin your printer. Although the low price of inkjet printers versus the high cost of ink almost makes that risk worthwhile (you can buy a brand new inkjet printer for the cost of 10 multicolor ink cartridges), the deterring factor is that you may be most likely to refill and ruin a printer when you are racing to print out a job to make a client deadline. Be safe, and buy new cartridges each time. Or keep a spare printer around.

Print Solutions

Today's color printers let you produce full color printouts that look as good as those produced by a print shop if you use good quality paper. The fly in the ointment: if you're using a low-cost color printer, the printer may take excruciatingly long to print your pages and may use up so much computer memory that it causes your cursor to move slowly or not respond at all. Or, you may find the print operation crashes when pages are only partially printed, making you start over from the beginning. If your computer is set up on an ethernet network, there's a solution at hand: a print server such as the Intel InBusiness Print Station. When you have a print server installed, your print jobs are sent directly to the print server, instead of being spooled to disk. That frees up the resources on your computer and allows you to work without interruption or slowdown while the printer is chugging out your documents.

Fix Clogged Ink Cartridges

An inkjet printer puts ink on pages by forcing the ink through tiny nozzles in the printer cartridges. Sometimes, however, one or more of these nozzles will clog, causing printouts to have white streaks through the type. If you are sure there is still ink left in the cartridge, look in your printer manual for instructions for clearing nozzle blockages. If the instructions in the manual don't clear the blockage, or if the printer manual doesn't give you instructions for clearing the nozzles, try these tips:

▶ Use whatever drawing software you have to create a document that contains a large, filled-in square. Print the document several times to see if that clears up the blockage

Shake "Empty" Laser Toner Cartridges

Don't be too quick to toss a laser printer cartridge (or send it to the recycling center) when you think it's out of ink. As soon as you start to see white stripes in the printout or other signs that the ink is low, take the cartridge out of the printer and gently shake it from side to side a few times. Replace it and try printing again. I often get several hundred extra printed pages this way out of an "empty" cartridge.

▶ <u>Note</u>

<u>Toner may fall out of the cartridge when you shake it. To avoid staining your clothes or flooring with the toner, when you shake the cartridge, hold it at arms' length over a sink or other surface that can be easily cleaned.</u>

Keep Fax Cover Sheets Simple

If you send many faxes, the cost of the telephone call to transmit the documents can mount quickly. To keep those costs down, make sure your fax cover sheet is simple and uncluttered. Large dark areas, pictures, and big bold typefaces all take more time to transmit than plain text on a white background.

Do Without the Cover Sheet

By law, your outgoing faxes must include the name and telephone number of the sender. But there's no law that says that information has to be on a separate sheet of paper from the document you are sending. If you're sending a very short note, send it as a fax memo. Put the fax data at the top of the sheet, and put your text below that as you would with a paper memo.

The Right Way to Save on Ink and Toner Costs

The best way to keep ink costs down whether you are using an inkjet printer or a laser printer is to use economy or draft mode for personal viewing. Switch to high resolution or "best" output to print out final copies of any materials you will be giving to other people to view.

Don't Store Copier Paper in a Damp Basement

Photocopiers and other devices are fussy about the paper they use. They won't print right if the paper has too much moisture content. If you keep your photocopier in your basement and your basement is damp (especially in the summer), store the paper in a drier part of your home and just take a supply with you each time you need to run photocopies. You'll get cleaner looking copies.

Back up Regularly

The one piece of advice that's given most often and heeded least often is to back up your compute files regularly. Hard drives do fail, and when they do, if you don't have a current back up of your work, and your billing and contacts databases, your business will be crippled. If you have a big hard drive, the easiest way to back up the systems is to buy a tape back up system. If you have only a small amount of data and files, you could use a zip drive or a rewriteable CD to back up your system. Whatever method you choose, do it regularly!

▶ **Tip**

If your hard drive should crash and you don't have a backup, a data recovery service may be able to get back some or all of your files. Look for such services in the display advertising in the back of computing magazines.

Chapter 17

MAKING MORE PROFITABLE CONNECTIONS

Businesses have long relied on telephone lines to link them to customers, suppliers, information, and their own sales staff. But in recent years, telephone connections have become more than links; they've become business life support systems. Your telephone connections will bring you orders, answer customer inquiries, get your mail, let you work with distant associates, let you retrieve information, send drafts of brochures or contracts, allow you to contact clients while you're stuck in a traffic jam, and pay your bills. And that's just for starters.

There's a price tag attached to all this connectivity, however. In fact, any one method of staying connected often carries several price tags. Among the possible charges: the initial purchase price for equipment, monthly subscription fees, hourly or per-minute usage charges, one-time service charges.

All these fees make staying connected expensive. It's not unusual, for instance, for profitable home businesses to spend $200 or more each month on telephone and wireless telecommunications bills. But today's need-it-yesterday business climate requires even the smallest businesses to stay connected. Here are tips to help you make cost-effective and productive use of today's telephone technology.

Use a Residential Phone Number as Your Home Business Phone

If you are running a business from home, you should use a separate telephone line for your business if at all possible. Besides helping you clearly separate business from personal calls (so you know how to answer the phone when it rings), the separate business line makes it much easier to track phone costs for tax purposes. Having the separate business line will also reduce the likelihood that customers, suppliers, or associates will get a busy signal when they call.

Unless you need a listing in the yellow pages, however, you do not want to order a business line when you call the telephone company. Instead, ask to have an additional residential line put into your home office. The reason? Local phone companies usually charge about twice as much for business telephone service as they do for residential service. Extra services such as call forwarding are usually more expensive on a business line, too.

The laws in most areas of the country allow you to use a residential telephone for a home business as long as you do not want a listing in the telephone company's yellow pages. To make certain this is permissible where you live, call the telephone company's business office and ask.

Use a Distinctive Ring as a Temporary Second Phone

If you're just testing the waters to see if you want to work for yourself, or if you just can't afford to have a second line installed, order a distinctive ring service from the telephone company as a stopgap measure. The name of this service varies somewhat from one phone company to another, but essentially it assigns two telephone numbers to one telephone line. Each "number" has a different sound when calls come in. Thus you know whether to answer the phone with your business name or just say hello. The cost varies by phone company, too, but is typically less than $5 a month.

Get Voice Mail from the Telephone Company

The telephone company's voice mail service has one big plus over using your own answering machine or even a voice mail board in your PC. It lets callers leave a message even if your telephone line is in use. That single feature makes telephone company voice mail so useful that it's worth ordering even if you have an answering machine or other voice mail system on your line.

There are other services you can order for extra monthly fees. Depending where you live, these may include voice mail boxes and paging. Pricing for voice mail services starts at about $5 a month.

Give Callers a Human to Talk To

If you frequently have your telephone in use for long periods, your customers may get annoyed at never being able to reach you. If that happens, consider using an answering service. Whenever you expect to be on the phone for a long time (or when you expect to be out of the office), forward your calls to the service.

Be Alerted When the Telephone Company's Voice Mail Has Picked Up a Call

The only disadvantage of the telephone company's voice mail is that you don't know you have received a call until you pick up the receiver and hear a stuttering dial tone, which alerts you that you have voice mail.

To be sure you know immediately when there's voice mail waiting, you can buy a device that lights up when you've gotten a call. Hello Direct is one source for this device. Check retail stores for other sources.

Have Calls Rolled Over from One Line to Another

If you have several phone numbers in your office, ask the telephone company about a service that hunts for an open line. That way, if the phone number they dial is in use when the call comes in, the call will just roll over to the next available number instead of sending the customer a busy signal.

Cut Your Local Phone Bill by Changing Your Local Billing Plan

When you have your residential telephone line installed, you may have chosen a rate plan that allows you to make unlimited calls in your local calling area without extra charge.

Although that sounds like a good idea, the local calling area may not include the phone numbers you call most frequently. Thus you may be getting billed by the minute for many of the calls you are placing. To find out, call the telephone company and ask for a detailed printout of all of your local calls for the last two or three months. (You may have to pay a small fee for the printout.)

Use a Business Line Only for Incoming Calls

If you need a yellow pages listing for your home business and you make a lot of outgoing business calls, it may pay to get two telephone lines put in: the business line plus an additional residential line. Use the business line only for incoming calls. Use the second residential line as the line you use to place outgoing calls. Phone companies usually let you have as many as three or four residential lines coming into a house.

Analyze the bills to see which numbers you call most frequently, the average time you stay on the phone during each call, and the general location of each call. Then contact the telephone company business office to see if they have a different rate plan that would save you money. If you call one number and stay on the phone a half hour at a time, for instance, a rate plan that charges a flat rate per call, if available, might save you money.

Consider Alternative Carriers for Local Service

As a result of the federal Telecommunications Act of 1996, you'll be able to shop for a local telephone service provider as well as for a long-distance carrier. The major long-distance carriers, smaller telephone companies, and even cable TV stations may all be competing for your business.

The same law makes it possible for the large regional phone companies (often referred to as Baby Bells) to sell long-distance service.

Watch Out for Variable Flat-Fee Rates

Not all flat fees are created equal. In fact, one of the regional telephone companies sent out a promotion to all its customers in one state boasting about their new flat rate calling plan that would allow unlimited calls within a group of counties in the state. The flier did not state the actual amount of the flat rate, however. Customers had to call the phone company to find out what the price would be.

When customers did call for pricing information, they were quoted a price, but unless they specifically asked, they weren't told how the telephone company derived the rate they were quoted. Neither were they told that different customers would be charged different flat rates.

As it turned out, the so-called flat rate was more like a balanced billing plan. It was based on the individual phone customer's past usage patterns and was subject to yearly review (something else the customer wasn't told during phone calls to inquire about the service). Thus any customer who signed up for the plan and took advantage of the unlimited calling to make more calls than in the past would see his or her flat fee go up proportionately the following year.

On the Horizon

Telephones, like everything else in the digital age, are changing. The day may not be far off when many small businesses use Internet or Ethernet phones to place calls over the Internet instead of over traditional phone lines. And the video telephones may make video conferencing a routine business occurrence.

Call a Long Distance Number Instead of Making A Toll Call

If you have to make a toll call (call outside the lowest price calling area) to use an online service or the Internet, compare the per-minute fee you are paying for the toll call to the per-minute fee you'd pay to call a long-distance phone number. Many people in less heavily populated regions of the country have found it cheaper to place out-of-state calls to reach their favorite service than to place in-state toll calls.

Route In-State Toll Calls Through Your Long-Distance Carrier

Long-distance phone companies are allowed to carry toll calls in many states. Where they can, their prices for carrying the toll call are often less than the prices charged by the local telephone company. If you make many toll calls, jot down the numbers you call frequently and then contact your long-distance carrier to see what they would charge to carry the calls. Compare that to the price your local phone company charges.

Although you may have to dial a code to force the call to turn over to your long-distance carrier, the effort could pay off by saving you as much 10 to 15 percent off the price the local phone company charges for the toll calls.

High-Speed Computer Connections

If you use the Internet occasionally in your business you probably can make do with a high-speed modem and a traditional telephone line. If you need to stay connected to the Internet for long periods of time, or if you often access Web sites with video and audio, you'll want a faster, data connection—perhaps one that is always on.

At this writing there are several choices that may be available to you. These are a T1, ISDN, cable (as in cable TV), and DSL. The best one to choose will depend on your needs, geographic location and budget. You can find good explanations and a good comparison of these types of services at http://www.hellodirect.com.

Lower Your Phone Bill Without Changing Long-Distance Carriers

Most long-distance carriers offer their customers a variety of calling plans that could lower phone bills. But to take advantage of any of them, you have to sign up for the plan. If you've been ignoring the mailings and phone calls from your long-distance carrier, call them and ask them to help you determine which of their current rate plans would offer you the greatest savings.

Reduce Your Long-Distance Telephone Bill by Changing Long-Distance Carriers

If you make many long-distance phone calls and haven't changed your rate plan in several years, you may be paying two or three times more than you have to for long-distance phone calls. Thanks to deregulation of the telephone industry, numerous companies now compete—sometimes fiercely—for your long-distance telephone business. As a result, you should be able to make almost all of your out-of-state long-distance calls for 10 cents a minute or less. (In-state long-distance calls run about 15 cents per minute on one such plan.) If you are paying more than this for residential or business service, get ready to save!

All you have to do is shop around. Call your current long-distance carrier and ask for their lowest rates. Look at your usage patterns to see where you call most (in state or out of state?). Then, if you have a computer, logon to the Internet and look for ads, or logon to AOL and type keyword Long Distance to see the details of their long-distance plan. Compare the figures you see to your current rates.

Or get comparative information from Telecommunication Research and Action Center (TRAC). TRAC is a nonprofit consumer organization dedicated to educating the public about telephone rates. Visit its Web site for information about comparison shopping for telephone services, cellular service, and other telecommunication issues. Several useful publications are available; ordering information can be found on the TRAC Web site:

TRAC
P.O. Box 27279
Washington, DC 20005
202-4408-1130
http://trac.org

Once you've gathered some basic research, call the companies that seem most promising and ask for details about their offerings. Among the major long-distance carriers are:

America Online	1-888-TALK-AOL
AT&T	800-222-0400
Frontier	800-836-8080
MCI	800-444-2222
Sprint	800-746-3767

Ask if the figure the company is giving you is a flat rate (all calls are billed at that rate) or if rates vary by distance to the calling location. If you place many long-distance calls in the evening hours, ask if there are different rates for peak and off-peak service. If yours is a home office, ask if there are differences in rates for residential customers and business users. Some of the long-distance carriers require you to have a business line to get business discounts; others don't care.

Ask if there are any minimum monthly charges or signup fees. Also ask if you have to belong to any group to take advantage of the savings and how your fees will be billed. The AOL plan bills fees to a credit card.

Be sure to find out how your bill is calculated. Some companies bill in six-second increments; others charge in thirty-second increments or round up to the next minute. (In other words, if you are on the phone for a minute and six seconds, will you get billed for a minute and six seconds or a minute and thirty seconds? Over the course of a year, the difference can be significant.)

Qualify for Volume Discounts by Combining Bills from Multiple Phones

Long-distance companies discount rates for customers who use the service the most.

If you have multiple phone lines coming into your office, and are paying the bills separately each month, you're spending more time and money on your phone bills than necessary. Many companies offer a service that lets you combine the bills from multiple lines onto one bill. If you don't have this service now, call your company and ask if it can add it. You'll save the per-check fee the bank charges you and the cost of the postage for mailing the additional payments.

More important, combining the bills into one may allow you to qualify for long-distance discounts you'd miss out on because each bill, by itself, is too small to qualify.

Consider Getting Your Phone Service from a Reseller

Long-distance carriers, cellular services, beeper services, and even Internet providers often sell services in bulk quantities to businesses that resell the service to consumers. These resellers package the services up under their own brand names and sell them to consumers at discount prices.

Savings can be substantial. The Telecommunications Resellers Association says consumers can shave up to 12 cents per minute on day-time long-distance calls, depending on which reseller they use and what calling plan they have from a traditional long-distance carrier. Additional savings resulting from six-second incremental billing can help cut bills more.

Since calls are actually transmitted through the carrier from which the reseller buys the time, the quality of the transmission is the same as if the service were being purchased directly from the big carrier.

Although the transmission quality is the same, consumers looking for bargain rates may find differences in the levels of customer support and service provided by resellers. Many of the resellers are relatively small companies and may not be able to provide the full range of customer support services available from the mammoth long-distance companies.

You can get a list of resellers in your geographic area by contacting:

The Telecommunications Resellers Association
1730 K St. N.W., #12301
Washington, DC 20006
202-835-9898

Get All the Details Before Making Your Decision

To get the best deal on long-distance services for your needs, create a chart or spreadsheet of the type you see in magazines and compare costs and features of each carrier or reseller you contact. The Telecommunications Resellers Association suggests comparing services on the basis of answers you get to these questions:

▶ What are the monthly service fees?
▶ Are there any setup fees?
▶ Are there differences in fees by time of day?
▶ Are the quoted rates for out-of-state or in-state long-distance calls?
▶ Is there a volume discount?
▶ Who pays for the switchover?
▶ Will the service be billed through the local phone company just as your bills from AT&T or whichever carrier you use now are?
▶ What are the calling card rates?
▶ How does the per-minute fee compare to your current carrier after you apply all discounts?
▶ Will you need to dial an access code to make a call?
▶ Do they have twenty-four-hour customer service?
▶ Can you get the extra services your business may need such as 800-number service, management reports, teleconferencing, and voice mail?
▶ Is there a monthly or minimum fee?
▶ Can you cancel at any time without penalty?

Ask About Billing for Wrong Numbers

One problem with having an 800-number is that you will get billed for every call that comes to you whether it's for your business or not. If another business has an 800-number that's close to yours and dialed by accident, or if a wrong number is published in the media, you could be billed for hundreds of calls that aren't for you. One possible source for misdirected calls: The only 800- and 888-numbers available at the time of this writing are recycled numbers. That means they once were used by other businesses or individuals. Any customers or friends who still have those numbers stuck in database may call you—and you'd have to pay for the calls.

To protect yourself, make sure your phone number doesn't spell anything that anyone could use as an ad slogan. Ask the phone company what steps it will take should you suddenly get hit with a barrage of calls that aren't for you and if it will cancel charges for such calls. Wait at least a month before giving your number to customers or publishing it to make sure no other business has a number confusingly close to yours. Or consider getting an 877-number (the newest batch of 800-numbers to be available).

If you do start getting a slew of calls that aren't for you, contact the phone company immediately and ask to have a prompter put in to separate your calls from those of the business your number is being confused with, or change your number immediately.

Use Two Different Carriers if the Costs Would Be Lower

If you fax a lot of documents at night or make a lot of international calls, but also make a lot of daytime calls, you may find that no one plan is best for your needs. In that case, compare the savings you might get if you used two different long-distance carriers. (You'd need two separate phone lines for this.)

Get It in Writing

Sometimes what you hear isn't what sales representatives remember telling you. Therefore, take notes while the sales representative talks. When you think you've gotten the best deal he or she will offer you, summarize what you think you have heard and ask the sales representative if that is correct. Then ask the representative to send you something in writing confirming the prices you've been quoted.

The sales rep at one of the long-distance companies I called first told me that the company charged 15 cents per minute if you made $250 a month in calls or less, and lower prices for higher call volumes. A couple of minutes later, after he had mentioned minimum fees could be waived, the price was 15.5 cents a minute and more than $1,000 in calls to get a lower price. When I asked to have the rates mailed or faxed to me, he mumbled something about it being against company policy.

When he started to try to convince me of the service's benefits by telling me his mother used it, I figured I was dealing with a very inexperienced sales representative. But I couldn't help wondering how the company would be at resolving problems if they couldn't train their front-line sales representatives better than this.

Slam Down on Slammers and Add-on Services

Businesses and consumers occasionally find that their phone service has been switched to another long-distance carrier even though they never agreed to sign a contract or to change their service provider.

This practice is known as slamming, and it is illegal. It can also cost you money if you are switched to a company with a higher-rate plan than the one you now use. To make sure you don't get slammed, look at your local phone bill each month and make sure the long-distance carrier indicated on it is the one you usually use. If you find you've been slammed, contact your former long-distance carrier and ask to have your service and rate plans reinstated. This should be done at no cost to you. Additionally, you should not have to pay extra for calls made before you discovered the switch.

Watch out, too, for added "services" billed to your telephone bill. Make sure you aren't being charged for any services or fees you don't want and didn't order.

Stay in Touch with a Cellular Phone

If you travel frequently, you can keep in touch with customers or your office by using a cellular telephone. A cellular telephone lets you talk directly with anyone just as you would if you were using a telephone in your own office. Like conventional phone services, options available include call forwarding, voice mail, and call waiting. Depending on the phone and the computer equipment and modem you own, a cellular phone can also let you send and receive faxes, or e-mail or even logon to online services if necessary.

Although cellular telephones were once rather large and clunky, today's phones are small enough to fit in a pocket, purse, or the glove compartment of your car. They weigh less than a pocket full of quarters, too.

You pay for incoming calls as well as calls you place. Thus cellular phone use can be expensive. But if it lets you get or keep customers, the expense is worthwhile.

To keep costs down, carefully evaluate the various rate plans available to you and choose the one that best matches your expected usage. Ask what it will cost you to call from your local region (called the home service area) and what it will cost you to place or receive calls when you roam outside the home service area. (The fees you are charged outside your own area are called roaming fees.) Be sure to check where your home area starts and stops. Since you pay for the incoming calls, give your number only to the people who must have it.

The Future Is Now

E-mail on your telephone? That's right. You can now receive e-mail on some cell phones. On the horizon: instead of using a telephon to communicate with business acquaintances, you may be conversing using Instant Messages sent to your palm pilot or TV. Video conferencing for the masses isn't too far off either.

Use the Cellular Phone Instead of the Desk Phone at Night

If you have a cell phone plan that gives you free night and weekend dialing and if you work at nights or on weekends, use the cell phone for toll calls instead of your regular handset during those free times. Why pay for business calls if you can get them free? Just be sure to check what time nighttime begins and ends.

Use a Pager or a Beeper to Save Money

If all you want is a way to get important messages, consider using a pager or a beeper service instead of a cellular phone service.

A beeper service, as the name implies, beeps you when there is a message waiting. You retrieve the messages by finding a telephone and calling the beeper service, or your answering machine if it is capable of notifying you when messages come in.

A pager notifies you of incoming messages and displays the message as either a preassigned numerical code or as text, depending on the capabilities of the unit and service you've purchased.

Using beeper or paging services usually costs less than using a cellular telephone service. (The actual costs depend on what service frills you need.) Either is an effective way to cut cellular costs if you need only to be alerted to messages.

Use a Pager Service to Reduce Your Cellular Phone Bills

If you will need to talk live to some callers, but not to others, you may save money by having both a pager and a cellular service. The pager would let you screen messages and determine which calls to return immediately and which can wait until you reach a regular telephone.

Use Codes to Distinguish Urgent Messages from Others

If you have a paging system that just sends you a numeric code, urge your customers or your staff to prioritize the messages they leave. Wayne Wertz, President of Advantage International, an Internet marketing company based in Portland, Oregon, has programmed his voice mail to ask customers to leave a message in one of several voice mail boxes if he's out of the office. Callers are told to press the numbers 123 to leave a general message and to press the numbers 321 if they have a problem requiring immediate attention. When they hang up, the voice mail system sends a message to Wertz's pager with the number the caller chose. "If I see 321 on my pager, I know the call is urgent and I should get to a phone. If I see 123, I know I can call in at my leisure. I don't have to immediately find a pay phone."

Cancel Call Waiting Service

If you plan to use a modem or fax, cancel call waiting service. The call waiting signal interferes with data transfers and will cause data calls to disconnect.

If you must have call waiting, disable it before fax or modem calls by dialing *70.

Check Compatibility with Your Phone System

If you have multiple phone lines in your office, make sure the voice mail, fax, or telemarketing system you plan to install will work with the telephone system. Check with manufacturers of both the hardware and software you plan to buy and with the phone service. The phone service may have a list of recommended products. If you are just purchasing a PBX or other phone system for the first time, ask whether it is capable of voice mail if you want to add it later on. If it isn't, you may be in for a big expense if you ever do want to add voice mail.

Use Fax-Back or Fax-on-Demand Technology to Answer Caller Inquiries

Answering routine customer queries or mailing product literature or other facts to people can eat up a tremendous amount of time. You can minimize the time you and your staff spend responding to requests for information by setting up a fax-on-demand or fax-back system. Such systems present callers with a list of documents they can retrieve by fax. The caller punches in a number and starts receiving a fax (with fax-on-demand systems) or hangs up, and your equipment then calls the caller and faxes the requested information (fax back).

Though such systems were once quite expensive, the cost of the hardware is now low enough to make fax-on-demand systems practical for even small home-based offices.

Such systems can boost sales as well as productivity since the information gets to the caller immediately—not several days later when the caller may have forgotten why he or she even asked for information.

▶ **Tip**

If you have a Web site you can accomplish the same goal by setting up one or more auto responders to answer routing e-mail inquiries or by writing a Web page that contains answers to frequently asked questions.

Check Your Voice Messages and Automated Response Systems for Errors

While I was researching this chapter, I called all the major long-distance phone carriers to get service and rate information. Most of the calls were received by an automated routing system that asked me to select a choice from a menu of options. When I did, the call would be routed to the proper department based on that selection.

After punching in my selection at one of the companies, I heard a pleasant voice advise me there would be a slight delay because "All representatives are currently with another customer."

When I stopped giggling to myself about the image that sentence conveyed, I placed a call to another leading long-distance phone carrier. This time I got a recording that said: "In order to provide you with better service, we have changed our phone options. Please select one of these five options. To inquire about our long-distance service for your business, please press 1. . . ."

I pressed 1. When I did, I heard: "I'm sorry. Your call cannot be completed as entered. Please check the number and try again."

Don't just record your outgoing voice mail message and forget about it. Check it out and have several other people check it out, too. Ask them to listen carefully for errors in wording and to give you an honest opinion about whether the message sounds professional. Have them pay attention to voice quality, timing, and volume of beeps, and to check out all the options if you give callers numbered choices.

Don't Trap Customers in Voice Mail

Voice mail systems that tell the callers to press a number to access a particular type of information (for example, press 1 for product information, press 2 for order inquiries) are a great way to reduce the time you and your staff spend answering routine inquiries. To be effective, however, they have to be set up with the end user in mind. If callers have to follow too many directions or push too many buttons to get information they seek, they will just hang up and call one of your competitors.

To avoid this problem, keep outgoing messages brief and to the point. Make sure your callers know exactly what they should do at each stop along the way, and make it possible for them to get the attention of a real person if they need to talk to someone. Try to limit the number of options the listener hears to three or four to avoid confusion.

Help Customers Reach You When Area Codes Change

To meet the demand for new telephone lines, the telephone industry has had to add new area codes. These new area codes do not have a 1 or a 0 as the middle number of the area code, and as a result, some business phone systems can't connect to the new area codes. To prevent problems, if you are in an area that will be changed over to a new area code, let your customers know in writing about the impending change and ask them to contact you if they experience any difficulty reaching you.

▶ Tip

If you know your phone number will be changing, get a low-cost 800 number and give that number to your customers. If it's not practical to give your 800 number to all of your customers, give it to the most important customers.

Use Distinctive Ring Service to Identify Incoming Toll-Free Calls

Chances are you'll want to keep incoming toll-free calls as brief as possible. But if a customer is calling on his or her own dime, you may want to spend more time with him or her. To distinguish between the two types of calls when both come in on the same line, order distinctive ring service from your local phone company. This makes the telephone make one sound when the call comes in on your toll-free number and a different sound when it comes in on the regular number.

Use Distinctive Ring Service to Route Calls

If you have multiple extensions or devices on a single line, you can also use distinctive ring service to route your calls to the proper device. Look in mail-order catalogs such as Hello Direct or in stores like Radio Shack for simple switches that will recognize the ring and separate the calls.

Look for Toll-Free Numbers Before Placing a Long-Distance Call

Before you place a long-distance call to a business, call 800-555-1212 and find out if there is a toll-free number for the business. If there is, see if you can use the number to reach the company.

Call When No One Is Likely to Be in the Office

If your client is a big corporation, call when you don't expect your contact to be in and leave a message on his or her answering machine. That way, your contact will call you back and the time you spend discussing the assignment will be on his or her dime, not yours.

Take Advantage of Time Zone Differences and Off-Peak Rates

If your long-distance service charges you less for evening calls than for calls placed during the day, time your long-distance calls to take advantage of differences in time zones. For instance, if you live on the East Coast and off-peak hours start at 5 p.m., place your calls to phone numbers in the central or western time zones after 5 p.m. The person you are calling will get the call during regular business hours, but you'll be billed the lower evening rate. If you're calling from west to east, get up earlier in the morning to place your eastbound calls.

Send Faxes at Night When Rates Are Lower

If you send out many faxes or have long documents to fax, queue them up in your computer and let your computer fax software send them in the middle of the night while you sleep. You could save up to half the daytime telephone charges, and your fax will be waiting for intended recipients in this country when they get to work in the morning. If you have customers overseas, time zone differences may make your overnight fax land on their desk in the middle of their workday.

An added bonus: If you use your computer for e-mail or to access the Internet, sending the fax overnight will leave the computer free for other telecommunications chores during your working hours.

Schedule a Time of the Day to Make and Receive All Telephone Calls

Just because you have a telephone on your desk doesn't mean you need to pick it up and call someone the moment a subject you want to discuss comes to mind. Instead, set aside a block of time each day for phone calls. Keep a notepad by the telephone and write yourself a note about whom you want to call and why. When your call hour rolls around, make all the calls at once. Having to fit them all into the allotted time will help you minimize chitchat, saving you both time and money.

Let Your Answering Machine Remind People What Your Work Hours Are

One of the problems with working at home is that it's too easy to always be there for your customers. If you find you frequently get calls at night and can't resist the urge to pick up the phone, get an answering machine that lets you have two outgoing messages and lets you schedule when each will play. Record one message that will play during the day when you are not in, urging callers to leave a message. Record a second message to play after hours thanking people for calling and stating what your regular office hours are.

If your current answering machine won't let you play two messages, just turn down the sound on the answering machine and the business telephone at the end of your work day. The answering machine will still pick up the messages—you just won't know about it until the next day when you see the messages and turn the sound back on to hear them.

> ## Tip
> Leave yourself a note to turn the sound back up on both devices the next day so you don't think something has gone wrong with the telephone.

Check Those Access Numbers!

When you use an online service or an Internet service, you pay two charges. One charge is for the subscription or hourly fee the Internet provider or online service charges you. The other fee if what the telephone company charges you for the time you spend on the telephone line.

Before you choose an Internet provider or an online service, find out where the nodes (telephone numbers you call to connect with the service) are located and how much the phone call to reach the service will cost.

If there are no local telephone access points, consider choosing a different service. If none of the services have local access points, consider using a surcharged 800-number line. These are "toll free," in that you do not pay any fees to the telephone company to use them; however, you do pay a communications surcharge to the online service for accessing the service through the 800-phone line. Typically, the surcharge is $6 an hour. For people who live in remote areas of the country, that $6 an hour surcharge is often less than the toll charges or long-distance charges from the phone company.

Be Careful When You Temporarily Change an Access Number

To use an online service, you use your computer's modem to dial the telephone and to send signals over the telephone line. At the receiving end of the call, another modem answers the call and passes your signals on through the network. Since many people are calling to a central point at one time, it's not uncommon to experience busy signals for lengthy periods. Occasionally, too, technical difficulties prevent any calls from going through. Although all the online services and telephone networks are constantly striving to improve service, when you run into this type of situation, you may find it advisable to call a more distant access point so you can logon to the service.

If you do that, write on a Post-it note and stick it to your computer screen reminding yourself to reset the phone number back to the one you usually use when you are finished with this one call. If you don't leave yourself a note, you may forget to change the number back and continue to call out on it. If that happens, depending on what the cost of calling the more distant phone node is, you could chalk up $50 to $100 or more in extra phone charges before you realize the error.

Look Up Telephone Numbers on a CD-ROM Disk Instead of Calling the Phone Company

The telephone company charges you 75 cents every time you call directory assistance to request a phone number. If you make more than five or six requests for directory assistance a month, and if you own a computer with a CD-ROM drive, consider buying one of the CD-ROM products that contain national telephone directories. You can usually purchase directories containing names, addresses, and phone numbers of all businesses and residences in the United States for about $50. For about $100 more, you can buy other CD-ROM phone directories that let you search by more criteria and export the information you find into formats that can be used by mail merge programs. Chapter 3 lists several sources for telephone directories on CD-ROM disks. Check popular mail-order catalogs for others.

Look Up Telephone Numbers on the Internet or Online

If you don't know a phone number, you can look it up online. This is a great way to find companies and friends in distant states. All you have to do is search for the person's name or the store name, and the database will show you matches and near matches. They may even show you the e-mail address of the person you are trying to reach.

Look for telephone directories on AOL.com and Yahoo.com.

Find Out Where an Area Code Is Located Without Calling Directory Assistance

If you do business nationwide, you may get voice mail messages or electronic mail from customers, prospects, or salespeople who leave their phone number but don't say what part of the country—or which country—they are calling from. If you have Internet access, you can save a directory assistance call by using a free, searchable database called Area Code Finder. It's located at http://www.mmiworld.com/telephone.htm.

Keep Calling Card Usage to a Minimum

Every time you use your calling card, your phone company may ding your account for an extra 80 cents or so. Some of the long-distance carriers also charge you higher per-minute fees for calling card calls than they do for calls dialed normally from your own telephone. Before you use the calling card from your long distance-service, check the rates carefully. Compare them to the rates you can get by purchasing prepaid calling cards from shopping warehouses like Costco and SAMS.

Two other advantages besides price to consider:

1. Use of a prepaid card avoids the risk of criminals getting your calling card number by looking over your shoulder at public phone booths.
2. Having employees use a prepaid calling card instead of the company calling card will force them to limit calls and keep chitchat down while on the road.

Protect Your Calling Card Number

If a thief gets your calling card number, he or she can ring up thousands of dollars in fraudulently placed calls on your account in just a short time. Among the more common ways calling card thieves get victims' numbers are by watching numbers punched in at public phone booths (or listening to people giving the operator their calling card number), by posing as telephone company employees and asking for the number, and by scanning cellular phone calls. You can help prevent these crimes by taking the following steps:

▶ Don't give your calling card number to anyone who calls you and tells you he or she needs to verify your account. Scam artists often pose as telephone representatives and ask people they call to read their calling card number so they can verify it. Real telephone company representatives never call with such requests.

▶ Don't hold up your calling card to read the number when you are in a public place. Use your body to shield it from view of anyone looking over your shoulder or spying on you from a distance with binoculars. Try to make it difficult for anyone to see what numbers you punch in on the telephone keypad, too.

▶ Avoid reading your calling card number over a cellular phone. Scanning (listening in on) cellular telephone calls is yet another way crooks get calling card numbers.

▶ Report stolen cards immediately so the phone company can cancel the card and issue you a new one.

Watch out for Pay Phones

Some pay phones are serviced by very small long-distance carriers who charge exorbitant fees. Before placing a call from a pay phone, dial the operator and ask what phone company provides the service and what they charge. If the charges are too high, use your calling card to make the call. By dialing a special access code, you can force the call to be carried and billed by the long-distance carrier you use at home.

Block Calls to Unneeded Area Codes

If you have employees and work from an office, watch out for unauthorized use of phones on weekends and evenings. Consider blocking calls to area codes that the business never calls and to foreign countries.

Use Caller ID to Screen Calls

If you don't have a secretary to screen your calls, you probably spend more time than you'd like talking to salespeople who waste your time. Although you can turn on an answering machine and let the answering machine screen your calls while you work, some callers will hang up when the answering machine kicks in. Others may hang up just *before* the answering machine picks up, so they don't waste the cost of the call.

As a result, you could miss important calls. There's an easy way to solve the problem, though: Get caller ID from your phone company. (You'll also need to purchase a special telephone that displays the caller's phone number.) That way, when the phone rings, you can look at the number of the incoming call and, based on that, decide whether to pick up the call or let your answering machine pick it up.

> ▶ **Tip**
> Save money by using Caller ID to screen incoming cell phone calls too.

Get a Multiline Phone

If you've got two phone lines, invest in a multiline phone. Although you'll pay more to purchase a multiline telephone than you will to purchase an additional single-line telephone for the new number, the difference in price will be more than offset by the convenience of being able to answer two different lines from one phone. If you work from a home office, for instance, you won't have to run into another room to pick up the house phone if it rings while you are in your office. If you have two or more office lines, one handset saves space and also makes it possible to make conference calls without operator assistance.

Have an "After Hours" Message for Your Answering Machine

Don't want to be bothered by calls in the evening? Just switch tapes in the answering machine, or if your machine can play more than one outgoing messages, switch messages. Make the evening message say, "Thank you for calling. Our office hours are from 9 a.m. to 5 p.m. weekdays. Please call during our regular office hours, or leave a message and we will return your call on the next regular business day."

If you have a Web site, be sure to include the Web site URL in your after-hours information.

Find Gadgets for Almost Any Purpose

If there's anything you do regularly on the telephone, chances are someone has invented a device to make doing it easier. Check Radio Shack, office supply stores, and the telephone gadgets sections of superstores like Home Depot or Wal-Mart for gadgets to make your work life easier. Among the devices available:

▶ A gadget to let a single-line answering machine answer two phone lines
▶ Fax/phone/answering machine switches
▶ Call restrictors (to block calls to numbers you set)
▶ Caller ID boxes (for people with caller ID service who don't want to buy a new phone)
▶ Devices that work with caller ID to block incoming calls from specific numbers

Free Your Hands and Avoid Neck Strain with a Headset

If you use the telephone a lot in your business, consider buying a headset. A telephone headset lets you talk without having to hold onto the telephone. There are a wide variety of headsets to choose from, including models that plug into your telephone, cordless headsets, sets that hook over one ear rather than wrapping around your head, and headsets for cellular telephones. You can find headsets at stores such as Radio Shack or Office Max. They are also available by mail order. One mail order company that specializes in the sale of telephone equipment is Hello Direct. You can get a catalog by calling 800-444-3556. Or if you have access to the World Wide Web, you can view their catalog at http://www.hello-direct.com/scripts/hellodir.exe.

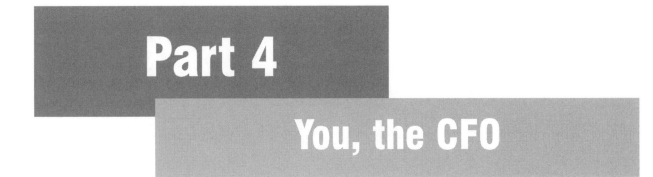

Part 4

You, the CFO

Chapters

▶ **18** **Travel**

▶ **19** **Playing Hardball**

▶ **20** **Keeping the Tax Collector at Bay**

▶ **21** **Making Cash Flow**

▶ **22** **Growing Your Business**

Chapter 18

TRAVEL

Corporate types with fat expense accounts aren't the only frequent travelers around these days. Management consultants, programmers, trainers, shop owners, sales representatives, Web developers, and other small and home-based business owners all can be seen lining up at ticket counters and moving through plush hotel lobbies where no one ever seems to sit.

You may not think of yourself as one of those beleaguered business travelers featured in airline, car, or hotel commercials, but you probably are—at least some of the time. And when you do don your traveling persona, the tips in this chapter will help you achieve your business goals with minimal inconvenience.

Get a Separate Credit Card for Travel Expenses

The cost of air fares, hotels, and car rentals can mount up quickly. To keep them from maxing out your other credit card balances, consider having one credit card that you use only for travel. A separate card will also prevent nonbusiness purchases from interfering with your business expense needs.

Watch Those Holds!

Car rental agencies and hotels often put a hold against your credit card when you make your reservation. The hold sets aside part of your available credit to be used for the service you are planning to purchase. Although you aren't actually billed for the amount of the hold until you use the service and give your okay to bill the fees to your credit card, the hold prevents you from using that amount of credit for any other purpose for a time unless the company placing the hold on your account releases it.

If you ultimately pay with cash rather than your charge card, have the hotel or car rental company immediately contact the credit card company and release the hold. If you don't remind them to take this step, it can be days—or even weeks—before the hold is released. If you're approaching your credit limit, that could prevent you from charging anything on your card until the hold is removed

Call the credit card company a day or two after the hold should have been released and ask what your current credit limit is. If it sounds too low, ask if there are holds against the card that haven't been cleared, and if there are, ask to have them removed.

Don't Travel on Impulse

Traveling to meetings, seminars, and trade shows is expensive. To keep costs down, ensure that all trips you and your staff take are really necessary. You can discourage impulse trips by establishing an annual travel and entertainment budget—and sticking to it.

Before approving trips for your staff or even yourself, determine what the trip will cost and whether this will make the best use of available travel funds.

For instance, is a prospect serious about purchasing your product or retaining your service or just window shopping? Is a seminar or trade show the only place you can get vital information or make key contacts, or can you get the same information some other way for a lot less money? Do the shows and seminars you're considering have solid track records pertinent to your customer base?

If the answers to these questions don't indicate a clear benefit for the trip, don't go.

Shop Around for Airline Tickets

Airfares follow no logical rule. Two people sitting side by side on an airline may have paid fares that differ by hundreds of dollars. The difference for similar seats on competing airlines can be even greater. On one trip I made from New York to Texas, the first two major airlines I called had each quoted a round-trip coach fare of about $1,400 because I was traveling midweek and didn't want to stay over a weekend. A third airline, however, charged only $460 for round-trip travel on the same dates. If you are ordering tickets yourself (or having your secretary order them for you), be sure to shop around. You may be able to save hundreds of dollars on your airfare by leaving from a different airport, by flying on a different airline than you normally do, or by making one or more stops en route to your destination.

Watch for Price Wars

The best time to buy a ticket is during price wars or times when promotional discounts are being widely offered. If a price war occurs after you've bought a ticket, call the airline and ask if they will refund the difference between the price you paid and the lower price being advertised.

Last-Minute Bargains

If you have to travel at the last minute, don't be too quick to pay full price. Airlines and hotels discount rates when they don't have a full house. Check the Web and your friendly travel agent to find bargains on last minute trips.

Make Reservations Well in Advance if Possible

Airlines and hotels frequently offer discounts for advance reservations. Although some advance purchase requirement can be as little as seven days, discounted tickets and accommodations often require a fourteen- to thirty-day advance purchase. These discounts can be as much as 50 to 60 percent off "regular" prices, but remember that the number of discounted seats or rooms available is usually limited, so the earlier you can make your travel arrangements, the more likely you will be to get a seat or a room at a savings.

Consider Small or Startup Airlines

If one of the small, economy-class airlines fly from a city near you, take a hard look at their prices. You'll get no-frills seating (and no seating choice), but here again you can save hundreds of dollars on each flight. An example: The lowest fare I could usually find for midweek, round-trip travel from New York City or Long Island, New York, to the Washington, D.C., area was more than $400 in early 1999. Then, Southwest Airlines started flying from Islip airport in Suffolk county Long Island. The cost: $135 round-trip from Islip to Baltimore/Washington airport. Even with car rental to get from Baltimore/Washington to Washington, D.C., the savings is more than $200.

Shop the Web for Bargains

Several sites on the Internet will help you compare airfare, hotel rates, and car rental fees. Several alert you to bargain fares and sales as well. These sites are useful for finding bargains and for estimating travel costs if you have time to browse around. If time is short, placing a few 800-number calls or calling your travel agent may be a better choice.

Here are several travel sites you can use:

Preview Travel
　　http://www.previewtravel.com or, on AOL, keyword Previewtravel

European Travel Net (good for U.S. fares also)
http://www.etn.nl/discount/index.html

A Trip by Modem
http://www.atbm.com

Priceline.Com
http://www.priceline.com/

Watch out for Holiday Weekends

Reserving far in advance is particularly important if your business travel will begin or end on a holiday weekend. If you wait until two or three weeks before the trip to reserve your plane and hotel tickets, discounted tickets and rooms are unlikely to be available. And full-price substitutes could cost you hundreds of dollars more than if you'd planned a little earlier.

If you must travel for business during holiday periods, allow extra time for delays. Flights are frequently overbooked at these times, and you could get bumped, so if it's imperative that you get to your destination on time, arrive early at the airport and select your seats well in advance of your scheduled flight to ensure you get a seat.

▶ **One caution**
If you volunteer your seat, you give up rights to any special seating preferences on the flight you were originally scheduled for. Thus, if there are no-shows and the airline doesn't need your seat after all, you'll have to board the flight and take whatever seat is available.

Give up Your Seat Voluntarily

If you have time to kill and a flight is overbooked, consider volunteering to be bumped. If they take you up on your offer and put you on another flight, they'll give you a free round-trip ticket for a future trip.

Ask What Restrictions Apply

Discounted travel fares generally come with strings attached. In addition to making reservations in advance, you may be required to travel on certain days or times, stay over on a Saturday night, or stay a minimum number of days to qualify for discounts. Furthermore, you may be told that your reservations can't be canceled or changed without incurring an additional fee. Be sure to find out what restrictions apply at the time you make your travel arrangements.

Carry Addresses and Phone Numbers with You

The only thing predictable about business travel is that it's unpredictable. Your plane may be delayed, making you several hours late for an appointment. Your meeting may finish up two hours earlier than expected (leaving you too much time to kill before your scheduled flight home, but not enough to go sightseeing). You may discover the car rental agency you thought was in the airport, isn't. Or when you climb into the cab and tell the driver, "Take me to the Sheraton," he may turn around and ask, "Which one? The Sheraton Washington? Or the one on Connecticut Avenue?"

To minimize stress and confusion, carry all important contact information with you and keep it handy.

Your list should include the airline name and phone number (in case you want to check on or change a flight) name, address, and telephone number of the hotel(s) you'll be staying at; name, address, and phone of the car rental agency; phone numbers for business contacts and any other individuals you might need to notify if you are delayed in transit.

Stay over a Weekend

If your trip is near the end of a week or the beginning, consider staying over on a Saturday night. The difference in airfares can be so significant that you still save a hundred dollars or more on the trip even after you pay for you hotel and meals for the extra night's stay.

Get Discounted Rates Without Staying a Weekend

If you know you will be making multiple, midweek trips to the same destination, you can save hundreds of dollars by buying both sets of tickets at once and overlapping the dates. Here's how it works.

You know you have to travel from Florida to Washington, D.C., on June 12 and return home on June 15, and that you have to be in Washington again June 20–21. You buy two round-trip tickets: One ticket will be leaving Florida on the 12 and returning to Florida on the 21st. The other ticket will be leaving Washington on the 15th and returning to Washington on the 20. On the first leg of your trip, you use the outbound portion of each of the two sets of tickets (that is, the one ticket leaving Florida and the one ticket leaving Washington). On the second trip, you use the remaining halves of each round-trip ticket.

Cut the Ties That Bind

Discounted tickets are often labeled "nonrefundable." Although some discounted tickets actually are nonrefundable, many can be changed if you are willing to pay a service charge of approximately $75. Thus if an emergency comes up and you have to change the dates or times of your trip, or cancel a trip altogether, don't assume the worse. Call the airline and explain your situation, and ask what can be done. If you're willing to pay the service fee, you may be able to make your change. Or if you have to cancel the trip altogether, you may be able to get a credit good for the purchase price (minus the service fee). Generally, such credits have to be used within a year.

Get a Frequent Flier Account

Frequent flier programs are promotional tools the airlines use to try to gain travelers' loyalty. If you sign up for an airline's frequent flier program, you earn credits for the number of miles you fly on that airline or on a partner airline. When you reach the number of miles specified in the frequent flier program, you are entitled to a free ticket.

▶ **Caution**
If you participate in a program whereby you get frequent flier miles based on credit card purchases, be sure to pay off the credit card at the end of each billing cycle. Otherwise, you could spend more in interest charges over a year than you'll save by getting a free airline ticket.

You typically have to accumulate 25,000 miles of credit to earn a free ticket. You don't have to fly frequently to accumulate those miles. Some programs give you extra miles as a signup bonus when you first join, and some plans have partnerships with other businesses allowing you to accumulate frequent flier miles based on your purchases with those other companies. Plans change over time, but typical partners include hotels, car rental companies, telephone companies, and credit card companies. Thus, talking on the telephone, paying for equipment with a credit card, or other purchases may help you quickly accumulate frequent flier miles.

In choosing a frequent flier plan, try to determine which airline you are most likely to fly on. If several airlines travel regularly to your expected destinations, compare the frequent flier plans benefits before choosing one. The phone numbers for major airline frequent flier programs are listed in Table 11-1.

▶ **Tip**
If you forget to sign up before you take your first trip, or if you forget to give the airline your frequent flier account number when making reservations, you may still be able to get frequent flier credit if you call the airline and ask.

Table 11-1

TRAVEL DIRECTORY

Airline and Name of Frequent Flier Program	Phone Number
Aero Mexico—Club Premier	800-247-3737
Air Canada—Aeroplan	800-361-8253
America West Airlines—Flight Fund	800-247-5691
American Airlines—Advantage	800-882-8880
Continental Airlines—One Pass	800-621-7467
Delta Airlines—Sky Miles	800-323-2323
Northwest Airlines/KLM—World Perks	800-225-2525
Trans World Airlines— Aviator Service Center	800-325-4815
United Airlines—Mileage Plus	800-421-4655
USAir—Dividend Miles Service	800-872-4738

Airline Reservations	Phone Number
Aero Mexico	800-237-6639
Air Canada	800-776-3000
Air France	800-321-4538
America West Airlines	800-235-9292
American Airlines	800-433-7300
British Airways	800-247-9297
Continental Airlines	800-525-0280
Delta Airlines	800-221-1212
Northwest Airlines/KLM	800-225-2525
Trans World Airlines	800-221-2000
United Airlines	800-241-6522
USAir	800-428-4322

Airline Ticketing Agencies	Phone Number
A Better AirFare	800-454-7700
800-FLY-CHEAP	800-359-2432
(Look in the yellow pages for local travel agencies as well.)	

Hotel and Motel Reservations	Phone Number
Best Western	800-528-1234
Comfort Inn	800-221-2222
Courtyard by Marriott	800-321-2211
Days Inns	800-325-2525
Econo Lodge	800-553-2666
Hilton	800-445-8667
Howard Johnson	800-446-4656
Marriott Hotels	800-228-9290
Omni Hotels	800-843-6664
Ramada	800-722-9467
Red Lion/Doubletree	800-547-8010
Red Roof Inns	800-843-7663
Ritz Carlton	800-241-3333
Sheraton	800-325-3535
Stouffer/Renaissance	800-468-3571

Car Rental Agencies Reservations	Phone Number
Alamo	800-327-9633
Avis	800-831-2847
Budget	800-527-0700
Hertz	800-654-3131
National	800-227-7368
Payless	800-237-2804
Thrifty	800-367-2277

Stretch Frequent Flier Miles with Your Residential Phone Bill

The three major long-distance telephone companies (AT&T, Sprint, and MCI) have programs that give you frequent flier miles when you make long-distance calls on your residential phone line or on a calling card billed to your residential phone line.

These programs can be especially lucrative to home businesses that use a residential line as the "business" line and make a lot of long-distance calls. Anyone with college kids, family, or friends in distant states or other countries is likely to benefit as well.

To get details of these plans, call the 800-numbers or visit the Web sites.

AT&T Global Travel
800-222-0260, ext. 603
http://www.att.com
MCI Frequent Flyer Program
800-999-1909
http://www.mci.com/worldphone/english/ffmiles/shtml

Sprint Bonus Award Travel
800-755-1093
http://csg.sprint.com/airline/index.html

Read the Small Print on Frequent Flier Programs

Frequent flier programs do have some limitations. Be sure you read and understand all the rules of the program(s) you sign up for.

Things to look for:

▶ How long you can leave credits sitting in your account before they expire (on some airlines, your mileage credit expires after three years if it's not used)
▶ How many miles you need to fly to earn a free ticket
▶ What destinations you can reach on free tickets
▶ Where else you can earn frequent flier credit (telephone company, partner airlines, hotels, car rental agencies)
▶ Blackout times (times during the year when you can't get a free ticket) and restrictions on flying during peak seasons
▶ Availability of seat upgrades for miles

Take a Discount Instead of a Ticket

If you don't have enough frequent flier miles for a free ticket or find that all seats set aside for frequent fliers have been sold out, consider cashing in frequent flier miles for trip discounts or upgraded seating.

Consider Driving Instead of Flying

If your destination is within a few hundred miles of home and if you expect to be there for at least several days, or if you need to carry a lot of paraphernalia with you, consider driving. Your out-of-pocket expenses will be lower since you save the airfare and the car rental costs. If you are traveling at a client's request, you may be able to bill them for car mileage at the IRS rate (31.0 cents per mile from 4/1/99 through 12/31/99). Whether you are reimbursed for mileage or not, you can take a tax deduction for the mileage on your tax return.

> ▶ **An added bonus**
>
> If your business destination is near a resort area, you could take the family along for an almost free minivacation. Your only costs for them would be the minimal add-on fees for more than one person in a hotel room and for their meals and personal expenses.

Keep Confirmation Numbers Handy

Hotels and car rental agencies give you a confirmation number when you make a reservation. Keep it handy. It's your proof you've made arrangements in advance. If the hotel or the car company loses your reservation, the confirmation number will help you get a car or room in a timely fashion. And if they don't have what you reserved available, they'll upgrade you to whatever they do have at no additional cost.

On a trip to Dayton, for instance, the car rental agency couldn't find my name in their computers and didn't have another budget-priced car available. When I was able to give them the confirmation number for my reservation, they found me in their computer. Their reservations people had reserved a car for me in Daytona. Since it was their mistake and they had no budget or midrange cars to rent, I spent my trip driving around in a white, climate-controlled Cadillac with blue leather seats—at a budget car price.

Find a Helpful Travel Agent

Letting a travel agent make arrangements for your trip can save you a bundle of time and may save you a good chunk of cash as well. A good travel agent should be able to find you the lowest fares and hotel rates available to the public, and may have access to discounts not normally available to the general public. Not all travel agents are created equal, however, so you may have to shop around until you find an agent with whom you are satisfied. Be sure to give any agent you work with as much information as possible about your preferences (is cost more important than comfort? for instance) and about memberships in large organizations that tout travel discounts as part of their membership benefits. The American Association of

Retired People (AARP) and the American Automobile Association (AAA) are two examples.

Even if a travel agent can't come up with any better deals on airfare, car rental, or hotels than you could on your own, when you consider the value of your time—or the cost of your secretary's time—you still come out ahead by letting a good travel agent make your reservations.

Combat Jet Lag

Traveling long distances by plane can play havoc with your internal clock. If you're traveling from east to west, you may be ready to hit the sack about the time everyone there is ready for dinner. Then, the following morning, you're likely to find yourself wide awake long before dawn. If you fly from west to east, the cycle is reversed, and "bright and early in the morning" will feel like the middle of the night.

George N. Vella works for the German Tourism Bureau. He frequently travels to and from Europe and throughout the United States.

Like many frequent travelers, George has found that he can adjust more quickly to time zone changes if he sets his watch to the time it is at his destination as soon as he takes his seat on the plane. Sleeping on the plane helps, too, particularly if you got too little sleep the night before your departure.

Finally, George advises, try to arrive at least one full day ahead of time for important business meetings. The extra day will help you get acclimated to local time and help ensure you'll be at your best when you give presentations or enter into negotiations with customers.

Get Paid for Your Travel Time

Many people who are starting out as consultants make the mistake of not charging clients for travel time. That's because they think of themselves as "working" only while they are actually meeting with the client or doing a task assigned by the client.

Don't fall into this trap. If you weren't traveling for the client, you'd be performing other income-producing work. To avoid problems with the client, make sure they know up front that you will charge for your travel time. If you don't bill on an hourly basis, be sure your day-rate includes sufficient leeway to cover the time you spend traveling.

Get Foreign Tax Refunds

Many countries have value-added taxes (VATs) that can add 15 percent or more to the cost of goods and services purchased in the country. If you buy goods for personal use or to give as gifts while you are in one of these countries, you may be entitled to a refund of the VAT. Typically, there are minimum purchase requirements you must meet to qualify for the refund, and the purchase requirements are per shopping trip at an individual store. Thus you can't add up all the purchases you make over a week to meet the minimum. You will have to fill out a form (available at the point of purchase or at the airport) and, in some cases, may have to wait several months for your refund.

Services such as hotel rooms, car rentals, and meals may also qualify for VAT refunds when they are purchased for business. Each country has somewhat different rules, but typically, you will need to submit VAT receipts and fill out a refund claim form in the language of the country you were visiting to get a refund. Additionally, your claim must exceed a minimum amount set by the country and must be filed within a certain period after the expense was incurred. Receipts can be saved up and filed all at once, provided they are filed within the allowable period.

Watch Carry-On Size

From time to time airlines get fussy about the size of your carry on items. Suitcases sold as carry-ons usually make it *if* you don't stuff the pockets.

Because of the hoops you'll have to jump through to get a VAT reimbursement, you'll probably find it practical only to request a refund if you are due several hundred dollars or more. You may also want to use a service bureau to process the claim for you. These bureaus have sliding fees that range from about 20 to 50 percent for processing claims. The higher the claim, the lower the percentage of the claim the service bureau keeps. Most will have a minimum fee or a minimum amount below which they won't handle your claim. One such service bureau in the United States is Meridian VAT Reclaim, Inc., at 800-727-4828. Your accountant or federal, state, or local government offices that offer international trade assistance may be able to refer you to other similar services.

Watch the Date on Midnight Flights

If you are booked on a flight for just after midnight, be sure to double-check the day and date of the flight. Keith Siddel, a business traveler, tells of the time he called an airline and asked to be booked on the last flight out of San Francisco on Friday, the 15th of the month. He was booked on a 12:05 flight. He drove to the airport Friday night, expecting to take off a couple of minutes after midnight, but to his dismay, was told he had missed his plane, and that he should have known that anything after midnight becomes the next day.

Don't Leave Home Without These

Leaving important items at home is easy to do when you're rushed. One man I know got to his hotel the night before a business meeting and discovered he had left his suit home. I forgot to take overhead transparencies with me on one trip, and on another, forgot the power cord for my notebook computer.

To make sure you bring everything you'll need with you, make two lists; one for business items and one for personal items you'll need. Store these lists along with any tickets, confirmation notices, directions, or maps you'll want to take with you in one place. (A pocketed file folder works well.)

As you think of items you'll need on the trip (handouts, overheads, business cards, reservations, phone numbers, clothing, and so on), add them to the list.

About a week before your trip, begin collecting the items you'll need. Store them in one location if possible. Then when you actually pack your bags, check off the items against your list.

On the eve of your trip, set your luggage and travel items by the front door, including any coat, portfolio, attaché case, notebook computer, garment bag, or other extras.

If you'll be driving to the airport and you live in a safe neighborhood or have a garage, pack the car the night before your trip.

> ▶ **Tip**
>
> Many credit cards give you add-on insurance protection for car rentals if you pay for the rental with their card. Call your credit card company to see if they do before you rent a car.

Reserve the Lowest Price Car or Room

If there is no real need to impress others with your wealth or prestige, always reserve the least expensive car if your stay is reasonably short. Doing so can save you $50 or more a day in expense. Furthermore, as I did on that Dayton trip, you may wind up upgraded to a better car or accommodations if the price-range car or room you reserved isn't available.

Don't Get Talked into Upgrades You Have to Pay For

Occasionally, you'll stumble on a branch of a car rental agency that seems hellbent on making or breaking sales quotas and will go to great lengths to get you to agree to trade up (and pay for) a higher-priced car model or to buy insurance you don't need. I ran into a sales agent from hell at an Alamo car rental franchise in Tampa late one night. I had flown in from St. Louis after day-long meetings in that city, and arrived at the Alamo office around midnight. There was a long line of people waiting for cars, and the line moved incredibly slowly even though there seemed to be more than enough agents in the office to help people.

When it was my turn, I found out why the line was moving so slowly. I had made a reservation for their $23-a-night special. When I got up to the counter and gave them my name, the conversation proceeded like this:

"You know, Mrs. Attard, this car is very small, you'd be much more comfortable in a midsized car."

"I'm traveling alone, I don't need a lot of room."

"Well, you know, Mrs. Attard, this car doesn't even have power steering. It will be hard to drive."

"This is a little car, right?"

"Yes."

"Then I don't need power steering. Look, it's late, could you just give me the car I reserved?"

"Certainly, Mrs. Attard. Now, would you like insurance?"

"How much is it?"

"Twenty-three dollars."

"A week?"

"A day."

"What? You've got to be kidding! That's as much as the car costs to rent!"

I got a song and dance about how that was a deluxe insurance plan. Then the agent said:

"Well, we do have another plan for $16 a day."

"That's still too much!"

"We do have another plan for $7 a day that covers . . ."

Unfortunately, we had just changed insurance companies, and I wasn't sure if the automobile coverage I had covered all damages on rented cars or had a deductible, so I went with the $7 per day add-on, which I was told would pay (if needed) enough to cover what the deductible on my own car insurance didn't pay.

Get Someone Else to Pay Your Way

If you are asked to consult with a distant client, speak at a meeting, or make on-site service calls in distant locations, get the

Minimize Out-of-Pocket Expense

If possible, get the client to book the flight and the hotel room for you and bill it to their account. You'll save the time and won't have to wait a month or more to be reimbursed by the client. Be sure to tell your client about any airline or hotel preferences or special accommodation needs. And if you have a frequent flier account, ask if they can arrange to have the mileage credited to your frequent flier account.

Not all companies will pay the travel fees up front. Some big corporations may have accounting procedures in place that require you to pay the travel costs and then include the travel expenses in your invoice. But it doesn't hurt to ask.

Note: If you are dealing for the first time with a small company, you may want to insist that they pay your airfare and hotel or give you an up-front payment to cover expenses. At very least, check their credit rating before spending your own money for travel arrangements.

organization making the request to pay your way. Be sure all contracts and consulting agreements make it clear that the client is responsible for paying for all travel and hotel costs in addition to your regular fees. Before each trip, ask the client to send a you a letter or fax authorizing the trip and confirming details you and they have agreed to.

Bill the Client for the Extra Night's Hotel Stay

If a client is paying your way, and if staying extra nights at a hotel reduces your airfare enough that the extra hotel expense plus the reduced airfare is less than the hotel and plane fare would have been if you didn't extend your stay, then bill the client for the extra nights at the hotel. If they realize a savings by having you stay the extra nights, what you do with your time shouldn't concern them. Thus, you get to visit that new prospect, attend a trade show, or take a weekend vacation without having to foot any of the costs for air transportation or hotel fees.

▶ Note

If your combined travel expenses are lower when you have to stay over additional time to qualify for lower airfares, the extra lodging, food, and incidental costs are tax deductible.

Check the Regular Rate as Well as the Conference Rate

If you're attending a conference, you may receive literature describing special conference rates on hotel accommodations or airfare. In some cases, the special conference rate is a good deal, but in other cases, you may be able to get much better prices on your own, so be sure to comparison shop before making your reservations.

Software developer Paul Mayer tells of a friend who tried to get a room at the last minute at the Comdex computer trade show in Las Vegas. The man was wearing a suit when he arrived. When he asked for a room, he was told there were none available. He went into a men's room, changed into casual clothes and went back to the registration desk. There he yelled in a loud, boisterous voice, "What are all these dudes doing dressed up in monkey suits? I thought this place was for letting your hair down and gambling." He got a room immediately, says Mayer, and at a lot lower rate than the guys in the "monkey suits."

---

* Under tax laws in effect in 1995, only 50 percent of food expenses incurred while traveling are deductible.

Beware of Shoulder Surfers

Shoulder surfers are thieves who hang out in airports, hotel lobbies, and other public places to steal telephone calling card numbers. What they do is to look over a caller's shoulder and record the calling card. To minimize the chance of someone getting your calling card number:

▶ Memorize the calling card number (so you don't have to pull out a card and look at it in a public place).

▶ Stand close to the telephone shielding your fingers from view with your body.

▶ Never give your calling card phone number to anyone else, even if he or she claims to be from the telephone company. (There have been scams where people say they are from the telephone company and claim to need access to the calling card number for testing purposes. Don't fall for these scams.)

▶ Purchase a generic calling card (one not tied to your phone number) and use that when you are traveling. Buying clubs like Costco often have these available with two hours or more time for under 20 cents a minute, and I've seen them as low as about 11 cents a minute. If any shoulder surfers bother to copy these numbers, all you'd stand to lose is the purchase price you paid for the card.

> ▶ **Warning**
>
> Just because there's no one standing close to you doesn't mean no one's watching what you do. Some shoulder surfers use distance viewing equipment that lets them see "over your shoulder" even though they are actually standing across the room.

Check out Room Rates at Several Facilities in the Area

Hotels and motels often have more than one facility in a particular area. Although the accommodations may be similar at any of the facilities, the cost of a room can vary tremendously. The closer a hotel within the chain is to a popular resort, business center, or the airport, the higher the rates usually are. When calling ahead for reservations, ask what the rates are at the hotel nearest your destination. Then, after the reservations clerk gives you that figure, ask if the chain has other hotels in the area. Ask how far away they are and what the rates are. When you get *those* rates, ask if there are any lower rates at other locations. You may be able to shave up to $20 a night, or more, off your hotel bill in this way, and still not be more than ten or fifteen miles from your destination.

Consider Distance and Work Hours

If you'll be working late into the evening or have to show up at the client's office very early in the morning, look for accommodations close to the work site when feasible. Juan Jimenez, owner of Micro Consulting Associates in San Juan, Puerto Rico, has paid as much as $1,500 a month for a studio apartment located near a client in New York City. Explains Jimenez, "It was expensive . . . for a studio, but I could walk to work, saving cab/train fares. More importantly, I could stay as late as I wanted to, knowing that I'd only have a four-block walk home in a safe area."

Consider Service and Convenience

On shorter trips, Jimenez prefers to stay at hotels such as the Sheraton or Hilton because "it pays for me not to have to worry about my safety (or the service). If I worry about that, my work quality suffers and so does my income. Getting a good night's sleep in an American-style bed is important when you're putting in long hours at $50 per hour or more, plus expenses."

Ask Hotels if They Have a Weekend Rate

Sometimes hotels have a weekend rate that is lower than the weekday rate. And, if you stay over the weekend, they may extend the weekend rate to weekday stay. On the flip side of the coin, if you are traveling to a conference and the conference rate is lower than the lowest weekend rate the hotel has, you may be able to extend the conference rate into the weekend.

Consider Travel Alternatives

You don't have to meet face to face to stay in contact with customers or to benefit from suppliers or other business contacts. Often you can accomplish your business goals without leaving home by using one or more of these strategies:

▶ Mail product literature.
▶ Make periodic phone calls to stay in touch with customers.
▶ Set up a conference call instead of a meeting.
▶ Consider setting up a videoconference.
▶ Buy training tapes instead of sending staff to distant cities.
▶ Videotape your sales presentation and send the videotape to prospects. Follow up with in-person sales calls only if the prospect shows a sincere interest in making a purchase.
▶ Create a multimedia presentation featuring your product or service and send your prospects a disk containing the presentation.
▶ Create a catalog on disk and mail the disk to customers.
▶ Locate sales agents or distributors to sell your products in other states.

Don't fall into the trap of trying to wine and dine customers into buying your products. Sell them with benefits instead. If you must demo your products to make sales, and have to do so frequently, consider having a video made and sending the video out to prospects. Or put a demo on disk.

Save Time and Avoid Airport Lines

Have the airline or your travel agent provide you with electronic tickets before the day of the flight. If you can fit everything you need for the trip in carry-on bags, you can go straight to the boarding gate without having to wait in line at the ticket counter.

If you have your boarding pass and have to check luggage, you can skip the lines by having skycaps check you in at curbside. The skycaps will expect a tip—about a dollar a bag is appropriate—but if you are carrying heavy luggage, being able to unload it without having to drag it around the airport to the ticket counter can be worthwhile.

Make Sure the Money's in the Budget

Bidding on a contract? If you'll be expected to travel as part of the contract be sure your bid—and the contract you get—allocates adequate funds for travel. If the money isn't budgeted or if you go over budget, travel costs could come out of your own pocket.

> ▶ **Tip**
> Always ask for the regular price before asking for the discount price. A friend of mine was making reservations for a motel in Florida and asked if the motel had special rates for AARP members. She was told, "Yes, we can give you a special rate of $69 a night." When she arrived at the motel, there was a young couple at the registration desk ahead of her. The couple asked if there were any vacancies and were told yes. The price? Sixty-nine dollars a night—the same as the "discounted" price my friend had been given.

Don't Accept the First Price

Even if you ask for the lowest price room in the hotel, the first price you are quoted won't necessarily be the lowest. To get the lowest price, wait until the hotel clerk has quoted a figure, then ask if they have any lower prices. Ask about specials for members of any group you belong to (AARP or an automobile club, for instance). If your client is a U.S. government agency, ask if they have rooms available at the government rate and then ask if *that* is the lowest rate. (Often the government rate is *not* the lowest-priced rooms in the hotel.)

Get Government Rates on Other Services

Hotels aren't the only places that offer government rates. Some airlines and car rental agencies offer special discounts, too. Though it isn't always necessary, you may be asked to prove your government connection, so be sure to have your contact send you a letter on government stationery stating what your assignment is.

Just as with the hotels, you shouldn't assume the government rate is the lowest possible rate. Often it isn't—particularly if you will be staying over a Friday or Saturday night. So, after you ask for the government rate, ask if there are any lower rates.

Staying for a While? Bargain the Rate Down

Hotels and motels make money only when rooms are occupied. Therefore, many of them—*if asked*—will discount their rate if you can guarantee a lengthy stay. William Arrott, an engineer who travels around the country from job to job, frequently gets motels to discount rates for long-term stays. Typically, he asks where others working on the project are staying, then calls and asks what the rate is. After getting the daily rate, he asks for a long-term rate. In some cases, he's gotten motels to knock hundreds of dollars a week off their quoted prices.

Ask the Locals

If your stay will be long or your budget small, ask someone who lives in the area or who has traveled to the area before to recommend a good, safe place to stay. For example, the first time I went to Boston to attend a conference, I stayed in one of the hotels listed in the conference brochure. The room cost more than a $100 a night and was a long metro ride from the main exhibit halls. The second time I went to Boston on business, I got smart. I called an acquaintance in the city. He referred me to a motel he had stayed in when he was moving to the city. It was clean, safe, a five-minute drive from my destination, and cost $60 a night.

If you are traveling for a client and don't know anyone else to ask for recommendations, ask the client if anyone in their office can suggest good places to stay in the area.

Sublet a Condo for Lengthy Stays

If you're working on an assignment that will keep you away from home for a lengthy stay, consider subletting a condo or apartment. Such listings can be found in the classified ads and real estate sections of newspapers. If you spot an ad that sounds promising, check with your client to see if the location is safe and convenient to the job assignment.

Cut Your Travel Phone Bill

Placing phone calls from your hotel room can be hazardous to your travel budget. That's because many hotels and motels add service charges to telephone calls that travelers make from their rooms. These service charges are a lucrative source of income for the establishments, bringing in as much as a quarter of a million dollars in profit each year at some hotels.

Typically, you'll encounter two kinds of charges on calls placed from your room: a per-call fee that usually ranges from 50 to 75 cents for each call (but may be higher), and a surcharge on direct-dialed, long-distance calls. The long-distance surcharge is generally a whopping 40 to 55 percent of the telephone company's charges. Thus, if the telephone company charges $2 for the call and the hotel charges a 50 percent surcharge, your out-of-pocket cost will $3 (the $2 phone company charge plus a $1 hotel service fee). Cut costs by using a calling card, an 800 number, or a cellular phone.

Keep Those Receipts!

Take a small envelope with you and use it to store all receipts for expenses you incur. As you incur the expense, put all expense receipts in the envelope, jotting down the date, time, and reason for the expense on the outside of the envelope.

When you get home, transfer the figures from the envelope to your expense report. Make photocopies of the receipts and send the photocopies to the client. Keep the originals for your own records.

Record Your Expenses Immediately

If you're traveling with a computer or a handheld device, don't wait until you get home to record your expenses. Write them down while they're fresh in your mind and the receipts are handy. A good time is right before you go to sleep or on the plane ride home.

If you hate saving receipts, or you are a real bargain hunter who enjoys finding the best deals in travel (and will benefit from using a generous per diem allowance), you might want to consider using the federal government per diem rate for travel rather than listing specific expenses. The U.S. rate, in general, is $50 per night for lodging, plus $30 per day for meals and incidental expenses, for a total of $80 per travel day. Higher-priced areas have higher per diem rates; for example, San Francisco's allowance is $129 per night for lodging and $46 per day for meals and incidentals. Check out the per diem rate for where your business travel takes you by visiting http://www.policyworks.gov/perdiem or call the Federal Information Center at 800-688-9889. Don't forget, you will still need to record your business travel and the reason for it in order to take these deductions, but with a per diem rate, you won't need to keep track of individual expenses.

Minimize the Bite

Avoid the hotel long-distance surcharges by using your telephone calling card for all long-distance calls. You can reach your long-distance carrier to place a calling card call by dialing one of these numbers:

> AT&T: 800-321-0288
> Sprint: 102220
> MCI: 800-999-9000

Some hotels don't charge the per-call fee if you place calls to an 800-number or if you bill the call to your calling card. If you expect to make many calls during your stay, ask about phone surcharges before you reserve the room. Compare fees at several hotels in the area. If room rates and distance to your business destination are similar, choose the hotel with the lowest phone fees.

Eliminate the surcharge by placing outgoing calls from a telephone booth in the hotel lobby. Look for a quiet corner so you can hear, and have paper and pencil handy in case you have to take notes. An added benefit: Since it's hard to get comfortable while you're making a call from a phone booth, your phone calls are likely to be shorter and, therefore, less costly.

Join a hotel or motel frequent traveler program, such as Marriott's, and get all of your local phone calls for free.

Rent a Car Phone, Wreck a Budget

Renting a car with a car phone can do even more severe damage to your budget. The combination of per-call charges, per-minute charges, and per-call minimums can put the cost of calls made from a rental car cellular phone at close to $3 per minute. If you must use a cellular phone while you travel, bring your own phone from home or keep close watch on the number and length of calls you make.

Get Through Security Checkpoints Faster

Wearing or carrying anything metal causes metal detectors to sound an alert when you pass through security checkpoints at airports. To avoid the delay of having to empty your pockets or the embarrassment of having to stand there while a security guard runs a metal-detecting wand up and down your body, leave big metal jewelry, belt buckles, pocket knives, unneeded keys, coins, and other items at home. Put any metal items (other than expensive jewelry) in your carry-on luggage and let it ride along the security checkpoint conveyor belt. If you are carrying a notebook computer with you, put that through the conveyor belt in U.S. airports, too. The x-ray device used to view the contents of carry-on items won't harm the data on the computer.

If you choose not to put the computer through the conveyor belt, you will have to hand it to an attendant, walk through the checkpoint, then turn on the computer to show the attendant that it is, indeed, a computer. Do not carry the computer through the area you walk through, since the metal-detecting device used there creates a magnetic field that could erase your hard drive or floppy disks.

Make Sure You'll Be Able to Use Your Modem

If you'll need to use a modem while you're away, ask in advance if the room has a data port on the telephone or a plug-in telephone jack. Carry along telephone wire with you (in case the telephone or jack is on one side of the room, and the desk or electric outlet on the other side) and a three-prong plug adapter (so you can recharge the computer battery if the sockets are only for two-prong plugs). Pack a few floppy disks, too. Use them to back up any new data you put on the computer during the trip.

Put Your Modem Call on Your Calling Card

If you must make a long-distance or toll call with your modem, you can avoid hotel surcharges by putting the modem call on your telephone calling card. The way to do it is to put all the information you would punch in by hand into your modem dialing routine. At places where you have to wait for a dial tone or computerized voice, insert one or more commas. (The commas tell Hayes-compatible modems to pause briefly before sending the next command.)

You can even put in the dialing command to use your own long-distance carrier. A typical dialing command to get out of a hotel, dial through your own long-distance carrier, dial the number you want to call, and plug in your calling card number is shown next.

If your calling card number is 212-555-1212-5000 and you need to dial 8 to make a long-distance call, it would look something like this:

```
@ATDT 8,,,800-321-0288,,,202-1232-4567,,,,,212-555-1212-5000
```

In this example,

ATDT tells the modem to dial using tones.
The number 8 is what the hotel phone system needs to let you make a
    long-distance call.

800-321-0288 puts the call through on your AT&T calling card.
202-1232-4567 is the number you are calling.
212-555-1212-5000 is your calling card number.

The exact routine you need will vary depending on what the hotel requires you to dial to get an outside line.

Dial Your Own 800-Line

If you work at home and have a personal 800-number set up to work with your business phone, call home for your messages on your 800-line. The cost of the 800-call is likely to be less than the total of the long-distance charge plus hotel or calling card surcharges.

Use Internet Services to Send Faxes

If your laptop computer has a fax modem (as opposed to just a plain modem), you could use that to send faxes from your hotel room. But you'll have to pay for long-distance charges. If the receiving fax machine is frequently in use, you may have to make several calls to get the fax through.

You can avoid some of the frustration of sending faxes by logging onto the Internet and using a service such as jfax.com to send faxes. Most will automatically redial the fax number at set intervals if they detect a busy signal. That frees up your hotel phone line, and frees you from having to sit next to the phone until the fax goes through.

Discover Kinko's

Kinko's is a copy and computer center that can be a lifesaver when you realize you need to add a couple of overheads to your presentation or have to run off more handouts. The centers generally have computers available that you can use for a fee, as well as printers and photocopiers. The prices are usually reasonable, compared to the price of similar services offered in hotel "business centers."

Chapter 19

PLAYING

HARDBALL

Business, like life, isn't always fair. Some of the problems one stumbles across in business are unpredictable. Some are fairly common. And some are completely avoidable. Here are some of the dirtiest little secrets of business and what you can or, in some cases, can't do about them.

Don't Promise What You Can't Deliver

The inability to fill orders is one of the leading problems that small businesses face when they try to grow. Either they can't raise money fast enough to cover all the costs of producing and distributing the products, they can't find enough employees to produce the work, or they can't do the work at all.

To minimize the problem, find out what will be involved in scaling up your production before lining up sales representatives or renting space for a trade show. Find out what quantities you'd need to purchase to get better wholesale prices, and what you'd need to do and what it would cost to secure the financing if you have to ramp up in a hurry. Check with employment agencies and talk to others in local business organizations to find out how much difficulty you are likely to have finding employees in the skill and salary range you will need.

A counselor at a local SCORE or Small Business Development Center should be able to help you work up the numbers and alert you to potential funding sources that may be available.

Remember, if you sign a contract to do a job or deliver a product by a certain date, you are legally bound to live up to the terms of that contract. If you don't, you could be sued and asked to pay the cost of having someone else complete the job, or for damages such as lost income due to your negligence. Depending on how your business is operated, you could lose not only your business, but your home and any other assets. So, be sure you really can do what you say before you sign that contract.

Be Sure You Get a Contract

Whether you are on the buying end or the selling end, be sure you have a contract and that it covers your needs. The contract should spell out what work will be done, what will be provided to you, what the deadlines are, who owns any intellectual property developed as a result of the contract, what fees will be paid and when they will be paid, and all other important details. If you are the one offering the contract, think the project through from the beginning to end. Make a list of what you expect to get out of the contract and what work you think needs to be done to get or document the results you are expecting.

If you are the one who will be performing the contract, make sure it clearly states what governs acceptance of work, how changes will be handled, and so on. More often than not, it is misunderstanding over those "little" details that causes problems.

If you are on the offering end of the deal, have your attorney draw up the contract based on your notes about what needs to be done. If you have need for similar work on a regular basis, have the attorney draw up one or more boilerplate contracts that you can use over and over again.

If you are on the receiving end, have your attorney read the contract and alert you to any potential trouble spots.

Don't Rely on Contracts Alone

Try to maintain a good working relationships with your customers and with your suppliers. Talk things out as soon as you see problems starting to develop. Don't wait until there are irreconcilable differences. If a relationship turns ugly, both sides lose, no matter what the contract says.

For starters, there's the cost of the lawsuit. If you sue another company, you can expect to spend a minimum of $20,000 just to get the case to court. If you're on the defending end, you'll incur high costs, too, even if you've done nothing wrong. The cost to have an attorney review a contract and review the circumstances of a dispute can quickly climb into the thousands-of-dollars range. And that's just to get a correspondence started between your attorney and the other party before a lawsuit is actually filed.

Second, if you go to court, sue, and win, you may not be able to collect. Collecting will be particularly difficult if the company or individual you sue is small. It's even harder if it's small and out of state.

Finally, if you are dealing with a corporation with deep pockets and an in-house legal staff, the bottom line on any dispute is going to be *their* bottom line. The contract is likely to have built in "outs" to cover or minimize their losses should they decide your products or services no longer meet their needs, even if you are performing the contract as specified.

If there is no easy exit from the contract for the big corporation, their attorneys will determine what it will cost the company if you decide to sue them. They'll also estimate what their costs will be based on how long you'd be able to hold out before mounting legal fees make you cry uncle.

The corporation may have another agenda as well. "Some corporations have a policy of fighting everything," says Kent Seitzinger, an attorney from Rosedale, California. "They do so because they do not want to be perceived as an easy mark for legal actions. It's not uncommon for big business to spend several times what they could settle a matter for just because they want to fight as a matter on principle. Their real agenda is to send a message to others about what they could expect to be up against should they also be foolish enough to sue the company."

Any decision or settlement offers will be based on issues like these alone. Being "human" or compassionate isn't something most big corporations are very good at. If you find yourself in this unfortunate situation, try to come to an agreeable settlement. Accept the circumstances, get the best settlement you can, and get out.

Don't Be Too Trusting

When you work regularly with people, you start to think of them not just as employees, contractors, or vendors, but as your friends. And, because they are your friends, you tend to trust them and not question what they do or why they do it.

Don't fall into that trap. As near and dear to your heart as you may think these people are, they may be ripping you off. It happens far more often than most small business owners realize.

Being too trusting, and not keeping accurate records of every transaction, is one way such problems arise. The owner of a gift basket business tells this tale of woe:

"I offered my employees a 20 percent discount on their own gift baskets. They had to design them on their own time and write up all the orders themselves. We were assigning SKU's to products, and they wrote them by hand instead of computer—I never checked them until it was too late. They wrote up wrong pricing, wholesale not retail cost, took a 30 percent discount on everything and never applied the 5 percent state sales tax to anything they bought."

> **Get Everything in Writing**
>
> If you are working with independent contractors be sure you spell out all the details of a job before they proceed. Think through the processes, and the way you want the finished job to look or perform. If you know the process will involve review and change to come up with a product or service that best meets your needs, let the contractor know up front. Creative types and others may get their nose out of joint otherwise if you aren't 100 percent happy with what they developed for you.

Keep Tabs on Your Employees

Don't wait until the deadline for a project is nearly at hand to see how your employees or independent contractors are progressing on it. If you do, you may learn the job has barely been started, or that it wasn't done right.

"When I entered the sales after the Christmas rush and discovered the loss, then took inventory and discovered items that didn't sell to customers were gone and not listed on their sales, they accused me of falsifying their sales records. The record-keeping on my behalf was sloppy and they got away with it. I simply couldn't recall all the details. One woman even attempted to charge me for three boxes of inventory that she insisted I store in her barn."

To make matters worse, the business was operating from the business owner's home. "You feel personally robbed. And unable to trust."

To avoid situations like this, be sure every sale is documented. State employee discount policies clearly, and don't let employees ring up their own sales. Be sure all inventory is carefully accounted for as well. If you can afford it, consider putting in surveillance cameras.

Cross-Train Your Employees

If you have employees, make sure more than one person knows how to do every job in your company. If you have only one employee other than yourself, make sure the employee documents his or her work thoroughly so that you or another hired person could do the job if the employee ever became incapacitated or left to work for another firm.

Getting your key employees to teach others what they do may not be easy. Often the employee will worry that doing so makes it easy for you to replace him or her.

If you sense that type of resistance, remind your employees that they are important to your business and that every job in your company needs to be documented. Without such documentation in a small company, the company could fail if an employee had an accident and couldn't work for several months. Then there would be no job to return to when the employee recuperated.

Don't Let the Night Cleanup Crew Clean You Out

Nighttime maintenance and security workers pose two potential threats to your company: loss of assets such as equipment or inventory and loss of confidential or critical information (customer lists, computer codes, drawings or designs, and so on).

If you are in a highly competitive industry, competitors may try to infiltrate maintenance crews or bribe people in maintenance to gain access to the contents of wastebaskets and to get a look at the stuff people leave on their desks or have taped to their computers. Surprisingly, many people tape computer system passwords to their computer monitor so they don't lose or forget them.

Before hiring maintenance personnel, carefully check all of their employment records and personal references. If you are using an independent contractor to clean your office, hire one that's bonded and insured. Find out how long they've been in business and check their references closely as well. Be sure all confidential information is locked away in a safe at the end of the day.

Be particularly careful about protecting portable equipment that is expensive or contains sensitive data. Removable hard-disk cartridges or microcomputer backup tapes containing sensitive information could easily be concealed and removed from your office if they aren't protected. Or if a nighttime maintenance or "security" person is left to his or her own devices and has access to your computer system, he or she could copy the proprietary or commercially purchased software onto backup media or send it out via modem and steal it without your knowing about the theft.

Don't Keep It All in Your Head

Take the time to write down all the information that would be needed to run the business if you suddenly became ill or were disabled. Be sure all procedures are documented and that all key contacts, including customers, attorneys, accountants, insurance agents, and employees are listed (with phone numbers). Make sure at least one person other than you knows what work is in progress; what contracts must be fulfilled; and where to find your list of contacts, employees, contractors, and operating procedures.

Store a copy of this list off-site so it can be accessible if some type of emergency occurs at your location.

Save Computer Backups Off-Site

Backing up your computer daily is essential to avoid loss of data in case anything happens to your computer hard drive. But have you ever stopped to think about where you are storing that backup? If the only backup copy of your computer system is stored in your office, what good would it be if the office burns down, floods, or is robbed?

To be on the safe side, make periodic backups of your data to store off-site. Be sure you include any important information such as computer logs on information, passwords, ISP phone numbers, e-mail addresses, and custom software you've written or had written for you.

Be Able to Document Your Losses

Having insurance doesn't necessarily mean you'll recoup all of your losses if you fall victim to fire, theft, or other losses. When an adjuster comes to assess damage from a loss, his or her mission isn't to pay you as much as possible. It's to save the insurance company as much as possible. Thus they look for proof there was an insurable loss. But proving some losses can be difficult. If your business or home burned to the ground, how long would it take you to remember all the software you had purchased over the last three years?

"In many instances, business owners and home owners don't recover the full value of their losses because they can't prove them," says Steve Toor, president of Videospec Information Programs, Inc. in Rockville Centre, New York. Toor was an insurance adjuster for twenty-four years before starting his company, which offers video documentation services to businesses and home owners.

One way to prove your loss is to document what you own. Take inventory of any physical inventory, of your equipment, furnishings, software, books, and other items that would be costly to replace. Record the purchase date and prices to help substantiate your claims. Periodically take video or still photos of your business, too. Those may help prove the existence of any items that hadn't yet been included in your inventory. If available, consider using an independent service like Toor's, which not only captures an image of your business property and possessions, but also transfers it to a CD-ROM that can't be altered.

Consider Business Interruption Insurance

If you would continue to incur business expenses even though the business were devastated by a disaster, consider purchasing business interruption insurance. It can help cover the costs of payroll, inventory, and other ongoing costs until you are back in operation again.

Get Federal Assistance After a Disaster if You Qualify

The Small Business Administration has a Disaster Loan Program that offers financial assistance to those who are trying to rebuild their homes and businesses in the aftermath of a disaster. The program offers low-cost loans to help small businesses and homeowners get back on their feet after a disaster. If your area has been hit by a hurricane, tornado, or other major disaster, watch the newspapers to see if it has been declared a federal disaster area, and if so, contact the SBA for information on your eligibility for loans. For more information on these programs, check the SBA Web site at http://www.sba.gov or contact the Disaster Information Helpline at 800-525-0321 or the Small Business Administration at 800-488-5323.

Protect Sensitive Data from Internet Snoops

If at all possible, don't keep customer lists, customer credit card numbers, employee data, or any data that you wouldn't want destroyed or delivered to your competitors on any computer hooked up to the Internet.

Maintain an Up-to-Date Copy of Your Web Site

If your Web site is an important part of your business, make sure you have a complete, up-to-date copy of the complete Web site, including all graphics, HTML files, scripts, programs, and databases running on it. If you are using a hosting service to store and serve your Web site to the world, don't rely totally on the service to make backups. Although a good service will, indeed, make backups every twenty-four hours, some services will tell you they make backups, but do not actually do so on a regular basis. If they have hardware problems on the server that contains your Web site, they may not be able to recover a recent version of the site. In a worst-case scenario, they might not be able to recover any of the site. If you have an outside contractor create design pages or write scripts and programs for you, they may not have saved copies of their work after you accepted delivery.

If you don't know how to copy the Web site files, ask whoever created the site for you to show you how or to make a copy for you and send it to you on a zip disk.

Watch out for Dumpster Divers and Trash Collectors

If you have a cutthroat competitor, if your business is targeted by thieves looking for credit card numbers to steal, or if you might be involved in a police investigation, be careful what you throw away. The innocuous-looking bum hanging out by the dumpster may not be what he or she seems. He or she may be a dumpster diver—a person who goes through your trash looking for credit card numbers, competitive information, or possibly evidence in a lawsuit.

The kinds of information you or your employees throw away that can be invaluable to unscrupulous competitors (or to attorneys, police, private investigators, and reporters looking to nail you) includes scraps of paper with customers' phone numbers, memos discussing how you plan to circumvent employment or other laws, printouts of computer code for products under development, notes about meetings you are having with a company that is planning to buy you out, sketches or blueprints of new products, credit card numbers, and virtually any information you don't want made public.

Your office isn't the only place that can come under attack, either. Joanna Strohn, who is president of Electronic Motorcyclists, Inc., and who worked for years in the marketing department of a Fortune 100 corporation, warns that meeting rooms, booths at trade shows, and hotel hospitality suites that are left unattended can be a target, too. "There's definitely gold in the trash," she says. "Notes tossed in the trash can or materials left out on tables may be viewed as fair game by competitors." Since some states consider trash placed in public places to be legally abandoned property, there may be nothing you can do to recoup losses incurred as a result of someone's picking through your trash.

Shred Confidential Material Completely

If you have printed data you need to destroy, be sure you do so in a way that the data can't be reconstructed. If you tear or cut up notes by hand and put all the pieces in a trashbasket next to your desk, anyone can easily reconstruct the pieces. If you are purchasing a shredding machine, look for one that shreds documents in such tiny pieces that it's difficult to put them back together again. If your data is sensitive, for instance, a strip shredder may not offer you much protection since it is relatively easy to piece the strips back together to reconstruct the document.

Don't Compete Head On with the Superstores

Trying to compete head to head with superstores is tantamount to commercial suicide. They can beat your prices and may be able to offer services you can't afford, such as free delivery.

But that doesn't mean you have to fold up your shop. Instead look for ways to serve different customer needs than the superstores do:

▶ Cater to the upper crust. Tailor your products or services to meet the needs of upper-income patrons. You can do this by offering special services or selling products that are different or much better quality than those the superstores carry.
▶ Offer free lessons to get people into your shop.
▶ Focus on personal service. Look for ways you can provide advice that the customer can't get in superstores.
▶ Be wary of customers who shop your store for information and then use it to buy products in a discount store. If you see that happening, consider whether you could turn your knowledge into training seminars, and charge admission to them.
▶ Look for related sales opportunities. Some travel agents who found airline ticket commissions slashed in the mid-1990s survived and grew by looking for cruises and tours to sell, by getting involved with meeting planning and special events, and by charging a fee for some services.

Chapter 20

KEEPING THE TAX
COLLECTOR AT BAY

Y ou work too hard for your money to give the government more tax dollars than necessary. But every year that's exactly what many small business owners and self-employed individuals do.

Some pay more than necessary because they fail to take advantage of all the
tax deductions and opportunities to shelter income that are available.

Others fail to pay their taxes on time (or at all!) or claim deductions to which
they aren't entitled. When the IRS catches up with them, they end up paying
penalties and interest charges that could have been avoided. In worst-case sce-
narios, bankruptcy, loss of one's home and possessions, or even a jail sentence
(if the IRS can prove tax fraud) can ensue.

You don't have to fall victim to these tax pitfalls. You can legally reduce your
taxes and avoid needless penalty and interest charges by familiarizing yourself
with tax laws and with tax-saving strategies that apply to you.

Here are some tips and hints to point you in the right direction. These tips
are based on the tax laws in effect as this book was being written.* Be sure to
check with your tax advisor to be certain that any specific suggestion is applicable to your situation and to obtain the latest tax information.

Start Out as a Sole Proprietor

From both a tax and a legal standpoint, the easiest method for starting up a business is to start out as a sole proprietor. Very little paperwork or cost is necessary
to start your business. Once the business has reached the point where it is profitable, you can consider changing your business over to a corporation or another

---

* This chapter presents only tips and hints. If you need basic information about taxable income, deductible expenses,
and estimated taxes, look at the tax help guides from J.K. Lasser, Ernst & Young, or other sources. You'll find them
in bookstores and public libraries. Be sure to talk to your tax advisor as well.

form of business. Besides the ease of startup, operating as a sole proprietor gives you these tax advantages:

▶ You can get cash out of your business easily without causing "double taxation." (Double taxation is discussed later in this chapter.)

▶ You don't have to pay unemployment insurance for yourself. In most states, you don't have to pay worker's compensation insurance for yourself, either.

▶ You can take deductions for the business use of your home if your work area qualifies as a home office. (C corporations can't take this deduction.)

Transfer Personal Assets to the Business to Save Taxes

If you have personal assets such as a computer, furniture, or books that you will use in your business, you can reduce your business taxes by transferring the assets to the business and depreciating them over their useful life.

The value of the assets at the time of transfer is called the basis and is the amount you can depreciate. For tax purposes, this value is pegged at either the fair market value at the time you transfer the assets to the business or their cost when you purchased them, whichever is lower. For example, a computer you purchased a couple of years ago is worth less now than when you purchased it. Your basis (what you can depreciate) is its current value, not what you paid for it, because the current value is lower.

▶ **Note**
Personal assets converted to business use aren't eligible for Section 179 treatment (but they are eligible to be depreciated using standard depreciation tables issued by the IRS). Section 179 is a special provision in the tax code that allows a large deduction in the year an asset is purchased and will be discussed later in this chapter.

Make Quarterly Estimated Income Tax Payments and Make Them on Time

Although you file an income tax return once a year, you are expected to make tax payments on a pay-as-you-go basis periodically during the year. If you don't, the IRS will charge you a late payment penalty based on the number of days late each payment is.

When you work as an employee, your employer withholds tax payments from your paychecks and sends them to the IRS periodically for you. When there is no income other than wages, the amount withheld from your paycheck is usually sufficient to cover most of your tax obligation and thus avoid late payment penalties.

But when you are self-employed (and in other circumstances where withholding won't fully cover your tax liability), you have to send tax payments to the IRS yourself. These payments must be made quarterly if your federal income tax and self-employment tax, minus any withholding sent in by an employer, will be $1,000 or more at the end of the year.

To avoid a late payment penalty, if you are an individual taxpayer, the total of these four estimated payments must be at least 100 percent of what you paid in taxes last year or 90 percent of your tax liability for the current year if your adjusted gross income for last year was under $150,000. If your individual adjusted gross income (AGI) was $150,000 or more last year ($75,000 if married filing separately), your quarterly payments need to add up to 110 percent of last year's tax bill or 90 percent of the current year's taxes.

In most cases, each installment payment should be one-fourth of the total estimated tax for the year. If you pay your taxes on a calendar year basis, the payments are due on April 15, June 15, September 15, and January 15. The April 15 payment is in addition to and separate from any payments due for the prior year's tax return, which is also due on April 15.

Don't Make Bigger Quarterly Payments Than Necessary

Many individuals with AGI under $150,000 attempt to pay 25 percent of their estimated taxes (based on 100 percent or more of the current year's tax) in each quarterly payment so they don't have to worry about big tax bills or penalties when they file their yearly tax return.

Paying in more than necessary, however, doesn't make much financial sense (unless it's impossible for you to keep from spending the money). In essence, paying more than the required minimum gives the IRS a free loan.

You will usually come out ahead financially by paying the IRS only the minimum due each quarter and keeping any additional amount you expect to owe in an interest-bearing account until it's time to file your return.

For instance, suppose your adjusted gross income last year was under $150,000 and you had to pay $10,000 in income and self-employment taxes. This year, your business did exceptionally well, and you expect your total tax bite to be $25,000. Instead of paying the IRS $6,250 each quarter (one-fourth of $25,000), you could comply with the laws and avoid penalties by paying the IRS $2,500 (one-fourth of last year's $10,000 tax bill) each quarter. You would then put the $3,750 ($6,250 − $2,500) difference each quarter away in your own bank account where it can earn interest for you until it's time to file your yearly tax return and pay the balance due.

▶ <u>Note</u>

<u>Estimated tax payments for C corporations must equal 100 percent of last year's</u>
<u>tax if the return had a tax liability; if no liability existed, then the corpo-</u>
<u>ration must pay in at least 90 percent of the current year's liability to avoid</u>
<u>late payment penalties. If you run a C corporation, be sure your quarterly cor-</u>
<u>porate taxes are estimated accordingly.</u>

Pay Whichever Way Saves the Most Money

For some high-income taxpayers, it costs more to pay an accountant to determine in advance what the current year's tax liability will be than it costs to pay the penalties if they actually owe more than the previous year. For such taxpayers, it may be cheaper to pay 100 percent of last year's tax plus resulting penalties (if you owe more than that) than it would be to attempt to avoid a penalty.

Others may find it's cheaper to pay 110 percent of last year's taxes and forgo the interest than it is to pay the penalty.

Increase Payroll Withholding to Avoid Penalties

Unlike individual estimated tax payments, the total amount paid in withholding taxes is treated as though it had been paid in equal installments through the year. Thus, if you realize midyear or later that you've underpaid your individual estimated tax payments, you could avoid penalty by having your employer or your spouse's employer withhold enough money for the remainder of the year to bring your total tax payments up to 100 percent of last year's tax bill or 90 percent of what you'll owe this year. If you operate as a corporation, you could increase the withholding tax on your own salary as well.

Make the Last Estimated State Tax Payment by the End of Your Tax Year

All the income taxes you pay your state and city governments can be deducted on your federal tax return if you qualify to itemize your deductions. You can deduct only the taxes in the year you actually pay them, however.

If you are a calendar basis taxpayer, your tax year runs from January 1 to December 31, but you don't have to pay the last quarterly state or federal tax installment until January 15. Paying it then pushes the payment into the next tax year, however, preventing you from taking a deduction on your federal return for the year to which the tax money applies. To avoid this situation, be sure to make your last state estimated tax payment by December 31.

Deduct All the State Tax You Are Entitled To

If your business did so well that you owed state income tax for the previous year, don't forget to take that payment off as a tax deduction on this year's return if you can itemize your deductions. For example, suppose in 1999 you make significantly more than you did in 1998. As a result, you owed more taxes than you paid in estimated income taxes. You paid the deficit in 2000 when you filed your 1999 return. When calculating the amount of state tax to be deducted on your personal federal tax return (schedule A, form 1040), be sure to add that payment to the amount of state estimated tax payments paid in 1999. Then add that combined total to any state tax withheld from paychecks you or your spouse received from employers during 1999.

> ## ▶ A Word of Caution
>
> If you are required to pay alternative minimum tax (AMT), you won't get a deduction for this payment. If you normally come close to having to pay AMT, you may trigger that tax by making this payment. Be sure of your tax situation before paying the tax early so that you don't unintentionally trigger AMT and lose the deduction for the state taxes paid.

Don't Underreport Deductible Expenses

Some people fail to report all of their deductible expenses for fear the IRS will challenge the deductions or disallow them. But underreporting deductible expenses doesn't make much economic sense.

"The government gets a substantial portion of your earnings," says Jack Slick, a CPA from Hagerstown, Maryland. "For example, if you are like many sole proprietors, you are in the 28 percent tax bracket. When you add the 15.3 percent self-employment tax rate to your federal tax rate and then add in your state tax rate, you can see that government in some form is a 50 percent partner in your business."

"The tax laws allow you to deduct all business expenses that are ordinary and necessary in the course of business. If you don't deduct every expense allowed, you are paying 50 percent of whatever you don't deduct to your 'silent partner.'"

Some deductible expenses are lost because the business owner decides that he or she doesn't have the time or can't be bothered keeping track of items like business mileage or out-of-pocket expenses. Others are lost because the business owner doesn't take steps necessary to qualify the business to take a deduction. "Failing to structure an office in the home properly to permit a deduction for it is one common way this occurs," says Slick.

But perhaps the biggest reason items aren't deducted is that record keeping is sloppy and haphazard. "Although it may be a hassle to record expenses as you incur them," Slick says, "at 50 cents on the dollar it more than pays off come tax time."

Take the Home Office Deduction if You Are Entitled to It

The home office deduction is a deduction you can take for using your home for business. When you take the home office deduction, you get to deduct depreciation for the portion of your home used in the business. You also can deduct a portion of your mortgage interest and real estate taxes as a business expense. This in turn lowers your business profit, and hence the amount of self-employment tax you have to pay on your profits.

In addition, when you declare a home office deduction, you are entitled to deduct a percent of gas, electric, and other utility costs proportionate to the percent of business use of the home.

You may also deduct depreciation on the business-use portion of your home. You will have to "recapture" the depreciation you've taken when you sell your home, however. Consult your tax advisor for more information on this type of deduction.

Added all together, these deductions can give you a nice tax break if you qualify for the home office deduction. To qualify, you need to use your office regularly and exclusively for business, and it needs to be your principal place of business. For taxable years beginning after December 31, 1998, a "principal place of business" includes the following: You use the office to conduct administrative or management activities of your business, and there is no other fixed location of your business where you conduct these activities.

This means that if you have a service-related business that you perform outside your home, you are now entitled to take a home office deduction for the part of your home or apartment that you use regularly and exclusively to run the business. (Prior to 1998, businesses such as cleaning services or repair services that performed work at clients' locations were not entitled to the home office deduction.)

Although the home office deduction is cited as a frequent trigger for audits, it makes

---

Don't Forget These Deductions!

Here are several deductions that business owners often forget to take.

- Cost of education to improve management or other business skills
- Tips given waiters, bellcaps
- Bank services charges
- Interest on business credit card purchases
- Cab fare
- Car mileage on short trips
- Train, cab, or bus fares
- Tolls and parking fees
- Postage

sense to take the deduction if you have a home office that qualifies and don't have anything to hide on your returns. The deduction could save you hundreds of dollars or more in taxes each year.

Let the Business Pay for Your Personal Travel Legally

You can give yourself nearly free, tax-deductible minivacations by tacking short personal trips onto legitimate business trips. Here's how it works.

The cost of business trips are tax deductible to your business as long as they are valid and necessary to the business. Thus, your air fare, cab fares, tips, hotel room,* and other travel expenses for the business portion of your trip are 100 percent deductible. Meals and entertainment for your business trip are 50 percent deductible.

As long as the main reason for your trip is business, you could go sightseeing or visit friends at your own expense during your business trip. Although you cannot deduct these personal expenses or any extra hotel fees incurred as a result of the personal aspect of the trip, you can still take all the business deductions you are entitled to for the trip, including the cost of the round-trip airfare.

For example, you have to travel to Orlando for five days to attend a convention and meet with potential clients. Your costs for attending the conference and meeting with the clients are deductible as noted.

> ▶ <u>Tip</u>
> <u>It's often necessary to stay over a Saturday night to take advantage of air fare</u>
> <u>and lodging discounts. If you can prove it's cheaper to stay the extra time than</u>
> <u>it is to make the business trip without staying over Saturday night, you can</u>
> <u>deduct the extra hotel costs. Thus, if your business trip ends on Friday and you</u>
> <u>stay until Sunday to take advantage of the discount, the hotel bill for Friday</u>
> <u>night and Saturday night would be tax deductible.</u>

After the convention and your business meetings are finished, you spend two days visiting theme parks. The costs of personal sightseeing, travel expenses incurred for personal side trips, and extra hotel costs for extra days spent on personal vacation are nondeductible personal expenses. However, as long as the primary reason for making the trip is business, your personal activities during the trip won't prevent you from taking the full deduction for air fare to Orlando and other expenses related to the business portion of the trip.

---

* Under the tax laws, you must be away from your "business home" overnight in order to take a tax deduction for a hotel room.

Important Reminders

▶ You must be able to prove that the primary reason for your trips was business. If you are audited, the amount of time you spend on business compared to the amount of time you spend on personal activities will be important in determining the primary reason for your trip. Therefore, you should keep good records showing who you saw, how long you spent, what business was discussed, what the results were.

▶ If you stay over a weekend, keep records documenting the price savings you achieved by staying the extra time. Be sure to get pricing from more than one airline and hotel to prove your case.

▶ Different rules apply to combined business/personal trips outside the United States. If you travel out of the country on business, don't spend more than one-fourth of your time on personal activities. The reason: If more than 25 percent of your time is spent on personal activities, the cost of travel has to be allocated between personal and business use even if the trip was primarily for business. For instance, if 30 percent of your time was spent on sightseeing in Germany, only 70 percent of your air fare to Germany would be a deductible business cost.

▶ You can't deduct the cost of attending investment seminars, and generally can't deduct the cost of traveling to a shareholders' meeting.

▶ Deductions for trips on luxury liners are limited to twice the per-diem rate allowable to federal employees on business in the United States. Conferences held on cruise ships are generally not deductible.

Let the IRS Pick Up Your Cleaning Bills When You Travel

When you go on business trips, don't bring dirty clothes home to be washed or to go to the cleaners. Take care of them while you are still away. The cost of cleaning clothes while on a business trip is fully deductible.

▶ **Warning**
Find out what the hotel charges for cleaning. Sometimes the prices are double what you'd pay in your local cleaner. (There's usually a cleaning price list in the closet. Most often it's inside a plastic bag on a hanger or on the top shelf of the closet.)

Deduct the Cost of Using the Internet and Online Computer Services

Online services such as America Online (AOL), Compuserve, Prodigy, and MSN are similar to business periodicals that you may subscribe to. The difference is that they contain not only business information but also personal information. As a business owner, you can deduct the costs of your online time if you use these services for research pertaining to your business or participate in forums that directly apply to your business.

For example, if you are connected to a service and you spend time in a software forum to get help using a program in your business, you can deduct the online charge for that time. If you also participate in forums that don't have a business connection or visit Web sites for personal reasons rather than business, you will have to prorate your online bill between business use and personal use.

> ▶ **Tip**
>
> If you use an ISP (Internet service provider) for access to the Internet, either alone or in combination with AOL or any other service, don't forget to deduct the fee the ISP charges.

Make Your Childrens' Allowance and Tuition a Deductible Business Expense

This is one fringe benefit that's easy for business owners to implement. Instead of giving your kids an allowance, put them to work in your business and let them earn the money. Their salary will be a deductible expense for your business. They will have to pay taxes on the income, but are likely to be in a lower tax bracket than you are.

You will have some additional paperwork to fill out. If you have no other employees, then you will need to get an employer identification number, and you will have to withhold federal and state taxes if your child earns more than the standard deduction. Your child is exempt from FICA and Medicare taxes if he or she is under eighteen years old and from unemployment taxes if under twenty-one years old. You will have to file form 941 quarterly and your state unemployment forms.

In addition, you will have to deposit the taxes withheld by you and your share of the employer's FICA and Medicare if it applies monthly by the 15th of the following month in most cases. If you have other employees and you have to deposit taxes on a schedule more frequent

> ▶ **Important**
>
> You can't take this deduction unless the child actually performs work for your business. Examples of the type of work they might do include cleaning the office, doing filing, typing letters, and so on.

than this, then you would include the taxes withheld for your child in your normal payroll tax deposit.

It involves a little more work on your end but you get a deduction for something you would have given your child anyway if you structure things properly. Additionally, your child gains work experience that may help him or her land a better job later on.

Employ Your Spouse and Deduct the Entire Amount of Your Medical Insurance Premiums

As a sole proprietor or more than 2 percent owner of an S corporation, your ability to deduct health insurance premiums is limited. As of 1999, you may deduct 60 percent of premiums paid for medical insurance as an adjustment to income (on form 1040). Any excess can be treated as a medical expense and may be deducted on schedule A if applicable. The adjustment to income is limited to your income (or salary for S corporations) from the business. It is not available to you if you are eligible to participate in an employer's health care plan available to you or your spouse.

There are no such limitations on the deductibility of medical insurance premiums you make on behalf of your employees, however. If your spouse is an employee of your business, the business can pay for (and deduct the cost of) his or her medical insurance. Your spouse would then add you as a dependent on his or her policy. This would make the entire premium deductible by your business as a business expense. If you don't have employees other than your spouse, and don't have any other good source of health insurance, this strategy offers significant tax savings by converting a personal expense to a business expense.

If you operate as a subchapter S corporation, a similar strategy can be used in conjunction with a medical reimbursement plan. (Medical reimbursement plans are self-insured plans that reimburse employees for medical expenses such as dental work or eyeglasses that may not be covered by health insurance plans.) Under normal circumstances, owners of S corporations don't qualify for medical reimbursement plans. However, if the corporation has a medical reimbursement plan for its employees and your spouse is an employee (but not an owner), he or she is covered by it and

▶ **Some Caveats**

As with hiring your children, your spouse must actually work in the business. If your spouse works only part time, or if there could be any reason for the IRS to doubt his or her involvement in the business, have your spouse keep a time card or other records to prove he or she works for you.

can add you and the children as dependents. The reimbursement payments would not be considered income to you in this circumstance.

If you have other employees, you may be required by the IRS to offer them the same pension and medical benefits package you offer your spouse.

Cut Payroll Taxes by Subcontracting Work or Using Independent Contractors

When you hire employees, you are required to pay unemployment taxes and a portion of their social security tax. If you have a Keogh, SEP, or other retirement plan, you will be required to put money into a plan for your employees, too, in many cases.

Depending on the work you need done, it may be possible to save these expenses by using independent contractors to do the work or by subcontracting the work to another company.

Because this is an area that is frequently abused, the IRS does scrutinize independent contractor arrangements. It has published a set of guidelines consisting of twenty items it considers in deciding if a worker is truly an independent contractor or not. The more your worker looks like an employee under these guidelines, the greater the possibility your claim for his or her independent status won't hold up.

The guidelines are as follows:

1. *Instructions.* An employee must comply with instructions about when, where, and how to work. Even if no instructions are given, the control factor is present if the employer has the right to give instructions.
2. *Training.* An employee is trained to perform services in a particular manner. Independent contractors ordinarily use their own methods and receive no training from the purchasers of their services.
3. *Integration.* An employee's services are integrated into the business operations because the services are important to the success or continuation of the business. This shows that the employee is subject to direction and control.
4. *Services rendered personally.* An employee renders services personally. This shows that the employer is interested in the methods as well as the results.
5. *Hiring assistants.* An employee works for an employer who hires, supervises, and pays assistants. An independent contractor hires, supervises, and pays assistants under a contract that requires him or her to provide materials and labor and to be responsible only for the result.

6. *Continuing relationship.* An employee has a continuing relationship with an employer. A continuing relationship may exist where work is performed at frequently recurring although irregular intervals.

7. *Set hours of work.* An employee has set hours of work established by an employer. An independent contractor is the master of his or her own time.

8. *Full-time work.* An employee normally works full time for an employer. An independent contractor can work when and for whom he or she chooses.

9. *Work done on premises.* An employee works on the premises of an employer, or works on a route or at a location designated by an employer.

10. *Order or sequence set.* An employee must perform services in the order or sequence set by an employer. This shows that the employee is subject to direction and control.

11. *Reports.* An employee submits reports to an employer. This shows that the employee must account to the employer for his or her actions.

12. *Payment.* An employee is paid by the hour, week, or month. An independent contractor is paid by the job or on a straight commission.

13. *Expenses.* An employee's business and travel expenses are paid by an employer. This shows that the employee is subject to regulation and control.

14. *Tools and materials.* An employee is furnished significant tools, materials, and other equipment by an employer.

15. *Investment.* An independent contractor has a significant investment in the facilities he or she uses in performing services for someone else.

16. *Profit or loss.* An independent contractor can make a profit or suffer a loss.

17. *Works for more than one person or firm.* An independent contractor provides his or her services to two or more unrelated persons or firms at the same time.

▶ <u>Caution</u>

<u>You can't just call an employee an independent contractor to avoid paying payroll taxes or benefits. Independent contractors must truly be independent. That means they must be free to work for other companies, should be able to complete the work using whatever means they choose (you determine the end result; they determine the method to achieve it), and should not need training or assistance from you in doing the work.</u>

18. *Offers services to general public.* An independent contractor makes his or her services available to the general public.

19. *Right to fire.* An employee can be fired by an employer. An independent contractor cannot be fired so long as he or she produces a result that meets the specifications of the contract.

20. *Right to quit.* An employee can quit his or her job at any time without incurring liability. An independent contractor usually agrees to complete a specific job and is responsible for its satisfactory completion, or is legally obligated to make good for failure to complete it.

▶ **Tip**

If you classify an employee as an independent contractor and you had no reasonable basis for doing so, you will have to pay employment taxes for that worker. Further, if you do not withhold income and social security taxes from his or her wages, you may be held personally liable for a penalty of 100 percent of the tax if you are the person responsible for the collection and payment of withholding taxes.

Reduce Taxes with Deductible Retirement Plan Contributions

You can reduce current taxes by making tax-deferred contributions to an Individual Retirement Account, Simplified Pension plan, Keogh plan, or other profit-sharing or qualified pension plan. Doing so lets you defer taxes on the amount of your earnings contributed until you take the money out at retirement. Taxes are also deferred on the interest the account earns.

The least complicated way to sock away tax-deferred money for retirement is through establishing an Individual Retirement Account (IRA).

If you are not covered by a qualified employer pension plan, you can make tax deductible contributions to your IRA of up to $2,000 even if your spouse is covered by a plan. (If your spouse is not covered by a plan, he or she can put up to $2,000 in a spousal IRA as well.) The deduction is phased out between $150,000–$160,000.

Since IRAs are available to any taxpayer with earned income, there is no requirement to fund an IRA for your employees.

An individual who is covered by a company pension plan is entitled to make a tax-deferred contribution of up to $2,000 to an IRA if his or her modified adjusted gross income (adjusted gross income before a deduction for the IRA) is under $51,000 for joint returns or under $31,000 for single returns for the 1999 tax year.

Once the modified adjusted gross income climbs above $51,000 for joint returns or $31,000 for single filers, the deductible amount is reduced, being phased out completely at $61,000 for joint returns or $41,000 for single returns in the 1999 tax year. Those dollar limits are scheduled to increase each year through 2005.

For example, Lisa is employed as a programmer and makes $65,000 a year. She participates in a pension plan provided by her employer. Her husband, Mike, is a self-employed consultant and makes $84,000. Because Lisa's modified adjusted income is above $60,000, she would not be able to make tax-deferred IRA contributions. However, Mike could make a tax-deferred contribution since he is not covered by another pension plan and his modified adjusted income is under $150,000.

Get Bigger Tax Deductions by Establishing a Qualified Pension Plan

If your business is profitable and you want a bigger tax savings than you can get with an IRA, consider establishing a Simplified Employee Pension (SEP) plan, or one or more qualified retirement plans.

A SEP is a cross between an individual IRA and a qualified pension plan. It lets employers contribute the lesser of 15 percent of employees' earned income or $24,000 to a pension plan. The contribution you are allowed for yourself is less. It is calculated on income minus the plan contribution. Your effective rate is 13.0435 percent on a maximum of $160,000 in earned income ($20,870).

Keogh plans are a bit more complicated. There are two basic kinds of Keogh plans: defined contribution and defined benefit.

With a defined contribution plan, you contribute a percentage of income to the plan each year. There are several methods for doing this. You can have a profit-sharing plan, which allows you to contribute up to 15 percent of compensation each year (as discussed elsewhere, the effective contribution is actually only 13.04 percent). Or you could choose a money purchase plan, which sets the contribution at a fixed rate when you establish the plan. A money purchase plan allows contributions of up to 25 percent or $30,000. Finally, you could have a combination of profit-sharing and money purchase plans. A common arrangement is for a small business to have a money purchase plan for 10 percent of income and a profit-sharing plan for 15 percent. This give them the ability to contribute up to the maximum amount, and the flexibility to lessen the burden (through not lowering the profit-sharing contribution or not making it at all) in years when profits slip.

A Keogh-defined benefit plan is one for which yearly contributions are based on the benefit that will be received at retirement rather than on the profits of the company. Calculating this amount requires a complex formula that takes into consideration the age of the individual, year to retirement, and other factors. Although it can potentially allow you to shelter much larger amounts of income each year, the complexity of the plan combined with the requirement to make contributions at set levels whether or not there are profits keep many businesses from adopting this particular form of Keogh plan.

Either a SEP or a Keogh plan is a good way to defer tax on income if you and your spouse are the only employees in your company. Their usefulness as a way to keep more of your income diminishes if you have other employees since you are likely to have to include them in the plan, too.

With a SEP plan, you have to include employees who are twenty-one or older, have worked for you in three of the five preceding years, and earn more than $400. Keogh plans give you a little more leeway regarding part-time employees and participation in the plan. The rules are complicated, though. Thus, if you have employees it's advisable to seek professional assistance in choosing the best pension plan for you and your company.

Boost Tax Savings the SIMPLE Way

The Savings Incentive Match Plan for Employees of Small Employers (SIMPLE) plan is yet another option. And it's one that lets some self-employed put away more money than they could with any other plan. Here's how it works.

Employees can choose to have their salaries reduced by up to $6,000. This amount is matched by the employer up to 3 percent of the employee's salary. This amount is not calculated as a percentage of income. If a self-employed person made $11,000, he or she could allocate the full $6,000 to the plan. Thus, some business owners come ahead with this plan.

Establish a Keogh Plan Before the End of the Tax Year

In order to take a deduction for a contribution to a Keogh plan, the plan must be in existence prior to the end of the year. But once it is set up (by making a very small deposit just to establish the plan, for instance), you can defer making the contribution to the plan until you actually file your return. Thus, you can take a deduction for retirement plan contributions and not actually make the contribution until as late as October 15 of the following year if you extend your personal return for the maximum allowable period.

Establish a SEP if you miss the deadline for starting a Keogh. If you didn't get a plan set up before the end of the year, you still have an option. You can set up a SEP up to the extended due date of your return. If you have employees, be sure to talk to your accountant before setting up the plan, however.

Pay Now, Save Later with a Roth IRA

If you expect to be in a higher income bracket after you retire than you are now, or if you don't qualify for a regular IRA, talk to your tax advisor about the advisability of a Roth IRA. The money you contribute to a Roth IRA is taxable in the year you make the contribution, but unlike a conventional IRA, as long as you meet the requirements, withdrawals and earnings are tax-free. There's one other difference, too. You can have a modified adjusted gross income of up to $95,000 as a taxpayer filing singly and still contribute the full $2,000 dollars to a Roth IRA.

Ask your tax advisor about nonqualified plans to reward key executives or to defer more money than allowed under qualified plans.

The IRS rules for qualified pension plans require you to set up plans that do not discriminate in favor of top executives. They also limit the total compensation on which benefits can be based to $160,000.

Depending on your business and personal circumstances, you may find it useful to adopt a nonqualified pension plan as a way to circumvent the antidiscrimination rules for pension plans or as a way to supplement retirement income for yourself or other highly-paid employees.

Essentially such plans, when properly set up, offer ways to defer compensation and taxes until retirement. The income is not tax deductible to the company, but is tax deferred for the recipient.

Nonqualified plans are unfunded (there's no requirement for the employer to set aside money to pay the pensions). So they can be risky for growing businesses where management might change. But depending on circumstances, they can be a good vehicle for putting aside money for retirement and rewarding key employees. Again, though, this is not a do-it-yourself project. Seek advice from an accountant or other tax advisor who can clearly explain all the rules and all of their possible effects on you and your business.

Do Your Personal Errands When You Run Business Errands

When you have to run errands for both business and personal reasons, combine your trips. This way the mileage you put on your car for the personal trip is deductible.

For example, you have to drop off a job at the printer. You also need to buy milk and eggs from the grocery store. The grocery store is on the way to the print shop. You can stop to pick up the milk and eggs without losing any business mileage deduction you were entitled to for the trip to the printer.

If the personal errand requires you to drive farther than you would have if you went only to get the printer, the cost of the additional miles is not deductible.

Route your sales calls so that you get the maximum deduction for mileage.

If you don't qualify to take an office in the home deduction, you won't be able to deduct all the miles you travel for business. The IRS considers the trip to your first work site of the day and the trip home from the last work site of the day to be nondeductible commuting mileage. You can, however, take a deduction for any miles you drive between the first and last trip of the day.

To make more of the miles you travel each day deductible, whenever possible schedule your first stop and your last stop of the day as close to home as possible.

Accelerate Expenses and Defer Income to Reduce Your Taxes

As a cash basis taxpayer, you have the ability to do some tax planning at the end of the year. You can pay for expenses that you normally wouldn't pay until after the year ends to get the deduction in the current year. In addition you can defer recognizing income. For example, you have the ability not to bill customers until after the first of the year for work you did in December.

Buy Customer Supplies and Parts on Demand to Avoid Tax and Accounting Headaches

Generally, a sole proprietor can operate on the cash basis. However, where inventory is material, you may be forced to account for your business on the accrual method. Under the accrual method, income is accounted for (considered received) as and when you earn it (as opposed to when you collect payment). Expenses have to be deducted when you incur them (for instance, when you order something) rather than when you pay them.

This makes accounting more complicated if you are doing your own books, and does not allow you to defer income or accelerate expenses to lower your tax bill. Therefore if you can eliminate inventory, you can keep your business from having to use the accrual basis of accounting and give yourself more options to save taxes.

Use the Section 179 Election to Lower Your Taxes When You Purchase Equipment

Purchases that can be expected to benefit your business for more than a year (a computer, for instance) are considered capital expenses. Under IRS rules, the cost of such items are depreciated (spread out over the estimated useful life of the item, which is often five years or more).

There is a special provision of the tax law, however, that allows you to deduct up to $19,000 in assets in the year you purchase them rather than depreciating them over time. This both avoids the need for maintaining depreciation schedules for your equipment, and also can result in substantial tax savings in the year an asset is purchased.

This provision is called the section 179 election. You make the election by filling out the section 179 on form 4562. The election can't cause a loss, but if you operate as a sole proprietor, the IRS considers all earned income on your tax return to be "business" income. Thus you can use income from any paid job you or your spouse has to qualify the expense and take up to the maximum deduction.

Items that will be expensed can be purchased right up to December 31. Thus if you see a large tax bill looming toward the end of the year, you may want to buy the items before the end of the year to take advantage of the tax savings. If you don't have the cash, put the purchase on a credit card. Credit card purchases are considered completed on the date of purchase, not when you pay the bill.

There are a few limitations you should be aware of:

▶ The expense deduction is prorated to business use. If you use the asset less than 100 percent for business, you have to reduce your deduction accordingly. For instance, if you purchase a computer for $2,400 and use it 75 percent of the time for business, you can expense only 75 percent of the cost, or $1,800.

▶ If you use the asset less than 50 percent of the time for business, you can't expense it. You can use normal depreciation methods, except for listed property, for which you must use straight-line depreciation to depreciate the business portion of the cost.

▶ Married individuals are treated as one taxpayer for the expense deduction whether they file a joint return or separate returns. That means if both a husband and wife have businesses, the two businesses together can't expense more than $19,000.

▶ You cannot expense purchases if you buy more than $200,000 in assets during the year.

▶ If you dispose of the asset before the end of what the IRS considers to be its useful life, you may have to recapture (add back as income) a portion of the amount you expensed for the equipment.

Deduct Interest on Business Loans and Credit Card Purchases

Interest you pay on personal loans and on charge card balances for items purchased for personal use aren't tax deductible. Interest you pay on outstanding business debt is deductible, however. Thus you can deduct the interest on a business loan, and you can deduct the interest you pay on credit card balances that result from business purchases.

Both loan interest and credit card interest can be prorated between business and personal when money borrowed or items purchased are used partly for business and partly for personal use.

For example, you take out a $4,000 personal loan to purchase a computer, software, and printer that you will use 100 percent for your business. You operate the business under your own name and don't have a separate business checking account. You get the loan and deposit it in your personal checking account. You wait two weeks after getting the loan to buy the computer. In the meantime, you pay your mortgage, utility bills, and other personal bills amounting to $2,000. Then you go to the computer store and spend $4,000 on the computer system. If you are audited, the IRS could declare that the $2,000 worth of personal bills you paid came out of the loan money, and therefore allow you to deduct interest only on the remaining $2,000 of the loan as a business expense.

Use the prescribed depreciation method rather than straight-line depreciation.

▶ **Caution**

If you take out a personal loan to make business purchases, immediately deposit the money into your business account to make the money deductible, or if you don't have separate personal and business accounts, make the very first purchase you make after getting the loan the business purchase. If you don't, the IRS can claim that all purchases made after the loan and before the business purchase came out of the loan proceeds, therefore making the interest a nondeductible personal expense.

If you must depreciate assets over time, use the rates prescribed by the IRS instead of straight-line depreciation. Although straight-line depreciation is simpler to calculate (you simply divide the cost of the item over the useful life allowed by the IRS), the prescribed method will give you a much higher tax deduction in the early years of an assets' life.

Keep Your Receipts

This can't be stressed enough. If you are ever audited, you will have difficulty proving your deductions and could have many of them disallowed.

The most heavily scrutinized expense on a tax return is for travel and entertainment. You can deduct business meals only if you are traveling away from home on business overnight, or if specific items of business are discussed before, during, or after the meal. (Entertainment is covered by a similar rule.) A general "good will" discussion does not qualify.

Your receipt for these items will prove you actually incurred the expense. They can also help substantiate the business nature of the expense if you make a notation on the receipt when you get it indicating who you entertained and the business matters discussed. The minute it takes to document your receipts in this way (and to put them in a safe place on return to your office) can save you money by preventing valid deductions from being disallowed on audit.

▶ **Tip**

The easiest way to separate business credit card interest expense from interest on personal credit card charges is to get a separate charge card and use it exclusively for business.

Don't Rely on Canceled Checks for Receipts

A canceled check is generally not valid documentation for a business expense. The invoice or receipt is what the IRS is going to want to see. The check doesn't provide the auditor with adequate documentation as to whether the expense was ordinary and necessary.

Another reason to hang on to receipts is that where you paid in cash for an item, the receipt is your only means of documenting your expense.

Deduct Sales Taxes on Business Purchases

When you make purchases for personal use, the sales tax is not a deductible expense. Sales tax is deductible, however, on business purchases. If you buy an item that you use partly in business and partly for personal use, be sure to deduct the business use percentage of the sale tax. For consumable supplies, the cost would be deducted as a business expense in the year the item was purchased. If the item purchased was an asset that is being expensed or depreciated, the sales tax would be included in the basis used to figure the expense or depreciation deduction. As with other deductions, if an item is being used partly for business and partly for personal use, you can deduct only the portion of the sales tax attributable to the business use.

When Income Warrants, Consider Incorporation

When your business becomes profitable, you may be able to derive some tax benefits by incorporating as either a C corporation or an S corporation.

A C corporation is the "regular" corporate structure. In a C corporation, the corporation is a separate taxpayer from its shareholders. The corporation is taxed on its income at special corporate rates. (The corporate income is the profits that are left over after all expenses and salaries, including owner or stockholder salaries, are paid.) If the corporation isn't a personal service corporation, these rates are lower than personal tax rates on income under $75,000.

Where you need to retain significant profits because you plan to invest in equipment or will need working capital in the foreseeable future, it may make sense to retain income in the corporation, reducing your tax liability on the retained income.

When you operate as a C corporation, you can give yourself a variety of benefits, including company-paid life insurance, health insurance policy, and company reimbursements for medical costs. These benefits are all tax deductible to the corporation, and tax free to you, the employee of your corporation. You must, however, follow IRS rules for including employees other than yourself in benefits plans offered by your company.

You can even use your C corporation as a bank, giving yourself an interest-free loan for amounts of under $10,000. (Be sure to document the loan and set up a repayment schedule or issue a promissory note to repay the loan on a certain date.)

The biggest disadvantage to a C corporation is the difficulty in getting cash out of it. There are essentially two ways to get money out of the corporation.

One is by taking it out in salary. The more salary the corporation pays you, the lower its profits and the lower its taxable income. If the business is doing very well, and doesn't need to retain earnings for future expansion or expenses, you might want to give yourself a very generous salary.

Unfortunately, the IRS has the ability to limit the salary a corporation pays employee/shareholders to "reasonable" compensation. In other words, if your compensation exceeds the average compensation for someone performing your duties in a business your size and in your general area, the

IRS can challenge the salary as being unreasonable and attempt to reclassify some of your salary as dividends.

Dividends are the worst possible means of getting cash out of a C corporation. A dividend is a distribution of profits that the corporation has earned and already paid tax on. When the profits are distributed to shareholders as dividends, the dividends are considered taxable income to the shareholders and are taxed at their tax rate on their personal tax return. This is called "double taxation" and is why your small corporation should avoid paying dividends if at all possible.

Choose an S corporation to Get Money out with Less Hassle

Every business that incorporates starts out as a C corporation. Once a business has incorporated, however, if it is eligible, its shareholders can elect to operate as a special form of corporation known as an S corporation.*

In an S corporation, all corporate profits pass directly to the shareholders, where they are taxed once—at each individual shareholder's tax rate. This avoids the double taxation associated with C corporations, making it much easier for shareholders to get money out of the corporation.

The corporate profits that pass through to shareholders are considered dividends, not earned income. Therefore they are not subject to self-employment or social security tax. If you set yourself a low salary and take the difference as a dividend, this loophole can potentially save you thousands of dollar over what you'd pay in self-employment tax (social security) as a sole proprietor.

For instance, if your profit for the year as a sole proprietor is $60,000, you have to pay $9,180 in self-employment tax† (15.3 percent self-employment tax × $60,000). This is in addition to the income tax due on your earnings.

If you operate as an S corporation, however, you might set your salary at $30,000 at the beginning of the year. You'd then take the remaining $30,000 as dividends. Although the entire $60,000 is still subject to income taxes, only $30,000 in salary is subject to social security tax. Thus you'd pay only $4,590 (15.3 percent × $30,000) instead of the $9,180 you pay on $60,000 of income as a sole proprietor.

The tradeoff, with an S corporation, is that under the current law you lose many of the tax breaks such as company-paid benefits that you can take as a C corporation.

---

* The key eligibility requirements for an S corporation are that there may be no more than seventy-five shareholders, it must be a domestic corporation, it must have only one class of stock, it can't own more than 80 percent of the stock in another corporation, and all shareholders must consent in writing to the S corporation status. For further information on S corporation eligibility, contact your accountant or the IRS.

† Self-employment is what social security tax is called when paid by a sole proprietor.

▶ **Note**
You have to set your salary at a reasonable level. If you don't, the IRS can step in and declare the dividend to be taxable salary. However, you only have to pay yourself what you'd pay anyone you hired to do similar work.

Watch out for the Built-In Gains Tax

If you have been operating for some time as a C corporation and then switch to an S corporation, the change could trigger something know as the built-in gains tax. This tax can be triggered in other ways as well when there is a transfer of property between the shareholder and the corporation. If you will be transferring property, liabilities, or receivables to your new S corporation, get advice from your accountant on how to structure the change so that you don't stumble into any tax pitfalls.

Consider a Limited Liability Company Structure Instead of Incorporating

A new form of doing business to emerge is the limited liability company (LLC). An LLC combines the best of a partnership with the limited liability of a corporation. The disadvantage to this form of business is that it is fairly new and not much case law exists to determine if the limited liability concept will hold up in court.

If more than one person owns the business, however, an LLC offers some advantages that S corporations don't. For instance, with an LLC, you can create an agreement that gives different shareholders different rates of return on their investment. You can't do that with an S corporation. You can also use an LLC if more than seventy-five shareholders are involved in the business or if any of the shareholders are nonresident aliens or corporations. LLC laws vary from state to state, so be sure to get advice from a professional in your state before adopting this form of business.

Profit as a Nonprofit Organization

Being a nonprofit organization doesn't necessarily mean that you can't make a living. A nonprofit corporation can pay you a salary for your services, and some executive directors of some nonprofits make quite substantial salaries. If the nonprofit corporation makes a profit, however, it can't distribute those profits to you. The only way you can get money from a nonprofit is as salary. Qualifying as a nonprofit organization is an extensive task. However, if you want to do something that benefits others and still earn a living, it is a viable option. You will have to jump through many hoops to get the organization formed and operating; because of this, not many people feel this is worth the effort.

Watch out for Hobby-Loss Rules

As a business owner, you are entitled to take deductions for all the expenses you incur in your business. If you have losses, you are entitled to use those losses to offset other income you have.

If you engage in an income-producing hobby, however, you are entitled only to deduct expenses up to the amount of income from the hobby. Furthermore, those deductions for hobby losses are miscellaneous deductions, and you can deduct only the amount that exceeds the 2 percent "floor" on miscellaneous deductions on form 1040, schedule A.

Businesses that show losses year after year stand a risk of having the IRS declare the business is really a hobby. Businesses at particular risk would be part-time businesses that require expensive equipment or purchases that might also be considered hobbies. The IRS might declare part-time photography businesses, computer consultants, or stamp dealers to be engaged in a hobby, for instance, if expenses were always higher than income.

The way to avoid the IRS from classifying your business as a hobby is to make a profit. The IRS will presume your activity is a business if you make a profit in three out of five years, including the current year, for most businesses. (For businesses involving horses, the time is extended to five out of seven years.)

If you don't expect to be profitable in three of five years, be sure to keep records of all of your business correspondence, your business plans, and any other documentation that you may have that will indicate the business nature of your activities and your intent to make a profit. Detailed record keeping, professionalism in the way you go about your activity, and other signs that you are treating it as a business and trying to make it profitable can help prove your case if you should be audited and the IRS should try to reclassify your business as a hobby.

Keep Accounting Costs Down

Making a legible notation on each receipt about the business purpose of an expense will help support the deductions, but that's not all you have to do to keep the IRS happy.

You must be able to give the IRS a clear record of income and expenses for your business. And, come tax time, the expenses have to be tallied up by category (advertising expense, insurance expense, office expense, and so on).

If you just hand your accountant or tax preparer deposit slips showing your income and a shoe box full receipts for expenses, he or she can probably sort it all out for you, but you will pay their rate or rate they charge for office staff assistance for the work.

You can save money by keeping records yourself either on paper in an acceptable format, or by entering income and expenses in an accounting program if you have a computer.

Many home businesses with no employees and no inventory can manage very well with a simple expense-tracking programs like Quicken, published by Intuit, or Microsoft Money. Others will want something a little more sophisticated, such as Intuit's QuickBooks Pro. QuickBooks Pro includes estimating, payroll, and time-tracking modules, along with a setup program that walks you through setting up the program to work for many specific types of businesses.

If you need a more sophisticated program, it would be advisable to ask your accountant for recommendations. Also ask if he or she offers a service to set up the program to work properly for your business.

You can also keep accounting costs down by following these suggestions:

▶ Keep phone calls to the point. You don't have to be abrupt or cold, but don't spend too much time chatting about the way your son scored the winning goal in last week's soccer game, either. "The only thing an accountant has to sell is his time," says CPA Jack Slick. "If your call lasts fifteen minutes or more that's a significant chunk of time and you're likely to get billed for it."

▶ Give your accountant all the information he or she needs to work with. Every time the accountant starts to do your work, there will be a certain amount of make-ready time involved to get out the records, find what's needed and get started. If your accountant has to stop in the middle of doing your work and put it away because some important piece of information is missing, you'll be paying for that make-ready time twice.

Use Popular Computer Software to Prepare Your Own Taxes if Your Business Needs Are Simple

If you are a cash-basis taxpayer, operate as a sole proprietor, and have a basic understanding of tax laws affecting your business and your personal return, you may save money at tax time by using one of the popular computer software programs such as TurboTax, MacinTax, or Kiplinger TaxCut to prepare your own tax return. You will need to buy two programs: a federal tax version of the program and a version for completing your state taxes. The price for both together is generally under $100. Although the programs are designed for novices, you should be familiar with using your computer as well as with the tax laws. April 15 is not the time to sit there and try to figure out what you have to do to hook up a printer to your computer and make it work.

Use a Professional When Your Return Is Complex or Your Income High

If you have a complicated return or made a lot of money, your best bet would be to have a professional prepare your tax return for you. The cost of a professional's work will be more than offset by the time and trouble they save you. More important, they may know of tax breaks you qualify for that you would otherwise miss, and could save you hundreds or even thousands of dollars in taxes. The professional can also advise you on steps you can take now to cut your tax bill in the future.

Get Free Help from the IRS

The IRS isn't likely to help you find loopholes in the law, but it does offer free help understanding the laws. If you need help with a specific question, you can call 800-829-1040. If you try to call that number near the time that tax returns are due, expect difficulty getting through, however.

If you have several questions, or can't get through on the 800-number, you can also get free assistance by visiting the IRS office located nearest to you. Try to arrive in the morning, and again don't wait until the end of March or April to go.

If you need more extensive information than a counselor can provide in a short time, call the IRS and ask if it will be holding a tax workshop in your area soon. These are conducted through the IRS Small Business Tax Education Program.

Make sure that you document any assistance you get from the IRS, including the name of the person you spoke to and the time and date. If the item you received help for is questioned in an audit, you can avoid penalties by showing that you relied on IRS advice.

Get Free Tax Help Online

If you have a computer and modem, you can also find free tax help available on the commercial online services. One section of the Business Know-How Forum on America Online (keyword, BKH) offers tax facts and help for small business owners and the self-employed. Intuit (http://www.intuit.com) has a variety of tax information available, and the Motley Fool (keyword, Fools on America Online) provides useful information on tax issues related to investments and pension plans. You can also view all the IRS taxpayer information publications on the IRS Web site at http://www.irs.treas.gov.

In many cases, the individuals who answer tax questions in online forums are professional tax preparers or accountants. Though their answers can be useful for gathering general information, they have no way of knowing all of your financial details and are not a substitute for getting help from your own tax advisor.

Get Copies of Forms or Instructions You Need at the Last Minute

If you need tax forms, you can get them online, too. They are available in Adobe Acrobat format on the IRS Web site, and in various online forums and Web sites that make tax information available. They can be read and printed using Adobe Acrobat Reader, which is available free of charge from the Adobe company Web site (http://www.adobe.com).

Work Out a Payment Schedule

As long as you file your tax return and aren't guilty of tax fraud, the IRS isn't going to arrest you if you can't pay your taxes. Neither are they interested in taking away your house and all of your possessions. What they want is to collect the money due to them.

If you can't pay your bill when the taxes are due and don't want to take out a bank loan or can't get one, complete your return and mail it without a check. The IRS will send you a notice in about a month asking for payment of the tax bill plus late payment fees. If you can't pay at that time, contact the IRS and ask to work out a payment schedule.

Ask for an Extension of the Time to File Your Return

If you don't file your tax return on time, the IRS will assess stiff late filing penalties. These are in addition to any late payment penalties you may owe.

Don't panic, though, if circumstances prevent you from completing your tax return on time. You can get an extension of the filing deadline from the IRS by filling out a simple form and mailing it to the IRS on or before April 15.

The extension gives cash-basis taxpayers until August 15 to file their return. To avoid interest charges accruing on money you owe to the IRS, you must estimate the amount of taxes you owe and send a check for any amount you may owe.

Chapter 21

MAKING

CASH FLOW

ash flow is a problem that plagues every small office from time to time. On paper, you look as if you're doing very well. Your sales are higher than your expenses. Things look as if you should be making a profit. But your creditors are breathing down your neck, and you're always playing catch up. What can you do about it? Here are some tips to get you moving in the right direction.

Raise Your Prices

When you started your business you may have priced your products or services on the low side as a way to attract customers, or because you didn't realize what all of your costs of doing business would be. Now, you may have plenty of work coming in, but it may not be profitable. You may find that you have to work eighty hours a week to get the work done, or that your costs for supplies or raw materials have increased. Or you may have expenses you hadn't planned on, like the cost of payroll taxes for employees, a need to move out of the home and to rent office space, or a need for new equipment or more physical space to run your business.

If you are in a situation like this, or if you are still charging the same prices you did four or five years ago, raise your prices. You can't stay in business if you don't charge enough to pay your bills and make a profit. Unless your business is very price competitive, you shouldn't lose many customers if you have good relationships with them.

Blame It on Your Accountant

Some clients, particularly those who were your first clients, may get annoyed when you announce you are raising your prices. They may believe you "owe them" for helping you get your start, and that your price increase is a betrayal. If the customer is one you want to keep, the way to defuse the situation is to take the personal element out of it. Instead of arguing about why you decided to increase your prices, sympathize with the client and then attribute the decision to your accountant. You might say, for example, "You know, John, I really didn't want to raise my prices. But my accountant said I had no choice."

Most professional advisors will be happy to go along with you, as long as you tell them ahead of time and as long as it sounds like something they'd really recommend.

Work on Retainer

One of the problems with self-employment is that income may vary drastically from month to month. When you wear all the business hats, the need to do the work often interferes with ongoing marketing. If you don't market steadily, there will be times when no business comes in, and as a result, times when no money comes in. Under this feast-or-famine scenario, you may get $20,000 in payments one week, and then not get another cent for two or three months.

One way to even out the irregularities in cash flow is to seek clients who will put you on retainer, paying you a guaranteed amount of money each month. Retainers are usually set up so that you guarantee you will set aside a specific number of hours to do work for a client each month. The client pays that amount whether they use up all the time or not. If they go over the time, they pay an additional, hourly fee. If they don't use up all the time, they lose it. The unused time does not accumulate from month to month.

Lawyers and accountants use arrangements similar to this. Public relations, computer consulting, and other businesses in which clients may need repeat attention are good candidates as well.

Watch Check Clearance Times

Money in the bank isn't money to spend—at least not immediately. Banks may take two business days to clear local checks. If your customers are out of state, your bank may hold deposits for up to ten business days. If sizable amounts of money are involved, those ten business days can seem like eternity.

▶ **Tip**

Tired of waiting a long time for checks to clear? Call several banks in your area and ask what their policies are. Some may clear checks much faster than others.

Accept Credit Cards to Speed up Cash Flow

You don't have to be a retail store to accept credit cards from your customers. Businesses and government agencies as well as consumers use credit cards to make a wide variety of purchases. Instead of waiting thirty days, sixty days, or more to collect payment from your customers, you can get paid in two or three days by asking them to pay you with a credit card instead of having you bill them. You'll have to pay a percentage of each sale to the credit card company, but that expense may be negligible when you consider the time and money you'll save by not having to send out monthly statements. This is a win–win arrangement. The customer can still string out payments, but you're not on the end of the string. An added bonus: Speeding up cash flow can help you speed up payments to your creditors, which may lower or eliminate interest payments you make on your payables.

Shift Your Receivables to a Finance Company

If your customers don't like to pay bills for your type of product or service with a credit card, or if the amount is too large for them to feel comfortable charging, look for finance companies that will offer loans to your customers. Again you get paid now, the customer or patient gets to string out payments, and you don't have to go to the trouble of sending out monthly statements.

Get Some or All of Your Money Up-Front

Don't spend weeks or months working without pay. When you negotiate deals, plan to get at least a third of the money up front if you are working on a long-term project. If possible, spread the remaining payments so you cover all of your ongoing expenses for the project.

If you don't know your customers and it would be difficult to collect if they didn't pay or if they never came to pick up work they ordered, insist on payment in advance. That way you don't have a collection problem.

Check Credit Ratings Before the Sale

One of the best ways to avoid collection problems after a sale is to make sure the customer is creditworthy before the sale. Take the time (and spend the money) to do credit checks on new customers.

Listen to the buzz in your industry, too. If you are unsure of the creditworthiness of a business, try to find others who have sold to the businesses. Ask is they have had any trouble collecting, and if they have, don't make the sale.

Catch Credit Problems Early

Keep an eye on aging accounts from existing customers. Don't wait until they are six months behind in payment to try to collect. Send out late notices if you haven't received payment by the next billing cycle. If a company that has normally paid on time still doesn't pay, call to find out if there is any problem with their order or with the service you are providing. If they say no, ask when you can expect payment.

Take Your Financial Pulse Regularly

Don't wait until the end of the year to look over your financial statements. Review those records monthly. Otherwise, you may not know until too late to make changes that you are losing money.

Helen O'Planick, an enrolled agent who operates HELJAN Associates in Manchester, Pennsylvania, tells of a client in the construction business who wanted to have his books done only once a year. "He would bring in all his check stubs, bills, and receipts. I'd do the work and he would peel off the big bills from a wad of cash to pay my bill," she recalls. "He was doing quite well, with 2.5 million in new construction his last full year. He had a wonderful house, a 25K natural pool, and just about everything he wanted. But since his wife was paying the bills and he never got a P&L or any other financial reports, he did not realize that his 15 percent gross profit margin had turned into a negative 20 percent as his supply costs went up 35 percent. He is now working under an assumed name down South, after losing everything to bankruptcy, and the IRS is still after him for back trust taxes."

Had the contractor been aware of the change, he could have raised his rates to cover costs, thereby preventing the bankruptcy.

Bring in New Business from Old Customers

If your cash flow problem is due to declining sales, get out your list of former customers and send a mailing to them. The mailing could be a reminder notice, a notice about new products you are offering, new store hours, or even your new Web site if you have one. Just be sure the mailing makes it clear that it is a mailing to people who have previously made a purchase. Make a habit of contacting them regularly in the future, too. People are more likely to do business with a company whose name they recognize than with a stranger.

Automate Your Billing System

If you have to go hunt up an address, calculate fees or find your hand-written notes about a job, you are likely to delay sending out bills. Avoid the problem by using an invoicing program or an accounting program to store and generate bills, track payments, and alert you to aging receivables. The faster you get the bills out, the faster you get paid.

Bill as Soon as a Job Is Done

Don't wait days to send a bill. Do it as soon as you deliver a job. This is particularly important when your customers are businesses. Businesses are likely to pay their bills on set cycles. If your invoice comes in after the checks have been cut for the month, you will have to wait an extra thirty days to get paid.

Don't Pay Your Bills Immediately

Look at the due dates on statements from your suppliers. If you have sixty or more days to pay, give yourself an interest-free, short-term loan by waiting until near the end of the time allotted to pay the bill. That added time may be enough to allow you to pay the bill out of your receivables.

> ▶ **Tip**
>
> Look your bills over carefully and don't pay for services that weren't performed, or that didn't meet the specifications you spelled out up front. If you tell an artist that your logo shouldn't show an image of men and you don't want coffee cups on it and he turns in samples of men drinking coffee, send the work back to be redone at no charge to you.

Don't Tell the World

Yes, it's tempting to get even with a scumbag creditor by telling their customers and suppliers how they didn't pay you. You may even be tempted to put up a Web site in hopes of saving some future unsuspecting dweeb from getting stung the way you have.

Don't do it.

If you do, you may find yourself on the receiving end of a lawsuit for slander. Even if you have done nothing wrong, and the suit is only a threat and no papers are filed at all, you may have to spend thousands of dollars to defend yourself.

Convert an Expense to a Profit

That's not as crazy as it sounds. Numerous businesses have done that by thinking outside the box. One expense that often can be converted to profits is the cost of disposing of waste products or scraps. Instead of throwing away scraps or, worse, paying someone to cart away scrap materials or waste, consider whether there is some other use for the material.

A Texas manufacturer, for instance, turned a $35,000 expense for carting away scraps of wood into a $15,000 profit by processing the wood scraps into a bedding material for use in poultry farms and horse stables.

Home businesses can often turn expenses and waste materials into profits, too. One person who does is Charlotte Cox of Charlotte's Dress Designs in Cleveland, Texas. Charlotte makes dresses and craft items. Instead of throwing away the leftover fabric or craft items or stuffing them away in a closet, Charlotte packages the leftovers for resale. She puts them in clear plastic bags, labels them and prices them, and then takes them to shows when she displays her craft items.

Reevaluate Your Purchasing Operations

If you haven't changed suppliers recently or if you are buying all of your supplies from one place because it's convenient to do so, you may be able to save money by making some changes in suppliers. For instance, could you save by purchasing toner from a supplier other than the one who sold you your photocopier? Has a new supplier opened a distribution center closer to your business? If so, could you save on shipping costs by ordering some or all of your merchandise through them?

Be Wary When Prices Are Too Low

If you get one price quote for work that's significantly lower than others, don't jump too fast at it, particularly if it's from a newcomer to business. They may not have the experience to understand what you really need done. For instance, the photographer who says he can shoot the photographs for your Web page and printed catalog for $8,000 less than the large photography house may not be able to achieve the quality for one job or the other. Get samples, get references, and go slowly if prices seem too low.

Streamline Your Operating Procedures

Before you add a new person to your staff, look at your operations to see if there are any procedures that could be streamlined or eliminated. If you can eliminate some of the tasks your existing staff performs, you free them up to do other work and may be able to avoid hiring anyone new. The way to spot potential areas for improvement is to write down procedures for each job that needs to be done on a repetitive basis. Include details about who handles or touches each piece of information or each item in inventory and what he or she does with it. Look for processes that require a single document, an inventory item, and so on to be handled multiple times. Then look for ways to cut down on the number of times the item is touched or read.

Reduce the Amount of Inventory You Carry

Take a careful look at your inventory. Are you ordering more merchandise than you can turn over quickly? Or are you ordering things that aren't selling? If so, look for ways to cut down on the expense. For instance, if a vendor sells only in carton-sized lots and you can't use an entire carton quickly, see if there is a competitor in your area with whom you could split orders from that vendor. Or can you make arrangements for any of your suppliers to drop-ship orders? If so, you eliminate the need to keep that item in inventory at all.

Reduce Your Costs by Purchasing in Quantity

If you know how fast your inventory turns over, ordering bigger quantities may save you money. If your current supplier can't give you quantity discounts, look through the supply chain and see if you can find a bigger distributor or deal directly with the manufacturer for better price breaks.

> ### ▶ Tip
> Buying in quantity pays when you know you can use the extra quantity. Don't get talked into buying large quantities of inventory or supplies if you don't know how fast you will use them up. For instance, if you are self-publishing a book, don't order 1000 copies just because the price is better than 100 copies. Order the smallest number, and if you can sell those, then order a bigger quantity.

Move Back Home

Consider whether you could save money without losing business by moving the business into your home. If it's a service business, do customers expect to visit your establishment? If it is a retail operation, could you sell just as well from the Web or by mail order? Calculate the amount you might save by eliminating rent, travel costs, extra lighting, heating, and telephone costs. Consider whether there may be employees you could let go because you won't have to have someone in the store during shopping hours.

Lease with an Option to Buy

If you are considering buying office space, but don't qualify for a mortgage, or aren't sure the space will be big enough a few years from now, see if you can lease with an option to buy. If the space proves adequate and you still want to buy at the end of the lease, you'd be able to do so without incurring moving costs. If the space is unsuitable or you don't have the cash flow to support a mortgage, you won't be stuck with a building you don't need.

Learn the Difference Between Profits and Cash

If you are like many small business owners, you probably think the best way to increase your cash flow is to increase sales. After all, if you double your sales, it's logical to assume your profits will double, too. And they may. But your profits may be only on paper, and you can't pay your employees or suppliers with paper profits. For that, you need cold hard cash.

To avoid unpleasant surprises, create a cash plan for your business that will show you just how your cash on hand will be affected by increased sales, increased expenses, late payments, changes in inventory turnover rates, and other critical factors. If your business is small service business, you can create a cash plan simply by determining your expenses and making realistic predictions about how long it will take you to get paid. If your are a retailer or manufacturer, consider using a software program called CashPlanPro to do your projections. The program, created by Palo Alto software, makes it easy to predict how changing cash factors might affect your cashflow.

Chapter 22

GROWING YOUR

BUSINESS

A business owner I know once remarked that owning a business was a way to owe more money to more people than he'd ever dreamed possible. Although he was somewhat stressed-out from running a high-volume, low-margin operation, his words have a lot of truth to them. The bottom line for business is that it takes money to make money. If you want to grow your business, you are likely to need more cash than you have on hand. Even when you have customers ready to order, there is going to be a lag between the time you have to pay for supplies, labor, and overhead costs and the time you collect payment and it clears your bank. That means borrowing money unless you have substantial savings of your own. Here are some of the basics you should know about borrowing for your small or home-based business.

Decide Where You Want to Go with the Business

If this is your first business, you probably think the sky's the limit. But before you borrow the money to get there, realize it's likely to be a very bumpy ride. You will have to balance sales against expenses and make it all work out so the cash comes in before you have to pay it out for leases, loans, and payroll. That won't be an easy trick.

If you apply for a loan or sign a lease, you will probably be required to personally guarantee that loan. Thus, even if you have incorporated your business, if the business goes belly-up, you still have to pay off the loan or lease—even if it means selling your home and possessions to do so.

And if those facts don't leave you looking for the antacids, here's one more: You will suddenly become responsible in part for not only your own family's well-being, but the well-being of your employees' families. That fact will hit home the first time one of them asks you to verify their earnings so the bank will process their mortgage or loan application.

Don't assume you'll have your family's full support behind you, either. You may not. You will be working long, long hours, sometimes for little pay. Your spouse may not offer any support, may try to undermine you, or may leave. If you work together, you may find that you don't see eye to eye on who controls what.

And if you can't make personal or family ends meet, everyone is going to be on your back to get a job and to forget about the business.

Entrepreneurs before you have coped with and survived all those things, of course. Bill Furiosi, of Ft. Lauderdale, Florida, left the Florida Highway Patrol to build a business based on a locking device he had invented for securing cylinders, ladders, and other devices onto trucks, boats, or anything that carries them. The product had a big market, but he couldn't bring in cash fast enough to ramp up to meet order. He put every waking moment into developing the business, and in doing so put his family in a hole. At one point he, his wife, two babies, two birds, and a dog were living in a 10-by-10-foot apartment. Furiosi slept on the toilet because there was no room any place else to sleep. (He eventually did get investors who were in the process of setting up offices for the business as this book was being written.)

But consider whether or not you can take the heat and what you and your family might have to give up, before laying it all on the line to start or grow a business.

Operate the Right Way from the Start

Most startups operate by the seat of their pants, putting procedures in place here and there without any planning for the future. If you have good products and are good at being flexible, you may be able to survive that way almost indefinitely.

But if you decide to grow your business, seat-of-the-pants operation isn't going to suffice. You'll need written policy manuals, job descriptions, and all the trappings of a "real" business. Without those things, your growth will be stymied by lack of direction, conflicting viewpoints on how to get things done, and wasted efforts. Furthermore, you may not be able to win the big contracts you'd like to win or need to win to stay in business.

Look for Microloans if the Need Is Small

If you need less than $25,000 and can't raise it or borrow it on your own, investigate whether there are any microloan programs in your area that can help. The SBA has a microloan program that makes loans to businesses in amounts of up to $25,000 to startups and other businesses needing money. These loans are handled through nonprofit intermediaries. The available funds are often reserved for those who would have trouble getting other sources of funding. A list of intermediaries who accept loan applications is located on the SBA Web site at http://www.sba.gov/financing/frmicro.html.

In addition to the SBA program, local community development agencies sometimes offer microloan programs.

Use Credit Cards to Finance Your Business

Sometimes the most expedient way to finance your business is to use credit cards. If you have a good credit history, and a couple of credit cards, you may have $25,000 or more in credit available to you just by signing your name (or by giving your credit card number to a mail-order company).

Some of that credit availability may be at high interest rates. But if your credit is good, you probably have offers showing up frequently that let you transfer existing balances to a new card at a special introductory rate. Or you may also be getting offers for cards with moderate interest rates that don't go up at the end of a brief introductory period.

These low-rate credit cards can be useful methods to finance your business if you can control your spending. Buy only the equipment or services that you have budgeted for and that you'll be able to pay back in a reasonable time. You won't have to wait for the bank to approve a loan, and if you make careful use of the low interest rate offers, you may wind up paying no more interest than you would have if you had a bank loan.

Be sure to read the small print on each credit card application to see how long the advertised rate is in effect. Check for clauses that allow the credit card company to bump the interest rate up to a much higher rate if you are late paying any bills. Some will bump the rate up if you are late paying just one bill.

> ▶ **Tip**
> If you can't get a credit card in your company's name, get a credit card in your own name that you reserve only for business use. If only business purchases are put on the card, you will be able to deduct any interest charges that accrue.

Write a Business Plan

When you are risking relatively little money, have no employees other than yourself, and have little overhead, you can get by with a simple outline of your ideas. Instead of an elaborate business plan, you can make basic predictions and business assumptions by gathering facts such as what it will cost you to produce a product or service, who will buy it, what they will pay for it, and what it will cost you to deliver it. (Be sure you take into consideration the money you, personally, will need to survive until you can pay yourself.) If this is the stage you are at, look for the business planning worksheet and marketing planning worksheet at http://www.businessknowhow.com/bkhstartup.htm. These will help you organize your thoughts and get the facts on paper if you don't want to do a more complete business plan at this stage.

But as soon as you plan to hire employees and risk more than the amount of money you can easily pay back out of other income or (heaven forbid!) by getting a "job," you need a more complete business plan. In fact, you won't be able to get a business loan or raise money from any other savvy investors without it. Neither should you attempt to do so.

Numerous resources will help you learn how to write a business plan. One of the best is a software program called Business Plan Pro published by Palo Alto Software. The software manual is as much an instruction manual on how to write business plans as it is a description of how to use the software. The software comes with a number of templates so you can see what a business plan should look like for various types of businesses. It's available in most stores, mail-order catalogs, and online sales outlets that sell software. The street price is about $90.

If you don't want to purchase software, you can get a free outline of a business plan and a free tutorial for creating your own plan on the Small Business Administration (SBA) Web site. The outline and tutorial is at http://www.sba.gov/starting/indexbusplans.html.

The More You Need, the More People You Need Behind You

No business is an island. Banks and private investors don't like to lend large sums of money to individuals. They want to lend only to an organization with a management team and plans that could go on if an individual left, had an accident, or for some reason was no longer involved. The bottom line is their bottom line. How would they get their money back if you were no longer part of the business? Therefore, when you apply for a big loan or seek investors, focus on the skills and strengths of the business and its employees, not just on your own skills.

Apply for Grants

Grant money doesn't flow nearly as easily as the "Get free money from the government" ads would have you believe. Most grant money goes to non-profit organizations and to educational institutions. But depending on your circumstances, and sometimes your willingness to fight for your rights, grant money or other assistance may be available to you.

Lorna Reynolds, of Watkins Glen, New York, learned that the hard way when she wanted to start a business selling leather clothing and accessories. Legally blind from macular degeneration, Lorna, who was a single mother, had been on social security for three years. The social security payments amounted to less per month than she had been making per week when she could work. "I couldn't live that way," she says.

The New York State Department of Rehabilitation was going to send her to a class to find out what kind of job she might be able to do, but she didn't want that. Before she had had her daughter, she and her former husband had run a business selling jewelry and leather goods at flea markets around the country. The business had been profitable, and now she wanted to start a similar business. Watkins Glen seemed a perfect place for it since it attracts many tourists.

Linda made a lot of calls and spent a lot of time at the library. After calling the New York State Commission for the Blind and getting a copy of the Disability Act, she was able to determine that grant money was available under the Disability Act for starting a business. "You have to be very demanding," she says. "The money is there to help with self-employment, but they don't let you know about it. The workers, themselves, don't always know about it."

In order to get the grant for self-employment, she had to write a business plan with a three-year projection and submit it to the commission. When she did, she was told she had to redo the plan because the punctuation wasn't good. "I can barely see the computer screen and they were going to make me type this over again on my own!" Linda recalls. From her research, however, she knew that they could provide assistance with the typing, and she insisted that they did. Eventually, she did get a grant of $12,500.

The Disability Act is not the only source for grant money. Many federal agencies, state and local organizations, and private foundations have grant money available if you can locate it, if you qualify for it, and if you go about it in the right way. Most the grant programs are designed to serve some public good, such as creating jobs in depressed areas of the country, retraining people whose skills have become outdated, or in some other way enhancing the general economy of a locality. Grant money isn't dished out in barrelfuls to people who want to start or grow a business for their own personal enrichment.

One way to find out about these programs is by using the *Catalog of Federal Domestic Assistance* (CDFA) to hunt for grant programs. The CFDA can be searched on the Web at http:// www.gsa.gov/fdac. It is also available in printed format and on CD-ROM. If you don't have a computer, your public library may have the current issue of the CFDA or access to it. Grant programs are also listed in the *Federal Register* when they are announced.

If you have access to the Web, there is a detailed listing of Web sites and e-mail lists for those interested in grants and grant writing. That is at http://www.sai.com/adjunct/nafggrant.html.

Large public libraries may also be a good source of information on grants. A reference librarian can help you find the information you need, including books on how to write grant applications.

But possibly a better source of information are contacts you make with state and local agencies. The people in these offices generally know what grant funds are available locally and what kind of organization and proposal will have a chance of winning any of the money. They will also know of other types of assistance programs you might investigate such as tax credits for hiring or training workers, or for starting a business in an economically depressed area.

Don't Forget About Federal Research Funding Programs

One of the most widely known "grant" programs for small businesses isn't really a grant at all. It's the Small Business Innovative Research program. The program awards funds to help develop products that the government has decided may aid national defense, protect the environment, manage information, or meet some other important national goal. Another program, the Small Business Technology Transfer (STTR) program, provides funding to foster collaboration between small businesses and nonprofit research institutions. If you win one of these awards, it can help underwrite the cost of developing a product you want to bring to market. (See Chapter 2 for a description of these programs.)

Understand Where Your Business Fits into the Overall Financing Picture

The type of funding available to you will be influenced by the stage your business is at in its life cycle. If you are just starting out and have no track record and no established product or service, you usually have to bankroll the business using your own resources. These may include your savings, income from a full-time job, personal loans, a second mortgage on your home, money you can borrow from relatives, or even what you can borrow on credit cards. If you are buying an existing business, you may be able to get the seller to finance all or part of the loan. And if you're buying a franchise, the franchisor may offer help by leasing equipment to you or by helping you get a bank loan.

As your business grows, you are likely to need more money than you can finance out of your own pocket. Depending on how much you need and the nature of your business, banks or venture capitalists may be the source of capital.

There are no hard and fast rules in business, though, so there are exceptions to all this. Sometimes, for instance, bright ideas for new businesses, particularly in the technology sector, do get outside funding while they are in the idea stage. And neither banks nor venture capitalists nor other outside investors may be willing to put up the money to get you to the next stage in your business.

Raise Money Before You Really Need It

Don't wait until you are in a hole to try to raise money. Raising money takes time. If you wait to start until the wolves are nearly at the door, or until customers actually place orders, you'll have difficulty surviving. If you are desperate for money to keep your business afloat, you look—sometimes rightly so—like a poor credit risk to banks and traditional lenders. And poor credit risks don't get loans.

Get to Know Your Local Resources

The single most important thing you can do before you apply for a business loan is to get to know the local resources available to help you. In the United States, there are a wealth of federal, state, and local resources such as the Small Business Development Center (SBDC), SCORE, and economic development agencies that exist specifically to help small businesses get started and grow.

Since cash is so necessary for growth and survival, the people in these local government offices usually know exactly which banks do business with small businesses. They also may be able to suggest ways to combine lending programs to come up with the money you need.

Get to know these people. They can often help loosen purse strings that are otherwise shut tight to you.

The same is true of trade associations and small business associations. Active associations will attract the leaders in your business community. They will attract your competitors, and they will attract people you want to do business with. They are also magnates for investment bankers, attorneys, accounting firms, and investors.

Locate these groups and become involved. Get to be a familiar face. And keep notes on the backs of business cards you collect about who does what and whom they might know. Even if you never get any new business directly from your participation in these groups, you gain new insights into the ways to do business in your community and beyond.

Look Before You Leap

If you are thinking about raising substantial money, take the time to learn everything you can about the process. Attend meetings at which people who have made it talk about what it took to get them there. Or find those people yourself. You'll hear about the things that work to raise money and manage employees in a growing organization, and some of the pitfalls to avoid.

Hire and Promote Based on Ability, Not Friendship

That may be the hardest thing you have to do as your business grows. The people who helped you get started and build your business to the point it is at today may not be the people you need to move ahead. Thus, you may need to bring in people from outside into positions over those long-trusted employees.

Trade a Share of Revenues or Stock for Work

If you need software developed or other work done, you may be able to get other businesses to work at lower rates or for free in return for a piece of the action. Be careful in setting up such deals that you don't give away a bigger percentage of the business than is wise. If there will be share in revenues, make sure there's still enough room in your pricing to allow for sales and marketing costs and still make a profit. If the deal involves stock, have someone experienced advise you so don't give away more equity than necessary.

Sell Your Invoices for Cash

You can turn your incoming orders to cash before you fill them by using the services of a factor. What a factor does is to purchase invoices from manufacturers and other businesses that need to raise cash in order to fill their orders. You may have gotten orders for all the widgets you have in stock. You've shipped the order, but won't have the money to buy the supplies to make more product until you collect from this last sale. If you can't get credit from a bank to produce the products to fill the new order, a factor may purchase your invoices at a discount, giving you the money you need to fill the next order now.

To qualify for factoring, you need to have customers who are creditworthy and have enough of a profit margin built into your pricing structure to allow for the discount rate the factor charges.

Knock 'em Dead One by One

Everyone wants instant business, but in the long run, almost every successful business owner will tell you that becoming an overnight success takes years of building relationships one by one, one on one. Each contact you make may either be able to help you or may know someone else who can help you.

Snickelways Interactive, a multimillion-dollar company that provides ecommerce solutions for retailers, created their first Web site for a jeweler who was a friend of Paul Cimino, CEO of the company. The site, Gemzone.com, was set up for less than their normal rates, but they were then able to use the site to demonstrate how businesses could cut costs using the Web. As a result, they won a contract to produce an extranet for Fruit of the Loom. "That put us on the map," Cimino says.

You don't have to have your sights set on corporate customers to grow, however. Businesses of all sizes grow one customer at a time. Yours can, too.

GLOSSARY

8(a) (SECTION 8A PROGRAM). A business development program authorized under Section 8(a) of the Small Business Act designed to develop small disadvantaged businesses for Federal and commercial marketplace. Administered by the Small Business Administration. who qualifies and monitors all firms in the program.

Access fee. A fee charged for use of a telephone network.

Affiliate program. A program whereby a company offers a commission on sales made as a result of referrals. Used by many ecommerce Web sites to get other Web sites to send customers to them.

Air time. When used in conjunction with cellular telephones, air time refers to all of the time the telephone is in active use. You are billed for air time whether you place or receive a call.

Alphanumeric. Using both letters of the alphabet and numbers in a print out or code.

Analog. A means of transmitting sound by converting sound waves to electrical impulses. This is the technology used in conventional telephones.

ATM. Automated Teller Machine. Also used in the telecommunications industry as the acronym for asynchronous transfer mode, a technology that allows video phone calls and video on demand.

Autoresponder. Software that will automatically reply to an e-mail message by sending out a document that you have written in advance. Frequently used on the Internet to respond to initial sales inquiries. The response mechanism is triggered whenever mail gets sent to a selected e-mail address.

Backgrounder. A backgrounder is a profile of you or your company.

Bandwidth. A term used to describe the amount of information or data that can be transmitted.

Bandwidth. The amount of data transferred across a Web site. Often used to calculate the cost of Web site hosting.

Banner advertisment. A rectangular or square box on a Web page containing an advertisement.

Barter. To use goods or services to purchase other goods and services.

BBS. An electronic bulletin board which allows people with a computer and modem to communicate with one another by leaving messages that can be read by anyone who uses the bulletin board. The term can mean a privately owned bulletin board system run on a home computer or it can mean one section of a forum on a commercial online service.

Bid opening. The public announcement of all the bids submitted in response to an Invitation for Bid.

Bidder's list. A list that contains the names of vendors from whom an organization.

Blanket purchase agreement. An agreement that gives a purchaser (often the government) the option to purchase goods or services from a vendor when needed on an on-call basis.

Boolean search. A database search capability that allow you to search for information and include or exclude results based on specified relationships such as "and," or," or "not." For instance, if you searched a news database for the term "home office" you would get a list of articles that included stories about offices in people's homes and articles that referred to the "home office" of companies that operate from more than one location. In a database with Boolean search capabilities, you could eliminate many of the articles about corporate home offices by searching for the phrase "home office NOT headquarters."

Break-even point. The point at which revenues equal expenses.

Browser. A software program used to view the Web.

BTW. By the way. Used as an abbreviation online,

Buddy List. An America Online program that lets you create a list of friends and show which of them are online at the same time you are.

c.i.f. Cost, insurance, and freight.

Cache. A storage area on your computer that holds recently viewed Web documents as temporary files.

Call forwarding. A telephone company service that transfers your phone call to a different phone number than the one the caller dialed.

Call waiting. A telephone company service that places incoming phone calls on hold and alerts you if you are on the phone when a call comes in.

Capabilities brochure. A brochure describing a company's products, services and qualifications. Sometimes includes case histories or descriptions of problems and how the company solved the problems for their clients.

CBD. *See* Commerce Business Daily.

CDRL. Contract Data Requirements List—A form that lists each item to be delivered under the terms of a contract.

CD-ROM. Compact Disc-Read Only Memory. A disk that looks like a music CD that stores computer data. Requires a CD-ROM drive to read.

CD-ROM drive. A computer disk drive that lets you insert and use CD-ROM disks and music CDs.

CE device. A small computing device that uses the CE operating system.

Certificate of current cost or pricing data. A document submitted to the contractor attesting that the cost or pricing data provided to the Government were accurate, complete. and current as of the date negotiations were completed.

CGI. Common Gateway Interface. A programming language that helps browsers and servers communicate on the Internet.

Change Order. A written order to make a change in an existing contract.

Click-through. The term used to describe what happens when a visitor clicks on an ad on a Web site and is taken to another location.

CO. Contracting officer. The only person who can bind the Government to a contract.

COB. Close of business.

COC. Certificate of Competency. A document issued by the Small Business Administration that certifies a small business as being responsible for the purpose of receiving and performing a specific Government.

COD. Cash on delivery. A payment method whereby the company or person making a purchase pays for it in cash when the merchandise is delivered.

Commerce Business Daily (CBD). A U.S. Federal Government publication containing listings of contracts going up for bid, names of companies that have won contracts and other information.

Competitive intelligence. Finding out what your competitors are planning.

Consignment. A method for selling where the manufacturer puts items on display in a store and gets paid a certain percent if the retailer sells the product. Often used for the sale of craft items.

Consumer Price Index (CPI). Measures the price levels of various goods and services purchased by consumers

Contract. A legal agreement between two parties. The contract may describe the work to be done, specific procedures to be followed in performing the work, the date the work or product is due, the amount to be paid for the work Other details such as size of the finished product, quality standards, ownership of copyrights and trademarks, may be included where applicable.

Contracting. A term usually used to mean doing business with government agencies.

Cookies. Files that carry data regarding your usage of the Web. The files are created by programs on the Web and placed on your hard drive. They are used to store passwords, remember what links you've seen, and to store other data about your activities.

Cooperative advertising program. Advertising programs whereby manufacturers give retailers back a percentage of the money they spend of advertising the manufacturer's products.

Cost or pricing data. Cost or pricing data submitted by an offeror or contractor enable the Government to perform cost or price analysis and ultimately enable the Government and the contractor to negotiate fair and reasonable prices.

CPM. Cost Per Thousand. Used in advertising to determine the cost of an ad based on the number of times the ad will be displayed. For instance, if you are placing an ad on a Web site that charges $20 CPM and wanted your ad displayed 50,000 times, the cost would be $1000.

CPM. Cost per thousand. Used in advertising determine the cost of an ad, If ad space sells for $20 per thousand and your ad is viewed or heard by 100,000 individuals you pay $20 x 100 for your ad.

Cross-train. To teach employees how to do more than one job.

Cyberspace. The term used to describe the electronic "universe" where people communicate with one another using computers and modems. The term was first used in the book, *Neuromancer*, by William Gibson.

Default. In contracting, the failure or anticipated failure of a contractor to perform contractual obligations.

Deliverable. In contracting, the specific item(s) that you will deliver to a customer as part of a contract. May include such items as reports, data or inventory.

Demographics. Common characteristics of a group. May include information such as the age, sex and marital status of a group of people.

Discount rate. A percentage of each sale that you have to pay for the privilege of accepting credit card transactions.

Distinctive ring. A technology that allows one telephone to accept two different phone numbers.

DOD. Department of Defense. Military departments (Army, Navy, Air Force), and defense agencies.

Domain name. A name given to a specific computer and address on the Internet. The most common domain names are those with .com at the end of the name, as in businessknowhow.com.

Double taxation. Being taxed twice on the same income. This can occur in C corporations when corporate profits (what's not paid out in expenses and salary) are taxed at the corporate rate. When the profits are distributed as dividends to shareholders they are taxed again as income to the shareholder.

Download. To transfer information from remote computer to your computer. Analogous to taking something down off a high shelf. (Also see upload)

Drayage. The cost of moving trade show exhibits into and out of an exhibition hall.

Drop-ship. A procedure whereby a mail order company takes orders for goods and then sends the individual order to the manufacturer, who then ships the order. The mail order company never has possession of the drop shipped goods.

Durable goods (durables). Items with a normal life expectancy of 3 years or more, such as automobiles, furniture, and major household appliances. Sales of durable goods are generally postponable and therefore are the most volatile component of consumer expenditures.

DVD. A disk that looks like a computer CD, but holds more data and can be used to store movies as well as traditional computer data. A DVD-ROM drive is required to read the disks.

E & O insurance. *See* errors and omissions insurance.

Ecommerce. The transaction of business on the Web.

EDI. Electronic Data Interchange— The transmission of documents and information from computer to another using a standardized format (ANSlxl2) via a Value Added Network (VAN).

Electronic mail. Mail sent electronically.

E-mail. Electronic mail. Mail sent via computer and modem. Used to send mail instantaneously within an office, to distant branches of a company, around the country and around the world. Used both for business and personal communications.

E-mail address. A specific mailbox for receiving individual electronic mail.

E-mail alias. A fake e-mail address.

Endorsement. An add-on to an insurance policy, expanding or modifying coverage. Also called a rider.

Endorsement. Personal testimony saying a product or service is worth buying.

Errors and omissions insurance. Insurance that protects you if you make a mistake. Similar to malpractice insurance for doctors.

Ezine. Electronic or e-mail magazine. A magazine distributed using electronic communications. May be sent in e-mail or appear on a Web site.

Factoring. The purchase of accounts receivable for less than the face value of those receivables.

FAQ. Frequently Asked Questions. FAQs are compilations of answers to questions that are often asked in a newsgroup or online forum.

FAR. Federal Acquisition Regulations—The regulations controlling all purchases made by the Federal Government.

Fax on demand. An automated system for sending frequently requested information by fax.

FCC. Federal Communications Commission. The government agency that regulates the telecommunications industry in the US.

Firewall. Security measures attempt to block access to sensitive computer data from those who shouldn't see it. Most commonly used in conjunction with blocking computer hackers from access to company data stored on computers tied to the Internet.

Firm-fixed price contract. A contract that establishes up front a fixed price which is firm for the duration of the contract and the only adjustments that can be made are authorized changes. Under this type of contract, you receive the maximum profit but you also assume the maximum risk of profit or loss.

Fiscal Year (FY). Designation of a year for budget and accounting purposes. The U.S. Government's fiscal year runs from October 1 to September 30.

Flame, Flamed, Flamewar. Flames are angry, criticizing messages sent in e-mail or posted in public electronic discussion areas. They often concern improper use of the Internet, but can be on any topic. A flamewar is when two or more people engage in prolonged, public exchange of angry, critical messages.

FOIA. Freedom of Information Act. A law that permits the public to obtain Government records.

Foreign trade zones (FTZs). Designated areas in the United States, usually near ports of entry, considered to be outside the customs territory of the United States. Also known as free trade zones.

Forum. As used by online services, a meeting place for people with a shared interest. Usually consists of several components such as message boards, feature articles, downloadable files and chat areas.

Forum manager. The person responsible for managing an online forum. Usually the person who plans what goes into the forum as well as overseeing any paid help or volunteers who work in the forum.

Frames. Divisions of a Web page that are attached to one another, but each are operate like separate, scrollable windows.

Free alongside ship (f.a.s.). The transaction price of an export product, including freight, insurance, and other charges incurred in placing the merchandise alongside the carrier in the U.S. port.

Free on board (f.o.b.). Without charge for delivery of export merchandise to and placing on board a carrier at a specified point.

Freelance. To work as an independent contractor.

Freeware. Copyrighted software that is available for use without payment to the author.

FTC. Federal Trade Commission.

FTP. File Transfer Protocol. A specific method for transferring files from one computer to another. Often the method of transferring files from your computer to a service that hosts your Web site. Also used as a verb, as in "He FTP'd the files to the Web site."

Fulfillment. The process of packaging and mailing an order to a mail order customer.

FWIW. For What It's Worth. Used as an abbreviation online.

Gatekeeper. A person who screens calls and filters calls and visits to an executive or other important person in an organization. The gatekeeper is often a secretary or staff assistant.

General Agreement on Tariffs and Trade (GATT). An international organization and code of tariffs and trade rules that has evolved out of the multilateral trade treaty signed in 1947. GATT is dedicated to equal treatment for all member trading nations, reduction of tariffs and non-tariff barriers by negotiation, and elimination of import quotas. (See Uruguay Round.)

GIF. Graphic Interchange Format. One of two common compression formats used to make graphic images smaller and more quickly viewable on the Web.

Grant. Money given to accomplish a specific goal. Does not have to be paid back.

Gross national product (GNP). The value of all goods and services produced in a country plus income earned in foreign countries less income payable to foreign sources.

GSA. General Services Administration.

Hacker. As it's commonly used, an individual who breaks into computer systems.

HBCU. Historically Black Colleges and Universities. Accredited institutions of higher learning.

Hit. An access to a single item on a Web page. For instance, a Web page that consists of two graphics and a text article would consist of three separate documents. Each document would be "hit" when the page was viewed. A hit count would therefore show 3 hits. A page view count would show 1 page view for those three hits. (See page view.)

Home page. The default URL for a Web site. The page used to enter the Web site.

HTML. Hypertext Mark-up Language. Coding used to create Web pages.

HTTP. Hypertext Transfer Protocol. The standard protocol used to transfer data between a computer and Web browser.

HUB. Historically Underutilized Businesses.

Hyperlink. Text or a graphic on a Web page that, when clicked on, takes you to a different (linked) page.

IM. *See* Instant message.

IMHO. In my humble opinion. Used as an abbreviation online.

Impression. *See* Page view.

Incubator. A facility, often affiliated with colleges or universities, that provide help new business get on their feet by providing a package of services that may include benefits such as lower normal rent, shared office equipment, shared office support services.

Independent contractor. A small, independently owned business. Often used to refer to one-person, unincorporated businesses.

Ink-jet. A type of printer which puts type on pages by squirting ink out of microscopic openings.

Instant message. A message that is sent directly from one person logged on to an Internet service to another. Instant messages do not go through e-mail accounts. Instead, they pop up on the screen of the recipient and allow the recipient to respond immediately.

Intellectual property. Includes trademarks, copyrights, patents, and trade secrets.

Internet. A world-wide information network that links hundreds of thousands of computers.

Internet fax. A technology that makes it possible to send or receive fax messages through the internet. An e-mail message, for instance might be sent to a fax machine. Or a faxed document could be sent to an e-mail box.

Intranet. A Web-like communications system set up for internal or private use by a company.

Invitation for bid. The solicitation method used when conducting sealed bid procurements.

IO. Insertion Order. A formal request to have advertising placed in the media. The insertion order specifies all the details including price, frequency and placement of the advertising.

ISDN. Integrated Services Digital Network. A high speed, telephone network that supports supports voice,data, fax, and other telephony applications. ISDN uses digital signals rather than the analog signals most phone systems today use. It allows multiple tasks such as faxing and making a telephone call to occur on the same line at the same time.

ISO 9000. A series of five standards (9000-9004) of the International Standards Organization (ISO), an international agency that promotes quality standards in products and systems.

ISP. Internet Service Provider. Any company that provides a service that lets you access the Internet.

IT. Information Technology. The use of computer technology to manage and manipulate information.

JPEG. One of two common compression formats used to make graphic images smaller and more quickly viewable on the Web.

Just-in-time (JIT) delivery. A management technique in which a manufacturer works closely with its suppliers to assure that critical components are delivered as needed to avoid disruptions of the production process and the costs of maintaining excessive inventories.

Land Line. Traditional, land-based (as opposed to cellular) telephone networks. When you place a call from your office to someone across the street or across the country you are using land lines.

Laser printer. A type of printer that uses laser technology to affix toner to pages.

Leads. Names of people who might want to buy your products or services.

Leads network. A group of people who gather regularly to exchange the names of people who might be likely sales prospects.

Line-card. List of products sold by a company or distributed by a manufacturer

Link. A clickable spot on a Web page that takes you to a different Web page. *See* hyperlink.

Liquidator. A company that buys excess or old inventory in large quantities and then sells it off at bargain prices.

LISTSERV. A particular brand of list server software.

List server. Software that lets you store e-mail addresses and deliver messages to all the names on the list by sending one piece of e-mail.

LOL. Laughing out loud. Used as an abbreviation online.

Long distance carrier. A provider of long distance services.

LRAE. Long Range Acquisition Estimates. Some Federal agencies publicize estimates of unclassified proposed acquisitions.

Lurker. A person who reads messages in electronic bulletin boards and newsgroups but who doesn't leave messages or participate in the electronic conversation in any way.

Mail Order Business. A business in which customers order products without actually seeing them. Orders for most mail order products these days are placed by telephone or on the Web. The order is usually then delivered by mail.

Mailto. A command used in hypertext markup language (HTML)on Web pages to cause an e-mail program to open up with the e-mail address of the recipient filled in. Used to make sure the e-mail address is entered correctly and to help the recipient route the mail to the proper department for reading and handling. For instance, a Web site might have a page on their Web site with contact information for various departments in the company. Mail requesting customer support might go to support@companyname.com sales inquiries might go to Sales@companyname.com and reports about problems using the Web site might go to Webmaster@companyname.com.

Majordomo. A type of listserver software.

Market segment. A small, identifiable section of your market.

Mass mailing. A large mailing usually consisting of advertising.

Merchant account. A special type of bank account that allows you accept credit card payments.

Message boards. Another name for electronic bulletin boards.

Microloan. A government program offering very small loans to businesses that might otherwise not qualify for a loan. Typically microloans are for $25,000 or less.

Minority Institutions. Educational institutions having significant minority enrollments. Designated minority groups include Blacks, Native Americans, Hispanics, Asian Americans/Pacific Islanders.

MPEG. Motion Picture Experts Group. A software compression scheme that facilitates transfer of and storage of video images on computers

Multifunction device. Usually a computer peripheral device that can perform tasks that might otherwise require several different machines. For instance, a multifunction printer might also serve as a scanner, fax machine, photocopier and telephone answering machine.

Multimedia. Information presented as a mixture of graphic, text and sound elements.

Multitasking. Doing more than one task at once.

NAICS. North American Industry Classification System. A numerical coding system used by the government and industry to categorize businesses by the type of goods and services they provide.

Newsgroup. A type of electronic messaging system used on the Internet.

Newsletter. A written document containing any combination of news, feature articles, check lists or other helpful information. Newsletters usually contain 32 or less printed pages, with 4 to 8 pages being typical.

NLT. abbreviation for Not Later Than.

Nondurable goods (nondurables). Items which last for less than 3 years, such as food, beverages, and clothing. Nondurables are generally purchased when needed.

North American Free Trade Agreement (NAFTA). Agreement to create a free trade area among the United States, Canada, and Mexico. Implementation was scheduled to begin January 1, 1994.

Offer. A response to a Request for Proposal that would bind the offeror to a contract should it be accepted.

Online. Being connected to an online service or to the Internet.

Online community. A forum or Web site where people with shared interests gather.

Online service. Commercial, subscription-based services that group many special interest areas and features together. Typically online services offer product support, special interest discussion areas, file libraries, live conferencing, news and weather.

OTH. On the other hand. Used as an abbreviation online.

Outsource. Hiring small, specialized firms or individuals to do work that was once done by corporate employees. This may include providing services such as training or manufacturing components for products.

Pacific Rim. A term that technically means all countries adjoining the Pacific Ocean, although it often refers only to East Asian countries.

Page view. A display of all the elements on a Web page. Equivalent to looking at a single page in a magazine or newspaper. Used for counting the number of time an advertisement is displayed. Also called an impression.

Palm pilot. A small computing device that can be held in the palm of your hand.

PCMCIA. A device about the size of a business card that adds functionality to notebook and smaller computers. A typical use of PCMCIA card is to add a modem to a notebook computer. Other uses include adding memory and adding hard drive space. PCMCIA is an acronym for Personal Computer Memory Card International Association.

PDA. Personal Digital Assistant. A small, computerized, hand-held device that can be used for things like maintaining contact lists, recording appointments and taking notes.

Peripheral. A product (such as a printer)that adds functionality to a computer system.

Plug-in. A computer program that adds functionality to another, larger computer program and requires the other program to work. For instance, drawing programs might have plug-ins that allow you to add special effects to the drawing.

POC. (Point of Contact)—contact person.

Portal. On the Internet, an entry point to the Web that collects a variety of resources in one place. Typically there will be a search capability, news, e-mail, information categorized into key topics such as computing, business, entertainment, and bulletin board capabilities.

POTs. Plain Old Telephone service.

Pre-Award Survey. A review of a company's ability to perform a contract.

Presenter. An individual who gives a seminar or a speech.

Press kit. A collection of information about a company, product, service, or individual. Usually consists of a folder with pockets containing one or more press releases, background information about the company and/or the founders, success stories, product descriptions or other information that might give reporters and editors information they need to write a story.

Press release. News about your company, products or services that is sent to reporters and editors as source material for news articles. Used as a means to promote products, explain what companies are doing to when newsworthy events involving a company arise, and in other situations where companies want to give reporters and editors information that can be made available to the public.

Press room. A room where members of the press go to rest, write articles or get and send information.

Prime contractor. The company responsible all the details on a contract. That company may contract with other companies or self-employed workers to do parts of the total job.

Procurement. Purchasing.

Producers Price Index (PPI). Measures the price levels of commodities produced or imported for sale in commercial transactions in the United States.

Professional liability insurance. See errors and omissions insurance.

PTAC. Procurement Technical Assistance Center. Offers small businesses free help with learning to sell to the government.

Public domain. Free of copyright restrictions. Anything that is in the public domain may be used free of charge.

Rate card. The published rate for advertising. This will be the highest rate the publisher charges for advertising. The published rate can often be negotiated downward.

Response rate. The percentage of people who call or make a purchase after seeing an ad.

Responsible bidder. A bidder who has adequate financial resources to perform a contract, a satisfactory performance record, and who is otherwise qualified to do the work specified in a contract.

Responsive bidder. One who submits a bid that conforms to the essential requirements of the invitation for bid.

Restocking fee. A fee charged by some stores when you return items for a refund. The fee is often 15 percent of the original purchase price.

Revenue stream. Income from a specific source such as retail sales, Internet sales, services, etc. A company that makes money from selling Web hosting services and also from Web design would be considered to have two income streams (hosting, being one and design the other).

RFP. Request for Proposal . A document asking for proposals for performing services or doing work.

Rider. An add-on to an insurance policy, expanding or modifying coverage. Also called an endorsement.

Roaming charge. The rate charged by cellular phone companies for use of a cellular phone outside of your home service area. The roaming rate is higher than the rate in the home service area.

S corporation. See Subchapter S Corporation.

Sales representative. Anyone who sells your products or services for you. The term usually refers to independent sales representatives (also called sales reps). These individuals are self-employed and sell the products of other businesses for a commission. They get orders for products and services and pass the orders on to the client company. They do not take possession of merchandise.

SBA. Small Business Administration. The Government agency whose function is to aid, counsel, provide financial assistance, and protect the interest of the small business community.

SBDC. Small Business Development Center.Located throughout the United States, these are centers that are jointly sponsored by the SBA and by state governments and which offer free assistance to small businesses.

SBIC. Small Business Investment Companies.

SBIR. Small Business Innovative Research program. A federal government program that provides funding for targeted research programs.

SCORE. Service Corps of Retired Executives. An SBA program made up of retirees who volunteer their time to help small business owners.

SDB. Small Disadvantaged Business. A small business that is at least 51 percent owned by one or more socially and economically disadvantaged individuals.

Search engine. A software program, usually residing on a public computer network, that lets you find files on the network.

Section 179. A part of the tax code that lets you deduct the cost of equipment or furniture instead of depreciating them.

Server. A computer that is set up to allow other computers to access its files.

Shareware. Software that you try before you buy.

Shopping cart software. Software that lets online shoppers buy multiple items using one order form.

Shrink wrap. Plastic wrapping that is heat sealed over items.

Slammers. Companies that change your telephone access provider without your consent.

Sole proprietor. A business that is not incorporated and not part of a partnership.

SOW. Statement of Work—A detailed project description describing work to be done, items to be delivered, methods to be used, and schedules for completion of work.

Spamming. To spread (send) unwanted messages or ads across many bulletin boards or e-mail boxes.

Spider. A program that automatically searches the WorldWide Web. They are used, among other things, to gather the information for the searchable directories available on AOL.COM, Lycos, Yahoo, Excite and other Web portals.

Standard Industrial Classification (SIC) system. The standard established by the Federal Government for defining industries and classifying individual establishments by industry.

Standard mail. New name for the merger of third-class mail and fourth-class mail as one class under Classification Reform implementation of July 1, 1996.

Stock balancing. The ability to return old, unsold inventory and have it replaced by new inventory.

STTR. Small Business Technology Transfer Program. A federal government program that fosters research and development conducted jointly by small businesses and research institutions.

Subchapter S corporation. A type of corporation under which all profits flow through to the shareholders and are not retained in the corporation. Often used for small corporations.

Subcontractor. A company that performs work on a contract on behalf of the company that is ultimately responsible to the client for the entire project. For instance, a company that paints buildings may be a subcontractor to the construction company that signed a contract to build the structure.

Tax deferred income. Income on which you won't pay taxes until a time in the future. Usually used in conjunction with contributions to pension plans.

TDY. Temporary Duty (travel).

Telecommute. To work at a distance, using telephone, computer or other means of communications.

Telecommuter. A person who works away from the main company office. Usually refers to an employee of the company, not a business owner.

Telemarket. Use of a phone to solicit sales appointments or sales.

Telephony. An adjective used to describe products and services that make use of telephone lines.

Template. Blank forms or documents created with a word processor, database, spreadsheet or page layout program that contain stylistic elements and any standardized text used in the type of document to be created. They are typically used for memos, invoices, letters, and other documents produced frequently on a computer. are set up so all you have to do is add your own text.

Test market. To try out a new product or service on a small scale before investing heavily in advertising and promoting it.

Testimonial. Praise for a product or service given by customers who use that product or service.

Time-and-materials contract. A contract that provides a fixed hourly rate for direct labor. That rate includes all appropriate wages, overhead, and profit and you are reimbursed at the fixed rate for each labor hour worked on the task. The material costs incurred in forming the work are reimbursed at the actual cost. resulting from inflation. material shortage, etc.

Toner. The dry ink used in laser printers.

Total quality management (TQM). A management technique to improve the quality of goods and services, reduce operating costs, and increase customer satisfaction.

Trade magazine. A magazine that carries articles and advertising geared to the specific needs of businesses in a particular industry.

Trade show. An event at which members of an industry or trade gather to display and demonstrate products.

Upload. Transferring information from your computer to a remote computer. Analogous to putting something up on a high shelf.

UPS. United Parcel Service.

URL. Uniform Resource Locator. A method for determining the location of data available on the Internet. It consists of four parts: the Protocol (HTTP, for instance), the domain name, the directory path, and the file extension. A typical example is http://www.businessknowhow.com/Startup/checklist.htm.

USPS. US postal service.

Value added. The difference between the value of goods produced and the cost of materials and services purchased to produce them. It includes wages, interest, rent, and profits. The sum of value added of all sectors of the economy equals GDP.

Virus. A computer program that destroys computer data and other computer programs and may render a computer useless.

Web page. A document on the Web containing any combination of text, graphics, photos, and links.

Web site. A computer that is hooked to the Internet and that supports the HTTP protocol used by the Web.

Wholesaler. A company that that purchases merchandise in bulk, takes delivery on it, warehouses it and resells it.

WOB. Women-Owned Business

Workshop. A training session during which the audience performs some type of activity as part of the training session. For instance, a workshop on writing advertisements might have the audience write a headline and write the text of an ad.

World Wide Web. A network of computers and documents on the Internet that use the HTTP protocol and allow visitors to jump from one document and computer by clicking on specified spots called links within the documents.

WWW. Acronym for World Wide Web.

WYSIWYG. An acronym for what you see is what you get. Used to refer to the way text looks on a computer screen compared to how it will print out. Pronounced wissy-wig.

Zip. To compress a file or group of files to save space.

ZIP disk. A specific brand of disk that holds a large amount of computer data.

INDEX

A

accounting methods, 349–350, 356–357
advertising, 101–130
   see also direct mail
   banner, 250–251, 255–256
      media, 124–128
   classified ads, 109–110
   comarketing agreements, 117
   cooperative programs, 116
   design of, 107, 108, 110, 114
   features vs. benefits, 135–136
   free, 106, 123–124
   incentives, using, 114–115, 119,
      122–123, 128
   on Internet, 127, 129, 231, 255–257
   laws, 120–122
   media buying services, 117
   money saving tips, 109, 118,
      125–126, 231
   planning, 101–104, 108–109, 113,
      117
   revenue from Web site, 234–236, 258
   timing and placement of, 115, 117,
      119
   tracking results of, 112, 129–130
   using automobile for, 119–120
   word-of-mouth, 124, 233
   in yellow pages, 111–116
advertorials, 98
affiliate programs, 236, 270
air travel, 304–310
American Wholesalers and Distributors
   Directory, 40
artwork. *See* clip art
automobile
   as advertising billboard, 119–120
   tax deductions for use of, 348–349

B

backgrounder, 95–96
bargaining/bartering, 47, 125–126
binding (documents), 68–69
borrowing money, 369–372
broadcast media, 124–128
built-in gains tax, 355
bulletin boards. *See* discussion groups
business associations, 77
business cards, 53, 57–58, 169
   foldover cards, 82–83
   magnetic, 83
   as marketing tool, 81–83
   Rolodex, 82

business frauds/scams, 10–11, 48, 115,
   123, 234
business hours, 268, 295–296, 300
business image, 51–71
   creating, 53, 54, 64, 70–71
   and mailing address, 55–56
   office space, 56
   and product packaging, 69–70
   on the telephone, 54, 56
business incubators, 13
Business Know-How Forum, 136, 219,
   249, 371
business name, 51–53, 117
business opportunities, 3–18
   consulting/teaching, 6, 7, 8
   environmental market, 9, 10
   exports, 10
   franchises, 5, 16–18
   hobbies, 6
   purchase an existing business, 13–15
   seizing, 15–16
   services and trades, 5, 6
   spin-off products, 4, 5
business plan, 371–372
business practices, unscrupulous, 33
business problems, 215, 325–332
business stationary, 57–67
   see also business cards
   clip art for, 58–60
   prices, 61–62, 63–64
   using color in, 58, 62, 65–67

C

CAGE code. *See* Commercial and
   Government Entity code
calling cards. *See* telephone calling cards
capital expenses, 350
card decks, 139–140
cash flow, ways to improve, 361–368
   accept credit cards, 363
   automate billing, 364–365
   bill paying, 365
   cut expenses, 366–367
   get money up-front, 363
   increase revenues, 361–362, 364
   recycle, 365–366
   reevaluate suppliers, 366
   streamline operating procedures, 366
   use a finance company, 363
   work on retainer, 362
Catalog of Federal Domestic Assistance
   (CDFA), 373

catalog vendors, 41–42
CDFA. *See Catalog of Federal Domestic
   Assistance* (CDFA)
CD-ROM directories, 39–40, 84, 297
classified ads, 109–110
clip art, 58–60
comarketing agreements, 117
Commerce Business Daily, 183–184,
   186
Commerical and Government Entity
   (CAGE) code, 185–186
company literature, 66, 68–69,
   168–169
comparitive financial data, 28
competitors
   acquiring information about, 29–31,
      34–36, 191, 254
   and advertising, 104
   alliances with, 15, 32, 44–45, 71, 78,
      252–253
   creating your own, 112–113
computer backups, 329
computer software
   for business plans, 372
   for cash planning, 368
   discounts on, 275
   installing new, 273–274
   for Internet, 226
   for mailing lists, 138–139
   for printing, 64–65
   shareware, 275–276
   for tax preparation, 357–358
   templates, 267–268
   for viruses, 275
computers, buying, 270–271
consignments, 46–47, 212–213
contract negotiations, 209–210
contracts, 326–327
   see also government contracts
copywriting, 104–105, 135–137
craft shows, 175–176
credit cards
   accepting, 247–248, 363
   to finance business, 371
   making purchases with, 273
   and tax deductions, 351–352
   using for travel, 303–304, 315
customer(s)
   acquiring, 122–123
   feedback, 28, 33, 35, 199
   retention, 130, 134, 188–189, 364
   surveys, 102–103

D

Data Universal Numbering System
(DUNS), 186
deductible expenses. *See* tax deductions
demographic data, 12–13, 26–27, 30
depreciation, 334, 350–352
direct mail, 131–143, 364
see also advertising; shipping
card decks, 139–140
cost effectiveness of, 131–132,
134–135, 140
goals for, 133–134
help with, 136, 148
money saving tips, 139, 142, 143,
150
Netpost, 153
postage meters, 153
postcards, 141–142, 151
strategies, 132–133, 142
timesaving tips, 148, 152, 153
tracking responses to, 143
directories, 38–42, 84, 158, 186–187,
297
Directory of Wholesalers, Importers and
Liquidators, 41
Disaster Loan Program, 330
discussion groups, 223–224, 237
drop-shipping, 45–46
DUNS number. *See* Data Universal
Numbering System

E

e-mail, 221, 225, 246, 290
advertising via, 256–258
aliases, 238
cost effectiveness of, 227
versus fax, 85
managing, 228, 236–237
for press releases, 226–227
to promote Web site, 255
sending files via, 229–230
employees, 189
see also freelancers; independent
contractors
dealing with, 327–329
for grunt work, 254–255
hiring, 375–376
using family as, 148, 341–343
ways to avoid, 366

F

factor, 376
family members
as employees, 148, 341–343
support of, 369–370
fax
cover sheets, 85, 278
on demand, 292
versus e-mail, 85
number, 56
federal research funding, 374

Federal Supply Classification (FSC)
code, 185
Federal Trade Commission, 11, 121,
123
finance companies, 363
finances, 369–376
factoring, 376
grants, 372–274
loans, 369, 370–372, 375
financial risks, 369–370
flea markets, 175–176
franchises, 5, 16–18
freelancers, 108–109
frequent flier programs, 308–310
FSC code. *See* Federal Supply
Classification

G

gatekeeper(s), 202–205
General Services Administration
schedule, 180
government contracts, 179–195
8(a) contractor, 193–194
bidding on, 182–184, 190, 191–192
classification systems, 185–186
free help with, 181–182, 189–191
General Services Administration
schedule, 180
marketing strategies, 180–181,
186–188
procurement conferences, 189–190
and Small Business Administration
(SBA), 193–194
tips for winning, 191–195
and women-owned businesses, 194
government publications, 23–24
grants, 372–374

H

hobby-loss rules, 356
home offices, 261–268
and business hours, 268
and business image, 266–267
dealing with interruptions, 267
deductions for, 338
equipment and supplies for,
261–262
ergonomics of, 263–364
insurance for, 264–265
money saving tips, 262–263
safety precautions, 268
space considerations, 262

I

incorporation, 353–355
independent contractors, 189, 327, 328
IRS guidelines, 343–345
Individual Retirement Account (IRA),
345–346
see also Roth IRA

information, organizing, 21, 83–84,
222, 329
information sources, 23–36
business/trade associations, 28–29
competitive intelligence, 29, 32, 34–36
customer feedback, 28
local resources, 30
market research, 31, 33–34
networking, 31–33
news-clipping services, 30
online, 26–27, 33
publications, 23–24, 28, 29
insurance, 264–265, 330, 342–343
Internal Revenue Service (IRS)
see also tax deductions; tax(es)
free help from, 358–359
independent contractor guidelines,
342–345
International Trade Administration, 10
Internet
see also Web sites; Web, using the
access numbers, 296–297
as communications tool, 225
directories, 39
fraud/security on, 248, 331
learning about the, 220–221
servers, 241
storefront, 232
tax deductions for use of, 340–341
Intranets, 226
inventions, 10–12
inventory, 46–47, 367
IRA. *See* Individual Retirement Account
IRS. *See* Internal Revenue Service (IRS)

K

Keogh plan, 346–348
Kinko's, 324

L

leads networks, 79–81
leasing, 367
legal issues
in advertising, 120–122, 253
contracts, 326–327
with creditors, 365
noncompete agreement, 14–15
libraries, using, 26, 28, 38, 40, 41, 373
limited liability company (LLC), 355
link exchange services, 255–256
listservs. *See* discussion groups
LLC. *See* limited liability company
loans, 351, 369, 370–371, 375
logos, 57

M

mail, classes of, 146, 149–150
mailing address, 55–56
mailing lists, 133, 137–139, 151, 178
see also discussion groups

market research, 11, 27, 31, 33–34
marketing, 73–87
  building name recognition, 76–78,
    85–87
  and business cards, 81–83
  cross-promoting, 77–78
  to government, 179–185
  leads networks, 79–81
  newsletters, 86–87
  plan/planning, 73–76
  referrals, 78
  trends, 78–79
mass production, 7–8
media buying services, 117
media contacts, 89–94
medical insurance premiums, 342–343
merchandise, 47–48
message boards. *See* discussion groups
microloans, 370–371
minority businesses, 193–194

N

NAICS. *See* North American Industrial
  Classification System
name recognition, building, 76–78,
  85–87, 118–119, 176–177, 197
National Business Incubation
  Association, 13
networking, 31–33, 34, 74, 83–84, 200
  with business associations, 44, 77, 183
  at trade shows, 157, 171, 177–178
news-clipping service, 30
newsgroups. *See* discussion groups
newsletters, 86–87
noncompete agreement, 14–15
noncompeting businesses
  alliances with, 71, 123, 139, 140
  cross-promoting, 77–78, 252
nonprofit organization, 355–356
North American Industry Classification
  System (NAICS), 185

O

office equipment/supplies, 269–279
  leases, 273
  maintaining, 274–275
  money saving tips, 262–263, 270, 278
  new products, 269
  peripherals and add-ons, 270–271
  printers, 276–277
  researching, 270
  returns on, 272, 273
  warranties for, 272
office space, 56, 367
online forums/newsgroups, 33
online services, 26–27
order fulfillment, 141, 147

P

pension plans. *See* retirement plans

personal touches, 84–85
photocopies, color, 66–67
postage. *See* direct mail; mail, classes of;
  shipping
presentations, 85–87
press kits, 96
press releases, 27, 90–93, 95, 226–227
price and merchandise comparisons, 122
price-shoppers, 112–113
print shops, 60–62
printers, 65–67, 276–277
printing
  doing it yourself, 63, 64–65
  money saving tips, 61–63, 67, 230
  prices, 63–64
  using color in, 58, 62, 65–66, 97,
    113, 142
Procurement Technical Assistance
  Centers (PTACs), 190–191
products, 4, 9
  distribution patterns, 36
  exporting of, 10
  misrepresentation of, 120
  packaging of, 69–70
  pricing, 361–362
  test-marketing of, 35–36
PTACs. *See* Procurement Technical
  Assistance Centers
publicity, 89–99
  advertorials, 98
  backgrounder, 95–96
  media contacts, 89–94
  press kits, 96
  press releases, 90–91, 92–93, 95
  radio and televison shows, 98–99
  responding to, 97
  using, 94, 98, 99
  writing articles for, 97–98

R

receipts, keeping, 352
referrals, 77–78, 188–189, 214–215
research, 19–36
  business/trade publications, 28–29, 30
  and competitors, 29, 32, 34–35, 36
  cost cutting strategies, 21–27
  marketing, 74–75
  money/information from
    government, 22–26
  objectives, 19–20
  online, 26–27, 33
  surveys, 33–34
  using libraries for, 21, 28, 29
retainer, working on, 362
retirement plans, 345–348
Roth IRA, 348

S

safety precautions, 172, 238, 298, 317
sales literature, 69
sales presentations, 207–208

sales representatives, 159, 211–212
sales strategies, 197–215
  business-to-business, 198–199
  customer contact, 201–206
  follow-up, 205–206, 213–214
  and gatekeepers, 202–25
  nonreferral "referrals', 205
  overcoming objections, 210–211
  presentations, 207–208
  seminars, 199–20
  structured approach, 199
  tracking results of, 198
Savings Incentive Match Plan
  (SIMPLE), 347
SBDC. *See* Small Business Development
  Center
SBIR. *See* Small Business Innovative
  Research program
search engines, 253–254
section 179 election, 350–351
security issues, 328–329
seminars, 171, 199–200
SEP plan. *See* Simplified Employee
  Pension (SEP) plan
shipping, 145–153
  see also direct mail
  cost of, 145–146
  fulfillment services, 147
  money saving tips, 146, 147, 149,
    229–230
  protection for products during, 146
  services, 147, 152–153
  tracking packages, 152–153
SIC code. *See* Standard Industrial
  Classification (SIC) code
SIMPLE. *See* Savings Incentive Match
  plan
Simplified Employee Pension (SEP)
  plan, 346–347, 348
simulations, in advertising, 121–122
Small Business Association (SBA)
  Disaster Loan Program, 330
  free business plan help, 372
  and government contracts, 193–194
  microloans, 370–371
Small Business Development Center
  (SBDC), 12, 375
Small Business Innovative Research
  (SBIR) program, 22, 374
Small Business Technology Transfer
  (STTR), 22–23, 374
software. *See* computer software
sole proprietor, 333–334
Standard industrial Classification (SIC)
  codes, 185
Statistical Abstract of the United States,
  The, 25
statistics, government, 24, 25
STAT-USA (U.S. government agency),
  24–25
stock balancing, 46
STTR. *See* Small Business Technolgy
  Transfer

subcontracts, 78–79, 193
suppliers
    alternate sources, 42, 43, 48
    auctions, 43
    bargaining with, 47
    cost cutting strategies, 44–45, 46–48
    and drop-shipping, 45–46
    local, 38
    locating, 37–48
    organizing information about, 45
    reevaluate, 366
    stock balancing, 46
    superstores, 43
    at trade shows, 42
    U.S. government as, 44

T
tax deductions, 336–349
    for family employees, 341–343
    hobby-loss rules, 356
    home office, 338–339
    interest, 351
    Internet/online services, 340–341
    medical insurance premiums, 342–343
    receipts for, 352
    retirement plan contributions, 345–348
    sales tax, 352–353
    section 179 election, 350–351
    travel, 339–340
tax(es), 333–359
    see also Internal Revenue Service; tax deductions
    alternative minimum tax (AMT), 337
    assett depreciation, 334, 350–351, 351–352
    built-in gains tax, 355
    computer software for, 357–358
    forms/instruction online, 359
    free help on, 358–359
    incorporation, 353–355
    payment schedule, 359
    payroll, 336, 343–345
    penalties, 336
    personal assetts, 334
    preparing, 357–358
    quarterly estimated income tax payments, 334–335
    state, 336–337
    value-added, 312–313
Telecomminucations Resellers Association, 287, 288
telephone answering machines, 55, 295–296, 300
telephone answering services, 54, 282–283
telephone calling cards, 298, 317, 322, 323–324
telephone connections, 281–300
    800 numbers, 56, 288–289, 294, 324
    business vs. residential, 281–282, 283
    long distance carriers, 285–286, 288
    money saving tips, 283–287, 289, 294–295, 297
    phone features, 282, 283, 294, 299
    rates, 284, 285–286
    service resellers, 287
    slamming, 289–290
    time management of, 295–296
    voice mail, 55, 205, 228, 282–283, 293
telephone directories, 38, 39, 84, 181
telephones, cellular, 290–291, 322
testimonials, 121, 122
Thomas Register of American Manufacturers, 39, 40, 41
time management, 173, 248–249, 267–268, 295–296
toll-free numbers, 56, 288–289, 294
trade associations, 28–29, 32, 183
trade shows, 155–178
    attending, 160–161
    choosing, 157–159
    company literature for, 168–169
    cost effectiveness of, 156, 159
    directories of, 158
    goals for, 155–156, 170
    making an impression at, 162–168, 172–173, 174
    money saving tips, 160, 163
    networking at, 157, 171, 174, 177–178
    planning for, 160–163, 166, 169–170, 176
    preshow promotion, 166–168
    safety precautions at, 172
    seminars at, 171
    using sales reps for, 159
travel, 303–324
    air, 304–310
    alternatives to, 318–319
    by car, 310–311, 314–315
    combining personal and business, 339–340
    money saving tips, 304–307, 316, 317, 319, 320–321
    planning, 304, 306, 313–314, 323
    rates, 304, 307, 316, 317, 319–320
    receipts, 321–322
    reimbursement, 312, 315–316
    safety precautions, 317
    using a travel agent, 311–312
    using credit cards for, 303–304
travel directory, 309

U
unsubstantiated claims, 120–121
U.S. government
    see also government contracts
    as information source, 23–26
    publications, 23–24, 25–26
    research programs, 22–23

V
vertical ads, 125
voice mail, 55, 205, 228, 282–283, 293

W
waranties and guarantees, 122, 272
Web sites, 239–259
    design/planning, 239–245
    hosting prices, 243
    maintaining, 250, 259, 331
    promotion of, 250–258
    sales strategies for, 245–246
Web, using the, 219–238
    to find information, 222–225, 297
    to generate income, 231–236, 258
    goals for, 221–222
    to improve productivity, 228–229, 233
    to network, 223–224
    saving money doing business, 225, 229–231
WebFerret, 222–223

Y
Yeabook of Experts, Authorities and Spokepersons, The, 91–92
yellow pages, advertising in, 111–116, 128–129

FIND MORE ON THIS TOPIC BY VISITING
BusinessTown.com
The Web's big site for growing businesses!

☑ **Separate channels on all aspects of starting and running a business**

☑ **Lots of info of how to do business online**

☑ **1,000+ pages of savvy business advice**

☑ **Complete web guide to thousands of useful business sites**

☑ **Free e-mail newsletter**

☑ **Question and answer forums, and more!**

http://www.businesstown.com

Accounting
Basic, Credit & Collections, Projections, Purchasing/Cost Control

Advertising
Magazine, Newspaper, Radio, Television, Yellow Pages

Business Opportunities
Ideas for New Businesses, Business for Sale, Franchises

Business Plans
Creating Plans & Business Strategies

Finance
Getting Money, Money Problem Solutions

Letters & Forms
Looking Professional, Sample Letters & Forms

Getting Started
Incorporating, Choosing a Legal Structure

Hiring & Firing
Finding the Right People, Legal Issues

Home Business
Home Business Ideas, Getting Started

Internet
Getting Online, Put Your Catalog on the Web

Legal Issues
Contracts, Copyrights, Patents, Trademarks

Managing a Small Business
Growth, Boosting Profits, Mistakes to Avoid, Competing with the Giants

Managing People
Communications, Compensation, Motivation, Reviews, Problem Employees

Marketing
Direct Mail, Marketing Plans, Strategies, Publicity, Trade Shows

Office Setup
Leasing, Equipment, Supplies

Presentations
Know Your Audience, Good Impression

Sales
Face to Face, Independent Reps, Telemarketing

Selling a Business
Finding Buyers, Setting a Price, Legal Issues

Taxes
Employee, Income, Sales, Property, Use

Time Management
Can You Really Manage Time?

Travel & Maps
Making Business Travel Fun

Valuing a Business
Simple Valuation Guidelines